BUILDING STONES
FOR AN UNDERSTANDING OF THE
MYSTERY OF GOLGOTHA

BUILDING STONES

FOR AN UNDERSTANDING OF THE
MYSTERY OF GOLGOTHA

Human Life in a Cosmic Context

Seventeen lectures given in Berlin between 6 February and 8 May 1917

TRANSLATED BY SIMON BLAXLAND-DE LANGE

INTRODUCTION BY MARIE STEINER

RUDOLF STEINER

RUDOLF STEINER PRESS

CW 175

The publishers gratefully acknowledge the generous funding of this publication by the estate of Dr Eva Frommer MD (1927–2004) and the Anthroposophical Society in Great Britain

Rudolf Steiner Press
Hillside House, The Square
Forest Row, RH18 5ES

www.rudolfsteinerpress.com

Published by Rudolf Steiner Press 2015

Originally published in German under the title *Bausteine zu einer Erkenntnis des Mysteriums von Golgatha* (volume 175 in the *Rudolf Steiner Gesamtausgabe* or Collected Works) by Rudolf Steiner Verlag, Dornach. Based on shorthand transcripts and notes, not reviewed by the speaker. This authorized translation is based on the latest available (third) edition of 1996 edited by H. Wiesberger and Ulla Trapp

Published by permission of the Rudolf Steiner Nachlassverwaltung, Dornach

A catalogue record for this book is available from the British Library

ISBN 978 1 85584 420 9

Cover by Mary Giddens
Typeset by DP Photosetting, Neath, West Glamorgan
Printed and bound by Gutenberg Press Ltd., Malta

CONTENTS

HUMAN LIFE IN A COSMIC CONTEXT

LECTURE 1
BERLIN, 6 FEBRUARY 1917

Materialistic or spiritual attitudes towards the spiritual world in relation to a book by Oliver Lodge. The relationship to the dead in spiritualistic seances. The appearance of the etheric Christ in the twentieth century. The preparation for this event since 1909.

LECTURE 2
BERLIN, 13 FEBRUARY 1917

Development of inner forces. Engagement with the dead in ancient times and now. Man as a part of the cosmic order: the correspondence between the Platonic year (25,920 years), a day in a person's life (25,920 breaths) and a human lifetime (25,920 days).

LECTURE 3
BERLIN, 20 FEBRUARY 1917

The three meetings of the human soul with the Spirit, the Son God and the Father God. Their influences until the end of life and after death. The nature of the third meeting in the event of early death and suicide. The development of a feeling for the holiness of sleep.

cepts that Saint-Martin and Oetinger did not think through consistently and their continuation in modern thought-forms through spiritual science.

BUILDING STONES FOR AN UNDERSTANDING OF THE MYSTERY OF GOLGOTHA

LECTURE 8
BERLIN, 27 MARCH 1917

Palestinian mysteries. The Pauline distinction between 'psychic' and 'spiritual' man. Gnosis, historical materialism and scientific world-view.

LECTURE 9
BERLIN, 3 APRIL 1917

Pagan mysteries. The Phrygian Attis cult. Trichotomy of body, soul and spirit. The elimination of the idea of the spirit. Original sin. The Risen One.

LECTURE 10
BERLIN, 10 APRIL 1917

The mysteries of the kingdom of heaven. The inner Word. The fourfold aspect of the Gospels as a manifestation of the coming Christ impulse.

LECTURE 11
BERLIN, 12 APRIL 1917

The deeply Christian impulse of Goethe. Physical and moral aspects. The 'lost Word'. The power of faith as a miraculous quality.

LECTURE 17

BERLIN, 8 MAY 1917

The eye of the soul. The appearance of clairvoyant forces in the present. Swedenborg's imaginative perception. Views about immortality before and after the Mystery of Golgotha. Faith and knowledge.

pages 301–321

TRANSLATOR'S PREFACE

Marie Steiner's introduction was written in the fateful year of 1933 for the first publication of lectures eight to fifteen of this book, lectures which form the core of the cycle generally known in English under the title given to the present volume in both German and English. However, from both external and internal evidence there is every reason to think of these lectures as a single whole. In the first place they were given in Berlin in an unbroken sequence of three months, mostly on a weekly basis but with additional lectures around the period of Easter, and clearly represented a fresh impulse on the part of Rudolf Steiner (who had not lectured in Berlin since July 1916) and were separated by three weeks from any subsequent lectures in that city. More fundamentally, however, Rudolf Steiner's real intentions on focusing in these central lectures on the historical background and esoteric context of the Mystery of Golgotha only become apparent from a study of the preceding first seven lectures, the theme of which is recapitulated in lectures sixteen and seventeen. This becomes particularly clear from the fourth lecture of the group of lectures entitled here 'Human Life in a Cosmic Context'; and it may be helpful to illustrate this by means of a more detailed analysis of the first part of this lecture.

After referring to the three meetings that the human individual has in varying rhythmic frequencies with spiritual beings in the course of earthly life, which he has described in the third lecture (one of which takes place every night, the second once a year and the third once in a lifetime), Rudolf Steiner breaks off his study of the spiritual context of earthly life in order to turn his attention to the extent to which conventional scientific ideas have not only come to dominate the way that people think about their lives but also, more importantly, how they feel and act. His particular concern here is to emphasize the alarming nature of the gulf between a conception of the world of outward facts which 'states that the Earth and the whole fabric of the heavens was formed in accordance with purely physical and also chemical earthly laws from a purely material cosmic mist . . ., that it has been developing in accordance with these laws and will, so it is thought, come to an end which will be determined by these same laws', on the one hand, and, on the other, 'the moral world, the world of moral feelings'. He goes on to indicate that if these materialistic assumptions become sufficiently ingrained,

> there is room for a more spiritual dimension—and especially for the moral element—only in a certain way. For just consider: if the world really did arise in the way envisaged by [a] theory [of this nature] and if it were to come to an end through physical forces alone and all human beings with their ideas, feelings and will impulses were to perish with it, what . . . would become of the whole moral dimension of the world if everything else is disregarded? Of what significance would it be that—on the basis that the world as we know it had perished—we had once said that this is good, this is evil; this is right and this is wrong? These would be nothing but ideas from a forgotten era, swept away as something which, if this theory were correct, could not live on even as a dim memory. Then the situation would be that the world would perish through the same mechanistic causes, the same physical and possibly chemical causes, whence it arose. From these same forces phenomena swell up like bubbles, which represent human beings. Within these human beings moral concepts of right and wrong, good and evil arise. Nevertheless, the whole world returns to the silence of the grave. The whole edifice of right and wrong, of good and evil, has been an illusion of human beings; and it is forgotten and vanishes without trace when the world has become a 'grave' . . . Indeed, these moral forces hover as a great illusion over the mechanistic world-order and will vanish into oblivion when the world is transformed into a grave.

This illusion, which, as Rudolf Steiner goes on to say, is sustained by the inner need to believe in something, will be powerless to stave off the enactment of such a future reality.

Except, of course, that—as it is the purpose of these first seven lectures to demonstrate—this whole materialistic scenario is untrue (although, as Rudolf Steiner indicates later on in the fourth lecture, it would already have become true if the Mystery of Golgotha had not taken place). In recent centuries, people have largely lost any real conception of the Christ mystery such that 'it irradiates the whole of their thinking and feeling'. For 'if one is unable to conceive of the Christ mystery as a true reality, one also cannot develop any ideas and concepts relating to the rest of world existence which are imbued with reality, which really penetrate to the truth'. It is the main purpose of this whole cycle of seventeen lectures to interpret the Christ mystery, or the Mystery of Golgotha, in the light of this statement; and Rudolf Steiner goes on to emphasize in this fourth lecture that this has to do not with Christ's moral teachings, however sublime they may be, but with 'the realization that in the Mystery of Golgotha something was accomplished which has to do not with the moral order alone but with the whole world-order in its entirety'.

Rudolf Steiner gave these lectures in Berlin in the course of a world military conflagration which he frequently laments with deep sorrow in the lectures; and when Marie Steiner wrote her introduction Europe was about to plunge the world into a further conflict of massive proportions, one particular feature of which was the endeavour to annihilate that race which historically had the task of preparing for the incarnation of the human bearer of the Christ. One effect of this was to darken the light of wisdom without which neither the Incarnation itself nor the mission of 'anthropos-sophia' in our own time is inherently possible. A century after these lectures were given it would seem that there is an even more overwhelming need to understand the essential message of these lectures, which is to recognize that man and his earthly home have now been wholly impregnated with a spiritual consciousness which formerly had to be sought elsewhere in a realm of wisdom (currently degenerated into mere information). Moreover, the existential dilemma reflected in the words of Friedrich Nietzsche from the sixteenth lecture, which applies no less to our own century, continues to find a response in the words of affirmation from the first lecture, where Rudolf Steiner is testifying to the active presence and companionship for modern humanity of the etheric Christ: 'As Christ approaches in His etheric reality, the time will come when people will learn to consult Christ not only on behalf of their own inner being but in connection with what they want to undertake here on Earth through that part of them which is immortal ... So let us endeavour to make spiritual science our own not merely as a teaching but as a language, and then wait until we find the questions in this language that we may address to Christ. He will answer, yes He *will* answer!'

Simon Blaxland-de Lange, Easter Sunday 2015

INTRODUCTION[*]

In these lectures the central event of human and earthly history, the Mystery of Golgotha, is considered from a historical perspective, on the basis of what spiritual-scientific research has established as to the fact of man's origin from the realms of the spiritual hierarchies, his Fall and his ever greater entanglement in matter, his awakening to sense-perception and his being burdened by what the Holy Scriptures call original sin; and then also his gradual ascent through a series of repeated earthly lives which develop his self-consciousness and give him the possibility of moral purification, a strengthening of the ego and a return to the spirit.

The significance of Earth existence can be found only in this steady, constant path of soul development. The lofty aim of human perfection can be attained only in many lives, which through the manifold trials and tests that they bring lead to a consciousness where wakefulness is increasingly enhanced. This knowledge was withdrawn for a while from the West in order that the individual personality within man might be both sought and found. A sharpness and precision of the practical intelligence had to be developed in order to make use of matter, to get to grips with its inherent possibilities in order in this way to discern something of its mysteries, and by virtue of the intellectual discipline thus acquired to gain a sure support for the investigation of spiritual laws. Only in this way could the earlier passive perception of super-sensible cosmic realities be transformed into knowledge and research through the strengthening of soul forces. The fading vision of the spiritual worlds disappeared in the course of time specifically amongst those peoples at the forefront of these developments; and it must now be rediscovered on a new level through an inner activity that is strengthened by the ego. We stand now at this great turning point. The

---

[*] Written for the first edition of 1933.

limitation of our view of spiritual reality has now extended to the point where it is threatened with turning into blindness. The immense destructive phenomena of western culture are a consequence of this intellectual blindness.

A new way of observing history from the aspect of the spirit must be given to mankind. Rudolf Steiner has assembled the building stones for this. Into the very midst of world history he places the Mystery of Golgotha, which from the context of the sovereign might of divine justice provides the balancing influence to the Fall of man into original sin. He sheds as much light on this mysterious event as is accessible to our intuitive understanding today. In this way something that we had virtually lost—the significance of the moral order over and against the natural order—comes once more to the fore. Through human guilt the paths of the Gods and human beings went their separate ways; but through the deed of atonement wrought by the man who had become God they were restored to unity and mutual interpenetration. Until this point the mysteries and the cultic ceremonies associated with them had formed a bridge from God to man and had created the places whence the will of the gods was able to exert its influence upon the destiny of a humanity that was becoming ever more engulfed in matter. They gave those seeking knowledge—after a long series of trials—the possibility of reuniting their spiritually awakened consciousness with the divine will. They contributed towards preparing the way for the descent of the divine Being who had resolved to protect mankind from the ultimately destructive consequences of original sin and to take them upon Himself, thus fulfilling the deed of redemption for the Earth. This deed of rescuing the Earth and the future of mankind makes it no less necessary for the human individual to work independently from the very foundations on his own moral redemption. It lies in man's free will to grant Christ access to his own being, to receive Him in an inwardly enlivening way to the point where the forces of healing take hold of his guilt-laden inner being and free it from the consequences of original sin.

If they are to will this, people today need to understand and know. A pious feeling life is no longer enough. They have to take into their consciousness what is later to be transformed into will. Obedience to the decrees of authoritarian powers where the requisite insight is lacking will all too surely stir rebellion in the human conscience. Not even the harshest means employed to wipe out heresies have been able to eradicate them. Where there seemed to be success outwardly, a germinal element continues to live on in secret and tries with renewed force to make itself felt. Today we are confronted by a worse danger than ever threatened even the most arduous path of a heretical movement: cynicism, the impulse of godlessness, the sharp, caustic scorn of anything spiritual. In order to withstand this impulse which destroys true human dignity already at a young age and to conquer it, we must enter more deeply into a knowledge of ourselves and of the world than has been possible until now; we must delve into the origins of human existence and appreciate the superficiality of the modern way of viewing history; we must penetrate the veils of Church history and investigate the extent to which the Churches have fulfilled their task and to what extent they have been unfaithful to it. We must also gain an insight into how much of their worthy spiritual heritage the authoritative power of the clergy have suppressed through forcible external measures and have not allowed to exist alongside them, and the reasons that have played into this. We need to understand, for example, why the ancient mystery centres were destroyed with such a radical zeal and thoroughness and their documents consigned to oblivion, whereas the formative nature and the juridical spirit of Rome have so strongly and surely dominated the way that the Church has developed—so strongly that those who were associated with the original Christian Church of Palestine, which still had an intimate connection with the mysteries, felt obliged to bring their impulses to the world through a spiritual stream different from that emanating from Rome. They became the representatives of a parallel esoteric stream which—as for example in Ireland and its Scottish spiritual colonies—was able until a certain point to develop freely and vigorously but soon provoked the anger of the Roman clergy and was then opposed and annihilated. It was in this way that first Gnosticism was eradicated and Arianism stifled, and something similar happened with those movements emanating from Manichaeism which entered Europe by way of the Balkans. These streams are lost in the mists of history; they are presented to the ignorant and the credulous by their opponents in a distorted form. A true consideration of history must attribute the very greatest significance to these phenomena, if it is to lay any claim to seriousness and soundness.

Any such historical survey must be grounded in anthroposophy, which can alone enable us to enter into the depths of history and can offer an overview of and a proper context for what has taken place in the world and amongst mankind. It is where nature and spirit, the natural world and the divine and human world, are united that we find the key to the mysteries of existence and to that greatest of mysteries, which world history in its present form seeks totally to evade but the fathoming and elucidation of which is a primary aim of anthroposophical research, seeking as it does the gradual development of an intuitive understanding of the depths of the Mystery of Golgotha. The life's work of Rudolf Steiner was devoted to the fulfilment of this aim.

Marie Steiner

HUMAN LIFE IN A COSMIC CONTEXT

During the war years the following commemorative words were spoken by Rudolf Steiner before every lecture that he gave to members of the Anthroposophical Society in the countries affected by the war:

My dear friends, we call to mind the guarding spirits of those who are out on the battlefields where war is now raging:

> Spirits watching over your souls,
> May thy wings bring
> Our petitioning love
> To the human beings on Earth entrusted to thy care,
> That, united with thy power,
> Our plea may radiate help
> To the souls
> Whom we seek lovingly to reach.

And as we turn to the guarding spirits of those who have, because of these tragic events, already passed through the gate of death:

> Spirits watching over your souls,
> May thy wings bring
> Our petitioning love
> To the human beings in the heavenly spheres entrusted to thy care,
> That, united with thy power,
> Our plea may radiate help
> To the souls
> Whom we seek lovingly to reach.

And may the Spirit whom we have for some years sought to approach through our spiritual science, the Spirit who passed through the Mystery of Golgotha for the salvation of the Earth and for the freedom and advancement of mankind, may He be with thee and thine arduous duties![1]

LECTURE 1

BERLIN, 6 FEBRUARY 1917

L ET me first express my deep satisfaction that I can be with you once again. This would have happened before had there not been an urgent need to bring the work on the Group that has often been referred to here,[2] which is to stand in the east of the building in Dornach and portrays the Representative of Humanity in relation, respectively, to the ahrimanic and luciferic powers, to the point where it can be worked on further without me. In our present time it is necessary to have fore-thought for the future; and in view of such events as may be impending it seemed to me absolutely necessary to take the work on this Group to where it is now. Moreover, times such as these must necessarily bring home to us in a quite particular way that being together in a spatial sense on the physical plane is not the only means of maintaining the strength and integrity of our relationship to spiritual science; for sharing in the thoughts and convictions of our spiritual-scientific endeavours—even if only in the realm of thoughts—has the potential to bring us through this difficult time of tribulations and sorrow and, hence, be a test for the strength of our spiritual-scientific aspirations.

Since the last time that we were together here, we have had to lament the loss from the physical plane of our dear Fräulein Motzkus[3] and other dear friends who have left the physical plane because of the events overshadowing our times. It is particularly painful no longer to see Fräulein Motzkus amongst those dear friends who have for so many years participated in our spiritual-scientific endeavours. She has belonged to our movement since its beginnings. From the first day, from the first gathering in the smallest circle, she has throughout been in our midst as a member devoted in a very heartfelt way to our movement, participating in a most intimate way in all its phases, all its developmental trials; and above all she has maintained through all the events that have come our way an invincible loyalty in the deepest sense of the word to what we have set out to do, a loyalty which sets an example to those who really want to be devoted members of the anthroposophical movement. And so we look upon this great and beloved soul in the worlds of spiritual existence to which she has ascended, maintaining that bond of loyalty with her that has grown and strengthened over many years, in the knowledge that we are united with her soul for ever. It was not long ago that Fräulein Motzkus herself suffered the loss of a dear friend whom she will now so soon have found again in the spiritual world; and the manner in which she accepted this loss was characteristic of the way that a person bears such a blow out of a true conception of the spiritual world. The active interest with which Fräulein Motzkus participated until her last days in the most important events of our time was indeed something to admire. She would often tell me that she would like to continue living on the physical plane until the momentous events in the midst of which we are now living have been resolved. So she will now in her present state be able to follow these events to which she was so intimately and avidly attached with a freer vision, with a firmer sense for the evolution of mankind. And so may our hearts be entrusted with the commitment that, to the extent that we are able, we will unite our thoughts and the active forces of our soul with this faithful spirit, with this faithful and much-loved member of our movement, so that we may know that—because of the very particular connection with us on the physical plane—we are one with her also in times to come, when she will dwell among us in another form.

The times in which we are living are such that we are given ever greater and greater incentive to ask ourselves what significance the aspiration towards higher knowledge necessarily has for the human race both in the present and in the near future. The events going on around us call forth a condition of stupefaction in many people today, even though there is little awareness of this; while what is actually going on, and how deeply influential what is happening is on human evolution, are things that those who survive such a catastrophe on the physical plane come to be fully aware of only after a certain time. So much the more must we endeavour to call to mind thoughts which are able to shed light on the tasks and goals of this spiritual-scientific movement which is so necessary for mankind. And since we are now again together after quite some time, it will perhaps be especially fruitful to express some specific aspects of our view of this spiritual science in a few brief thoughts—or, to put it somewhat more clearly, the kind of view that can emerge quite naturally from this spiritual science which we have now been cultivating for many years.

It is noticeable that there are individuals scattered everywhere today who are developing the longing to draw near to the spiritual world, even though unfortunately materialism is not diminishing in intensity. Precisely because of the various forms in which the longing for the spirit manifests itself, there is a need for us to call to mind the specific nature of our quest for spiritual life and activity. In England at present the search of a prominent scholar for the spiritual world is making a considerable impression upon a large number of people there. It is indeed an extraordinary phenomenon that a man who is reckoned to be a scientist of the highest order should have written a comprehensive book—with a quite distinctive form—about the relationship of humanity on Earth with the spiritual world. Sir Oliver Lodge,[4] who has been working for years in a variety of ways to extend the scientific knowledge that he has acquired in such a way that it can give him information about the spiritual world, has written a thick book about a particular instance of a relationship that he is wanting to cultivate with the spiritual world. This particular instance can be described as follows.

Sir Oliver Lodge had a son, Raymond Lodge, who in 1915 was fighting on the English side in the war in Flanders. Although his parents knew that their son was still at the front, they received some strange news from America, news which spiritualists with a materialistic attitude must without doubt have found most striking. The news was presented in such a way that one was led to understand that the English psychologist Myers,[5] who many years ago had studied the relationship of the physical world to the spiritual world and had by this time been in the spiritual world for several years, would shortly be looking after young Raymond Lodge. At first it was not clear to what this might relate. There was some delay in the news reaching Sir Oliver Lodge. It arrived when Raymond Lodge, his son, had already fallen—I think it was a fortnight later, but I cannot be exactly sure. So the news of his death was received, and in addition there was this information from America—imparted by mediums—advising his parents to go to English mediums. And so they did so, approaching mediums towards whom Sir Oliver Lodge had a critical attitude. (I shall have more to say presently about the significance of this.) Sir Oliver Lodge is a scientist and is trained to examine such things in a scientific way. He went to work in the way that he approached his work in his laboratory. What emerged from this was an indication given not by one but by several mediums: Raymond's soul wanted to communicate with Sir Oliver and his family. All sorts of communications followed, including automatic writing and knocking, which not only Sir Oliver Lodge himself but other members of his family—who had hitherto had a thoroughly sceptical view of such matters—found wholly convincing. Raymond Lodge's soul indicated, among other things, that Myers, who had long predeceased him, was acting as his guardian; and he told his family many other things about his last days before he died, together with much else which was of significance to his parents and his family, and made a great impression, especially because the various things that Raymond Lodge imparted through the mediums were directly addressed to the family and parti-cularly to Sir Oliver. I should add that not only his family but also Sir Oliver found that the way that the seances were conducted was most strange, and the wider public—in so far as they were able to follow them—found them most extraordinary. They would not have surprised someone who has experience of such things, for in actual fact anyone with any sort of familiarity with the technique and process of such seances would know about the way that communication with the dead was conducted by mediums. One factor in particular, however, made an especially deep impression in England, and it was doubtless calculated to evoke conviction among large numbers of educated Englishmen and also Americans—the sort of conviction that in our sceptical age had previously been largely absent but was ignited among these people by this affair and will continue being ignited. The factor that made so strong an impression on the Lodge family (and on Sir Oliver Lodge in particular) as well as on the wider public can be characterized as follows.

Photographs taken while Raymond Lodge was still alive were described by one of the mediums. The way that they were described was that Raymond Lodge himself was expressing to the medium through rapping sounds what the photographs were about. By this means a group photograph was described; that is to say, it emerged through the medium that the soul of Raymond Lodge wanted to describe a photograph that had been taken of him in a group shortly before he passed through the portal of death. From beyond the threshold he was saying that he had had himself photographed with some of his comrades, who had been photographed in two groups one behind the other; this was how they were arranged, and *this* was his position. He then went on to indicate that several photographs were taken one after another, as photographers tend to do. He described exactly how these photographs taken in rapid succession differed from one another. He was—he said—always sitting on the same chair, also with the same approximate gesture, though the position of his arm and other similar details were slightly different. This was related with great precision. Now the Lodge family knew nothing of these photographs, they had no idea that photographs had been taken. So there was this situation, that through the agency of the medium a series of group photographs had been described which portray Raymond Lodge with several of his comrades. After some time, approximately a fortnight, these photographs were sent to Sir Oliver Lodge from France, and they corresponded exactly to the way they had been described through the medium in accordance with the indications given by the soul of Raymond Lodge. This made a particularly strong impression. And indeed, anyone who is something of a dilettante in such matters—and it is clear that all those concerned fell into that category—would inevitably have such a strong impression. It was a fool-proof test. A soul describes from beyond the threshold a series of photographs in a number of different poses which reach the family only a fortnight later and correspond precisely with the information that had been given. Thus one can say that there was not the slightest possibility that the medium or someone involved in the seance—and these were all members of the Lodge family—could have seen any of these photographs. So you see that we have a case here which really bears thinking about, both from the scientific standpoint and also as a phenomenon of cultural history. For it is not merely possible to anticipate that something of this nature might make a considerable impression; this is what indeed occurred, it did make a considerable impression. In so far as one could see, it was this description of the photographs, which could not depend on thought-transference, that was so deeply convincing.

We really need to give consideration to the whole of this case. For we must be quite clear that when a person passes through the portal of death the situation is such that the human individuality is at first briefly enshrouded by the astral body and ether body, and that after a period of varying length but always measured in terms of a few days the ether body is given over to the etheric world, where it pursues its further destiny, so that the individuality sets out on its further journey in the spiritual world together with the astral body. Just as the physical body here on the Earth is separated from the individuality, so too is the human ether body. Now we must be clear about the fact that in spiritualistic seances—and the whole of Sir Oliver Lodge's work is pervaded with his interest in them—only someone with the requisite knowledge is able to distinguish whether the communication is being conducted with the actual individuality or merely with the discarded etheric corpse which has been left behind. This etheric corpse is none-theless in constant communication with the individuality. Now if a connection is established with the spiritual world through the agency of a medium this is formed initially with the ether body, and one can never be sure whether one is really in contact with the individuality. There is, to be sure, the aspiration in our time to explore spiritual existence rather as one would engage in an experiment in the laboratory, to find something that one can really take hold of and see before one in the material world. Our materialistic age has little inclination to embark upon the inner path, the purely spiritual path which the soul will follow into the spirit land. It wants the spirit to manifest itself materially, to descend into the material world. We are experiencing all kinds of materialistic spiritualism, a materialistic way of relating to the spiritual world.

Now it is perfectly possible for the etheric body which has been separated from the human individuality as such to manifest a certain life of its own, which to the uninitiated can easily be confused with the life of the individuality. One should not think that once this ether body has been given over to the etheric world it would exhibit only reminiscences, recollections, echoes of what the individual concerned experienced here on Earth; rather does it manifest an ongoing individuality of its own. It can communicate and give rise to altogether new things. Nevertheless, anyone who thinks that this connection with the ether body also entails being in touch with the individuality is on the wrong track. This would be especially possible if the people sitting in a circle—and in this circle of the Lodge family they were all members of the family—were directing their thoughts (which were formed to varying degrees) to the dead person, as was naturally the case with each of these members of the Lodge family. Thoughts of the dead person and memories of various kinds were being shared through the agency of the mediating power of the medium, and the ether body from time to time responds with wholly astonishing answers which really give the impression that the dead man's individuality were giving them. Nevertheless, it may be that they derive merely from his discarded etheric corpse. Those who are familiar with such things find it to be the case that whenever the medium is describing a communication of some nature from Raymond Lodge to the members of his family it will actually only be coming from the etheric corpse; and so no communication will have been taking place between the individuality of Raymond Lodge and his family circle. Similarly, anyone who is accustomed to the way that such seances proceed would not find anything particularly remarkable about all these communications.

This story would probably not have made so much impression on a wide circle of people or continue to reverberate further were it not for the photographs. For the issue of the photographs is indeed a quite remarkable phenomenon. After all, it is impossible that any transference of thoughts would have taken place from people in the circle to the etheric body through the medium, as would have been possible with everything else that took place at the seances. No one in England could have known anything about the photographs; they had not reached

England when the communications were made through the medium. Nevertheless, it is very strange that someone who has been interested in these matters and is, moreover, such a learned scientist as Sir Oliver Lodge does not know how such a circumstance is to be regarded. I have gone to quite some trouble to look at this case more closely, and that is very possible because Sir Oliver Lodge is a learned man and a scientist and his descriptions are therefore reliable. So what we have here is not the record of an ordinary spiritualistic seance but the account of a man who writes with the certainty of a scientist, who is accustomed to the conscientiousness with which a chemist works in his laboratory. From the highly conscientious nature of the description it is possible to form a complete picture of what it is all about; and that is what it is necessary to know.

It is strange that a learned man like Sir Oliver Lodge, who has been interested in these things for many years and has a very particular interest through the circumstances concerning his own son, knows nothing of the descriptions that have often been given through our spiritual science where the atavistic forms of clairvoyance are referred to as a form of premonition, as deuteroscopy. For in this case we are clearly dealing with a quite particular instance of deuteroscopy. The fact of the matter is that a medium is involved here. To such a medium the spiritual world is in a certain sense accessible, albeit through atavistic forces. Such mediums can reach beyond space in their visionary perception. But not only do they reach beyond space with their so-called second sight but also transcend time. Let us take a very simple case, a case which has been described hundreds and hundreds of times (you can read descriptions of such cases if you have not yourself experienced something of this kind yourself or through someone you know), whereby someone who has a particular disposition for this sees his own coffin or funeral procession as a future event as though in a dream or a dim visionary perception. He dies a fortnight later. He has seen something which was to occur only in 14 days' time. It is possible for one to see not only one's own coffin or funeral procession but, for example, the funeral of a complete stranger, an event with which one has no personal connection. Or—to relate a particular instance—one may see oneself called out in two or three weeks' time into the country and falling from a horse. This did actually happen. Someone saw this very thing and was very careful to take every precaution; but despite every precaution this event still came about. Here we are concerned with transcending time. What Sir Oliver Lodge describes is none other than the bridging of two phases of time, a temporal second sight. This is quite simply what it is. His description is so precise that a thorough investigation is possible. Through her mediumistic power the medium saw the future event. When the medium spoke, the photographs did not exist; but they did in a fortnight or approximately so. They were then shown round. This happened only after a certain time, but the medium saw this in advance. It was a prophetic vision, a case of deuteroscopy. It was a premonition; that is the explanation. Hence it has nothing to do with a communication between those on the physical plane and the one who was in the spiritual world.

You see how thoroughly confused one can be by endeavouring to give materialistic explanations of spiritual circumstances in the world, how very blind one can be towards what is actually going on. In truth, it is nevertheless a proof for the reality of a world lying behind the ordinary sense-perceptible world that such a premonition is possible. The case is interesting, even if one cannot use it in order to establish connections between the living and the dead. The dead must be sought—if we are to, and may be enabled, to seek them at all—on a truly spiritual path. In the near future we shall have much to say about these matters, for I intend to say quite a lot about the question of the relation of the living to the dead.

I spoke about this book by Oliver Lodge regarding his son Raymond in order to show you that although there is indeed a longing for the spiritual world the form in which it manifests itself is one that one can call materialistic. Oliver Lodge is a materialistic scholar. Even though he longs for the spiritual world, he wants to gain knowledge of it as one would the physical or chemical world. Just as he investigates chemical laws in the laboratory, he also wants to have visible proof of what relates to the spiritual world. Similarly, the path that we must necessarily recognize as the right one—the inner path of the soul to the spiritual world which we have so often described—is far removed from his; although we have devoted no less time to describing what we recognize as of the most immediate concern to us today and underlies the world of the physical senses in which we live. The efforts made to reach the spiritual world in a materialistic way are a particularly clear sign of the whole materialistic character of our age. If our movement is to have any significance, that is, the significance that must accrue to it from the laws governing human evolution, it must sharply emphasize the inner, spiritual nature of reality as opposed to these materialistic—that is to say, absurd—aspirations towards the spiritual world.

Why is it necessary that in our present time an attitude that is completely different from a materialistic one, that is, a purely spiritual attitude, should prevail in human hearts? We need to consider this question in relation to a fact to which we have frequently referred over the years, one that must closely concern us especially in these times of suffering and tribulation. I have indicated that this twentieth century must bring to humanity a perception of the etheric Christ. As I have often said, just as at the time of the Mystery of Golgotha the Christ was physically present amongst human beings in a particular place on the Earth it is equally true that in the twentieth century the etheric Christ will live and move amongst human beings over the entire Earth. It is essential for the sake of the Earth's evolution that mankind should not let this event pass by unobserved; it must have the attentiveness necessary that a sufficient number of people will be prepared truly to behold the Christ who will come and must be beheld.

Just as the event of Golgotha did not come all of a sudden but was prepared over the course of 33 years, such an event will not come suddenly. The time when something will happen—albeit now of a spiritual nature—that will have a similar significance for mankind to the event of Golgotha on the physical plane is now very near. Hence if you acknowledge in general terms the fact referred to above, you will not find it incredible if I say that He is already present in the form in which He will be beheld in the great moment of evolution in the twentieth century, that this great moment of evolution is being prepared. You will not find it difficult to believe if, in view of the great moment that is impending, it is already being anticipated. Indeed, one can say that the extent to which humanity would appear to be far from being imbued in its present deeds by the spirit of Christ on the physical plane is matched by the closeness of Christ, He who is now approaching, to human souls, if they would but open themselves to Him. The occultist is able to point out that since the year 1909 or thereabouts what is to come is being prepared in a clearly discernible way, and that since 1909 we have been living in a very special time. If we do but try to approach Christ to the extent that we are able, it is possible to find Him in an altogether different way than was possible in earlier times.

However simple it may seem, there is one thought that occurs to me which I must pass on to you out of a deep feeling for the times. It is unfortunate that people do not usually have sufficiently clear ideas about the past, specifically about what took place in human souls in previous centuries. They do not any longer have any real conception of the strength of the impression made by what lives in the Gospels that we are familiar with today (irrespective of what has actually been handed down to us) in the early Christian centuries albeit on a limited circle of people; they have no idea of the infinite power that took hold of people's souls in this way. In the ensuing centuries the impression made by the inner content of the Gospels grew weaker and weaker. And today one can honestly say that, although individuals with certain intuitional powers can through the words of the Gospels gain an insight into what happened at the time of the Mystery of Golgotha, the immense power that the words of the Gospels once possessed is diminishing to an ever greater extent and one has to accept that the influence of these words on the majority of people is now very weak. There is a resistance to acknowledging this; but it would be as well to do so, since this is the truth. How did this come to be the case?

The fact of the matter is that what pervades the Gospels are not mere earthly words but cosmic words, heavenly words which have an incomparably greater inner force than anything else on the Earth; but it is nevertheless no less true that people have in our present time become estranged from the form in which these words have been set forth in the Gospels from the time of the Mystery of Golgotha. Just consider how very difficult it is for you to understand the language of four or five centuries ago if you happen to chance upon it. It is very difficult to draw out from the words what they actually mean. The Gospels in the form in which they are available to anyone today are not the original Gospels;

they do not have the original power. One can enter into them through a certain intuition, as I have often said; but they do not have the same force. But the words that Christ spoke which should be deeply engraved in human souls, 'I am with you always, to the end of the earthly age,' represent a truth, a reality; and He will be in close proximity to us in various forms in the twentieth century at the time that has been indicated.

From what I have said, you may suppose that someone who as an occultist feels inwardly involved in these things may say: He is here; and He makes His presence felt so that we clearly know from Him that He wants more from His human children than He did in previous centuries. The Gospels have hitherto addressed human beings in an inward way. Their task was to take hold of people's souls. It was therefore possible to rest content with faith and not venture towards knowledge. This time is now over, it lies behind us. The Christ now has quite different plans for His human children. His intention is that the kingdom that he refers to as being 'not of this world' should become wedded to those aspects of man's being which are themselves not of this world but are of another world. For that part of man's being which is not of this world lies within each one of us; and this aspect of our being must undertake an intensive quest for the kingdom of which Christ has said that it is not of this world.

We are living at the time when this needs to be understood. Many such things in human evolution are proclaimed through profound contrasts; and likewise in our time something of grandeur and deep significance is being proclaimed through contrast. For as Christ approaches in His etheric reality, the time will come when people will learn to consult Christ not only on behalf of their own inner being but in connection with what they want to undertake here on Earth through that part of them which is immortal. The Christ is not only a ruler of human beings, He is their brother who wants to be asked with respect to life's every detail. When people want to undertake anything today they act in a totally contrasting way. Deeds seem to be accomplished today where people are as far removed as possible from appealing to Christ. We may well ask whether anyone poses the question: What would Christ Jesus say about what is taking place today? Who asks such a question? Many say that they do, but it would be sacrilegious to believe that they ask in such a way that their questions are really addressed to Christ Himself. Nevertheless, the time must come and cannot be far away when people will, out of the immortal aspect of their being, ask Christ with respect to whatever they want to undertake: Should we do this or should we not? Human souls will then see Christ accompanying them as a loving companion in life's every detail, not only receiving strength and consolation from the Christ Being but also information guiding them as to what needs to happen. The kingdom of Christ Jesus is not of this world, but it must exert an influence upon it; and human souls must be the instruments of the kingdom that is not of this world. From this point of view we must be mindful of how little today people raise the question that must be posed to Christ with regard to individual deeds and events. However, mankind must learn to consult Christ.

How is this to come about? This can happen only if we learn His language. Anyone who has an insight into the deeper significance of our spiritual science sees in it not merely a theoretical knowledge of all manner of problems that humanity encounters, of the various members of man's being, of reincarnation and karma, but views it as having a quite particular language, a particular way of speaking about spiritual things. It is far more important that we learn through spiritual science to have an inner discourse in our thoughts with the spiritual world than to acquire theoretical thoughts. For Christ is with us always until the end of the epochs of earthly time. We need to learn His language. And through the language (however removed from everyday experience it may seem) that enables us to hear of Saturn, Sun, Moon and Earth, and of the different periods and ages of the Earth and of many other mysteries of evolution, we are teaching ourselves a language in which we can frame the questions that we pose to the spiritual world. If we learn inwardly to speak in the language of this spiritual life, what will then arise, my dear friends, is that Christ will stand beside us and give us answers. This is the basic attitude, the underlying feeling, that we should receive from our spiritual-scientific endeavours. Why do we concern ourselves with spiritual science? It is as though we were learning the vocabulary of that language through which we approach Christ. If we really try to learn to think about the world as spiritual science has sought to do, if we make the kind of mental effort that is asked of us by spiritual science to gain insight into the mysteries of the world, the figure of Christ Jesus will emerge from the dim, dark foundations of these mysteries and give us the strength and power that will imbue our lives; He will stand at our side in a brotherly way in order that we may be able in our hearts and souls to have the strength to gain the necessary maturity for the tasks of the future evolution of mankind. So let us endeavour to make spiritual science our own not merely as a teaching but as a language, and then wait until we find the questions in this language that we may address to Christ. He will answer, yes He *will* answer! And anyone who—amidst the spiritual depths through which mankind is currently passing in its evolutionary journey—receives guidance from Christ, which He will give in the near future to all who seek it, will be richly endowed with inner forces, inner strength and renewed impulses of soul.

THE thoughts that we formulated a week ago were focused on the insight that anyone with a knowledge of spiritual realities is well aware that, even though outwardly a materialistic view, a materialistic outlook on the world, has reached its culminating point, we are nevertheless inwardly at present in the initial phase of a dematerializing of thoughts and of the world of ideas, and that in the course of time this will lead to a spiritualizing of earthly life, an imbuing of Earth existence with the spirit. This renewing impulse which is to take hold of outward life on the physical plane must first be understood and formulated by some and then by increasing numbers of people in a spiritual way; and spiritual science needs in this respect to begin the process whereby human beings are inwardly uplifted to what can become accessible to human souls today if they do but will it, to that of which outward physical life is not as yet a reflection—though it must become so if the Earth is not in a certain sense to be engulfed in the decline of materialistic evolution. One could describe man's present situation by saying that his soul is in general terms actually very close to the spiritual world; but the ideas and especially the feelings deriving from a materialistic conception of the world and a materialistic attitude towards it have cast a veil over what is in actual fact closely affiliated to the human soul. The connection between physical Earth existence—where people today, in spite of many assertions to the contrary, are firmly rooted with their whole being—and the spiritual world can be found by human beings if they try to develop the inner forces of courage to understand not only what nature displays before their outer senses but also what remains invisible to sensory perception; for it is possible to unite with and experience this supersensible domain if one intensifies the inner forces of one's soul to the point where one becomes aware that something of a superhuman and spiritual nature lives in these inner forces of the soul.

This connection should not be sought in the way that human connections are sought and pursued in the coarse world of outward sensory existence; for the connection between the human soul and the spiritual world will be found in the intimate forces which the human soul develops when it acquires the inner quality of quiet, calm attentiveness—a quality that cannot be achieved without training, for in this materialistic age people have grown accustomed to paying attention only to what is thrust at them forcefully from without and what in a certain sense cries out to their faculties of perception. The spirit that now needs to be experienced inwardly does not cry out but, rather, has to be awaited; and it can be approached only by preparing oneself for it as it draws near. Whereas one can say that the phenomena of the outer world which appear before our senses and demand the attention of our faculties of perception come towards us and address us directly, one cannot refer in a similar way to the manner in which the spirit, the spiritual world, approaches us. As the language of modern times is, as I have often said, more or less moulded for the outer physical world, it is difficult to find words that are an exact reflection of whatever aspect of the spiritual world appears before our soul. But one can nevertheless try to show approximately how differently the spiritual and physical worlds approach man. One could say that the spiritual world is experienced through the feeling of gratitude that one has when experiencing it. Take special note of these words; we owe a debt of gratitude to the spiritual world.

Our relationship to the physical world is such that we say that the mineral kingdom is spread out before our senses, and from it proceed the plant kingdom, the animal kingdom and then our own human kingdom. Within this human world we feel ourselves in a certain sense as being in a superior position in the sequence of these kingdoms of the outer world. With respect to the spiritual realms we are aware of our inferior position and of the other realms—those of the Angeloi, Archangeloi, Archai and so on—as being far above us. We feel that at every moment we are supported by these beings and continually summoned into life by them. We are grateful to them. We look up to them and say: our own life, all that lives in our soul, flows down to us from the will-impregnated thoughts of the beings dwelling in these realms and constantly forms us. This feeling of personal gratitude to the higher realms should be just as alive in us as the feelings that outer impressions arouse within us as we perceive them physically. If both these feelings— those that outer sensory phenomena exert upon us and our awareness that what lives in the very centre of our being is owed to the higher hierarchies—are equally alive in our soul, we are then in that state of balance whereby we can continue rightly to perceive the interplay between the spiritual and physical domains, a collaborative process which is taking place continually but which cannot be perceived without the feelings that have been characterized being in a state of balance.

An evolution that leads into the future must proceed in such a way that, through the presence of these two feelings in the human soul, additional forces enter into earthly evolution which are not able to prosper there in the present materialistic age. Such a statement clearly implies that there have been considerable changes in the course of human evolution. Only in the earliest period of human evolution was there a connection with the spiritual world, albeit in a dimly conscious form. In the early stage of their evolution human beings did not only have the two states of consciousness that they have now, namely waking and sleeping together with a chaotic dream life, but they had a third state of consciousness which did not merely consist of dreams but was a capacity to perceive the world in pictures out of a dulled condition of consciousness, in pictures that corresponded to a spiritual reality. As we know, it was necessary for this way of perceiving the world to give way to the development of a fully Earth-bound consciousness. Man would not have become free if he had not been exposed to all the dangers, challenges and temptations of materialism. However, he must also find his way back to the spiritual world, whose mysteries he must fathom in full earthly consciousness.

This is connected with far-reaching changes in the way that people have perceived the world in the course of human evolution, on the lines that we have just indicated. Living in constant communion with souls that had departed from physical existence was a purely natural state of affairs for people in ancient times, which did not require any proof; for in that state of consciousness where they perceived the spiritual world in pictures they lived together with those who through their karma were connected in some way with them in life and had passed into the spiritual world through the portal of death. They knew quite simply that the dead are there; they are not dead, they are alive, albeit in a different form of existence. Something that one perceives does not need to be proved. There was no need to ponder about immortality in former ages of human evolution, for people experienced the so-called dead for themselves. However, this communion with the dead had other consequences of a far-reaching nature. It was at that time easier for the dead than it is now—I am not saying that it is impossible at present but that it was easier then than now—to collaborate with people here on the Earth with what is going on and thus enable things to proceed as they should. Thus in these early times of human evolution, what took place on the Earth happened in such a way that the dead were active in people's will impulses, in everything that they did and sought to accomplish.

Materialism has not only brought forth materialistic ideas (this would be the least harmful of its legacies, for materialistic ideas as such represent its least harmful aspect); it has given rise to a completely different form of co-existence with the spiritual world. It has become far less possible for the so-called dead to take an active part here in the evolution of the Earth through the so-called living; and a connection with the dead of this nature is a relationship that mankind needs to re-establish. However, this will only be possible if people learn to understand the language of the dead; and the language through which one can communicate with the dead is none other than that of spiritual science. It may certainly seem initially that what spiritual science imparts to us is for the most part concerned with matters pertaining to spiritual erudition, such as world evolution, human evolution and the various members of man's being, and many people may well say that such things are of little interest to them: they want something that kindles their enthusiasm and warms their hearts. This is a very laudable demand, but the question is how far satisfying such a demand to a certain extent can take us. It seems that we are only learning how the Earth has evolved on Saturn, Sun and Moon, how the various cultural epochs on the Earth have run their course and how the members of man's being can be distinguished; but by focusing our thoughts on these seemingly abstract, but actually very real matters, by endeavouring to think in such a way that these things can really be beheld in pictures, we are learning to preoccupy ourselves in a particular way with thoughts and ideas which we could not bring before our souls in any other way. If we come truly to feel how our ideas are transformed when we study these spiritual-scientific insights, a time will come when we will find it just as absurd to say that we are not interested in concerning ourselves with these things as it would be for a child to say that it had no interest in learning about the trivialities of the ABC but wants to be able to speak! When compared with what a living language can impart to us, the process that the child has to undergo in its bodily existence when learning to speak is no less abstract than are the ideas of spiritual science when contrasted with the thoughts, ideas and feelings aroused in the soul under the influence of these spiritual-scientific concepts.

This does of course require patience; for it is necessary to assimilate spiritual science not as an abstract body of ideas but as a living substance. With regard to what we now have in view, this is quite a remote possibility for people today. In a somewhat different way, however, they also have a certain affinity for it; for they are accustomed to being more or less content when they have focused their attention on a particular object or theme, such as a work of art of some sort or a scientific study. But if they see something for a second time, the tendency today is to say: I know this already, I have already dealt with it. This is life lived in the abstract. But in other domains where life is evaluated in accordance with its actual realities, its essential substance, one does not proceed in such a way. Thus one is not likely to meet someone to whom one offers lunch and who then excuses himself for not wanting to eat on the grounds that he has already eaten yesterday or the day before yesterday. Where such things are concerned one keeps on repeating the same action, life is a constant repetition. If the spiritual realm is to become truly alive (and unless it does so it is unable to bring us in touch with the universality of the world of spirit), we must imitate in our souls what the laws of life have formed in the physical world, which for all its ossified nature has a spiritual origin. In particular, we shall become aware that, if with a certain rhythmic regularity we allow such impressions to affect us as presuppose a certain freedom of thought, an emancipation of thinking from the physical world, much is going on within our inner being. The saving grace—if I may use these emotive words—of man's spiritual development will be that people do not settle into relating to spiritual ideas in the way that this tends to happen today, an attitude that can be characterized by statements such as, 'Oh, I know that already, I have heard it all before,' but instead regard these ideas as being like life itself, which is always associated with repetition, with what I might call a recurrence of the same phenomenon at the same place. Thus if we work towards imbuing our soul with spiritual life, our inner attentiveness also increases. It becomes so intimate that we are able inwardly to call to mind those important moments in which the connections with the spiritual world that speak most directly to our heart can be nurtured.

Significant moments for engaging with the spiritual world are, for example, those of falling asleep and waking. The moment of falling asleep will be less fruitful for most people at the beginning of their spiritual development, because immediately after going to sleep their consciousness will be so dulled that they will not perceive the world of spirit. But the moment of passing from sleep into a waking state—if we do become accustomed not simply to let it pass by unobserved but try to pay attention to it by endeavouring to wake up in such a way that, although consciousness has dawned, the world around us does not immediately approach us with its raw brutality—can be highly productive. In this respect there is much of value in the folk customs of olden times that is little understood today. Simple people who have little acquaintance with intellectual culture will say that when you wake up you should not look immediately at the light. Thus instead of having an immediate raw impression of the outside world one should remain in a state of wakefulness without receiving impressions of one's surroundings.

If this can be achieved, it is at this moment of waking possible to see those dead people with whom we have a karmic connection approaching us. They do not only approach us at such times, but this is the best opportunity to perceive them. At such a time we do not only have perceptions of this nature but we also see what is taking place between us and the dead people concerned in the time outside these moments; for one's perception of the spiritual world is not bound up with time in the same way as one's perception of the physical world. Herein lies a difficulty with respect to comprehending the essential nature of the spiritual world. One moment of perception can momentarily and fleetingly reveal to us something from the spiritual world that extends over a wide expanse of time. The difficulty lies in having sufficient presence of mind to grasp in the moment what is spread out over greater periods of time; for as is indeed generally the case, the moment may pass by in *status nascendi*. It is forgotten as soon as it arises. This is an inherent difficulty in comprehending the spiritual world. Were it not for this, a large number of people would especially in our present time already be receiving impressions of the spiritual world.

There are also other moments in life when it is possible for the spiritual world to reach through to us. One example is when we form a thought in such a way that it springs forth from us. If we simply abandon ourselves to life and flow with the stream, there is little like-lihood that the real, true and inwardly vibrant spiritual world will be active within us; whereas in the moment when we inwardly take an initiative, when we are confronted with a decision that we have to make ourselves (even if only about something very trivial), this again is a particularly favourable moment for the dead people who are karmically connected with us to enter our sphere of consciousness. Such moments do not need to be important in the sense of what one terms 'important' in outward material life. Indeed, what is important as a spiritual experience may sometimes not appear to have any great significance in one's outer life. But to someone who has insight into such matters it is absolutely clear that these experiences which—while perhaps having little outward significance—are inwardly of such great importance have deep karmic associations. Thus it is necessary to observe soul processes of a more intimate nature if one wishes to arrive at an understanding of the spiritual world. It may, for example, occur that someone is walking along the street or sitting in his room and is startled by an unexpected bang or a sound that he had not anticipated. After his shock he may have a moment of quiet reflection which makes him aware that something important was revealed to him from the spiritual world during this shock. One needs to pay attention to these things. Generally speaking, people do not have any awareness of this aspect, since they are preoccupied with the shock that they received and are only able to dwell on this. This is why it is so important to acquire an inner sense of balance, as indicated at the end of my book *Theosophy*[1] or in *Knowledge of the Higher Worlds*;[2] for if this can be acquired one will not be so perplexed after such a shock that one dwells merely on one's sense of alarm, and the nature of what one has experienced in such an apparently insignificant but nevertheless—in an inward sense—highly important moment will become clearly apparent, albeit in an intimate way.

These are of course only initial steps, which must be developed further; for by developing these capacities of being attentive to the moment of waking and being attentive to the moment when we are disturbed by an outward event of one kind or another, we learn to discover our connection with the wider cosmos—comprising as it does both material and spiritual aspects—to which we belong and from which we have become separated (with the object, to be sure, of becoming free human beings but which is indeed the source whence we originated). The truth is that, as was an accepted fact in ancient times, man is not a sort of cosmic hermit who wanders about the Earth like a lost soul, as people believe now. On the contrary, he is—as was acknowledged in ancient times—part of the great cosmic whole, just as a finger is a member of our bodily organism. People today, or at any rate the majority of people, no longer feel themselves to be members of the great organism of the cosmos, in so far as it comes visibly to expression as a spiritual reality. Nevertheless, a reflection on ordinary scientific insights could teach us today that we—and our lives—are members of the whole cosmic order of which our own organism is a part. Let us take a very simple example, which anyone can confirm for himself through a simple calculation.

We all know that in spring, on 21 March, the Sun rises at a definite point in the heavens. We call this the vernal point. However, we also know that this vernal point is not the same every year but that it moves forward. We know that the Sun now rises in the constellation of the Fishes. Before the fifteenth century it rose in the Ram. (Astronomy continues to say 'in the Ram' or 'in Aries', which is not correct. However, this incidental remark can be disregarded for now.) So the vernal point progresses; the Sun rises a little further on in the zodiac every spring. It is easy to see from this that over a certain period it will have moved through the whole zodiac, that the position of the dawn will have travelled through the entire zodiacal circle. Now the time that is necessary for the Sun to move through the whole zodiac is approximately 25,920 years. So if you calculate the vernal point for any particular year it will have moved forward in the following year. When 25,920 years have elapsed the vernal point returns to the same point. Hence 25,920 is a highly significant period for our solar system; the Sun takes what I might describe as a cosmic step when the position of the dawn returns to the same point. Plato, the great Greek philosopher, referred to these 25,920 years as a cosmic year—the great Platonic year. All this is already very remarkable, but if we consider the following we can see the infinite depth and significance of the whole remarkable picture.

A human being normally takes 18 breaths in a minute. This varies in that in childhood they are somewhat more frequent and in old age less so, but on average it would be correct to say that a normal person takes 18 breaths. If on this basis we work out how many breaths are taken in a day, it is a simple calculation: 18 times 60, which makes 1080 in an hour; multiply that by 24 and we arrive at 25,920 breaths in a day. You see from this that the same number governs the human day with respect to our breaths as the great cosmic year is governed by this number in the passage of the vernal point through the zodiac.

This is one of the signs which shows us that we are not just talking in a general, vague and dimly mystical way when we say that the microcosm is an image of the macrocosm, but that as regards an important function on which his life depends at every moment man is governed by the same number and measure as the course of the Sun within which his own life is also lived.

Now let us consider another aspect of this. The patriarchal age, as it is generally called, is 70 human years. Of course this does not mean that every person has to live for 70 years. Some people may live much longer, for man is a free being and such thresholds may well be exceeded. Nevertheless, let us keep to this patriarchal age and say that a human being lives on average for 70 or 71 years. Let us work out how many days that is, on the basis that there are 365.25 days in a year. If we multiply this by 70 we get 25,567.5; if we multiply it by 71 we arrive at 25,932.75. From this you can see that the point of time when human life encompasses exactly 25,920 days lies between the ages of 70 and 71; so the patriarchal age lasts for 25,920 days. So a human day is defined as having 25,920 breaths, and a human life as having 25,920 days.

Let us now investigate something else, which can now be done quite simply. You will see quite easily that if I divide the 25,920 years that the vernal point of the Sun needs to pass through the zodiac by 365.25, I shall arrive at approximately 70 or 71 (in that I arrived at the same figures through multiplication). That is to say, if I regard the Platonic year as one great year and divide it in such a way that I define the length of a day, I discover what a day is in terms of a Platonic year. What is it? It is the course of a human life. The course of a human life is related to the Platonic year as a day in a person's life is related to a year.

The air is all around us. We breathe it in and breathe it out. The numerical rhythm of this process is such that 25,920 breaths are equivalent to one day in our life. What, then, is a day in our life? It has a rhythm whereby our ego and astral body leave our physical and ether bodies and return to them again. Thus day after day the ego and astral body leave and return, leave and return, just as our breath is exhaled and inhaled. Many of our friends will recall that in order to make this clear, I have in public lectures compared this alternation of waking and sleeping to a deep breath. So just as we exhale and inhale air when we breathe, our astral body and ego leave and return to our ether and physical bodies when we go to sleep and wake up again. This amounts to saying that a being exists, or can be presumed to exist, that breathes in and out just as we fulfil this function in an eighteenth of a minute, and the breathing of this being is directly related to the leaving and returning of our astral body and ego. This being is none other than the living being of the Earth. In that the Earth experiences day and night it is breathing, and its breathing process bears our sleeping and waking on its wings. This is the breathing process of a greater being. And now let us consider the breathing process of the greater being of the Sun, encircling the heavens. Just as for the Earth a day elapses as the ego and astral body depart from and re-engage with man's physical and etheric bodies, the great Being corresponding spiritually to the Sun brings us human beings into existence; for our 70 to 71 years are, as we have demonstrated, a day of the Sun year, of the great Platonic year. Our entire human life is an out-breathing and in-breathing of this great Being, to whom the Platonic year is assigned. Thus, you see, we draw one small breath in an eighteenth of a minute which regulates our life; we are involved in the life of the Earth, whose breathing rhythm encompasses day and night, and this corresponds to the rhythm whereby our ego and astral body leave and return to our physical and ether bodies; and we are ourselves breathed out by the great Being whose life corresponds to the course of the Sun, our life is a breath of this great Being. You see, then, that as microcosms we are fully part of the macrocosm and are subject to the same laws as regards the beings of the universe as our breathing is subject with respect to our own human nature. Everything is governed by number and measure. But what is so amazing, deeply meaningful and profoundly moving for our hearts is that number and measure govern the wider cosmos—the macrocosm—and the microcosm in a similar way. This is not merely a figure of speech, not merely something that is mystically felt, but something that a wisdom-filled contemplation of the world teaches us, namely that we stand as microcosms within the macrocosm.

If one makes these very simple calculations (for they can of course be arrived at by means of the most ordinary methods of arithmetic) and if one does not have a heart like a block of wood but one is sensitive to the mysteries of cosmic existence, a statement such as 'we are part of the cosmic whole' ceases to be purely abstract and becomes deeply alive. A knowledge and a feeling will blossom and flourish and bear fruit in impulses of the will, and the whole of humanity will live the all-encompassing life of divine cosmic existence. This is the path on which we may find to some extent a means of forming a link to the spiritual world, and it must be found—as already indicated in the previous lecture—during the time when Christ will dwell etherically on the Earth. I have even referred to the year when He began to move about etherically on our Earth. He must be found! But people must become accustomed to perceiving the connection, the very intimate connection, that is already established with cosmic existence, a connection which—when it is perceived—will ensure that the need, the intense longing, arises to seek this union with the spiritual world. For it will not be long before people will be compelled to realize one thing, which is the following.

If one is dulled by materialism it is indeed possible to deny the spiritual world; but one cannot kill the inner forces which have the capacity to seek a connection with it. One can delude oneself as to the existence of a spiritual world, but one cannot kill the soul forces which have the potential to bring man into communion with the spiritual world. This has a very significant consequence of which one needs to be aware especially in our time, namely that where forces exist they have an effect, even if one denies them. The materialist does not forbid the forces in his soul that incline towards the spiritual world from having an effect; he cannot do so, for they have an effect anyway. You may ask whether someone who has these spiritually inclined forces within him can be a materialist. Yes, he can. They are active within him. Whatever he may think about it, they are at work within him. But what effect do they have in such a case? Forces that are present in any situation can indeed be suppressed as regards their own original influence, but they are then transformed into other forces. And if one does not use the forces that would reach towards the spiritual realm in order to seek an under-standing of this domain (I speak now only of 'understanding', since that is all that is necessary to begin with), they are transformed into forces of illusion in human life. Their effect is then such that people in ordinary life abandon themselves to all manner of illusions with respect to the world around them. That this should be so is not without significance in our time, for at no time have people indulged their imagination as they do today, even though they have no love for imagination. Imagination is not restricted to particular areas. If one were to begin to give examples of what people who want to be mere realists and materialists imagine, one could shed light on all sorts of things and there would be no end of it. Although I do not want to engage in heresies, one might by way of an example begin to take a look at what certain people, statesmen for instance, have prophesied no more than a few weeks ago about the probable course of events in the world and then cast one's eye over what has actually happened. If one compares these things one will find that the capacity for illusion has for quite some years been far from small.

If one investigates all areas of life in this way, it is quite remarkable to note the extent to which this capacity for illusion exists everywhere today. This capacity for illusion at times endows the attitudes and opinions of materialistically inclined people with a childlike, even perhaps a childish, quality. When one sees what is needed for people to understand one another or to try to spell something out to them, one will get some idea of what I mean when I say 'childlike' or even 'childish'. Well, this is how things are. If people turn away from the spiritual world, they must pay for it by becoming prone to illusions, by losing the capacity to have appropriate concepts about outward physical reality and the course of outward events. Their imagination is then directed towards another realm, because they have a disregard for truth, irrespective of whether it relates to spiritual or physical reality.

I once gave you an obvious example which, even though it relates to matters within our own circles, is nevertheless quite typical. One frequently experiences discussions where the spiritual science advocated by me is the subject of negative judgements. These judgements are based on the assertion that everything that I have said is pure fantasy, and such flights of fancy are not permitted! So these people do not want to accompany us into the true spiritual world, because they consider it to be purely fanciful, and they despise such fanciful imaginations. And then they formulate all sorts of arguments whose relationship to the reality in question is no greater than that of white to black—for example, about my own antecedents,[3] about the way that I did this or that in my life. In this way they develop the boldest fantasies. Here you see the coexistence of a repudiation of the spiritual world and a capacity for illusion! The people concerned do not notice this, but it accords with an absolute law. A certain amount of energy is directed towards the spiritual world and a certain amount towards the physical world. If the quantum of energy available for the spiritual world is not used for this purpose it is directed towards the physical world not in order to grasp the truth of earthly reality but to plunge people into illusions concerning their lives today.

This cannot be similarly observed in each individual case, so that one can necessarily say in every instance that this person has fallen prey to illusion through his rejection of the spiritual world. Such examples can indeed be found, but they have to be searched for; and the reason that they cannot so easily be detected is that life is complicated and one person influences the other. It is always the case that a stronger soul influences weaker souls, so that if one finds a certain capacity to cherish illusions in one person the reason for this tendency lies in a hatred for or a rejection of the spiritual world; but this does not necessarily reside in the soul of the person who is swayed by illusions and may have been suggested to him. In spiritual domains the danger of infection is far greater than in any physical domain.

In the next lecture, when we shall take what we have been considering today further and connect it with the Christ mystery and the mystery of our present time so as to gain some insight into the significance of the spiritual outlook as a whole, we shall endeavour to discover how what has been under discussion here is connected with the general karma of humanity and how these matters—when considered in the light of the important law of the metamorphosis of soul forces oriented towards the spiritual world into forces of illusion—exert an influence in the whole context of life and are associated with the developmental circumstances of our present age and of the immediate future.

LECTURE 3

THE fruits of spiritual science can, through their essentially practical orientation in the highest sense of the word, enable us to feel that the ordinary, outer aspect of man's being has within it an inner aspect which to all intents and purposes is completely distinct from the former outward aspect. In this respect we as human beings consist of two beings, one of which is composed of our physical and etheric bodies and belongs more to the outer world—outer in the sense that this physical body and to a certain degree also the etheric body are forms and images, that is to say manifestations, of the divine spiritual beings by whom we are constantly surrounded. Our physical and etheric bodies in their true essence—as opposed to how we as human beings know them initially—are images not of us, of our real being, but are images, shall we say, of the gods, who find fulfilment in giving rise to and developing our physical and etheric bodies, just as we as human beings bring about our own actions. The inner aspect of man's being is more closely related to the astral body and ego. In the context of the universe the astral body and ego are younger than the physical and etheric bodies. We know this from the information that has been recorded in the book *Occult Science*.[1] Our ego and astral body as it were reside within the protective sheath that is prepared for us by the divine spiritual beings who pervade the outer universe and make it manifest; and through the experiences, trials and fluctuations of destiny that they undergo as a result of their association with the physical and etheric bodies they are intended gradually to ascend to the stages of development with which we have already become familiar.

As I indicated to you in the previous lecture, we have a very intimate connection with the entire universe, with the whole cosmos; and this connection is such that—as we saw from a brief exploration of numerical relationships—it can even be calculated and expressed in numbers. Although there are many, many ways in which this becomes apparent, it is to our great astonishment expressed by the fact that the number of breaths that a person takes in a day equals the number of years that the vernal point of the Sun needs to return to the point where it began. If we ponder these numerical discoveries with our feelings, they can fill us with awe, with a holy awe of the way that we belong to the divine spiritual universe as it is manifested in all outward phenomena.

This fact of our being the microcosm, the little world fashioned and manifested out of the macrocosm, out of the big world, is shown at a far deeper level if we consider the realities that I want to put before you today, which I might refer to as the three encounters of the human soul with the essential nature of the universe. This is, therefore, what I should like to speak about now.

We all know that as earthly human beings we bear within us the physical body, the ether body, the astral body and the ego. Each of the two aspects of man's being to which I have referred has within it two subordinate elements: the more outward aspect has the physical and etheric bodies, the more inward aspect has the ego and astral body. We also know that man will develop further through a Jupiter, a Venus and a Vulcan planetary evolution. During this time man will rise from one stage to another. We know additionally that a higher being will be manifest within him that will develop beyond his ego. This will be the Spirit Self, which will come to full manifestation during the Jupiter evolution which will follow Earth evolution. The Life Spirit will fully manifest itself within man during the Venus age, and the actual Spirit Man during the age of Vulcan. Thus as we anticipate the great cosmic future of mankind, we see before us this threefold evolution of the Spirit Self, Life Spirit and Spirit Man. But these three further stages which in a certain sense await us in our future evolution already have a relationship to us today, even if they are not the least bit developed; for they are encompassed within the bosom of the divine spiritual beings whom we have learnt to know as the higher hierarchies. We will be endowed with them from out of these higher hierarchies. Today we already have a relationship to these higher hierarchies, who will in the future bestow upon us the Spirit Self, the Life Spirit and the Spirit Man. Thus instead of saying in a somewhat complicated way, 'We are related to the hierarchy of the Angels,' we can simply say, 'We are related to what is to come in the future, to our Spirit Self.' And instead of saying, 'We are related to the Archangels,' we say, 'We are related to the Life Spirit, which will come in the future,' and so on.

Indeed, we human beings already have a predisposition—and in the spiritual world predispositions have a far greater significance than in the physical world—to be more than merely a fourfold being with a physical body, ether body, astral body and ego. We already bear the germinal essence of the Spirit Self within us, also that of the Life Spirit and Spirit Man; they will evolve from us in the future, but we already possess them in this rudimentary form. Moreover, the manner in which they are present within us has nothing abstract about it; and when I say that we bear them within us I mean this in a very real way, for we have actual encounters with these higher members of our being. These meetings take place in the following way. We would as human beings increasingly come to feel estranged from the spiritual world—something that people find difficult to endure in our present age—if we were not able to encounter our Spirit Self from time to time. Our ego must meet with that higher member of our Spirit Self, which we have yet to develop and which in a certain sense is of a similar nature to beings from the hierarchy of the Angels. So as one says when speaking in a Christian context: we must from time to time meet a being from the hierarchy of the Angels who is particularly close to us, because when this being meets us it brings about a spiritual change in us which enables us at some future time to receive a Spirit Self. Similarly we also need to have an encounter with a being from the hierarchy of the Archangels, because this being brings about something within us which leads to the development of the Life Spirit, and so on.

Whether in a Christian sense we assign this being to the hierarchy of the Angels or whether we speak more as the ancients did when they spoke of the daemon, of a person's guiding genius, makes no difference.

We know that we are living at a time when only a few people—though this will soon change—are able to behold the spiritual world, and perceive its beings and other phenomena. The time has now passed when people beheld the beings of the spiritual world together with its various developmental processes to a far more extensive degree; and at the time when people spoke of the genius of an individual person, they were also able to have a direct perception of this genius. It was not so very long ago that this clarity of perception was so strong that it was possible to describe it quite concretely and objectively, and in terms that people today would regard as poetic, although nothing fanciful was intended. Thus Plutarch describes man's relationship to his genius in the following way (and I should like to quote the actual passage).[2] Plutarch, the Greek writer, says that aside from the part of the soul that is immersed in the earthly body another, pure part of it remains hovering above a person's head and is like a star in appearance; and this part is rightly called his daemon, his genius, who guides him and whom the wise man willingly follows. Thus Plutarch describes in this distinct way what he so much wants to be taken not as a poetic fancy but as a clearly perceptible outward reality that he states explicitly: 'The rest of the spiritual part of man's being can in a certain sense be perceived simultaneously with the physical body, so that the spiritual part normally occupies the physical body in the same space; but as for the genius, man's guiding and ruling spirit, it can be beheld as something special outside the head of every human being.' And Paracelsus,[3] one of the last who, without any special training or talents, had powerful insights into these things, said on his own account roughly the same about this phenomenon. Many others gave a similar picture. This genius is none other than the budding Spirit Self, though borne by a being from the hierarchy of the Angels.

It is deeply meaningful to immerse oneself in these things; for the particular nature of this genius can be discerned when it becomes perceptible, as one will come to understand if, for example—for this subject could be considered from a completely different point of view, but we will adopt this particular viewpoint—we arrive at a conception of the mutual relations of human beings. This theme has something to teach us—something that is by no means without significance with respect to the spiritual members of man's being. When two people encounter one another, and one is only able to observe this encounter with one's physical vision, one notices that they come together and perhaps greet one another and so forth. But if one has the ability to observe such an event spiritually, one finds that with every human encounter a spiritual process is associated, which comes to expression in that, for as long as two people are standing next to one another, the part of the ether body which forms the head becomes an expression of the most refined sympathy and antipathy that these two people who have come together feel for one another. Let us suppose that two people meet who cannot bear one another. We are taking an extreme case, but this undoubtedly happens. Suppose two people meet who cannot stand one another, and that this feeling of extreme antipathy is mutual. What then happens is that the part of the ether body that forms the head projects beyond the head of both individuals, and the etheric sheaths of the heads incline towards each other. When two people meet who cannot endure one another's company, their antipathy is expressed etherically as a continual inclining of the head. Whereas when two people come together who love one another, a similar process can be observed. However, the etheric head in this case withdraws, it inclines backwards. And so what arises in both these cases—whether the ether body inclines forwards as if in greeting where antipathy is felt or whether it inclines backwards where there is a bond of love—is that the physical head becomes freer than it would otherwise be as a result of the balancing gestures of the etheric head. These movements are always only relative; the ether body does not reach out completely but it shifts to some extent and then returns, so that some continuity can be observed. But in this way a more rarefied ether body now fills the head than if one were on one's own. The consequence of this is that, by virtue of the fact that this ether body that fills the head has become more rarefied, the astral body remaining within the head becomes more clearly visible to clairvoyant perception. So not only is there this movement of the ether body but a change takes place in the astral light of the head. Hence the reason why, in circles where such things are understood, people who are capable of selfless love are portrayed with an aura around their heads known as a halo is not that artists are indulging in creative licence but that an actual truth is involved. When two people meet one another in the ordinary way, so that in their love there is always a strong element of egotism, this phenomenon is not so apparent. But when a person comes in contact with others at moments where he is not concerned with himself and his own personal relationship to another individual but with humanity in general, with an all-pervading love for mankind, such phenomena do indeed become visible. At such times the astral body in the region of the head becomes clearly discernible. If people are present who are capable of clairvoyantly perceiving selfless love in another person, they will see the halo and are obliged to paint the halo as a reality or in whatever way may be appropriate. These things are associated with objective facts of the spiritual world; but the objective elements of this situation, in so far as they are part of the ongoing reality of human evolution, are connected with something else.

A human individual must from time to time enter into an inner communion with his Spirit Self, with the Spirit Self which is brought into being, in an undeveloped form, in the astral aura that becomes so visible in what I have indicated to you, raying down from out of the future. He must from time to time be brought in touch with his Spirit Self. When does this occur?

We now come to the first meeting of which we have to speak. When does this happen? It takes place during normal sleep, roughly in the middle of the period between the time of going to sleep and waking up. With people who are close to nature, the simple country people who go to sleep when the Sun sets and rise with the dawning light, this mid-point more or less coincides with the middle of the night. With someone who is more detached from natural rhythms this is less the case. However, human freedom requires that this should be possible. In present-day culture people can organize their lives how they want, even though it is bound to have a certain influence on their lives that within certain limits they can do so. Nevertheless they can in the middle of a long sleep experience this intimate communion with the Spirit Self, with the spiritual qualities from which the Spirit Self will be derived, a meeting with their genius. So this meeting with one's genius takes place more or less every night, every time one goes to sleep. It is important that this happens; for the sense of contentment that one feels regarding one's connection with the spiritual world is dependent on the after-effect of this meeting with one's genius during sleep. The feeling that we are able to have in our waking state of our connection with the spiritual world is an after-effect of this meeting with our genius. This is the first encounter with the higher world; and it takes place initially unconsciously for most people, although they become increasingly conscious of it the more they become aware of its influence through refining the waking consciousness in their feelings by absorbing the ideas and concepts of spiritual science, to the point where their souls are sufficiently sensitive to be able to observe these after-effects. This meeting with the genius comes frequently to consciousness in some form or other; but the present materialistic environment, which is full of concepts deriving from a materialistic view of the world, and quite particularly the life of today, pervaded as it is with a materialistic attitude, do not enable the soul to be attentive to what is brought about as a result of this meeting with the genius. As people fill their minds with concepts that are more spiritual than any that materialism can offer, the perception of these nightly meetings with the genius will become more and more self-evident to them.

The second meeting of which we must now speak is of a higher nature. You will be aware from what I have already said that this first meeting with the genius is associated with the course of the day. If we were to adapt our outward lives completely as people who do not have the freedom that we possess in our modern culture, this meeting would coincide with midnight. At the hour of midnight every person would have this encounter with the genius. But it is in the nature of freedom that this meeting when the ego encounters the genius is no longer fixed. The second meeting, however, is not so movable; for what is connected more with the astral body and ether body is less movable with respect to the macrocosmic order. What is connected with the ego and physical body has a strong degree of mobility for people today. Thus the second meeting is connected more with the great macrocosmic order. Just as the first meeting is connected with the daily rhythm, this second meeting is associated with the course of the year. At this point I need to draw your attention to various things that I have already indicated in this connection from different points of view.

Man's life in its entirety does not run its course in a similar way throughout the year, and there are certain distinct changes.

In the summer, when the Sun is at its hottest, man is far more strongly engaged with his physical life and, hence, also with the physical life of his surroundings than during the winter, when he has to battle against the outer elements of nature and is thrown back on his own resources. The spiritual part of his nature is also freer, both in itself and from the Earth; and he is connected strongly with the spiritual world, with his whole spiritual environment.

Hence the particular feeling that we associate with the Christmas mystery and the Christmas festival is by no means arbitrary, but it forms part of the timing of the Christmas festival. During those winter days appointed for the festival, both man and the entire Earth give themselves up to the spirit. Man is therefore inhabiting a realm where the spirit is very close to him. The consequence of this is that around Christmas time, thus until our modern New Year, man experiences a meeting of his astral body with the Life Spirit, just as the first meeting entails an encounter of his ego with the Spirit Self. The possibility for Christ Jesus to draw near depends on this meeting with the Life Spirit; for Christ Jesus reveals Himself through the Life Spirit. He reveals Himself through a being from the realm of the Archangels. He is, of course, an infinitely higher Being, but this is not what we are concerned with at present; what we have to consider is that He manifests Himself through a being from the realm of the Archangels. Thus with respect to modern evolution—evolution since the Mystery of Golgotha—we draw particularly close to Christ Jesus through this meeting; and we can in a certain sense also call the meeting with the Life Spirit the encounter with Christ Jesus which takes place in the very depths of our soul. Now when a person—whether by developing spiritual consciousness in the realm of religious study and practice or, as a supplement to the religious feelings nurtured in this way, by absorbing the concepts and ideas of spiritual science—has intensified and spiritualized his feelings in the manner described, he will, in the same way that in waking life he is able to experience the after-effects of the meeting with his Spirit Self, experience the after-effects of the meeting with the Life Spirit, that is, with the Christ. And it is indeed the case that in the time following the period of Christmas until Easter the conditions are particularly favourable for bringing clearly to consciousness the encounter that a person has with Christ Jesus.

The period of Christmas is connected with earthly processes at a profound level (and this should not become blurred today through a materialistic way of looking at things); for man accompanies the changes taking place in the Earth at Christmas. The time of Easter is determined by processes in the heavens. Easter Sunday falls on the first Sunday following the first full Moon after the vernal equinox. So whereas Christmas is governed by earthly circumstances, Easter is determined from above. Just as we are—through all that has been described—connected with earthly circumstances, so are we connected, through what I shall now relate, with heavenly circumstances, with what is going on in the wider expanses of the spiritual cosmos; for Easter is that time in the yearly cycle when everything that has been brought about in us through the meeting with Christ at Christmas time is fully united with our physical earthly humanity. And the great mystery of Good Friday, which brings the Mystery of Golgotha to a focus for us as human beings at Easter time, has in addition to much else the significance that Christ, who has as it were been walking beside us at the time that I have been describing, now approaches us most strongly in that—to put it in a vivid picture—He disappears into us during the ensuing period of summer, when in the ancient mysteries human beings sought to unite themselves at St John's tide with the macrocosm in a way that was not possible after the Mystery of Golgotha.

From this you can see that we are a microcosm, and that we are incorporated in the macrocosm in a deeply meaningful way; and in the cycle of the year there is a continual union with the macrocosm, which is brought about through man's inner relationship to the year's course. In this way spiritual science seeks gradually to reveal the insights that can be acquired through spiritual-scientific research regarding the pervading and permeating of our earthly lives by Christ since the Mystery of Golgotha.

At this point I need to make an interpolation which is important and needs to be thoroughly understood by those sympathetic to spiritual science.[4]

It should not be thought that our spiritual-scientific endeavours should be a substitute for religious life and practice. Spiritual science can to the highest degree, and especially with respect to the Christ mystery, be a support for—and a foundation of—religious life and practice. But one should not turn spiritual science into a religion, and one needs to be quite clear in one's mind that religion in its living form and when practised in a living way kindles a spiritual consciousness of the soul within the human community. If this spiritual consciousness is to become a vital presence within man, he cannot continue to have abstract conceptions of God or Christ but he must be constantly renewed through involvement in religious practice and activity (which can take the most divergent forms for different people), in something that surrounds him as a religious environment and speaks to him out of this background. And if this religious milieu is of sufficient depth and has the means of stimulating the soul, such a soul will also come to feel a longing for those ideas that are developed in spiritual science. Moreover, if spiritual science is—as it surely is—in an objective sense a support for religious edification, the time has now come when from a subjective point of view a person with true religious feelings is driven by these very feelings also to seek knowledge. For spiritual consciousness is acquired through religious feeling and spiritual knowledge through spiritual science, just as knowledge of the natural world is acquired through natural science; and spiritual consciousness leads to the impulse to gain spiritual knowledge. From a subjective point of view one can say that an inner religious life can spur a person on today to spiritual science.

A third meeting is when a person approaches the Spirit Man, which will be fully developed only in the far future. This meeting is mediated by a being belonging to the hierarchy of the Archai. We may say that people in ancient times (as people also do in our present time, although when they speak of these things they no longer have an awareness of the deeper truths involved) experienced this meeting as an encounter with that which pervades the world, a presence which we are barely able to distinguish any longer in ourselves or in the world but where our selfhood is absorbed in the world as in a unity. And just as in the case of the second meeting one can speak of an encounter with Christ Jesus, so with the third meeting one can speak of an encounter with the Father principle, with the 'Father' who represents the very ground of the world, with that Being whom one experiences when one has a true feeling for what the various religions mean by the 'Father'. This meeting is of such a nature that it reveals our intimate relationship to the macrocosm, to the divine spiritual universe. The daily course of universal processes, of world processes, includes our meeting with our genius, the yearly course includes our meeting with Christ Jesus, and the course of the whole of a human life, this human life of ours which can generally be designated as the patriarchal life of 70 years, coincides with the meeting with the Father principle. For a certain period of our physical earthly life—by rights through education although at present largely unconsciously— we are prepared for and then experience (in the case of most people unconsciously between the ages of 28 and 42, though in a very real way in the intimate depths of the soul) this meeting with the Father principle. The after-effects of this may extend into later life, if we develop a sufficient degree of sensitivity in our feelings to be aware of what emerges from within ourselves as an influence in our lives deriving from this meeting with the Father principle.

During the period of our lives when we are being prepared, our education should—and this can happen in a variety of way—be making this meeting with the Father principle as profound an experience as possible. This can happen if during the period of his education a person is urged to develop strong feelings about the splendour and magnificence of the world and the sublime nature of its processes. We considerably deprive children and adolescents if we fail to draw their attention to the beauty and grandeur of the world for which we feel the greatest reverence and devotion, so that this passes them by. If we enable young people to feel a real connection in their hearts with beauty and with the greatness of the world, we are preparing them for a real meeting with the Father principle. For this meeting has a considerable significance for the life between death and a new birth. This meeting with the Father principle, which generally occurs in the years indicated above, signifies that a person has a considerable degree of strength and support when, after he has passed through the gate of death, he has, as we are aware, to retrace his life's path, his earthly journey, retro-spectively as he passes through the soul world. This retrospective journey, which as we know lasts for one third of the time spent between birth and death, can and should be a powerful experience if the person concerned is able to see: here at this point I met with that Being whose existence comes to expression in dimly intuitive, stammering words when people speak of the Father of the cosmic order. This is an important picture which—together with the picture of death itself—a person needs to have once he has passed through the portal of death.

There is, of course, an important question that arises in connection with this. Some people die before they have reached the middle of their life, which is when the meeting with the Father principle normally takes place. We need to consider the situation where someone dies because of some outward cause, through illness (which is indeed such an outward cause) or weakness of some kind. If because of this early death the meeting with the Father principle in the subconscious depths of the soul has not as yet become possible, it happens in the hour of death. This meeting is experienced when death occurs. At this point it is of relevance to speak in a somewhat different way of what I have already brought to expression in, for example, my book *Theosophy*,[5] where there is a reference to the invariably tragic phenomenon of people bringing their lives to an end through their own will. No one would do this who was aware of the significance of such a deed; and once spiritual science has really fully entered into people's feelings, there would no longer be any suicide. For in order that a person may perceive the Father principle directly after death occurs, in a case where death takes place before the middle of life it is necessary that death approaches him from without rather than through being self-inflicted. The difficulty that befalls the human soul, and which is described from another viewpoint in my *Theosophy*, might be described from the standpoint from which I am speaking today if I were to say that through a death that is self-inflicted the individual concerned deprives himself of the meeting with the Father principle in this incarnation.

Because they are so intimately involved with our lives, the truths that spiritual science is able to impart to us about human life have such infinitely serious implications in instances of particular importance.

They bring us clarity about our lives in a serious way, and this serious illumination regarding their lives is needed by people at a time when they need to extricate themselves from materialism, which governs the present world order and the prevailing world conception, in so far as these depend on human beings. More powerful forces will be needed to overcome the strong connection with the purely material powers that have taken hold of people today, in order once more to give them the possibility of recognizing their connection with the spiritual world from their immediate experience of life.

Whereas one speaks in a more abstract way of the beings of the higher hierarchies, one can speak in a more concrete way of how the human individual himself can ascend in three stages through experiences which, while being initially unconscious, may be brought to consciousness during his life between birth and death: through the meeting with the genius; through the meeting with Christ Jesus; and through the meeting with the Father. Of course a great deal depends on our acquiring as many ideas as possible that call forth feelings, ideas which refine our inner soul life in such a way that we do not heedlessly and inattentively fail to notice these things which are simply part of the reality of our lives, if we did but know it. Education will have a very considerable part to play in this respect in the near future.

There is something else that I still need to mention. Just think how infinitely life would be deepened if, to the overall knowledge of karma, one could add such details as the meeting with the Father principle that a person whose life ends relatively early has when he dies; for it then becomes clear that it was a karmic necessity for this person to experience an early death in order that a meeting of abnormal intensity with the Father principle might take place. For what actually occurs when a meeting of such a kind with the Father principle takes place? The person concerned is destroyed from without; his physical being is undermined by outward forces. Indeed, this is also the case with an illness. The scene where the encounter with the Father principle is being enacted is then still here in the physical world. Through the destruction that this external physical earthly world has wrought upon a person, the meeting with the Father principle is manifested at that very place; and when viewed in retrospect it does of course continue to be visible. The individual concerned is thereby also enabled throughout the entire life that he leads after he has passed through the portal of death to keep firm hold of the thought of the place where, descending from heavenly heights to this earthly location, the Father principle met with him. This does, however, lead him to want to bring a strong influence from the spiritual world into the physical earthly world.

If we consider our present time from this viewpoint and try to experience the weighty feelings that have been aroused within us now at the very mentioning of the meeting with the Father principle as feelings and not as a mere abstract idea, and if we endeavour to contemplate the numerous premature deaths now occurring with feelings of this nature, we have to say that these were predestined as a preparation for the considerable influence that can stream down from the spiritual world to the physical earthly world in the near future. This is another aspect of what I have been saying for some years when confronted by these tragic events, that these people who are passing prematurely through the portal of death will become helpers in a quite particular way for the future evolution of mankind, which needs powerful forces to extricate itself from materialism. However, all this needs to be brought to consciousness; it must not take place unconsciously or in a subconscious state of mind. It is therefore necessary that there are human souls on Earth who can make themselves receptive for this (as I have already indicated), since otherwise the forces emanating from the spiritual world will go in other directions. In order that these forces, which are predestined to be available, can become fruitful for the Earth, it is necessary for there to be souls on the Earth who imbue themselves with knowledge of the spiritual world; and there must be more and more souls imbued with such a knowledge. So let us try to enable what has to be expressed initially in words, namely the content of spiritual science, to bear fruit; and let us try with the help of the language that we learn through spiritual science (I mentioned this here in the last lecture but one) to re-enliven the old insights and ideas that are not for nothing embedded in our modern life. Thus, for example, let us breathe new life into Plutarch's idea that as human beings we are, as physical beings, also imbued with a spiritual aspect, but that, in particular, a person has a higher member which belongs to him spiritually outside his head and which, if he be wise, he follows. Let us try to allow the feelings to which I have referred help us not to pass these phenomena of life by unnoticed.

In conclusion, I shall leave you today with a thought which is particularly suited to awaken the necessary feelings in our souls. It is unfortunately difficult for many people today in our modern materialistic life to have a feeling for something that mitigates the sorrows of this period of trial, although what is needed is something that goes beyond mitigation (which might be a forlorn hope if materialism continues to prevail at its present level, and its strength is already considerable and it is likely to become more and more so). It is very, very difficult for many people in our materialistic age to have a feeling for what I might describe as the holiness of sleep. It is a cultural phenomenon of far-reaching significance when one can experience that among those who are regarded as intelligent there is an absence of any respect for the holiness of sleep. Such things are not said here by way of blame, and they are also not intended to drive people towards some unattainable ascetic goal. We must live with the world, but we must do so with our eyes open; for only in this way can we wrench our bodily nature ...[6] One needs only to consider how many people who spend their evening hours preoccupied with purely material things go to sleep without developing any awareness—and there would be no more than a very dim awareness of this in a materialistic mind—that sleep unites us with the spiritual world, sleep sends us over into the spiritual world. People should at least gradually become able to develop an awareness of what they can express in words such as these: 'I am going to sleep. Until I wake my soul will be in the spiritual world. There it will meet the guiding power of my earthly life who hovers around my head, there it will meet the genius. And when I awake, I shall have had the meeting with my genius. The wings of my genius will have come in contact with my soul.'

As regards the overcoming of the domination that materialism has over life, a great deal depends on whether or not one makes such a feeling alive within one. The overcoming of this domination can happen only through the awakening of intimate feelings which are also in accordance with the spiritual world. Only if we make such feelings alive within us will our lives in sleep become so intense—and the contact with the spiritual world so strong—that our waking life will also gradually be strengthened; and we shall then have around us not merely the world of the senses but also the spiritual world, which is the true, real world. For the world that we generally call the real one is, as I have indicated in the last public lecture,[7] only a reflection of the real world. The real world is the world of the spirit. The little community that is currently devoted to anthroposophically oriented spiritual science will gain the fullest impression of the serious symptoms, the harsh suffering of our time if in addition to all the other trials to which man is subject today it learns to feel this time as a test as to whether there are sufficient resources of inner strength and true courage to unite what we need to absorb through our reasoning and intellectual powers in the form of spiritual science with our whole being.

With these words I wanted once more to emphasize what I have often said here: that spiritual science will find its right place in human hearts only when it is not mere theory and knowledge but when, symbolically speaking, it pervades and enlivens our whole being as the heart's blood of the soul as intimately as our physical blood pervades and gives life to our bodily organism.

LECTURE 4

I spoke to you last time about the three meetings which the human soul has with the regions of the spiritual world. I shall have a few more things to say on this subject, and this will give me the opportunity to answer a question asked by our friends at the end of the last public lecture in the Architectural Hall regarding the forces which lead to the fulfilment of karma and outward destiny from a previous incarnation. I have been told that this is very difficult to understand. I shall therefore return to this theme in the course of these lectures; but it will be better to do so only after we have spoken about something which will perhaps bring about a fuller understanding of this question. In order, however, that what was said about the three meetings in the spiritual world may be further clarified, I shall today insert by way of an episode something that seems to me to be particularly important to discuss with you just at this very time.

When we consider the ideas that have been embraced by the souls of all people—people of all educational levels—as a result of the intellectual developments of recent centuries, we become clearly aware that these developments have given a powerful impetus towards shaping world evolution and man's place within it solely in accordance with the ideas of natural science. To be sure, there are many people today who are of the opinion that their mental constitution and inner attitudes have not been formed by scientific ideas. Nevertheless these people do not observe the deeper foundations of their mental attitudes; they do not know the extent to which scientific ideas have crept in a one-sided way into their minds, not only governing the way they think but quite especially also their feelings. Anyone who reflects along the lines of the concepts generally available in ordinary educational centres and whose mind is formed in accordance with these concepts cannot possibly feel the right, and true, relationship between the moral world, the world of moral feelings, and the world of outward facts. When, in accordance with modern thinking, we reflect upon how the Earth and indeed the whole firmament of heaven is supposed to have developed and how it might come to an end, we are thinking along the lines of purely out-ward, sense-perceptible facts. Just think how deeply significant it is for people's souls that there is the so-called Kant-Laplace theory of the origin of the universe (even if they do not always form a clear picture of it),[1] which states that the Earth and the whole fabric of the heavens was formed in accordance with purely physical and also chemical earthly laws from a purely material cosmic mist (for it is envisaged in a purely material way), that it has been developing in accordance with these laws and will, so it is thought, come to an end which will be determined by these same laws. A state of being will eventually come about whereby this whole cosmic structure will mechanistically come to an end, in the same mechanistic way that it arose.

It is true that, as I have said before, there are many people who resist this modern tendency to think in this way. But this is not the point; for what really matters are not the ideas that we formulate but the attitude of mind out of which they come. The notion to which I have just alluded is a purely materialistic one; it is the sort of idea regarding which Herman Grimm[2] says that a piece of carrion encircled by a hungry dog is a more appetizing sight than this picture of the world arising from the Kant-Laplace theory. Nevertheless, it arose and could become estab-lished. Indeed, it not only became established but the great majority of people who come across it find it illuminating. There are only a few people who, like Herman Grimm, ask how future generations of scholars will account for the emergence of this crazy idea in our time, how it was possible that such a barmy notion of the origin of the world could ever have seemed illuminating to so many. There are indeed few individuals who, out of a healthy soundness of mind, ask such a ques-tion; and those who do so are—at any rate in these circles—simply regarded as weird. But as I say, what really counts are not the ideas that are formulated but the mental attitudes out of which they come—this is what really matters. These ideas derived from certain intellectual tendencies; and although they were promulgated by learned people and have been disseminated more widely in such a way today that most people still believe that the world did not originate solely through such mechanistic impulses but that divine impulses must also have played a part, the fact is that it was possible for such ideas to be formulated. That is to say, there is a fundamental tendency in people's souls to formulate ideas of a materialistic nature; and this tendency exists not only in the few scholars and other individuals who believe in such ideas but it exists on a wide scale in all manner of people. Nevertheless, most people today are still wary of plunging courageously into becoming followers of Haeckel and of conceiving of all spiritual realities purely in a material form. People do not have the courage. They think of spiritual matters as having a certain significance, but they do not think about them.

If the idea that has been characterized is generally accepted, there is room for a more spiritual dimension—and especially for the moral element—only in a certain way. For just consider: if the world really did arise in the way envisaged by the Kant-Laplace theory and if it were to come to an end through physical forces alone and all human beings with their ideas, feelings and will impulses were to perish with it, what, for example, would become of the whole moral dimension of the world if everything else is disregarded? Of what significance would it be that— on the basis that the world as we know it had perished—we had once said that this is good, this is evil; this is right and this is wrong? These would be nothing but ideas from a forgotten era, swept away as something which, if this theory were correct, could not live on even as a dim memory. Then the situation would be that the world would perish through the same mechanistic causes, the same physical and possibly chemical causes, whence it arose. From these same forces phenomena swell up like bubbles, which represent human beings. Within these human beings moral concepts of right and wrong, good and evil arise. Nevertheless, the whole world returns to the silence of the grave. The whole edifice of right and wrong, of good and evil, has been an illusion of human beings; and it is forgotten and vanishes without trace when the world has become a 'grave'. The only thing that then remains as regards the moral order is that people feel that, for as long as the whole episode lasts from its initial state to its end, they need such concepts in order to live together, they have to develop moral concepts of this nature; but these moral concepts can never be rooted in a purely mechanistic world-order. The forces of nature, such as heat and electricity, have their place in the context of the natural world, where they also make their presence felt, whereas moral forces, which if the mechanistic view were true would exist only in people's minds, would have no involvement there. They would not be like heat, which expands bodies, or light, which illuminates them and makes them visible by permeating the world of space. Indeed, these moral forces hover as a great illusion over the mechanistic world-order and will vanish into oblivion when the world is transformed into a grave.

People do not think these thoughts through sufficiently. Because of this, they do not resist the encroachment of a mechanistic view of the world but instead they allow it to continue in existence not so much out of benevolence but out of indolence. And if they feel the need for a certain intellectual stimulation they may say: 'Yes, our scientific knowledge does not demand that we think through the implications of such a mechanistic conception of the world; but our wish to believe demands something else from us, so we put our faith alongside our knowledge and believe in something other than a mechanistic natural world, in that we have a certain inner soul-need to believe in something.' That is a convenient way of dealing with the problem! There is no need to rebel against what Herman Grimm, for example, feels to be a crazy idea of modern science. There is no need to stage a rebellion. But this attitude cannot be justified by someone who wants to think his thoughts through to their logical conclusion.

If one were to ask why people live so blindly in this impossible intellectual position and, moreover, put up with it, the answer is—however strange it may sound if one hears such a thought for the first time—that they have in the course of recent centuries more or less forgotten to conceive of the Christ mystery, which should be at the focal point of modern life, in its true sense. For the way that people should think about the Christ mystery in modern times is that it irradiates the whole of their thinking and feeling. It really is the case—and I shall have more to say about this in the near future—that the position that man has adopted towards the Christ mystery since the Mystery of Golgotha represents a standard according to which his whole world of concepts and feelings can be measured. If he is unable to conceive of the Christ mystery as a true reality, he also cannot develop any ideas and concepts relating to the rest of world existence which are imbued with reality, which really penetrate to the truth.

This is what we need to be particularly clear about today. If people really do think in the way that I have described (and this is how most people today think more or less unconsciously), the world splits into a mechanistic natural order, on the one hand, and, on the other, a moral world-order. Now timid souls, who nonetheless often think themselves to be very courageous, make the Christ mystery into something that is only part of the moral world-order. These are people who see nothing in the Christ mystery other than that at a certain time a great, perhaps even the greatest Teacher of the earthly world appeared, and that it is His teaching which is of the greatest importance. However, if one regards Christ merely as even the greatest Teacher of mankind, this view is in a certain sense wholly compatible with this division of the world into a natural order and a moral order. For of course even if the Earth had been formed in the way envisaged by the mechanistic world-conception and were to be destroyed such that there would be nothing left of it, it would nevertheless be possible for a great teacher to appear who could indeed do much to make people more moral and to teach them. His teaching might be of a sublime nature, but this would not alter the fact that at the end of the day everything would perish and that, similarly, the teachings of Christ would have faded into oblivion, with not even a trace in anyone's memory. The fact that one does not like to think this through does not affect the issue. If one declares one's absolute belief in a purely mechanistic world-order, one really has to deal with thoughts such as these.

Now everything depends on the realization that in the Mystery of Golgotha something was accomplished which has to do not with the moral order alone but with the whole world-order in its entirety; something that belongs not solely to moral reality, which according to the mechanistic world-conception cannot really exist, but to the full intensity of reality as a whole.

We shall arrive at the clearest possible perception of what is involved here if we turn our thoughts once more to the three meetings that I mentioned last time, though in a different sense from the way that I explained them on that occasion. I told you that whenever a person sleeps he encounters, in this state between going to sleep and waking up, beings of the spiritual world who are of a like nature to his Spirit Self, as we have grown accustomed to calling it. This means that when he wakes up he emerges from sleep in such a way that he has encountered a spiritual being, and he carries the after-effects of this meeting—even though the experience remains on an unconscious level—with him into outward physical life. Now what takes place within us while we have this daily meeting also has a definite effect on our future. Someone who does not concern himself with spiritual science has little knowledge of what actually goes on in the depths of the soul when one is asleep. Dreams, which to the ordinary way of thinking could betray certain aspects of sleep processes, give some kind of an inkling of this, but in such a way that the truth cannot so easily become visible. When someone wakes up during a dream or out of one or else recalls his dreams, these dreams are mostly connected with ideas that he had already acquired in his life, with reminiscences. However, this is only the outer garment of what lives in dreams or in one's sleep life. When your dreams are clothed with ideas deriving from your life, these ideas are merely the outer garment; for in a dream what is actually taking place in the soul during sleep is manifested in a veiled form, and what is actually going on in the soul during sleep is related neither to the past nor even to the present but it has a relationship to the future. In sleep the forces are formed which in a human being can be compared with the germinal forces developing in the plant for a new plant. As the plant grows the germinal forces for the coming year are already developing in the plant for the future offspring. These germinal forces culminate in the seed-formation process; this is where they become visible. But as the plant burgeons forth in this way, the germinal forces for the next plant are already there. The germinal forces within man, whether they be for the next incarnation or even for the Jupiter period, are present in this same way, and they are primarily formed during sleep. The forces that are thereby developed are not directly associated with specific events but are related more to the basic forces of the next incarnation among other things but quite especially to these forces of the forthcoming incarnation. Thus in sleep a person is working on the seeds for his next incarnation in a future-oriented way. Hence when he is asleep he is already in the future.

As I do not want to leave a vague impression in your minds about this, I should say that for the state of sleep the next incarnation is like our knowledge of the next day. We know simply from experiences that when tomorrow comes the Sun will rise again and also roughly what its course will be, although we do not know what the weather will be like or what particular events will happen in our lives. So the soul is like a prophet in sleep, but a prophet who only looks upon things on a broad, cosmic scale and not upon the weather. Hence anyone who were to have the idea that the soul would be able to visualize the details of the forthcoming incarnation in sleep would be making the same mistake as someone who thinks that because he knows for certain that the Sun will rise and set on the following Sunday and because he knows certain other things he would also be able to know what the weather will be like. However, this does not alter the fact that while we are asleep we are concerned with our future. So the forces that we encounter during our sleep, which are essentially of a similar nature to our Spirit Self, work on the forming of our future.

Another, further meeting—if I omit the second encounter—is the third meeting, which, as I indicated in the previous lecture, occurs *once* in the whole course of human life and around its mid-point. When a person is in his thirties he meets with what can, as I have said, be called the Father principle, whereas every *night* he encounters the Spirit principle. This meeting with the Father principle—which as you know from what I have already said also has to occur for those who die before the age of 30; if they live through their thirties they encounter it in the course of life, whereas in the case of a premature death it occurs sooner—has a very great significance, because as a result of this meeting the person concerned is enabled to have so deep an impression of the experiences of his present life that they are able to exert an influence upon his next incarnation. So the meeting with the Father principle has to do with the earthly life of the next incarnation, whereas our encounter with the Spirit principle radiates into our entire future life and also into our life between death and a new birth.

The fact is that the laws within which this meeting that we have once in our lives is interwoven are not earthly laws but laws which within Earth evolution have remained as they were during the Moon evolution. These laws are on the physical side associated with our physical descent, essentially with everything signified by physical heredity. This physical heredity is only one side of the matter; as I have already amply indicated, it is underpinned by spiritual laws. Hence everything that renders the meeting with the Father principle a necessity points back to the past. It is the legacy of the past; it points back to the Moon evolution, to previous incarnations, just as what takes place every time one goes to sleep points towards the future. Just as what takes place during sleep forms the seed for the future, the process that is enacted whereby human beings are born as the descendants of their ancestors and also carry from previous incarnations what has to be transmitted from these earlier lives is a remnant from the past. Both of these aspects—that which relates to the future and that which relates to the past—are as it were wresting themselves free from the natural order. The farmer still goes to sleep at sunset and rises at dawn; but with the progressive advances in our so-called culture the connection with the natural order is loosened. In cities one even meets people—perhaps not so very often—who go to sleep in the morning and get up in the evening. Man is freeing himself from the limits of the natural order; this is an inherent part of his development of freedom. Thus because he is preparing for a future which has not yet come, he has in a certain sense separated himself from nature. Similarly, by bringing the past, and in particular the lunar past, into the present, he is breaking his connection with the natural order. No one, for example, can point to any need arising from natural laws for John Smith to be born in, say, 1914; such an event is not governed by necessity as is the rising of the Sun or other natural events. During the Moon period everything was ordered in a similar way to our birth on Earth.

Nevertheless, with respect to anything that has a direct significance for the present and is directly related to his earthly existence, man is fully part of the natural order. Whereas with respect to the Father principle and the Spirit principle he bears past and future within him, with regard to that meeting of which I said that it occurs in the course of the year and is, moreover, associated with an encounter with the Christ, he is firmly linked to the natural order. If he were not connected to the natural order in this way, the consequence would be that one person would celebrate Christmas in December and another in March and so on. And yet in spite of the fact that the various nations differ in many respects as to how they celebrate the Christmas festival, an integral part of the festivities, which always have some bearing on the meeting to which I have been referring, falls during the last days of December. With respect to this meeting which is fully part of the yearly cycle, man is wholly present and therefore directly associated with the order of nature; whereas with regard to both past and future he has separated himself from it, as has been the case for thousands of years.

In ancient times man was fully linked to the natural order also as regards past and future. Thus in the Germanic countries, for example, birth was in such times governed in accordance with the natural order; for birth, which was regulated by the mysteries, was only allowed to take place at a quite specific time of the year and belonged to a particular season. In these ancient times long predating the Christian era, conception and birth were regulated in Germanic lands by that of which only as faint echo has been preserved in mythical form through the worship of Hertha. The worship of Hertha[3] in those days consisted in that when Hertha approached human beings in her chariot this was the time for conception; and when she had withdrawn it was no longer allowed. The result of this was that anyone who was not born within a particular season was considered to be dishonourable, because as regards his human existence he was not in harmony with the natural order. This was in olden times just as much a part of the order of nature as going to sleep and waking up. People went to sleep when the Sun set and woke at dawn. These things have shifted in their rhythms; but what cannot be shifted is the central question of adapting to the course of the year. Through this deed of adapting to the course of the year, something is preserved—and needs to be preserved—in the human soul.

What, then, is the whole significance of man's earthly evolution? Its significance lies in that man adapts himself to the Earth, that he embraces the conditions of Earth evolution, and that he brings to the future of his evolution what the Earth can give him—I do not mean merely in one incarnation but throughout all his incarnations. This is the significance of earthly evolution; and it can be made a reality only if man has in a certain sense gradually learnt on the Earth to forget his connection with the cosmic and heavenly powers. This he has learnt to do. We know that in olden times human beings possessed an atavistic clairvoyance through which the heavenly powers exerted an influence upon them. Man still retained his connection with the heavenly powers, and the heavenly world was able as it were to reach down to his inner being. This had to change in order that he might develop his freedom. In order that he might become related to the Earth there was no longer to be any trace of the kingdom of heaven in what he beheld in his direct visionary perception. It was for this reason that at the time of his closest relationship to the Earth, in the fifth epoch in which we are now living, the possibility arose whereby man became materialistic. Materialism is merely the most radical, most extreme expression of man's relationship to the Earth. This would, however, mean that he would be completely subjected to the Earth if nothing else were to have happened. He would have had to become related to the Earth and gradually share in its destiny; he would have had to follow the same path as the Earth itself and become completely wedded to earthly evolution, if nothing else were to have intervened. He would have to have become segregated together with the Earth from the entire cosmos and unite his destiny wholly with that of the Earth.

However, this was not what was intended for mankind; something other than this was planned. He was on the one hand to be fully united with the Earth, but a message was to be imparted to him from the heavenly world of spirit which would, in spite of the earthly affinity of his nature, raise him up above this relationship to the Earth. The bringing down of this heavenly message came about through the Mystery of Golgotha. Hence on the one hand the Being who passed through the Mystery of Golgotha had to take on a human nature, while on the other hand bearing within Himself the nature of a heavenly being. This means that we should not merely conceive of Christ Jesus in such a way that He develops within human evolution like anyone else (albeit on a higher level), but that He develops as one who possesses a heavenly nature, someone who does not merely propagate a teaching but who brings to the Earth that which comes from heaven. That is why it is so important to understand what the Baptism by John in the Jordan actually represents, and that it is not a moral act—I am not saying that it is not a moral act but that it is not merely one—but a real deed, and that something took place then which is as real as events in the natural world, as real as if I warm something through some source of heat and this heat is transferred to what is being warmed. It was in this same way that the Christ Being entered into the human being Jesus of Nazareth at the Baptism enacted by John. This is, to be sure, a highly moral act, but also a real event in the natural world, just as natural phenomena are real. The important thing is that it is understood that one is dealing not only with something deriving from rationalistic human concepts, which always merely accord with mechanistic, physical or chemical laws, but that it is an idea which is at the same time just as much an actual reality as are the laws of nature or indeed the forces of nature themselves.

Once this has been understood, other ideas will also become much more real than they are at present. Although we are not now going to enter into a discussion about alchemy, we want to observe what the old alchemists had in mind (whether they were justified or not we will leave aside for now, and it could perhaps be the subject for another discussion), which was that their ideas should not be mere abstract notions but that something should actually result from them. Thus when an alchemist burnt incense and had an idea or experienced it out loud, he was trying to imbue this idea with such a power that the smoke of the incense took on a certain form. He sought such ideas as have the power to take hold of the outward reality of nature, not merely to remain within the egotistic aspect of man's being but to intervene in the natural world. Why? Because he still had the idea that something occurred at the Mystery of Golgotha which intervened in the course of natural events, and which is just as much a fact as a natural process is a fact of nature.

In this respect there is a significant difference which entered in during the second half of the Middle Ages and towards modern times, towards our fifth epoch which followed the Graeco-Roman age. During the time of the Crusades, in the twelfth, thirteenth, fourteenth and fifteenth centuries and even in the sixteenth century, there were some people, especially women, whose minds had such a mystical quality that the inner experience which their mysticism brought them was for them like a spiritual marriage, whether with Christ or with another being. Many ascetic nuns celebrated mystical marriages, for example. I shall not enter today into the nature of these intimate mystic unions; but something took place within their inner being which could only be expressed in words, which lived within the ideas, feelings and also the words in which the feelings were clothed. Valentin Andreae wrote his *Chymical Wedding of Christian Rosenkreutz,* which was derived from certain specific ideas and spiritual-scientific associations, as a contrast to this.[4] The chymical wedding, or as we would say today 'chemical wedding', is also a human experience. However, when you read this *Chymical Wedding of Christian Rosenkreutz* you will see that it is not only about an inner, soul experience but has to do with something that encompasses the whole of man's being and is not merely expressed in words; something that does not simply live in the world as an inner, soul experience but, rather, as a real occurrence, a natural event, where a person accomplishes something that is like an event in the natural world. Thus Valentin Andreae's intention in his *Chymical Wedding of Christian Rosenkreutz* is to present something that is more permeated with reality than the purely mystical marriage of, for example, Mechthild von Magdeburg, who was a mystic.[5] Through the mystical marriage of the nuns something was done merely for a person's subjective nature; whereas through the chymical wedding the human individual gave himself to the world, something was being accomplished through him for the whole world through processes in nature. This is, moreover, to be thought of in a truly Christian sense. People who thought in a more real way—even if only in the one-sided sense of the old alchemists—wanted ideas through which they would be able to deal with reality in the right way and really take hold of it, ideas that actually have something to do with reality. The age of materialism has initially cast a veil over ideas of this nature; and whereas people today believe that they think with absolute preci- sion about reality, they live far more in illusions than, for example, the old alchemists whom they so much despise and who sought ideas through which reality can be mastered.

What, after all, can people do with the ideas they formulate today? We are experiencing especially in our time that these ideas lead them to illusions, to the empty husks of ideas, to the idols that they chase after today and which have nothing to do with reality. For reality is reached only by plunging down into it, and not by forming all manner of ideas about it. It is, after all, possible to distinguish between ideas that are imbued with reality and those that are unreal in the most ordinary, everyday occurrences. Most people, however, cannot manage this. They are so completely satisfied with the mere shadows of ideas which are altogether lacking in reality. Imagine, for instance, that someone today gets up and makes a speech in which he says: 'A new age must come and is already approaching when a person will be measured only according to his own worth, when everyone will be valued for what he can do!' Anyone would say that that is something arising from the deepest understanding of our time! But for as long as the ideas remain mere husks, however fine the sentiments may be they do not live in the real world. For it is of little significance that someone should advocate the principle that people should be given the jobs appropriate to their capacities if he is convinced in hindsight that his own nephew is the person best fitted for the task. What really matters is not the ideas and conceptions that one cherishes but that one is able to participate with one's ideas in reality and get to know it! It is all very well and also a great delight to have principles and ideas, and it is often an even greater delight to express them. But what is needed is that we really enter into reality, understand it and penetrate it. We are plunging ever more deeply into what has brought about the infinite sorrow of the time in which we are living if we continue to worship the idols of the husks and shadows of ideas, if we do not learn to see that it is not of the slightest value to have and express beautiful ideas and fine concepts if this is not connected with the will to plunge down into reality and get to know it. If we indeed immerse ourselves in reality we find there not only material substance but we also find the spirit. It is the worshipping of the idols of mere shadows and husks of ideas that leads us away from the spirit. Moreover, it is the great misfortune of our time that people are intoxicated with fine words. This is at the same time also unchristian; for the fundamental principle of Christianity is that Christ did not only impart teachings to Jesus of Nazareth but entered fully into him, that is to say, He united Himself with earthly reality in such a way that He entered fully into this earthly reality and thereby became the living message from the cosmos.

The book which, if it is read properly, is the best possible educational tool for reality is the New Testament. However, it needs to be put little by little into our own language. The existing translations do not fully convey the original meaning, but if the real meaning is expressed in everyday language the Gospels will then be the best means of evoking a thinking that is imbued with reality, since in their every line they lack the kind of thought-forms that lead to shadowy ideas that are devoid of any real content. What is necessary today is to grasp things in their deeper reality. It might sound almost trivial to speak of being intoxicated with ideas, but this state is so widely prevalent today that it is not so much concepts and ideas—however fine they may sound—that are important but that the person who utters them should be grounded in reality. People find this infinitely difficult to understand today. Virtually everything that appears in the public arena is judged purely on its content, on its conceptual content. If this were not so one would never have considered documents which are totally devoid of ideas such as, for example, the Peace Programme of Professor—or should I say President—Wilson,[6] which is a vacuous conglomeration of conceptual shadows, as having any bearing on reality. Anyone who has any sense of discernment for murky ideas could well know from this assembly of mere conceptual shadows that it could function at best as an absurdity, which might then represent a certain kind of reality. What is really needed today is to search for ideas and concepts that are imbued with reality. This presupposes, however, that people can be deeply related to reality, that they are sufficiently selfless to unite themselves with what lives and weaves in reality; and there is much to be observed in our present age that leads people completely away from this quest for reality, although these things are not noticed.

Many lamentable things are going on now, as anyone with any awareness can see. For example, it is possible at present for people to be

impressed, simply through the way that words are put together, by a
number of speeches (which have even been printed) which for someone
who goes not by words but by realities are absolutely appalling.
Speeches are being given by a highly respected person of our time who
in one of his first speeches proposes the view that with respect to the one
side of his nature man belongs absolutely to the natural order and
theologians are not behaving as they should if they do not leave the
natural order to the scientists. Then the speaker goes on to say that with
respect to the natural order man is purely a mechanism; but the
functions of the soul also depend on this mechanism, and what he
specifies these functions to be are essentially all the functions that the
soul possesses. Theology is then left with the consolation that although
everything has been ceded to science, we can nevertheless still give talks!
But these talks are littered with empty phrases; and they are full of
discontinuities (I shall return to this aspect in the coming lectures and
look at it in greater detail), such that if one studies a thought in conjunction with the previous thought with which it is supposed to be
associated there is no real connection between them. Nevertheless, the
whole talk sounds absolutely fine! In the preface to these lectures about
'The Moulding of Life' it is stated that these lectures were given recently
before thousands of people and that many more thousands will without
doubt feel the need to find comfort in these lectures at this serious time.
These lectures were given by the famous theologian Hunzinger,[7] and
appeared in the Quelle and Meyer series on 'Science and Culture' and are
highly dangerous material, because although they read well and have
something quite enchanting about them one's thoughts become utterly
confused; the ideas have no connection with one another, and once one
has probed what lies beneath the fascinating words the whole thing is
revealed as being absolute nonsense. (In a future lecture I shall say more
in detail about the confused nature of these thoughts.) Nevertheless,
these lectures have been praised very widely; and no one paused to
examine the thought-forms but instead everyone dwelt only on the
word-shadows.

It is indeed the case that what manifests itself outwardly is wholly a
reflection of what man develops inwardly. If he develops concepts that
are alien to reality, reality itself becomes confused; and then conditions

arise such as we have now. It is no longer possible to judge things by what one encounters by way of outward conditions; rather must one form one's judgements by studying what has often been developing in human minds not merely for years but decades and perhaps for considerably longer. It is there that the cause lies; and it is there that one needs to look. Everything depends on Christ being accepted not merely for His teachings; for it is essential that the Mystery of Golgotha is perceived in its true reality, and that there is the clear awareness that something of a super-earthly nature was united with the earthly realm through the person of Jesus of Nazareth. For the awareness will then dawn that morality itself will not fade into oblivion when the Earth and even the fabric of the heavens perish, just as a plant becomes dust; and that just as in a plant there lies hidden the seed for a future plant, so in the present world does the seed for the next world lie concealed—and human beings are connected with this seed. However, this seed needs the connection with Christ, so that it does not—in the same way that the seed of a plant that has not been fertilized dies together with the plant—perish with the Earth. That the moral world-order in the present is the germinal force of a future order of nature is the most real idea that there can possibly be. Morality is not merely something that has been thought out; and if it is imbued with reality it lives now as a seed for later outward realities.

A world conception such as that of the Kant-Laplace theory, of which Herman Grimm[8] said that the spectacle of a hungry dog prowling around a piece of carrion would be a more appetizing sight, is not an idea of this kind. The mechanistic view of the world can never arrive at this thought that morality in its essence has the power to become a phenomenon of nature, that it is the seed of a future natural order. And why not? Because it is essentially an illusion. For if you were to imagine that the Mystery of Golgotha had not taken place, the situation would be as the Kant-Laplace theory describes. You simply need to think away the Mystery of Golgotha from the Earth, and this theory would be correct. The Earth had to reach a condition which would, if left to itself, inevitably lead to human existence ending in the desolation of the grave, because at the critical moment the Earth was fructified by Christ, because Christ—who represents the opposite power to that which leads to the grave, a power that is of a germinal quality—descended to bear man up into the spiritual world. This means that when the Earth becomes a grave, when it fulfils its destiny in accordance with the Kant-Laplace theory, the seed that resides within it is not subject to destruction but is carried over into the future. Thus the Christ-inspired moral world-order presupposes what Goethe calls the 'higher nature in nature';[9] and one can say that anyone who can conceive of the Mystery of Golgotha as a reality in the right way is also able to think in a real way and form concepts and ideas that are imbued with reality.

This, however, is necessary, and it is also what human beings must learn before all else. For people have wanted to incorporate into this fifth post-Atlantean age either ideas which intoxicate them or ideas which make them blind. Ideas of the intoxicating kind mostly derive from religious spheres; those which cause blindness largely arise in the scientific domain. A conception which, while acknowledging the validity of the purely natural order, has only the moral element in view—such as that of Kant, who places these two worlds of knowledge and faith alongside one another[10]—must result in intoxication. Ideas of this nature, which are developed on a moral foundation, are able to intoxicate, and because of the intoxication one does not see that one has actually involuntarily succumbed to the stillness of the grave, where all trace of a moral order fades and vanishes away. Alternatively, ideas can make people blind, as do those of modern science and economics, and—something that it is especially hard to come to terms with—the political ideas of our present age. These ideas make people blind if they are not formulated in connection with a world that is understood from a spiritual standpoint but only from the shreds of the so-called real—that is, the outwardly sense-perceptible—world. The result is that everyone only sees as far as the end of his nose, and blindly forms opinions about what he can see with his eyes and grasp with the concepts that he has acquired, without the benefit of having formed ideas which—through being permeated by the spiritual dimension, by an understanding of spiritual realities—are indeed imbued with reality.

It is important to re-emphasize what is so absolutely necessary for our time; for a historical perspective is often limited now to mere conceptual shadows. A great deal is proclaimed today about what Fichte[11] has said to the German people. However, one only understands what Fichte said if one surveys Fichte's entire life, a life that is so deeply rooted in reality. In my book *The Riddle of Man* I have tried to portray Fichte's life in its entire development, showing how closely linked he was with reality from his childhood onwards. It would be really good if statements such as these about ideas being imbued with realities were not only heard in a superficial way but were received on a deeply intimate level—and I really mean deeply intimate. Only in this way will one acquire a free and open perception—an inner, soul perception—of what our age so urgently needs. Everyone needs such a free, open inner perception of this. Anyone who has not made a particular point of pondering the facts that have been touched upon here is far too little aware that in our time the ideas and words that we exchange are but shadows and empty husks, and that everything has a tendency to lead people in the direction of ideas and concepts that either intoxicate them or make them blind.

Do not take anything that I have been saying today as the words of some sort of fanatic but rather as expressing an actual reality. We all have to live with our times, at any rate we should; and when something is being spoken about one ought not to regard it as implying that absolutely everything should be done away with. Nevertheless, some sort of balance needs to be established. It is quite natural that everyone is being confronted with impulses leading entirely towards materialism. There is nothing that we can do about this, for the drive towards materialism is connected with the deep needs of our time. All the same, a balance must be created. I have to say that everything is geared towards leading man firmly in the direction of materialism. This cannot be prevented; it is part of the nature of the fifth post-Atlantean epoch. But there needs to be some kind of balance. A particularly powerful means of driving people towards materialism is something that has hardly been viewed from this angle at all: the cinematograph. For what one perceives in films is not reality as it is actually seen. Only an age that has so little idea of reality as ours, which worships reality as an idol in the materialistic sense, could believe that the cinematograph represents reality. A different age would consider whether people walk along the street as they do in films, whether—if one were to ask oneself what one has seen—the images that one sees really correspond to reality. Ask yourselves very honestly: is what you have seen on the street closer to a picture painted by an artist, which does not move, or to the ghastly flickering images of the cinematograph? If you are really honest, you will say to yourself: what the painter portrays in a state of rest has a much stronger resemblance to what you yourself see on the street. So when people are sitting in the cinema, what they see there comes to reside within them not through their ordinary faculties of perception but at a deeper material level than is normal for the process of perception. A person becomes etherically goggle-eyed. His eyes begin to look like those of a seal, only much bigger, when he watches lots of films. I mean etherically bigger. This has an effect not only on what lives in his conscious mind but it has a materializing influence on his subconsciousness. Do not interpret this as a denunciation of the cinematograph. I should like to make it quite clear that it is perfectly natural that there should be cinematographs; and the art of cinematography or film-making will be developed to an ever-increasing degree. This will be the road leading to materialism. But a counterbalance needs to be sought. This can happen only if the addiction for the kind of reality that is being developed through films is connected with something else. Just as with this addiction there develops a tendency to descend below perception by way of the senses, so must there develop an ascent above sensory perception, that is, into spiritual reality. Then it will do no harm to go to the cinema, and one can see such images as often as one wishes. But if no counterbalance is created, people will be led through such things to relate to the Earth not in the way that is necessary but to become more and more closely related to it to the point where they are completely cut off from the spiritual world.

LECTURE 5

I have spoken to you about the three meetings that feature in the human soul's biography in the course of its life between birth and death, and which bring it in the course of this life into connection with the spiritual worlds. We shall today return to this subject, which on the previous occasion we touched upon in a preparatory way in the form of an interpolation, in somewhat greater detail.

I pointed out that during the time between going to sleep and waking up we experience a meeting, which usually takes place in the middle of the period of sleep. (I say 'usually', because the state of sleep is normally equivalent to the night.) Thus between going to sleep and waking up we generally have an encounter with that world to which our Spirit Self is related, the world in which we place the beings from that hierarchy whom we refer to as the Angels. So every time we pass through a period of sleep we traverse that world where these beings dwell, a world which lies immediately above our physical world; and we refresh and strengthen our whole spiritual being through this meeting. Because this is so, because during sleep man is related to the spiritual world, a purely materialistic explanation such as is attempted by ordinary science can never provide a satisfactory interpretation. Much of what goes on within man can be explained from the changes that the body undergoes from waking up until going to sleep, and the attempt may be made to explain sleep from these changes; and yet there will always be something unsatisfactory about this, because sleep has to do with the meeting referred to and, hence, with a person's relationship to the spiritual world. Thus it is precisely when we consider the state of sleep that we can see that where a person does not consciously seek a relationship to the spiritual world he arrives at half-truths, which— since ideas become deeds—bring a disturbing element to life and also eventually in a very real way bring about great catastrophes in life.

Half-truths! These are in some respects even worse than ideas that are completely erroneous, because people who formulate half-truths are very insistent about them, for they are able to prove them (on the grounds that if they are even half-true, they can be proved). Moreover, they cannot be refuted, since the ideas are, after all, partly true. Such ideas distort life even more than completely erroneous ones, for their falsehood can be immediately discerned and recognized. One such half-truth, which has to some extent been abandoned by science today but continues to have a considerable degree of support, is an idea that I have often alluded to before: that we sleep because we are tired. It is, we may indeed say, a half-truth, and it is supported by a half-true observation to which people appeal, namely that the life of the day tires the body and so one needs to sleep because one is tired. I have often drawn your attention in previous lectures to the fact that this interpretation of sleep can never explain why people with a private income, who have never done a stroke of work, often fall asleep at once when they hear stimulating discussions about events in the world around them. There is certainly no way of proving that they are tired, and that they have had to go to sleep because they have been slaving away is quite simply an erroneous—or half-true—observation. If we believe that we are compelled to go to sleep because we are tired, we are only half-observing. We only see the limitations of our observation when we compare what we are observing from the one side with what can be observed from the other side, thus coming in contact with the other side of the truth. You will see presently what I mean.

Going to sleep and waking up is a process of constant rhythmic alternation in an individual human life. However, man is a being who possesses freedom, and who can therefore interfere with this rhythm (more through circumstances than through anything that could be construed as free will, but such circumstances are the foundation of freedom). He can intervene in the course of events, and is sometimes only all too glad to do so in the context of the rhythm of going to sleep and waking up. Another rhythm, which we have often combined with that of sleeping and waking (even though in ordinary consciousness they are not linked together in the right way) is the one that manifests itself in the course of the year: the alternation of summer and winter, if we leave the intermediate seasons out of account. It will not occur to anyone to say that during the summer the Earth is making great efforts and is developing those forces which lead to the growth of plants and to much else besides and that it then becomes tired, and needs to have a rest in winter. Everyone would find such an idea to be absurd and will say that the coming of winter has absolutely nothing to do with the efforts of the Earth in summer but is caused by the Sun being in a different spatial relationship to the region of the Earth where winter makes its appearance. In the latter case everything is being derived from outside, while with sleeping and waking it is all a question of tiredness, which derives from within. Now the one is just as incorrect as the other, or one could also say it is just as half-true as the other. The rhythm of sleeping and waking is the same kind of rhythm as that between winter and summer. It is no more true to say that we go to sleep only because we are tired than it is true that winter arrives because the Earth has worn itself out during the summer; for both these events arise through the independent influence of a rhythm which is brought about by certain circumstances. The rhythm of sleeping and waking is governed by the need of the human soul to bring about the meeting with the spiritual world. If we were to say that we want to go to sleep and therefore feel tired, or if we were to say that we are entering a stage when we are in need of one part of the rhythm, the state of sleep, and therefore feel tired, we would be saying something more correct than to say that we must go to sleep because we are tired.

Things become even clearer if we simply ask what the soul actually does when it is asleep. The unspiritual science of the present day does not have the right understanding, or even any real possibility, to answer such a question. When we are awake we enjoy the outer world; for enjoyment accompanies us throughout our life. We do not merely enjoy the outer world when we experience a good meal by way of our palate, in which case the word 'enjoy' has a quite particular connotation, but we enjoy the outer world throughout the time that we are awake, and the whole of life is at the same time enjoyment. Although there is much in the world that is unpleasant and which is apparently not enjoyment at all, this is only an illusion; and we shall speak of this in a different context in the forthcoming lectures. When we are awake we enjoy the outer world; when we are asleep we, quite literally, enjoy our own selves. Just as we enjoy the outer world through our body when our soul is dwelling in our body, so do we enjoy our own body when our soul is outside the body; for during the life between birth and death we are connected with the body, even when as souls we are outside it. The essential point about the state of sleep, of ordinary, normal sleep, is that we are deeply immersed in our body, that we enjoy our body. We enjoy our body from outside. And dreams, ordinary chaotic dreams, are rightly interpreted if one says that they are the reflection of that bodily enjoyment which a person has in dreamless sleep.

This explanation of sleep comes closer to the need for sleep that I spoke about in the case of the person with private means; for whereas it is not easy to believe that he is tired, we will have no difficulty in believing that he is so fond of his body that he would rather enjoy that than what often comes towards him from the outside world. He takes such endless pleasure in it and enjoys himself so much that he greatly prefers this than, say, a lecture that he listens to perhaps out of a certain sense of shame, or a difficult piece of serious music, where he goes to sleep immediately if he has to listen to it. Sleep is self-enjoyment. However, as in sleep, in normal sleep, we have the encounter with the spiritual world, sleep ceases to be mere self-enjoyment and becomes also a means of acquiring understanding of oneself to a certain degree, a process of self-discovery. In this respect our spiritual training is really needed in order that people may come to understand that in normal sleep they do indeed become immersed in the spiritual domain and re-emerge from it when they wake up again, and that they learn to approach this meeting with the spirit with reverence.

Now in order that we are fully presented with the facts, I should like to return once more to the so-called enigma of fatigue; for anyone looking from a superficial standpoint might very well pick up on this point. Such a person may say that we really do experience feeling tired, and the need for sleep arises from this sense of tiredness. This is a point where a really clear distinction needs to be made. We do indeed become tired as a result of the day's work, and while we sleep we are able to get over our fatigue. So this aspect of the matter is true: we are able to get rid of our tiredness through sleep. But sleep is not in any sense the result of tiredness but consists in a person's enjoyment of himself; and through this self-enjoyment he acquires the forces through which he drives away the tiredness that has arisen. Thus to this extent it is true to say that sleep can enable us to get over our fatigue. However, it does not follow that all sleep can do so; for whereas it is true that all sleep is self-enjoyment, it is not the case that all sleep drives away tiredness. For a person who sleeps unnecessarily, who goes to sleep at every opportunity, is really able to manage to go to sleep when there is no tiredness to be driven away, when nothing but self-enjoyment is involved. It is of course true that, because one is accustomed through one's normal life to get over tiredness through sleep, one will through a sleep of this nature also constantly be making efforts to drive away one's sense of fatigue. But if there is no actual tiredness, as is the case with the person with a private income who goes to sleep in the concert, one will simply be busying oneself with one's body in the way that one would do if one were actually tired. As, however, there is no tiredness involved in this case, the person concerned will be busying himself unnecessarily, with the consequence that he incubates all sorts of ancillary conditions in the body. That is why these well-to-do people who sleep so much are tormented to such an extreme degree by all manner of conditions known collectively as neurasthenia.

Through one's connection with spiritual knowledge it is possible to imagine a situation where one is conscious of living in a rhythm where one is alternately in the physical world and in the spiritual world. In the physical world one has encounters with outer physical nature; in the spiritual world one meets with the beings who live in that world.

We shall be able to understand this more fully if we study the entirety of man's being from a certain point of view. As you know, the science of biology normally views man as a unity, roughly dividing him into the head, chest region and lower abdomen with the various limb appendages. In those ancient times when there was still an atavistic knowledge, people associated other ideas with this division of man's being. The great Plato, the Greek philosopher, attributes wisdom to the head, courage to the chest region and the lower impulses of human nature to the lower abdomen. Moreover, what belongs to the chest region can be ennobled if wisdom is united with the courage that is linked to the chest region, thus becoming wisdom-filled courage, wisdom-filled activity. And if what may be regarded as man's lower part and is associated with the lower abdomen is irradiated with wisdom, Plato calls this prudence or circumspection or, quite literally, a state of being clothed with the Sun.[1] Thus we see how the soul is divided and related to the various parts of the body. With the benefit of spiritual science, which was not as yet accessible to Plato in the same way, we can speak about these things in much fuller detail.

As we are speaking about the whole of man's being, we will now—starting from the highest of his four members—speak about his ego. Everything that man calls his own in a soul-spiritual sense works in his physical life between birth and death through the instrument of his physical body. With respect to each member of man's being, we can ask through which parts of the physical organism does the member in question work. What manifests itself to us through really thorough spiritual observation is that what we call the human ego is between birth and death—however strange it may seem, but the truth is usually very different from the way that a superficial awareness might imagine it to be—connected physically with what we call the lower abdomen. For the ego is, as I have often said, the baby of human nature. The physical body had its origins in the era of Old Saturn, the ether body in that of Old Sun, the astral body during the Old Moon period and the ego during that of the Earth. It is the youngest of the members of man's being. Only in the future period of Vulcan will it be at the stage where the physical body is now during the earthly era. The ego is linked to the lowest part of man's physicality, and this lowest aspect is actually in a state of constant sleep. It is not organized in such a way that what takes place within it can be brought to consciousness. What is enacted in this lower region is in ordinary waking consciousness governed by sleep. We are just as little conscious of our ego as such in its true nature, its real essence, as we are of the processes of our digestion. The ego of which we are conscious is the image of what is reflected by way of our head. We do not ever really perceive our ego, neither in sleep, where we are normally completely unconscious, nor when we are awake; for the ego is then also asleep. The true ego does not come to consciousness; all that does so is the idea, the concept of the ego, which is reflected there. On the other hand, during the time between going to sleep and waking up the ego really comes into its own, though someone who is in a normal state of deep sleep knows nothing of this because he is still unconscious in this deep sleep during the Earth era. So the ego is to all intents and purposes connected with the lowest part of man's bodily organism—during the day and for the duration of waking consciousness from within, and during sleep from without.

If we now move on to the second member of human nature, to what we call the astral body, we find that as regards the instrument through which it works the astral body is from a certain point of view connected with the chest region of man's being. In actual fact we can really only dream about what goes on in the astral body and comes to expression through the region of the chest. In so far as we are earthly human beings we can perceive something of the ego only when we are asleep, that is to say, we cannot perceive anything consciously; whereas we can dream of what the astral body brings about within us. That is why we continually dream about our feelings, about the sentiments that dwell within us. Indeed, they lead a sort of dream life within us. Thus the ego is outside the region that we human beings encompass with our ordinary sensory consciousness; for it is continuously asleep. The astral body is also still in a certain respect outside what we encompass with our sensory consciousness, for it can only dream. With respect to both of these we are, in reality, in the spiritual world, irrespective of whether we are awake or asleep.

What we call the ether body is, however, with regard to its physical aspect connected with the head. Through the particular organization of the head the ether body is able to remain constantly awake when it is within the human body, when it is connected with the physical aspect of the head. Thus we can say: the ego is connected with the lowest parts of our body, and the astral body with our chest region. The heart, the functioning of which lies outside our full consciousness (we have only a dream consciousness of it), beats and pulsates under the influence of the astral body. When the head thinks, it does so under the influence of the ether body. We can then in addition differentiate the physical body as a whole, where everything comes together; for its connection is with the entirety of the outside world.

You can now see a remarkable set of relationships: the ego is connected with the lower parts of the body, the astral body with the heart region, the ether body with the head, and the physical body with the whole of the outside world, with the world around us. The physical body as a whole also has a relationship in waking consciousness with the surrounding outer world. In the same way that with our whole body we have a relationship with the external environment, so does our ether body have a connection with our head, our astral body with the heart and so on. From this you can see how truly mysterious are the connections linking man with the world. These relationships are indeed virtually the opposite of what a superficial understanding of these matters might suppose. The lowest parts of human nature are at present the aspects of man's being which are as yet imperfect; and this is why they correspond as parts of the body to what we have referred to as the baby of our being—the ego.

Infinite mysteries of human life lie hidden in what I have been saying to you. If you enter fully into all of this you will above all else understand how the whole of man's being has been formed from the spirit, though at different stages. The human head is formed from the spirit, but its formation has been taken further; it belongs to a later stage of formation than does the chest, of which we might say that it is just as much a metamorphosis of the head as, in the sense of Goethe's theory of metamorphosis, the leaf is a metamorphosis of the flower. If we consider the rhythm between sleeping and waking from this point of view, we may say that during our waking life the ego actually dwells in all the lowest activities in the human body, which finally culminate in the formation of blood. The ego is present in these activities during the waking state. These are those activities of the body which are in a certain sense at the lowest level of spirituality, for everything to do with the body is also spiritual (even though what we are speaking about now is at the lowest spiritual level). However, through the fact that during waking consciousness the ego is at the lowest level of spirituality, during sleep—and it is important to note this—it is with respect to man's being at the highest level of spirituality. For consider the following. When we observe the head, and the way that we as human beings bear it on our shoulders, it is as regards its outer form the most fully a manifestation of the spirit. It is to the fullest degree a reflection, a revelation of the spirit; the spirit has in the head entered most deeply into matter. For that very reason it has left the least behind in the spirit-world itself. Man has expended so much effort on making the outer form of the head a revelation of the spirit that little has been left behind in the spiritual domain; whereas because what is outwardly manifested in the lower parts of man's physical organism is the least spiritualized, far more of what is related to these lower parts has been left behind in the world of spirit. The head, as head, has to the smallest degree a spiritual counterpart, because it has the most spirit within it; the lower abdomen has the greatest spiritual counterpart, because it has the least spirit within it—and in this greater abundance of spirit which does not reside in the bodily organism there dwells the ego during the hours of sleep.

Just consider this wonderful balancing process: whereas man has a lower nature with respect to his physicality and the ego immerses itself in this lower nature at the moment of waking, this lower nature is only a lower nature because the spirit has worked least upon it, because the spirit has kept so much behind in the spiritual domain. And yet during sleep the ego is present in what has been kept back. Thus during sleep the ego is already now together with what man will develop and unfold only in the future; for it is at present only barely indicated and very little developed in man's bodily organism. Thus when the ego becomes conscious of the situation in which it dwells during sleep, when it really becomes conscious of this situation, it may say to itself: 'During sleep I am in the holiest situation that I can be in as a human being. And as I emerge from sleep, when I wake up, I am going from the world of my holiest situation to what is today only a feeble indication of it.'

Yes, it is important that through spiritual science such things can really begin to live in our feelings, in our inner thoughts. Our lives will then themselves be imbued with a magical breath of holiness. We will then be able to associate a definite and positive idea or concept with what is called the grace of the Spirit, of the Holy Spirit. We will then connect this totality of human experience which takes its course in the rhythm between sleeping and waking with the idea: 'You may participate in the spiritual world, you may dwell in it.' When we have really taken this idea into our feeling life—'You may be in the spiritual world, you will receive the grace of being imbued with the spiritual world, which is inaccessible to you through your ordinary consciousness'— when we have really lived with this thought, we have also learnt to look up to the Spirit who is revealed to us, I might say, through every detail of life and, indeed, just as much as outer nature manifests itself to our outward eyes and ears. But the age of materialism has separated man from the consciousness of being irradiated and permeated in the totality of his existence by the grace of the Spirit. It is of immense importance that this is overcome; for in the depths of our souls we are more aware in our time of the prevailing materialism of our age than one might think. Nevertheless, the human soul is in our present age generally far too weak to bring these ideas which can lead beyond materialism to an inner awareness. One such idea is that of the holiness of sleep. For once we have understood this idea of the holiness of sleep, we ascribe all the thoughts and ideas in our waking state that do not bind us to matter to the influence of the spirit which follows during sleep. We would then be seeing what is important for us as human beings not only in our waking state, which connects us with matter—which would be like considering that only winter is of any importance for the Earth—but we would be seeing everything as a whole. For the Earth we see the whole if we consider winter together with summer; and we see the whole for man if we consider the daytime, i.e. the connection with matter, together with sleep, i.e. the connection with the spirit.

Now a superficial observation might say: 'So when someone is awake he is connected with matter and can therefore know something of the spirit even when awake!' Of course, man has a memory, and this memory functions not only in his consciousness but also in his subconscious mind. If we had no memory, no amount of sleep could help us. This is very important, and I want you to keep it firmly in mind—if this were so no amount of sleep could help us. For if we had no memory we would be led inevitably to the firm belief that there is nothing but material existence. It is only because we preserve in our subconscious mind a memory of what we experience during sleep (even though we have no knowledge of this on the surface of our consciousness) that we think in a way that is not purely materialistic. If people do not only think materialistically, if they have spiritual ideas of any sort during the day, it is because they have a memory. For man is now constituted as an earthly human being in such a way that he comes in contact with the spirit only while he is asleep.

The point at issue here is that if, on the other hand, we were to develop so strong a consciousness of what takes place within us during sleep, of the nature that under certain circumstances people in former times were able to develop, it would never occur to us to doubt the spirit; and we would, in contrast, remember what we encountered in our sleep not only subconsciously but also in a conscious way. If someone has had a conscious experience of what he lives through during sleep, it would be just as absurd to deny the spirit as it would be absurd for someone to deny the existence of tables and chairs while he is awake. The crucial point is that humanity should once more really come to appreciate the meeting with the spirit during sleep. This can only happen if the ideas and concepts developed during the day have suffi-cient force to make this possible; and this can be achieved by entering deeply into spiritual science. In spiritual science we are working with ideas that are derived from the spiritual world. We discipline our head, that is to say the ether body in our head, to conceive of things that do not have anything to do with outward materiality and which have reality only in the world of spirit. A greater effort is needed for this than for forming mental pictures of things which have their reality in the material world. This is the real reason why people do not involve themselves with spiritual science. They come up with all sorts of reasons against it. They say that it is not logical. If they were urged to prove its illogicality, they would run into difficulties; for it cannot be proved that spiritual science is illogical. But the rejection of spiritual science, the refusal to acknowledge it, derives from something altogether different, namely—and I'm not sure whether one may also be somewhat impolite in a scientific debate—from sheer laziness. And although certain learned people are ever so industrious when it comes to all the ideas that relate to outward material things, with regard to the energy that one needs to apply in order to understand things of a spiritual nature they are idle and lazy; and it is because they do not want to call forth in themselves the necessary energy that they do not acknowledge spiritual science. For it simply requires more effort to think spiritual-scientific thoughts than to formulate ordinary ideas associated with material realities. Ideas of the latter nature arise out of themselves, whereas ideas that are not bound to the material world must be thought; one has to gather up one's forces and really make an effort. This reluctance to apply oneself is the reason for the rejection of spiritual science; and one has to realize this. But when the effort is made to assimilate such ideas and to think them through, one's soul enters into such a state of inner activity that it will gradually begin to develop a consciousness of what goes on between going to sleep and waking up and of the meeting with the spirit that takes place then. A certain amount of unlearning of some ideas will surely be necessary. Just think to what a small degree many spiritual leaders today have the capacity to develop such ideas. Although the following scenario is less pronounced than it used to be, those who have now become leaders were for the large part of their apprenticeship, or what one would call their student days, so deeply immersed in the life of their day that they learnt to drink themselves into a stupor.[2] Well, an idea and a whole wealth of feelings as to what goes on during sleep that such a person may develop are certainly not an appropriate way of clarifying the whole significance of sleep. One may be very learned as regards everything that is associated with matter, but it is naturally not possible for such a person to gain an insight into what one experiences between going to sleep and waking up.

When people make the effort to think through ideas that are not connected with material substance, they develop an understanding of what I have called the first meeting, the meeting with the spirit during sleep. However, if the world is not to fall into decadence, it will be important for this understanding to shine into our lives with a sunlike radiance in the not too distant future. For if people do not take up these ideas, how will they be able to arrive at ideas of any kind? The only way they will be able to do this is by observing the outer world. However, ideas that are arrived at in this way alone leave the inner aspect of man's being, his soul, in a state of inertia; and what needs to exert itself through spiritual ideas is left inert, is unused and unfulfilled and becomes degenerate. What is the consequence of this? The result is that people become blind in their whole relationship to the world, spiritually blind. By developing ideas and concepts under the influence of outer circumstances and impressions, they become spiritually blind; and spiritual blindness is the defining characteristic of the materialistic age. In science this is only damaging up to a point, but in practical life this blindness with regard to the real world is extremely harmful. You see, the further we descend into matter, the more things correct themselves in this materialistic age. If a bridge is being built, the people building it will be forced by the circumstances involved to adhere to the proper rules of construction, otherwise when the first vehicle crosses it the bridge will collapse. It is more possible to apply erroneous ideas in the realm of medical care, for the reason that a person dies or is made well can never be proved; but it is by no means necessarily the case that the ideas acted upon were the right ones. However, in the world of ideas as such and where one is active in the cultural domain,[3] matters are far more serious. That is why things are looking really serious in what one generally calls the practical sciences such as economics and politics. In the materialistic age people have become used to being guided with respect to economics by ideas and impressions coming from the outer world; and as a result their ideas have become blind. Everything that is developed in the realm of economics consists for the most part of intellectually blind ideas. The inevitable consequence of this is that people who have these blind notions in their heads are carried along by events as though in leading-reins; they allow events to take hold of them. And when in this state they become involved in them the result is hardly surprising.

This is the result of one of the ways in which one arrives at ideas *without* taking up spiritual science, namely that one's ideas are blind. The other approach to ideas is that, instead of being guided by outer circumstances, one's ideas are stimulated from within—which is to say that only what lives in one's emotions and passions is allowed to germinate in one's soul. This gives rise to ideas that are far from being blind but are, one might say, of an intoxicating nature. And so people of the present day who believe in materialism are forever swinging to and fro between blind ideas and intoxicating ideas: blind ideas, where they in effect let themselves be bossed around by what is going on, so that when they become involved they do so in the clumsiest way possible; intoxicating ideas, where they give themselves over solely to emotions and passions and relate to the world in such a way that they do not really understand anything but either love or hate everything, passing judgements in accordance with their love or hatred, their sympathy or antipathy. This is especially so in this materialistic age. For it is only by, on the one hand, making inner efforts to formulate spiritual ideas and, on the other hand, developing one's feelings for the wider concerns of the world that a person arrives at ideas and conceptions that shed any light on anything. If we are able to embrace what spiritual science has to say to us regarding the wider connections with the ages of Saturn, Sun and Moon and our connection with the universe (which are ridiculed by people who uphold the modern materialistic conception of the world), if we can fructify our moral feelings through these wider purposes of humanity, we will reach beyond the mere emotions displayed in the form of sympathy and antipathy for everything in the world around us and, moreover, in the only way available to us.

It is undoubtedly necessary for much that is living in our time to be purified through spiritual science; for man will not allow himself to be cut off so completely from the spiritual world. He does not really allow himself to be cut off but only apparently so. I have already made you aware of how this apparent cutting off process is achieved. When, on the other hand, people swear only by matter and by the impressions of the outside world, the inner forces which are intended for the spirit remain within them; but they then direct them to a false realm and give themselves up to all manner of illusions. This is essentially why the most down-to-earth, materialistic people are also most prone to indulging in illusions. Thus we see many people who go through life denying the spirit and roaring with laughter if anyone speaks to them of someone having spiritual experiences. 'He is seeing ghosts!' they say, and they are uttering words of condemnation if they are able to say of someone that 'he is seeing ghosts'. *They* certainly do not 'see ghosts', as they would say. But they only *think* that they do not see ghosts, because they are actually seeing them all the time. One can put such a person who is so firmly rooted in his crudely materialistic view of the world to the test, and one will be able to see how he indulges in the most extreme illusions as regards what the following day may bring. This giving way to illusions is merely a substitute for the realm of spirit, which he denies. He inevitably falls prey to illusions if he rejects everything of a spiritual nature, and he cannot avoid doing so. As has been said, it is not so easy to demonstrate the existence of illusions in the various areas of life, but they are all over the place, absolutely everywhere. And the thing is that people like illusions. One can, for example, very often come across someone saying: 'Shall I invest my money in this or that enterprise? This one is a brewery. I don't want my money being used for that, so I won't invest it here.' He takes his money to the bank. Without his knowledge the bank invests the money in the brewery. It makes no difference whatsoever in the objective fact, but he is under the illusion that his money is not being used for such debased purposes.

It might be thought that what I am saying is somewhat far-fetched. However this is not so; it is a very common phenomenon. People today do not take the trouble to study life properly and penetrate its surface. It is, however, important to do this; for it is quite crucial that one should come to know what position one is in. This is not easy nowadays, because life has become complicated. Nevertheless, what I have been pointing out is true. For, you see, under certain circumstances an absurd situation may easily arise. I shall illustrate this by means of an example. There was once an arsonist—I am giving you an actual instance—who ran out of a house that he had just set on fire. He had organized everything so that he was able to get away in time. He was caught and was held responsible. And then he said that he had done a really good job, for it wasn't his fault that the house went up in flames but that of the workmen who had just left the house, leaving a lighted candle glowing in the twilight. If the candle had burnt down during the night, the house would have gone up in flames in the middle of the night. He had therefore set the house on fire before it became totally dark. The house would have caught fire in any case, and he had only done what he did because if there was still some daylight when the house went up in flames it would still be possible to put the fire out quickly; this would have been more complicated at night and the whole house would have burnt down, whereas with some daylight the fire could be quickly extinguished. Then he was asked why he had not extinguished the candle. His reply was: 'I am a teacher of humanity. If I had blown the candle out, the workmen who were the ones to blame would have carried on being careless, but now they can see what happens if they forget to extinguish the light.'

We may laugh at such an example but we fail to see that we are continually doing the same thing. People are constantly doing similar things to what this man did when instead of blowing out the candle he set fire to the house. It is simply that we do not notice how a situation relates to the spiritual world, either because we are dulled by our feelings and passions or because we are enticed by intoxicating ideas. If we become inwardly accustomed to the elasticity and flexibility that are necessary for the nurturing of spiritual ideas, we shall also develop our thinking in such a way that it can really penetrate into our lives and adapt itself to them. If we fail to do this, our thinking will never be able to deal with life and will not even come in contact with it, except in a superficial way. That is why—to turn to the deeper issue—the materialistic age really leads people away from all connection with the spiritual world. Just as one undermines one's bodily well-being if one does not sleep in the right way, so does one undermine one's soul life if one is not awake in the right way. And one is failing to be awake in the right way if one gives oneself up to outer impressions, if one lives without being conscious of one's connection with the spiritual world. Just as someone who for one reason or another tosses and turns in his sleep undermines his physical health, so does a person who in his waking hours gives himself up solely to his outward impressions of the world and to physical matter alone undermine his spiritual health. This will prevent him from rightly experiencing that first meeting with the spiritual world of which I have spoken. However, through this he ceases to be able to relate to the spiritual world in the right way during physical existence; and as a result the connection with that world in which we are dwelling when we are not incarnated in a physical body, that world which we enter when we pass through the portal of death, is severed.

People need to understand once again that we are not here simply in order to involve ourselves in the physical universe during our physical existence, and that in the course of our whole existence we have a connection with the totality of the world. Those who have passed through the portal of death want to work with us on the physical world. This collaboration is only apparently of a physical nature, for everything physical is but an outward expression of the spirit. The materialistic age has estranged human beings from the world of the dead; spiritual science needs to enable them to befriend this world once more. There will have to come a time when we no longer make it impossible for the dead to carry out their work for the spiritualization of the physical world by estranging ourselves from them. After all, the dead cannot take hold of things and affairs in the physical world with their hands and become directly involved in physical work. That would be unthinkable. They are able to work in a spiritual way. For this, however, they need the tools that are available to them here; they need the spiritual substance that lives here in the physical world. We are not merely human beings, we are also at the same time instruments for the spirits who have passed through the portal of death. For as long as we are incarnated in a physical body we use pens or hammers or axes; once we are no longer incarnated in a physical body our tools are human souls themselves. That this is so arises from the particular nature of a dead person's perception, which I should like to touch upon once more. I have already mentioned it earlier.

Suppose you have before you—shall we say—a small vessel containing salt. As you look at it, you see the salt as white grains, as a white powder. But if you put the salt on your tongue and taste it, taste the distinctive quality of salt, it begins to be possible for the spirit to perceive it. Any spirit is able to perceive your tasting of the salt. Every spirit, and also every human soul that has passed through the portal of death, can perceive everything that takes place within man through the outer world. Just as nature reaches towards us when we taste and smell and see and hear, so does the world of the dead reach down to what we hear, see, taste and so on. The dead accompany us in our experiences of the physical world; for these are not only part of our world but also part of theirs. It belongs to their world when we imbue what we receive from the outside world with spiritual ideas. Unless we do this, what we merely experience as the effect of a material substance is as though incomprehensible to a dead person and is veiled in obscurity. A dead person experiences a soul that is estranged from the spirit as a dark soul. For this reason the dead have become estranged from our earthly life during this materialistic age, and this situation must come to an end. There needs to be an intimate community of life between the so-called dead and the so-called living. However, this can happen only if people foster within their souls forces of a vibrant, spiritual nature, that is, if they develop ideas, concepts and imaginations which emanate from the spiritual domain. If a person makes the effort to reach the spiritual domain in his thoughts, he will gradually also reach the spirit in the realities of life. That is to say, a bridge is built between the physical and spiritual worlds. This alone can enable the transition to be made from the age of materialism to an age when human beings will confront reality neither in a blind nor an intoxicated way but with vision and composure. These qualities will arise, on the one hand, through their capacity to see as it were with spiritual eyes and, on the other, through their ability to develop from their feelings regarding the wider concerns of the world a true balance between sympathy and antipathy, also with respect to what their immediate surroundings are demanding of them.

WE shall begin by devoting a little more time to what we have been saying about the three meetings referred to in earlier lectures. We have said that the alternating states in which man lives in the brief period of 24 hours, when he lives alternately in a sleeping or a waking state, are not what they outwardly appear to be from a physical point of view but that in the course of these alternating states a person has a meeting with the spiritual world. In this connection we indicated that the ego and the astral body, which are separated from the physical and ether bodies during sleep in that they are, as it were, breathed out into the spiritual world when one goes to sleep and breathed in again when one wakes up, have their meeting during sleep with that world which we associate with the hierarchy of the Angels, a world to which our own human soul will belong when the Spirit Self has developed and where the being who is referred to in a religious context as the Holy Spirit holds sway as the highest ruling principle. We have spoken in quite some detail about this meeting in the spiritual world, which accordingly takes place for every human being every time he goes to sleep.

Now we must clearly understand that as the human race has developed there have been changes in the course of earthly evolution with regard to these processes. What actually happens when a person is asleep? I would say that, from the standpoint of man's inner being, I explained this in the previous lecture. From the standpoint of his relationship to the universe, man in a certain sense imitates that rhythm of the world order which applies to any particular place on the Earth's surface through the fact that one half of the 24-hour period is day and the other half is night. Of course, it is always day somewhere on the Earth, but a human being inhabits only one place on its surface, and with respect to this one place what has been outlined above applies: wherever he lives, he imitates the rhythm between day and night in his own rhythm of sleeping and waking. The fact that this connection is loosened in modern life, so that man is not compelled simply to be awake during the day and to sleep at night, is associated with his freeing himself from the objective rhythms of the world in the course of evolution; and he therefore only has within him the one rhythm instead of the two rhythms, his own rhythm of sleeping and waking and that of day and night, running in regular parallel paths. These rhythms work in a certain sense at one time for the universe, for the macrocosm, and at another time for man, for the microcosm; they are no longer in unison. In this way man is, in a certain sense, a being who is independent of the macrocosm.

Now in olden times, in those former times when, as we know, human beings possessed a certain atavistic clairvoyance, they fitted in more closely as regards this rhythm with the great rhythms of the cosmic order. In former times people's sleeping patterns were such that they were awake during the day and asleep at night; and so the whole context of a person's experience was different in those times from how it is now. Man had in a certain sense to be wrenched free from this parallel path with the macrocosm in order through this process of separation to develop an active inner independent life. It cannot be said that the main point associated with this was that in olden times people slept in such a way that they actually hardly saw the stars at all. They did indeed observe them, despite what scientific research claims about star worship (which is something quite different). The essential point was that people had a completely different relationship to the whole cosmic order, in that while the Sun was on the other side of the Earth (and was therefore not exercising its influence directly on the part of the Earth where they were living), their egos and astral bodies, which were outside their physical and ether bodies, were given over in reverence to the stars. So they did not merely perceive the physical stars, they perceived the spiritual counterpart of the physical stars. They did not actually see the physical stars with their outward eyes, but they saw what belongs spiritually to the physical stars. So we should not understand what is related of the old star worship as signifying that these people in olden times looked up at the stars and then translated what they saw into symbols, formulating all sorts of lovely images and symbols. It is very easy to say in the sense of modern science that in these ancient times people had very fertile imaginations; they imagined gods amidst Saturn, Sun and Moon; through their fantasy they translated animal forms into the signs of the zodiac. One really has to give credit to the active imaginations of the modern scientific experts who fabricated such ideas! What is, however, true is that in that state of consciousness of the egos and astral bodies of these people in olden times, things really did appear in the way that has been described, so that they really saw and perceived such phenomena. This meant, however, that people had a direct perception of the spirit that pervades the universe; they lived with this spirit with which the universe is ensouled.

We are really only properly adapted to the Earth through our physical and etheric bodies. As for our ego and astral body, they are suited to the spirit that ensouls the universe in the manner just described. We may say that our ego and astral body belong to this realm of the universe, but man needs to develop himself in such a way that he can discover the innermost nature of his ego and astral body from his experiences within them. For this purpose the outer experience that existed in former times had to disappear for a while; it had to become obscured. The consciousness of communication with the stars had to recede, it had to be dimmed, so that man's inner being might be strengthened in such a way that at some future time he might learn to develop the inner strength to be able to find the spirit as a spirit. Just as people in former times were connected in the course of every night with the spirit of the starry world, so were they similarly connected with that same spirit in the course of every year; but in the course of the year they eventually came in contact with a higher Spirit of the starry world, with what actually takes place in that world. During the night the forms of the stars in their peacefulness exercised their influence upon them; in the course of the year they were affected by the change associated with the passage of the Sun during the year, and thereby also with the destiny of the Earth in its yearly cycle as it passes through the seasons, and especially through summer and winter.

You see, although there are still certain traditions with regard to the experience that people had in olden times when they were asleep at night, there are relatively few traditions—or to be more precise very few of which the origin is known—remaining of those still more distant times when man's life encompassed the mysteries of the course of the year. Nevertheless, the reverberations of these experiences of the yearly cycle still persist, although they are little understood. Among the myths of the different peoples you will constantly find those which testify that there was everywhere a knowledge of a battle of winter with summer, of summer with winter. Here again, present-day scholars view this as symbolizing the creative imagination of people in olden times, which in our progress and sophistication we have gone so far beyond. These were, however, real experiences that people went through, experiences which played a deep and significant part in the whole cultural environment of these ancient times. There were mysteries in which considerable emphasis was placed on acquiring knowledge of the secrets of the year's course. We need to have some idea of the significance of such mysteries. They were different in really ancient times from how they were in the historical periods of ancient Egypt or ancient Greece or even in the earliest period of Roman history. We will, therefore, consider those mysteries which faded into oblivion with the ancient cultures of Egypt, Greece and Rome.

In these mysteries there was still an awareness of the relationship of the Earth with the universe as a whole. Suitable individuals were therefore chosen and subjected to a quite particular psychic treatment (in accordance with a process that would no longer be allowed today); and at a particular time—over the course of several days during winter—they were sent to certain specially prepared locations in order that they might fulfil a receptive function for what the universe, the extra-terrestrial cosmos, is able to communicate to the Earth at such times when the Earth can offer an adequate receptive function of this nature. In these ancient times the decisive period for this was not precisely our modern Christmas but was fairly close to it; but the exact time is not so important. Let us assume the time to be from the 24th and 25th of

December through into the early days of January. This time is one when, because of the special position of the Sun with regard to the Earth, the universe conveys something to the Earth that it does not at other times. It is the time when the universe speaks more intimately with the Earth than at other times. This is because the Sun does not display the power that it has in summer at this time; for this power has in a certain sense withdrawn. Now the leaders of the old mysteries used this time, in conjunction with certain individuals who were trained for this purpose in specially prepared locations, to make it possible for deep secrets from the cosmos which came down to the Earth in the course of this intimate dialogue of the cosmos with the Earth to be received by them. This can be compared today with something far more trivial, but it nevertheless bears comparison with it. You know that so-called wireless telegraphy depends on electric waves being set in motion, which are further transmitted without wires, and that in certain places instruments are installed called coherers which by virtue of their particular structure offer the possibility of receiving the electric waves at the station and setting the coherers in motion. It all depends on the arrangement or, rather, the particular formation of the filings, the metal filings in the coherer, which are shaken back into place when the wave has passed through it. Now if we suppose that the mysteries of the universe, the extra-terrestrial cosmos, pass through the Earth at this particular time that I have indicated, a reception device will be needed; for the electric waves would merely pass by the receiving station if one did not have the particular instrument with the coherer. One would, as it were, need a coherer for what comes forth from the cosmos. The ancient Greeks used their Pythia, their priestesses, for this purpose; they were trained to do this and, through being exposed to what came down from the cosmos, they were able to communicate these mysteries of the universe. These mysteries then came to be interpreted by those who had, perhaps, not been able to fulfil the function of actually receiving them for some time. Nevertheless, the mysteries of the universe were still imparted. All this was, of course, carried out under the sign of the holiest mysteries, a sign of which our present age, which has lost all trace of anything sacred, has no conception. In our time the main priority would of course be to interview the priests of the mysteries!

Now what was actually demanded of these priests of the mysteries? It was in a certain sense necessary for them to know that, if they incorporated the fructifying wisdom for earthly life that was streaming down from the cosmos to their cognitive faculties, and especially their social understanding, they would through the greater degree of cleverness that they had imbibed be capable of establishing social regulations for the immediate future, of making the legal and other arrangements for the coming year. There were formerly times on the Earth when people would not have instituted social regulations or legal structures without first having sought guidance in this way from those whose task it was to receive the mysteries of the macrocosm. Later ages have preserved feeble and dubious echoes of this great wisdom in superstitious fancies. When on New Year's Eve people pour melted lead into water with the object of finding out about what the coming year has in store, this is the superstitious residue of that great holy task of which I have been speaking. Its aim was essentially so to fructify the spirit—the spirit of human beings—that what can only spring from the cosmos might become a reality on the Earth; for there was a wish that man should live on the Earth in such a way that his life is not merely the result of what one can experience on the Earth but a result of what one can learn from the wider world. In the same way it was known that during the summer the Earth cannot receive any intimate tidings from the cosmos. The summer mysteries, which had a totally different purpose that does not concern us at present, were based upon this knowledge.

Now, as I have said, ever fewer traditions have been preserved of those things that are associated with the mysteries of the cycle of the year than of everything related to the rhythm of day and night, of sleeping and waking. However, in those ancient times when man still had a high degree of atavistic clairvoyance, which enabled him to experience in the course of the year the intimacies that flowed between the cosmic regions and the Earth, human beings knew that what they experienced there had its origin in the meeting which they had—a meeting which does of course take place in every age, but at that time it was perceived through atavistic clairvoyance—not with that spiritual world that he can experience every time he goes to sleep but a meeting with the spiritual world in which those spiritual beings live who belong to the hierarchy that we know as the Archangels. This is that same world where man will dwell in his innermost essence when his Life Spirit has developed during the age of Venus; and it is also where in ancient times Christ, the Son, was thought of as being the guiding and ruling principle. This meeting, which man has with the spiritual world in the course of the year at any point on the Earth's surface, at the time when for this part of the Earth it is the winter season of Christmas, can therefore also be called the meeting with the Son. Thus in the course of a year a person indeed experiences a rhythm which reflects that of the seasonal round itself and in which he has a union with the world of the Son.

We know of course that through the Mystery of Golgotha that Being whom we call the Christ united Himself with the course of the Earth. At the time when this union took place a direct perception of the spiritual world was—as I have just explained—obscured. We see the objective fact that the Mystery of Golgotha is directly connected with the change taking place in human evolution on the Earth. But we can also say that there have been times in human evolution when, through becoming aware of the Earth's intimate dialogue with the macrocosm as experienced in the old atavistic clairvoyance, human beings have entered into a relationship with Christ. This is the source of what has with a certain justification been put forward by a number of intelligent learned people in recent times and students of religion: that a primal revelation has been given to the Earth.[1] So what I have been describing did indeed come about. There was a primal revelation. And all the separate religions scattered over the Earth are the decadent fragments of that primal revelation.

What, however, is the position of those who have accepted the Mystery of Golgotha? Their position is that they can express their innermost faith in the spiritual origin of the universe by saying that what in ancient times still had to be perceived by means of a dialogue of the Earth with the cosmos has now descended and has appeared in the course of the Mystery of Golgotha in a human being, in the human being Jesus of Nazareth. Recognition of that Being who was formerly perceptible to human beings in the course of the year through atavistic clairvoyance again in the Christ who dwelt in Jesus of Nazareth is something that must be increasingly emphasized as necessary for the spiritual evolution of mankind. For in this way one would be bringing the two elements of Christianity together which really do need to be united if, on the one hand, Christianity and, on the other hand, humanity are each to develop further in the right way. The fact that the legends of Christ Jesus have through old Christian traditions been annually included in the yearly cycle as the festivals celebrated at Christmas, Easter and Whitsun is connected with this, as is the further fact that, as I said in a previous lecture, the Christmas festival is celebrated on a fixed date whereas Easter is a festival whose date is determined by the movements of heavenly bodies. The celebration of the festival of Christmas in accordance with earthly relationships in the very depths of winter is associated with the meeting with Christ, with the Son, that does indeed take place then. However, Christ's nature as a Being who belongs to the macrocosm, descended from the macrocosm and is *one* with it is expressed through the fact that the timing of Easter—that festival which is intended to declare that Christ belongs to the whole world, just as Christmas indicates that Christ descended to the Earth—depends on when the spring equinox takes place and the positions of Sun and Moon. Thus it was right that what itself belongs to the seasonal round through the rhythmical presence of the human soul within it should be inserted into the yearly cycle. And because this is something with so deep a reflection in man's inner being, it is also justified that these festivals that relate to the Mystery of Golgotha should continue to be celebrated in harmony with the rhythm of the wider cosmos and not be subject to the kind of alteration that has taken place in the hours of sleeping and waking in modern cities.

So here we have to do with a situation where man is not as yet so free that he may raise himself out of the objective flow of the cosmos; every year he can be aware that, even though he cannot engage directly with the cosmos through atavistic clairvoyance, something lives within him that belongs to the universal whole and comes to expression in the cycle of the year.

Now among the things which certain religious faiths have most strongly censured about spiritual science is that through spiritual science the Christ impulse must once again be linked to the whole cosmos. As I have often emphasized, spiritual science does not take anything away from what religious traditions have contributed to the mystery of Christ Jesus; but it adds the relationship extending from the Earth to the whole cosmos which surrounds this mystery. It seeks Christ not only on the Earth—it seeks Him in the whole universe. Indeed it is difficult to understand why some religious groups again and again single out especially this connection of the Christ impulse with cosmic events for censure; for it would only be understandable if spiritual science were to take something away from the rightful traditions of Christianity. If it adds something, this should surely not be a reason for criticism. However, this is how things stand; and the reason is that there is a strong wish not to add anything to certain traditions.

There is, however, a very serious background to this, something which is of considerable importance especially for our time. I have often drawn your attention—in my first Mystery Play among other places[2]— to the fact that we are approaching the time when we are able to speak about a spiritual Second Coming of Christ. I do not need to expand more fully on this today as it is a familiar subject for all our friends. However, this Christ event will not merely be an event that satisfies people's transcendental curiosity but it will above all be an event which will place a demand on their minds for a new understanding of the Christ impulse. Certain basic sayings of Christianity, which should live throughout the world as holy impulses (at any rate amongst those who want to receive the Christ impulse), are not understood with sufficient depth. I should like to remind you of the significant and incisive words 'My Kingdom is not of this world'.[3] These words will take on a new meaning when Christ appears in a realm that is indeed not of this world, which is to say not of the world of the senses. For it will have to become an essential characteristic of the Christian conception of the world that it is able to relate to all other human views and attitudes with under- standing, with the exception of a coarse and crude materialism. If one can see clearly that all the religions on the Earth are the remnants of ancient visionary perception, it will simply be a question of taking them with the seriousness that they deserve. What can be perceived in them—and because mankind subsequently ceased to be in a position to see in a visionary way, what one finds in the various religious faiths and denominations is only of a fragmentary nature—can be recognized through Christianity. Thus through Christianity one can gain a deep understanding of every form of religious faith on the Earth, not only of the great religions but of every religious creed or confession. Admittedly, this is easily said, but although it is easy to say such things it is difficult for people to see it in this way. And yet it needs to become a general conviction of people over the entire Earth. For the way that Christianity has manifested itself on the Earth hitherto is as a religion among other religions, one faith among other faiths. That is not the reason for its existence. Christianity was brought into being in order to spread understanding over the entire Earth. Christ did not die, nor was He born, for a limited circle of people, but for all human beings. There is in a certain sense a contradiction between the requirement that Christianity should be for all human beings and the fact that it has become a faith in its own right. But it is not intended to be a separate creed, and it can only become one if it is not understood in its full depth. Its cosmic aspect is an essential part of the full depth of its meaning.

One struggles today for words to express certain truths, because they are so far removed from people that there are not the words with which to express them. It is often the case that one can only express them by way of a comparison. You will recall that I have often said that Christ can be called the Sun Spirit. From what I have been saying today about the yearly course of the Sun, one can already see that there is a certain justification for calling Him the Sun Spirit. But it is not possible to have any conception of a Sun-spirit unless one keeps the cosmic relationship of Christ in mind, unless one conceives of the Mystery of Golgotha as a true Christ mystery that has significance for the whole cosmos and is an event that took place for the whole cosmos.

Human beings quarrel about many things on the Earth; there is much that they disagree about. They disagree about their religious faiths, they think that they are at variance with one another because of their nationalities and for many other reasons. These disagreements lead to times such as the one that we are living in now, for example. People also disagree about the Mystery of Golgotha; for no Chinaman or Indian will simply accept what a European missionary says about the Mystery of Golgotha. Anyone who considers things as they are will not find this surprising. But there is one thing that people have not hitherto disagreed about. It seems scarcely credible, but it is a trivial matter and one simply has to accept it. If one considers the way that people oppose one another on the Earth, one cannot help wondering if there is anything that they have not disagreed about. But there are still some things of this nature, and one example is the opinion that people have about the Sun. The Japanese, the Chinese, and even the Americans and the English do not believe that one Sun rises and sets for them and another one for the Germans. People still believe that there is only one Sun; and indeed, they still think in common terms about everything lying outside the Earth. They do not have arguments about such things; they do not wage wars on their account. This can be taken as a sort of comparison.

As has been said, these things can be expressed only through comparisons. When people begin to understand the connection of Christ with these phenomena that they do not quarrel about, they will not argue about Christ; and they will then behold Him in the kingdom which is not of this world and is His Kingdom. But there will be no unity about those matters regarding which there needs to be common ground throughout the entire Earth until people have come to recognize the cosmic significance of Christ. For we shall be able to speak to the Jews, the Japanese, the Chinese and the Indians in the way that we speak to Europeans of a Christian persuasion. This opens up an enormously significant perspective both for the further development of Christianity on the Earth and for the further evolution of humanity on the Earth; for ways must be found of engendering inner qualities and attitudes which all people are able to understand in a similar way. This will, however, be a demand of the time in which the Second Coming, the spiritual Second Coming of Christ, will take place; and from this time onwards there will need to be a deeper understanding of the words 'My Kingdom is not of this world', a deeper understanding of the fact that there is not only an earthly part of man's being but a super-earthly part, which lives in the annual course of the Sun. We must come to feel that in the individual human life the soul aspect governs the bodily aspect, so that in everything that goes on out there in the ascending and descending stars, in the bright sunlight and fading twilight, a spiritual quality is living; and that, just as we are part of the air through our lungs, we are part of the spiritual life of the universe through our souls—not the abstract spirituality of a wishy-washy pantheism but a concrete spirituality such as lives in individual beings. Thus we shall find that, in inner connection with what lives in the cycle of the year (as do the breaths in a human being), there is something of a spiritual nature which belongs to the human soul and which is, indeed, the human soul, and that the Christ Being who passed through the Mystery of Golgotha belongs to the cycle of the year in all its mysteries. We must soar upwards with our imagination if we are to be able to connect what took place historically on the Earth in the Mystery of Golgotha with the great secrets of the world, with the mysteries of the macrocosm. But then something of immense importance will emerge from this understanding, namely a knowledge of what people need in a social sense. There is a lot of social science in our time, and many social ideals of all sorts. There is, of course, no objection to that; but all these ideas need to be able to achieve something, and this will have to happen through what will arise within man once he is able to bring a renewed spiritual impulse to the cycle of the year. For only by vividly experiencing each year the image of the Mystery of Golgotha alongside the course of the year can one be inspired with what lives as a potential for social knowledge and social feeling.

What I am saying now will certainly appear highly convoluted to most people today, but it is true nonetheless. When the course of the year is experienced by humanity as a whole in such a way that it is felt to be inwardly connected with the Mystery of Golgotha, this inner sensitivity to the cycle of the year and to the Mystery of Golgotha will make it possible for a true social feeling to be disseminated throughout the Earth. This will be the true solution or at least the further development of what is today so foolishly (in view of what is being considered here) referred to as the social question. Through spiritual science, however, people will have to acquire a knowledge of man's connection with the universe. This will surely make it possible for them to see more in this universe than what modern materialism sees in it.

It is precisely those things to which the least value is attributed that are the most important. Modern materialistic biology, indeed materialistic science in general, compares man with animals. It does, to be sure, find a slight difference. Of course, it is correct in its own terms; but what it totally disregards is man's relationship to the various directions of space. The spine of animals—and here the exceptions prove the rule—is directed out into the cosmic expanses in parallel with the Earth's surface. The human spine is directed towards the Earth. For this reason, man's relationship to above and below is quite different from that of an animal, and it is this that defines him in his whole being. In the case of an animal the spine reaches out into the infinite distances of the macrocosm; with man it is the upper part of the head, the brain that does so; and the human being himself becomes a part of the whole macrocosm. This has immense implications. For it determines the way that the relationship between the spiritual and bodily aspects of man's being is manifested; it means that his spiritual and bodily aspects are also related to one another in terms of above and below. I shall have more to say on this subject; but I wanted today just to mention it briefly. This 'above and below' relates to what we may refer to as the departure of the ego and astral body during sleep. For man with his ego and astral body is united through his physical and etheric bodies with the Earth while he is awake. During the night he is, through his ego and astral body, part of what lies above.

Now we may ask: how does it work with the other pairs of opposites in the macrocosm? There is also the contrast which can for man be defined in terms of forwards and backwards in the sense of in front and behind. Again, with regard to this dimension of space man is related in a different way to the whole macrocosm than, for example, animals or plants. This relationship is such that this front and back orientation corresponds to the path of the Sun. Moreover, this orientation corresponds to the rhythm in which man takes part in living and dying. Just as in sleeping and waking man in a certain sense expresses the living relationship of above and below, so does he manifest the relationship between in front and behind in his living and dying. This dimension of space is oriented in accordance with the course of the Sun, so that 'in front' signifies for man towards the East, and 'behind' towards the West. East and West form the second dimension of space, that dimension of which we are actually speaking when we say that the human soul leaves the human body (not in sleep but in death); for the soul leaves the human body in an easterly direction. This is only still to be found in those traditions where one speaks of dying in terms of his 'entry to the eternal East'. Such old traditional sayings will be regarded by learned people as merely symbolic (and they are perhaps even now). For example one may say something trivial such as this: 'The Sun rises in the East, that is a beautiful sight; so in speaking of the East people were also referring to eternity!' And yet this corresponds to a reality, and one more closely related to the yearly path of the Sun than to the course of the day.

The third difference is that between the inner and the outer. Above and below, East and West, inner and outer. We live an inner life and we live an outer life. The day after tomorrow I shall be giving a public lecture about this theme of the inner and outer life entitled 'The Human Soul and the Human Body'.[4] We live an inner and outer life. For us as human beings this theme of inner and outer is just as much a contrast as above and below or East and West. Whereas in the course of the year one has more to do with what I might describe as a representative picture of the whole course of life, one might say that when we speak of an inner and outer life in connection with the life and death of man we are referring to the whole course of his life, especially in so far as it has a descending and ascending development. As you know, approximately until a certain year man experiences an ascending development. His growth then ceases, and then after a while it regresses once more.

Now it is a feature of man's life that at the beginning of his life his whole bodily organism is most connected, in a natural, elemental way, with the spiritual world. I might say that man is constituted in a completely opposite way from when he has attained the climax of his ascending development in the middle of his life. During the first period of his life a person grows, thrives and develops his forces; then he begins to embark upon a descending phase of development. This is associated with the fact that his physical forces are no longer in themselves growth forces but that forces of decline or decay are also intermingled with the forces of growth. A person's inner being at that time has a similar relationship to the universe as has his bodily organism at the beginning of life, at his birth. A total reversal takes place. That is why it is at this time, in the middle of life, that a person experiences in what is today a state of unconsciousness a meeting with the Father principle, with that spiritual being whom we associate with the hierarchy of the Archai, with that spiritual world in which man will dwell when he has fully developed his Spirit Man.

We may now ask: does this have any kind of connection with the universe as a whole? Is there anything in the life of the universe that is connected with the meeting with the Father in the middle of life in a similar way that the meeting with the Spirit is connected with the rhythm of day and night and the meeting with the Son is connected with the rhythm of the year? This question can indeed be asked. Now we need to be aware that, just as is the case with the meeting with the Spirit, people are likewise out of rhythm as regards this meeting with the Father. The rhythm does not completely correspond. For people are not born at the same time but at different times; because of this their lives cannot run in parallel, but they can inwardly reflect some kind of spiritual, cosmic event. Do they do this?

If we call to mind what appears in the little volume *The Education of the Child from the Standpoint of Anthroposophy*[5] and also in other writings and lecture-cycles, we are aware that approximately in the first seven years of life a person forms his physical body, in the next seven years his ether body, in the next seven years his astral body, in the seven years after that the sentient soul and then the intellectual or mind soul between the ages of 28 and 35. The meeting with the Father principle falls within this latter period. It is spread over this time but it occurs during these years—not that it extends over this time but it occurs during these years; so one can say that a person is preparing for it during the ages of 28, 29 and 30. In the case of most people the meeting takes place in the deep unconscious regions of the human soul. We might therefore suppose that there is something taking place in the universe that corresponds to this time; we should find something in the cosmos representing a cycle or a rhythm. Just as the rhythm of day and night is one of 24 hours and the yearly cycle 365 days, so we should be able to find something similar in the cosmos, except that it would have to be more extensive. It would have a relationship to the Sun or at any rate the solar system; and there would, I would say, need to be something— some kind of orbit—on a larger scale connected with the Sun, something more extensive in the same measure that 28, 29 or 30 years are a longer period than either 24 hours or 365 days. Now the ancients rightly regarded Saturn as the outermost planet of our solar system. It is the most distant planet. From the standpoint of materialistic astronomy it is completely justified that Uranus and Neptune should be added, but they have a different origin; they do not belong to the solar system. So we can speak of Saturn as representing the limit of the solar system. Consider this, therefore: if Saturn is the limit of the solar system, we could say that in its orbit around the Sun it moves around the outermost limit of the solar system. So if you imagine Saturn orbiting the Sun it returns to the point from which it started, with the same relationship to the Sun. Now Saturn describes its course—as one can say today according to the Copernican system—in around 29 or so years, which corresponds to the time in question. Here then, in the orbit of Saturn around the Sun (it actually happens quite differently, but the Copernican system is not sufficiently developed to understand this) we have the set of circumstances and relationships—encompassing the totality of the solar system as manifested in the outermost path of Saturn around the Sun—with which man's life's path is associated, which is, therefore, a reflection of this path of Saturn inasmuch as the course of a human life leads to the meeting with the Father. This, too, leads us out into the macrocosm.

I believe I have in this way shown you that the innermost aspect of man's being can only be understood if one thinks of it in relation to the extra-terrestrial world. This cosmic world is, as a spiritual phenomenon, organized into that which presents itself to us also in a visible form. But what we can actually see is only the outward manifestation of these spiritual realities. Man will be able to free himself from materialism only if he develops his knowledge to the point where it is raised beyond conceptions of purely earthly relationships and is again able to encompass an understanding of the world of the stars and the Sun.

I have already pointed out that many things that modern book-learning does not even dare dream about are connected with these matters. People today imagine that they will be able to generate living beings in the laboratory from inorganic substance. Materialism makes the most of this today. One does not need to be a materialist to believe that a living being can be made out of inorganic substance under laboratory conditions, as is confirmed by the belief of the alchemists—who were certainly not materialists—that they could make homunculus [mannikins, miniature human beings]. Today this is interpreted in a materialistic way. But the time will come when one will have the perception, which is to say inwardly feel, on approaching a person at work in the laboratory (for it will come about that living things are brought forth from non-living things under laboratory conditions) that one is compelled to say to the person who is doing this: 'Welcome to the star of the hour!'—because this will not simply be possible at any time at random but it will depend on the positions of the stars. Whether life arises from the lifeless depends on forces that are not of the Earth but which derive from the cosmos.

There is much that is associated with these mysteries. Now it is possible—and we shall speak about these things in the near future—to say a lot about these matters, regarding which Saint-Martin, the so-called unknown philosopher, says in various passages of his book *On Truth and Errors* that he thanks God that they are veiled in secrecy. They cannot remain veiled in deep mystery, because human beings need them for their further development; but it is necessary that people once again develop a serious attitude to all these things and acquire that feeling for holiness without which one will not use this knowledge for the world in the right way.

We shall speak further about these matters next time.

LECTURE 7

BERLIN, 20 MARCH 1917

To d ay I should like to introduce a sort of historical survey into the process in which we are engaged, not so much in order to venture into history for its own sake but rather because there is much in the cultural life that surrounds us at present that can be brought to a clearer focus through a survey of this nature.

It was in 1775 when a very remarkable book appeared in Lyons, a book which very soon and at any rate by 1782 became accessible to certain circles of German cultural life and had a far greater influence than is normally supposed. Its influence was, however, of such an extent that it more or less had to be suppressed by the main impulse underlying cultural development in the nineteenth century. This book is of the highest interest for those wanting to inform themselves about what happened from earliest times until our own times. I am referring to the book *Des erreurs et de la vérité* by Saint-Martin.[1] Anyone trying to read this book today, whether in its original language or in the German edition by Matthias Claudius, who has also written a beautiful preface to the translation, will find it extremely difficult to understand. Even Matthias Claudius himself admits this[2]—and this was at the end of the eighteenth century. He says in what is, as I have said, his beautifully written preface: 'Most people will not understand this book. I do not understand it properly either. But it made such a deep impression on me that I think it should become more widely known.' No one will be able to make anything of this book who—without having the slightest knowledge of these subjects themselves—approaches it from the standpoint of those physical, chemical and similar world conceptions that are taught in schools today or which one imbibes through one's general education. Nor will the book appeal to someone who derives his knowledge of the present times—a phrase which is to be preferred to 'political views'—from ordinary newspapers or from the modern cultural attitudes influenced by them and reflected in various topical magazines.

There are several reasons why I am speaking to you about this book today, after the two public lectures that I gave last Thursday and last Saturday.[3] In these two lectures I spoke about the nature of man and the various members of his being and about the connection between the human soul and the human body in the way that one will eventually come to speak about this relationship when the scientific knowledge that is currently available but which cannot be appreciated for what it is can be perceived in the right way. Someone who is in a position to know about these matters from a spiritual-scientific standpoint will have the clear conviction that people will no longer speak about the relationship of the soul activities of thinking, feeling and will to the human organism in the way they do today. It is therefore my opinion that with these two lectures a beginning has been made with respect to what is bound to come, even though it may perhaps be postponed for a long time in the wider world through the considerable resistance which not science itself but scientists themselves exhibit. Even though it may take some time it will nevertheless eventually come about that the relationship between the human soul and the human body will be perceived as has been outlined in these two lectures.

In these lectures I spoke about these things in the way that I believe is necessary in 1917. What I mean is the way one needs to speak once one has taken into account all the scientific research and other relevant human experiences. It would not have been possible to speak about all these things in the eighteenth century, for example. In the eighteenth century one would have spoken about them completely differently. People are not sufficiently aware what an enormous significance it had that, as I have frequently indicated, roughly at the end of the first third of the nineteenth century—during the 1830s and 1840s—there was from a spiritual point of view a crisis of immense magnitude in the development of European humanity. I have often characterized this by saying that at this time the tide of materialism reached its highest point. I have also often drawn attention to the frivolous way that people talk about our time as a period of transition! Of course every age is a period of transition, and this expression 'our time is a period of transition' is entirely reasonable, because that is what every age is. But the point at issue is not that it is being said that a particular age is a period of transition but, rather, to establish what kind of a transition it is. There will always be particular turning points which represent deeply radical times of transition in human evolution; and one such fundamental transition in human evolution occurred at the time indicated, even though little attention is paid to it today. There is therefore a need to understand that we must speak today about the riddles that directly concern human beings with totally different words and completely different expressions and approach the subject in question from wholly different points of view than was the case in the eighteenth century.

There was perhaps no one in the eighteenth century who spoke with such an intuitive awareness and attentiveness about the scientific ideas of his time with respect to questions of a similar nature to the ones that we are speaking about now as Saint-Martin. In all that he said, however, Saint-Martin was not yet—as we are now—at the dawn of a new age but in the twilight of the old age, and he speaks with a twilight mood. So unless one keeps the point of view that I am about to express clearly in view, it might appear to be almost a matter of indifference whether one concerns oneself with Saint-Martin at all, whether or not one studies this distinctive form of the ideas aroused in him by Jakob Böhme. It might indeed seem to be a matter of indifference were there not a very different and deeply significant viewpoint to be considered, to which I shall refer in the course of today's lecture.

To mention a specific case, in the course of pointing out the errors to which people are prone through their philosophy of life and through what their path to the truth might be (for his book is after all called *Des erreurs et de la vérité*), Saint-Martin speaks in such a way that he uses certain concepts and ideas that were current in particular circles right into the eighteenth century in the most pertinent way possible. The way that he expresses himself makes it clear that he is very used to working with these ideas. So we find that as Saint-Martin launches into a consideration of man's relationship to the whole cosmos and to ethical life, he draws upon three principal ideas or conceptions which play such a big part in the thinking of Jakob Böhme and Paracelsus and through which people sought at the time to understand nature and also man: mercury, sulphur and salt. Through these three elements of mercury, sulphur and salt they tried to discover the key for understanding both outer nature and man. A person today who would want to speak in accordance with the way that a modern scientist speaks (and this is necessary if one is not to go back to the past) cannot think of the three words mercury, sulphur and salt in terms of the ideas with which people in the eighteenth century associated them. When people spoke about mercury, sulphur and salt they conceived of a threefoldness which someone today, if he is speaking out of a scientific insight, could only rightly represent by dividing man in the way that I have proposed: into the digestive system, the breathing system and the nerve system out of which the whole human being is composed; for everything belongs in one way or another to one of these systems. And if one supposes that any particular part does not fit into this picture (as one might in the case of the bones), this would only be apparent. People in the eighteenth century understood that the whole of man's being can be understood if one has the overall conception of mercury, sulphur and salt. Now of course, when an ordinary person—or a chemist—speaks about salt, he is referring to the white grains that he has on the table or to the salts that the chemist prepares in his laboratory. When he speaks about sulphur, the ordinary person thinks of matches and the chemist of all the experiments that he has carried out in his retort for the transmutation of sulphur. As to mercury, one thinks of ordinary quicksilver, and so on.

In the eighteenth century people did not think in this way. Today it is very difficult even to imagine what was living in their souls when they spoke of mercury, sulphur and salt. Saint-Martin put the question in his own way at that time: how do I divide man if I regard his bodily organism as a reflection of his soul? His reply was on these lines: I first need to consider man with respect to the instruments, the organs of his thinking (he puts it somewhat differently, but we must interpret it a little so that the explanation does not take too long). I first need to consider man with respect to the organs of his head. What is the main characteristic involved here? What do we need to consider? What is the active agent in the head (or, as we would say today, in the nervous system)? His answer is: salt. And by salt he means not the white grains, and also not what chemists understand by salt, but the totality of those forces at work in the human head when a person has an idea. Everything associated with the outward effect of salt he regards merely as a manifestation, an outward revelation of the same forces that are active in the human head. He then asks: which element works primarily in the human chest region? In accordance with the way that I distinguished the members of man's being in my lecture last Thursday, we would put it a little differently: what is at work in the region of man's breathing? Saint-Martin replies:[4] sulphur. So that according to him everything associated with the functions of the chest is governed by those active elements which have their origin in sulphur, or in that which is of the nature of sulphur. And then he asks: What is at work in the rest of man's being? (We would refer to this as the metabolic system.) His answer is: mercury. And so he has an overview of the whole of man's being. On the one hand one sees that, from the way that he formulates everything, he stands in the evening twilight of this whole way of thinking. But on the other hand it is apparent that from his position in the fading twilight he was still able to grasp a whole wealth of truths which were still understood at that time but are now buried, obscured from view—truths which he is able to express by making use of the three concepts of mercury, sulphur and salt. Thus this book *Des erreurs et de la vérité* consists of a very fine treatise—which for a modern physicist is complete nonsense—on thunderstorms, on thunder and lightning, in the course of which he shows that one can on the one hand use mercury, sulphur and salt in order to explain man's bodily nature, and that on the other hand one can use them to explain such atmospheric phenomena. At one time they are working together within man, at another time they are working out in the world. In man they give rise to the thoughts or will impulses that light up within him; out in the world the same elements engender phenomena such as thunder and lightning.

As has been said, what Saint-Martin explains is something that anyone imbued with the way of thinking characteristic of the eighteenth century could understand perfectly well. For a modern physicist it is total nonsense. But there is, I would say, something of a snag quite specifically as regards thunder and lightning in modern physics; for what it offers by way of an explanation for them is somewhat facile. It teaches that the lightning—and then the thunder in its wake—is brought about when the electric charges between two clouds, one of which is positively and the other negatively charged, are balanced out. A schoolboy who has his wits about him and has previously noticed that when the teacher carries out electrical experiments he carefully wipes away any dampness so that the instruments are dry, because nothing works with electricity whenever there is any dampness, may say: 'Yes, but surely the clouds are so damp that the electricity cannot function in them as you say it does?' The teacher would then say: 'You're a silly boy, you don't understand!' It would be difficult for him to answer in any other way today.

Saint-Martin tries to explain how mercury and sulphur are connected in a particular way through the salt in the air, and then he goes on to show how in a similar way saltpetre and sulphur are united through charcoal in gunpowder and, therefore, how explosions can arise through a particular transmutation of the elements of mercury and sulphur by means of the presence of salt. This explanation arising out of the way that the concepts of mercury, sulphur and salt were understood at that time is remarkably ingenious. I cannot enter into it more deeply now; but we shall consider the whole subject more from a historical point of view. Saint-Martin shows particularly well how the distinctive relationship of lightning to salt—or what he calls salt—is proved through certain properties of air after thunderstorms. In short, Saint-Martin battled in his own way against the materialism that was already looming through having behind him the foundations of a traditional wisdom, which found in him a highly significant expositor. By this means he aspired towards an explanation of the world as a whole and, after having given the interpretations that make use of the elements of which we have been speaking, he proceeded to an explanation of earthly evolution. In this respect he is not so foolish as those born after him, who believe in a primordial mist in their belief that one can arrive at the beginning of the world with physical concepts; rather does he have recourse to imaginations in his wish to explain the origin of the Earth. In the book we find a wonderful richness of imaginative ideas when he addresses this theme, ideas which—like his physical concepts—can only be understood out of the age in which he lived. We would not be able to make use of such ideas any longer, but they indicate that from a certain point onwards he endeavoured to grasp things with an imaginative perception.

Then, having explored this area, he moves on to developing an understanding of the historical life of man. He tries to establish that historical life can only be understood if one sees that from time to time spiritual impulses have been entering into the physical world from the spiritual world. He then tries to apply this general idea to man's deeper nature by showing that what is described in the biblical legend of the Fall from paradise derives—according to his imaginative perception—from definite facts and that man has arrived at his present condition from one in the primordial past. He endeavours to understand the historical phenomena of his time and of historical time in general from the Fall of spiritual life into matter. I am not necessarily defending this but am merely describing it. Of course, I am not wanting to replace spiritual science, our anthroposophy, with Saint-Martin's teachings; I merely wish to relate this in order to show how far advanced Saint-Martin was at that time.

As we read *Des erreurs et de la vérité* chapter by chapter, we keep coming across something quite remarkable. We find that Saint-Martin speaks out of a rich abundance of knowledge and that what he actually communicates represents, I would say, only the outermost layers of the knowledge that lives in his soul. He indicates this in several passages of his book. This is the gist of what he says:[5] 'If I were to explore this issue at a deeper level, I would have to divulge truths that I may not pronounce.' At one point he even says: 'If I were to say all that needs to be said on this subject, I would have to unveil certain truths that for most people are better left enshrouded in the deepest darkness of night.' A true spiritual scientist can discern a great deal from these remarks, and he also knows why these observations appear at particular points of certain chapters. One cannot speak unconditionally about certain things. It will only be possible to speak about certain things when the impulses that have been given through spiritual science have become moral impulses; when human beings have attained a certain high-mindedness through spiritual science, so that one is able to speak about certain questions in a different way than is possible when remarkable scientific figures such as Freud and his syndicate are at work.

In the last third of his book Saint-Martin moves on to discussing certain political topics. It is scarcely possible in our present time to do more than merely indicate how to relate the way that Saint-Martin thought at that time to the way that humanity as it were 'thinks' now; for that is a forbidden subject. I can merely say that the whole attitude that Saint-Martin adopts in this last third of his book is really quite remarkable. If we read this chapter, we must do so today in such a way that we are clearly aware that it appeared together with the rest of the book in 1775, and that the French Revolution followed only after this chapter had been written. This chapter must be thought of in con-nection with the French Revolution; and a great deal needs to be read between the lines. But Saint-Martin proceeds as an occultist. Someone who lacks the organs of perception to recognize the profound impulses living in this chapter of the book will probably be very appreciative of the introduction that Saint-Martin supplies for this chapter. For what he says is this: 'No one should think that I am trying to inveigle myself into anyone's presence. Anyone who has anything to do with the ruling powers of the Earth or is connected in some way with the government should be very far from thinking that I am trying to approach them. I am a friend of all and everyone.' But after excusing himself in this way he says certain things that make Rousseau's statements[6] seem like child's play. However, I cannot say more about this.

In short, we are dealing here with a person of great significance who was the leader of a school, and without whom Herder, Goethe, Schiller and German Romanticism in general can hardly be imagined, just as he is barely conceivable without Jakob Böhme. Nevertheless, if one reads him today and allows oneself to be influenced by what he says, the fact is that, as I have just said, there would not be the slightest point in speaking to some sort of public audience in the way that Saint-Martin wrote, as I did last Thursday and Saturday (and will do so again next Thursday),[7] when I was trying to delineate a picture of the world which on the one hand is absolutely correct from a spiritual-scientific point of view and, on the other, is equally correct from the standpoint of the most meticulous scientific discoveries of the present. The way that Saint-Martin formulated his ideas is no longer suited to the way that people need to think today and apply their thoughts. Just as someone travelling from one linguistic region to another needs to use not the language of the first region but that of the second, it would be absurd today to try to explain everything in the way that Saint-Martin did; and it would be particularly absurd because there is between us and them that mighty dividing wall in spiritual evolution which dates from 1842, thus at the end of the first third of the nineteenth century.[8]

From this you can see that it is possible for a certain way of thinking to fade into oblivion in the spiritual evolution of mankind. But if one studies Saint-Martin one does not really have the feeling that his thoughts have lost their relevance. This is certainly not the case, and one has on the contrary the feeling that there is such an enormous amount of undiscovered treasures of wisdom in his work that a great deal could still be extracted from it. Nevertheless there is, on the other hand, a need in the spiritual evolution of mankind for this way of thinking to come to an end and another to begin. This is indeed a reality. For in the former period the outer world was still in a rudimentary stage of its present development and its more extreme materialistic phase was only just beginning. We can therefore only really understand what actually happened then if we survey longer periods of time, when what spiritual science seeks to arouse within us today can be discerned over a wider span of time; for of course what Saint-Martin expressed at the end of the eighteenth century, when present developments were still in an incipient form, looked quite different from the way that it does today.

At that time in general something was coming to an end. Not only was this the case in the sense that the ideas still inspiring Jakob Böhme, Paracelsus, Saint-Martin and others in the later phase of the evening twilight of this whole way of thinking could no longer be implemented; but something highly significant was also taking place in the way people felt. Whereas in Saint-Martin we see in the context of this phenomenon of the evening twilight a human mind focused more upon nature, the same phenomenon manifests itself in a somewhat different way if we cast our eye on the almost parallel decline of theosophy, on the fading glow of the theosophical view of the world. It is true that Saint-Martin is also generally referred to as a theosophist, but I have in mind when I characterize Saint-Martin a theosophy that is focused more upon natural science, and a theosophy that was more widely prevalent as one of a more religious nature. In this very particular form it reached a culmination in Swabia (one cannot really refer to South Germany), where at the time of this period of general decline—when it also reached a quite particular maturity—two individuals in particular stood out among the various other figures, namely, Bengel[9] and Oetinger[10]. They were surrounded by a large number of others. I shall mention only those with whom I am more familiar: Friedrich Daniel Schubart,[11] the mathematician Hahn,[12] then Steinhofer,[13] the schoolmaster Hartmann,[14] who had great influence on Jung-Stilling[15] and was also personally acquainted with Goethe, then Johann Jakob Moser[16]—a large number of remarkable individuals in relatively modest positions who did not form a coherent group but who all lived at the time when Oetinger's star also shone. Oetinger's life almost spanned the entire eighteenth century. He was born in 1702 and died as a prelate in Murrhardt; a highly remarkable personality in whom was concentrated in a certain sense the essence of what lived in this whole circle.

This theosophy of the eighteenth century found an echo in Richard Rothe, who in addition to teaching at other universities taught mainly in Heidelberg and wrote a very fine preface to a book which Carl August Auberlen[17] published on *The Theosophy of Friedrich Christoph Oetinger*. In this preface Richard Rothe,[18] who represents an echo of all the traditions of this circle, on the one hand out of his theosophical convictions recalls the theosophy of those great theosophists whose names I have listed and, on the other hand, speaks in such a way that one can clearly see how he feels in looking back at the twilight period with regard to those mysteries of life with which he was concerned as a theosophist. Thus in this preface, which was written in 1847, Richard Rothe writes about Oetinger. I should like to quote some of it here, and I want to do so in order that you can see that Richard Rothe (who was then in Heidelberg) was someone who, in his review of Oetinger's work, saw him as a person who in his own way endeavoured above all to study the Scriptures, both the Old and the New Testaments, out of a theosophical understanding of the world. Richard Rothe looked back at this particular way of reading the Scriptures and compared it with the way that he (and he died only in the 1860s and was therefore very much of a latecomer) had learnt them, which was how it generally happened at the time. He compared this latter way of reading the Scriptures with the methods of Bengel, Oetinger, Steinhofer, the mathematician and astronomer Hahn and others.

In this regard Richard Rothe says something quite remarkable: 'Among the men belonging to this group, which included Bengel and his *Apocalyptica*, Oetinger occupied a foremost position. Dissatisfied with the academic theology of his time, he thirsted for a richer and fuller, but at the same time also a purer understanding of Christian truth. Orthodox theology did not satisfy him; he thought it shallow. He wanted more than this, not because it asked too much of his faith but because his profound mind needed more than it had to give. He did not have a problem with its supernatural aspect—the supernatural quality of the theology of his time—but with the fact that it did not take this aspect seriously enough. He inwardly rebelled very strongly against the spiritualism current at the time, which reduced the realities of the world of Christian belief to pale abstractions, to mere intellectual images. Hence his fiery zeal against all idealism . . .'

Such a sentence might seem strange, but one needs to understand what it means. By idealism a German understands a system that lives purely in ideas, whereas Oetinger—and, with him, also Rothe—had a truly spiritual aspiration; they were people who really wanted to move history forward, unlike what Ranke[19] and people like him and all the others with their colourless ideas referred to as so-called historical ideas. (As if it were possible for ideas—and indeed, no mere word is adequate if one is wanting to speak in a 'real' way—to wander through history and carry human affairs forward.) These people wanted to replace dead abstractions with a more vibrant quality. 'This is the reason for Oetinger's fiery zeal against all idealism, his realism which did as a matter of fact, contrary to his intentions, tend towards materialism, his energetic urge towards "massive" concepts.'

These are ideas which really take hold of spiritual realities, ideas which do not refer to an ideal archetype underlying everything but are really 'massive' or substantial thoughts and ideas that reach out towards spiritual beings themselves.

Rothe continues: 'Moreover, his way of relating to nature and to the natural sciences was closely connected with this fundamental scientific attitude. The contemptuous disdain with which the idealist treats the natural world was foreign to him; he sensed a very real existence behind its coarse material veneer and was deeply convinced that without nature there could be no true—because no real—existence, whether of a divine or created origin.' There was something surprising about this, as it gave a new strength to the historical verification of the view of which we have been speaking, that in this thirst for a real understanding of nature, not only in Oetinger but also in the earlier and the contemporary Protestant theosophists and especially in Jakob Böhme, the original *scientific* tendency of the age of the Reformation was bursting through once more.

'The kind of realism for which Oetinger yearned came to birth in its innermost essence in Christianity,' says Richard Rothe. 'If transplanted into a different spiritual stream it will inevitably develop weaknesses, especially as regards certain aspects of its very specific doctrine. It is also capable of sustaining a Christian world of miracles which has a completely different kind of richness from the idealism in which we have been educated from a young age, which is always governed by the fear of thinking in too real a way about divine things and of taking the word of God too literally. Indeed, this Christian realism demands such a world of miracles, as is manifested in the teaching about the last things. It will not be confounded in its eschatological hopes by a sympathetic shaking of the heads of those who deem themselves to be alone capable of understanding; for it has no conception of how a thoughtful understanding of created things and their history is possible without a clear idea about the ultimate result of world evolution, which—as the goal and purpose of creation—can alone shed light on its true significance. Finally, it does not shrink from the thought of a real, immediate and, therefore, truly living spirit-world and an equally real contact with that world on the part of man even in his present state. The reader will confirm how precisely all this accords with what Oetinger says.'

Here you have a reference to a time when there was a quest not for ideas of nature but for a living spiritual world; and indeed, Oetinger tried to bring together in his life all the treasures of human knowledge that were accessible to him in order to attain a living relationship with the spiritual world. What stood behind this man? He was not like a person of the present day. People in the present day have above all the task of showing how modern natural science must allow itself to be corrected by spiritual science, in order that a true knowledge might come into being. Oetinger strove for something different: he aimed to demonstrate the necessity of finding a relationship with the living world of the spirit if one is to arrive at an understanding of the Bible, the Scriptures, and especially the New Testament. Richard Rothe speaks about this in a very beautiful way: 'In order to understand this, one needs to take into account his'—that is, Oetinger's—'position or, rather, his inner inclination towards the Holy Scriptures, his living awareness that a right, that is, a complete and therefore also utterly accurate understanding of the Bible is still lacking, that the interpretations of the Bible given by the Churches do not do this justice.

'I can make what I want to say about Oetinger as clear as possible if I relate my own experience of working with the Holy Scriptures for over 30 years,' writes Richard Rothe, 'especially with the New Testament and above all with the words of the Redeemer and the Epistles of Paul. The impression that I receive from the Scriptures the more I study them, if I approach them with the help of our commentaries, is that I have an ever more lively sense of their exuberant fecundity, not merely as regards the inexhaustible ocean of feeling that surges through them (the παθη Sacrae Scripturae, as Bengel calls it) but no less in view of the thoughts expressed through their words. I stand before them with a key which the Church has placed in my hand as the fruit of the trials of many centuries. I cannot exactly say that it does not fit, but still less can I say that it is the right one. It just about opens the door, but only if I use force to release the lock. Our traditional exegesis—I am not referring to modern interpretations—enables me to understand the Scriptures, but it is not enough to enable me to arrive at a *complete* and *accurate* understanding of them. It is certainly able to evoke the *general content* of the thoughts, but it fails to imbue the *distinctive form* in which these thoughts appear with life. After a traditional interpretation has been made it always seems to me that a blossom is left hovering above the text. This is left behind as an unexplained residue from the words of the text which, however conscientiously they may have carried out their task, presents the Bible commentators and those who refer to them in what they say in a very unfavourable light. Indeed it is made to appear as if our Lord and the apostles wished to say *only this* and *precisely that* in accordance with what the commentators allowed them to say, and it was made unnecessarily difficult for those who heard and read what they said to understand them because they expressed themselves so clumsily and awkwardly, or—to be perfectly honest—in such a curious way. Our exegetic literature in its vast unfathomable compass represents in this respect a serious complaint about them, in that they spoke with so little clarity and objectivity and yet with ornate language about such incomparably important things and to such an incomparably important end. But who does not feel that this complaint is unwarranted? A careful reader of the Bible receives the totally unambiguous impression that the way it is worded is absolutely right, that there are no meaningless flourishes which our exegesis has to cut away like wild vines from the composition of the Scriptures before it is able to enter into their actual content, and that the long-established custom of these scholars of removing the dust from the words of Scripture—on the grounds that they are so old and inadequate—before interpreting them leads to the incomparable lustre through which they have shone forth for centuries in the imperishable springlike radiance of eternal youth being wiped away from them. The masters of biblical interpretation can smile as much as they want, but the fact remains that between the lines of the Bible text something is written which, despite all their skill, they are unable to read; and yet it is above all this that people need to be able to read in order to understand the *thoroughly distinctive form* in which the—among us—generally acknowledged thoughts of divinely revealed truth come before us *only in the Holy Scriptures*, in characteristic contrast to all other descriptions of such truths. Our interpreters merely point out the figures standing in the foreground of the panorama of the Scriptures, but they ignore the background with its beautifully formed mountain ranges in the far distance and its radiant dark-blue sky with wisps of clouds. And yet from it there falls on these scholars that unique, magical light in which they receive an illumination which is for us the most enigmatic part about them. The distinctive fundamental thoughts and perceptions that lie as the *unspoken premiss* of the way in which the Scriptures express what they have to say are lacking; and no less of an absence is the real soul of the Scriptures, the inner connection of the individual elements of the thoughts expressed in the Bible which is the bond organically linking all the separate thoughts of the Scriptures together. No wonder, then, that there are hundreds of passages in our Bibles which therefore continually elude interpretation and cannot be *properly* understood, in such a way that the details of the text are fully recognized as making sense in all their minute features. No wonder that in so many instances we have a whole wealth of different interpretations which have since time immemorial been in dispute with one another, without there being any outcome to the battle. No wonder; for they will probably *all* be wrong, because all of them are imprecise or approximate and only reflect the meaning in general terms. We approach the texts of the Bible with the alphabet of *our* basic concepts of God and the world, taking it for granted and in all good faith that the alphabet of the biblical commentators, which stands as a silent premiss at the background of everything that they think and write as individuals and shines through everything, will be the same as ours. But that is unfortunately an illusion, from which experience should have cured us a long time ago. *Our* key doesn't work, the right key has got lost, and until we find it again our Bible studies will not bear fruit. The framework of *basic* biblical concepts which is not outwardly expressed in the Scriptures but is merely present as an underlying premiss is lacking, it is not present among our scholars; and for as long as we undertake our research without it the Bible must remain a *half*-closed book. We must approach it with *different* basic concepts from the familiar ones that we are used to regarding as the only possible options; and whatever these may be and wherever they may be sought, one thing at any rate is absolutely clear from the whole sound of the melody of the Scriptures in its natural fullness, that they must be more realistic and more "massive" or substantial. I have here merely reported my own experience. I am far from wanting to force it on anyone for whom it is alien, but believe with full confidence that Oetinger would understand me and would assure me that it was also the same in his case. But there are also some of our contemporaries who *in this respect*, despite the objections that are raised against me, will stand alongside me. Among many I could name I refer to one in particular, the celebrated Dr Beck in Tübingen.'

Oetinger tried to arrive at an understanding of the Bible by endeavouring to find inner inspiration in the ideas that still retained some vitality in the evening twilight in which both he and Saint-Martin lived and to enter into a living connection with the spiritual world, for only then did he hope that the true language of the Bible might be revealed to him. His premiss was firmly of this nature—that with purely abstract intellectual ideas one will fail to understand the most important things in the Bible, especially the New Testament, and that one will only come near to the true meaning of the New Testament if one is able to understand that this New Testament has come out of a direct perception of the spiritual world itself, that no commentaries or exegeses are necessary but that above all one needs to be able to read the New Testament. To this end he sought a *philosophia sacra*. This was not to be a philosophy according to the model of what came after but one in which was inscribed what a person may really experience if he lives in communion with the spiritual world.

Just as we, who want to shed a scientific light on spiritual-scientific research, are not able to speak in the way that Saint-Martin did, so are we equally unable to speak like Oetinger, or still less like Bengel, if we speak today about the Gospels. Nevertheless, the edition of the New Testament brought out by Bengel will continue to be of use; but his *Apocalyptica*, of which he thought so much, is not of the slightest interest to anyone now. For Oetinger himself the apocalypse was fairly remote; for Bengel, who was the older man, it was very immediate. In his studies on this theme he attached a particular importance to calculations. He regarded one number as being of particular importance. And the mere fact that he considered this number to be particularly important is enough in itself for a modern thinking person—and of course I say 'modern thinking person' in inverted commas—to regard Bengel as a muddle head, a fanciful visionary and a fool; for according to his calculations the year 1836 was to be especially important in the evolution of humanity. He made very extensive calculations. Of course he lived in the first part of the eighteenth century, so he was separated from this year by a century. He worked this out by considering the historical phenomena in his own way. But if one looks deeper at the relevant phenomena without the 'cleverness' of the modern mind, one realizes that the good Bengel erred in his calculations by only six years. This error arose from an incorrect estimate of the founding of Rome,[20] and this can easily be verified. He had meant to arrive with his calculations at the year 1842, the year that I have given for the materialistic crisis.[21] Bengel, the teacher of Oetinger, was referring to that deep rift; but because he went too far in his search for really massive or substantial concepts he thought on too large a scale, and imagined the outward course of history in such a way that something special was going to take place which would be like a doomsday, an end of everything. But it was only a day of doom for the ancient wisdom!

Thus we see the decline of a theosophical age at a not so very distant date from our own time. And yet if someone is writing an account of history or philosophy he will—if he mentions these people at all—at most devote a few lines to them which will as a rule say very little at all. Nevertheless, these people wielded a very considerable influence. And if someone today asks what is the meaning of the second part of Goethe's *Faust* and answers in the way that many commentators have done, we cannot but be surprised that,

> He who cleaves to shallow things
> Can keep his hopes alive on empty terms,
> And dig with greed for precious plunderings,
> And find his happiness unearthing worms![22]

In this second part of *Faust* there is an enormous amount of occult wisdom and a reflection of occult facts, expressed in a truly poetic form. All this would be inconceivable if it had not been preceded by that world that I have been trying to characterize to you by means of two main examples. People today really have no idea of how much was still known about the spiritual world a relatively short time ago and how much has become obscured in recent decades. In any event it is very important that we are aware that we are only just beginning to read the Gospels again, because we are only just learning how to do so through what spiritual science is able to impart to us today.[23]

There is something very remarkable about Oetinger. There is in his writings a sentence which is quoted again and again but is never understood, a sentence which would alone enable anyone with the requisite insight to say that he is one of the greatest figures in cultural history. This is the sentence: 'Die Materie ist das Ende der Wege Gottes' (a literal rendering of which would be: 'Matter is the end of the ways of God').[24] Such a definition of matter, which so closely corresponds with what the spiritual scientist is able to know, could only be given by a very highly developed soul who was able to understand how the divinely spiritual creative powers work and concentrate their energies in order to bring a material structure into being (such as man, for example), which in its form expresses the ultimate manifestation of an enormous concentration of forces. If you read what is said in the conversation between Capesius and Benedictus at the beginning of the second Mystery Play[25] about the relationship of the macrocosm to man, which causes Capesius to fall ill, you will be able to form an idea of how through modern spiritual science one can express in our words those things that Oetinger was able to characterize by means of this phrase (which we can only understand once we have rediscovered its meaning): 'Matter is the end of the ways of God.' But it is also the same in his case: we are unable to speak in his words, no more than in those of Saint-Martin. Anyone who utters them must have a special fondness for preserving what can no longer be understood.

However, not only have ideas undergone a considerable transformation; the same can also be said of feelings. Just think of a typical person who exemplifies our modern age, someone who embodies its essential features and attitudes, and imagine what he would make of Saint-Martin's book *Des erreurs et de la vérité* if he were to open it and chance upon the sentence:[26] 'Man is protected from knowing the principle of his outward physical bodily nature; for if he were to know the principle of his physical bodily nature he would be too ashamed to be able to look at a naked human being.' In an age when people long for nudity on the stage—as the typical examples of modern humanity are the first to do—it is not possible to make anything of such a sentence. Just think, along comes a great philosopher called Saint-Martin who understands the world, and he explains that a higher sense of shame makes us blush when we see a human form. And yet for Saint-Martin this is totally understandable!

You see, I initially wanted to indicate today that something has become obscured which has immense significance, but my particular wish was to draw attention to the fact that people used to speak in a language that we are no longer able to speak. We have to speak differently now. Thinking capacities that formerly existed have been lost in order that we may speak in this language today. But we find both in Oetinger and in Saint-Martin that things have not been thought through to the end, and they can be taken further. One can continue to discuss them, but not with a modern human being. I should like to go further and say: one does not need to speak about them further if one raises questions today about the riddles of the world, because we need to develop our understanding not with ideas from the past but with ideas belonging to the present. This is why so much emphasis is placed here on linking everything arrived at through spiritual-scientific research with concepts of the present. It is a remarkable phenomenon that, however much importance one attaches to not returning to these ideas, their potential has not yet been fulfilled; it is apparent from the ideas themselves that there is much more to be thought about along these lines. People have no conception of how these ideas actually form part of a wider consciousness, because they are governed by the strange notion that the way of thinking that prevails today has always been as it is now.

The typical person of whom I spoke earlier thinks as follows: I call these little white particles, this white powder in the salt-cellar, salt. Now this typical person knows that salt has different names in different languages, but that people have always understood them as referring to what he sees today. This is simply assumed. But it is not true. Even the most uneducated peasant in the seventeenth or eighteenth centuries and for quite some while afterwards had a far broader conception of what he meant when he said the word 'salt'. His picture was one of which that of Saint-Martin was a more concentrated version; instead of the present materialistic conception he was aware of something connected with spiritual life when he spoke of salt. Words were not as materialized as they are today; they were not merely concerned with a separate material essence. We read in the Gospels that Christ says to the disciples: 'You are the salt of the Earth.'[27] Yes, when this is expressed in the modern words 'You are the salt of the Earth', it does not have the same meaning as it did when Christ spoke these words, because one inevitably experiences the word 'salt' through the whole inner relationship that a person has today with respect to the word 'salt'; and however broad his conception may be this will not be of any help. If a person today is to have the same experience that would have arisen at that time from the value attached to the word 'salt', it would be necessary to shift one's understanding of the meaning in such a way that what is there is not salt but something else. One has to do something similar with respect to a great many old documents, particularly with the Holy Scriptures; and many errors have been committed in this regard especially in connection with them. It is therefore not difficult to understand why Oetinger tried to make a large number of historical studies in order to arrive at the true value of the words and to gain an appropriate feeling for them. Of course, anyone with a mind like Oetinger's would be considered mad carrying out alchemical experiments and studying Cabbalistic books, simply in order to find out how the words of a sentence were really to be understood; for all his efforts were devoted to the words of the sentences of the Holy Scriptures.

I have spoken of these things today on the one hand in order to show that now, at the dawn of a new age, it is necessary to speak in a different way about them from how this was done in the twilight of a former age; but I should like, on the other hand, to return to the strange fact that, according to the prevailing view of our time out of which spiritual science also has to develop, it would appear to be a matter of indifference whether one studies the manner of thought of the time of Bengel, Oetinger, Saint-Martin and others. For if one is speaking to educated people today, one has to speak about the digestive system, the respiratory system and the nervous system; one cannot speak about mercury, sulphur and salt in connection with the body. These concepts, which were still understood by those who worked with them in the time of Paracelsus, Jakob Böhme, Saint-Martin and Oetinger, are no longer understood today. Nevertheless, it is by no means without value to concern oneself with these matters, and there would still be some point in doing so even if one does not have the opportunity to speak to cultured people out of a background of these ideas. I am willing to admit that it would not be very clever to introduce notions such as mercury, sulphur and salt into modern thinking. Not only would I regard this as unintelligent; it would also not be right. Anyone who feels the pulse of his time will not make the mistake of wishing to restore these old ideas in the way that certain so-called occult societies do which attach great importance to clinging on to old vignettes. All the same, it is of the greatest significance to acquire a facility in this language which is no longer spoken today and whose last word has by no means been uttered in the works of Saint-Martin and Oetinger, or in earlier times those of Paracelsus and Jakob Böhme.

Why is this? Yes, why? People of the present day do not speak in this way; they might abandon this language. And at the most one might focus one's mind on the historical phenomenon of how such a historical epoch was unable to find fulfilment, how it came about that there was something that could have been carried further but which came to a standstill despite its having this potential for further development. How can this be? What is at the bottom of this? It could well be that people will be completely unable to understand one another if, despite learning everything that has to be learnt, they have not taken these ideas into account.

There is something here of immense significance. The living no longer speak about these ideas; they neither have to speak about them nor need to do so. And yet the language of these ideas is all the more important for the dead, for those who have passed through the portal of death. If the need arises to make oneself understood by the dead or by other particular spirits of the spiritual world, one learns to recognize that in a certain respect it is necessary to become familiar with that unfulfilled language which at that former time died out as regards the physical earthly life of the physical plane. And it is precisely among those who have passed through the portal of death that what lives in these ideas will gradually become a vibrant force, for it will be for them the familiar language that they are seeking. And the more efforts are made to live into these ideas as they were thought, felt and imagined at that time, the more will one succeed in making oneself understood by the spirits who have passed through the portal of death. A process of mutual understanding is then able to develop. And then the extraordinary and remarkable mystery is disclosed that thought-forms of a certain kind have been living on the Earth but have been developed only to a certain point and are no longer being developed further on the Earth; but they are being taken further among those who enter into the life between death and a new birth. No one should think that anything can be done solely with what one can learn today about the formation of sulphur, quicksilver—mercury is not quicksilver—of sulphur, quicksilver and salt. If one only has these concepts, one finds that they are useless for acquiring a relationship with the dead through their language. But if one relates to these ideas in the way that Paracelsus and Jakob Böhme did and also as Saint-Martin, Bengel and Oetinger were able to do in what I might describe as their tendency towards superabundance, one notices that by this means a bridge is built between this world and the other world. Of course, people may laugh about Bengel's calculations[28]—after all, they have no conceivable value for outward physical life; but for those who are between death and a new birth these calculations make a great deal of sense. For rifts in development such as Bengel tried to calculate—and he was only six years out—are of far-reaching significance.

You see, therefore, that the world here on the physical plane and the world of the spirit are not connected in such a way that the link between them can be forged through abstract formulas, but they are connected in an utterly concrete way. The meaning that is becoming lost here in the physical world rises up into the spiritual world and lives on with those who have died, provided that on the part of the living it is succeeded by a new phase.

We shall continue with this next time.

BUILDING STONES FOR AN
UNDERSTANDING OF THE MYSTERY
OF GOLGOTHA

LECTURE 8

BERLIN, 27 MARCH 1917

AT this time I need to draw your attention again and again to one particular aspect of what our whole spiritual-scientific research must focus upon at the present time. This has to do with the fact that behind the various concepts, ideas and mental pictures that people form for themselves and within which they live there is not only what is generally referred to as logic but also the world of reality, which must be sought by means of ideas that are deeply imbued with reality. In the course of these studies which will be directed towards a particular aim that I shall characterize shortly, it may from time to time be necessary to indicate that it may easily happen that an idea or conception of some kind that has arisen in the course of life can be true in a certain way but does not reach down to reality. It will only gradually become clear what is meant by ideas that are imbued with reality; but it will become possible to acquire a picture of this through some simple comparisons. Today I shall therefore introduce what I have in mind by means of a comparison or analogy.

What I want to say now has apparently—but only apparently—no connection with our ensuing studies, but it is purely of an introductory nature. From the sixteenth century onwards until 1839, all Roman cardinals had to make an important vow. During the years of his pontificate Pope Sixtus V, who held office between 1585 and 1590, deposited a sum of five million scudi in the Castel Sant'Angelo as a fund to be used only in time of need. Because it was considered so important that such a bounty should be available for such a purpose, cardinals always had to swear that they would carefully protect it. In the year 1839 under the pontificate of Pope Gregory XVI, Cardinal Acton[1] raised an objection to this vow; he wanted the cardinals no longer to have to swear that they would preserve this treasure. If one were to hear nothing else about this story, one might form all sorts of excellent hypotheses as to why this remarkable Cardinal Acton did not want the cardinals to make the vow that was still required of them at this time, that they would guard the treasure that was of such potential importance to the Holy See. Moreover, everything that one would have to say could well be thoroughly logical; but all the very fine things that one might have ended up saying would be superseded by what Acton knew because of certain circumstances and the cardinals did not know. He knew that since 1797 this fund had no longer been there,[2] that it had been used for other purposes. So the cardinals had been required to swear that they would protect a treasure that was no longer there, and Acton did not want to demean himself by having to make a vow about something that no longer existed. So you see, all the ingenious discussions and hypotheses that someone would advance who did not know that the entire treasure had already been used up—all these hypotheses would collapse.

If one meditates on an example such as this—and it may sometimes seem unnecessary to meditate about things that are so patently obvious, but one needs to do so in order to compare something of a matter-of-fact nature with many other situations in life—one may come to see the difference between ideas that are rooted in reality and those that are not. I need to make you aware of the unreality of ideas prevailing in our present time for the simple reason that, as you will see later and perhaps only on the next occasion that we meet, this is directly connected with the theme that I must speak about once more in the course of these lectures from the standpoint of spiritual science. My endeavour in this respect is to relate our previous studies to the consideration of a particular aspect of the Christ mystery. What I said last time will be able to serve as a framework for that aspect of the Christ mystery that we are now wanting to consider. Even though much of what I should like to present to you today may appear unrelated to our essential theme, it will nevertheless provide a valuable foundation.

As you are aware, I tentatively began to indicate a particular way of approaching the Christ mystery in a book of mine which appeared quite some time ago, *Christianity as Mystical Fact*. This book—which was, incidentally, one of the last books to be confiscated in its new edition by the old regime in Russia a few weeks ago—is, I would say, a first attempt to understand Christianity itself from a spiritual point of view, a dimension which over the centuries has more or less disappeared in the development of Christianity in the West. I must first emphasize one thing in particular upon which all the arguments in the book stand or fall. A particular view of the Gospels is presented in *Christianity as Mystical Fact*. I do not want to say any more about this here, as you can read about it in the book. However, if there is any justification for this view, it is necessary to assume that the Gospels did not arise as late as Christian theologians often suppose today but that their origin must be placed somewhat earlier. You are aware that, according to this view, the elements of the Gospel teaching are to be found in the ancient texts of the mysteries and that the Mystery of Golgotha is a fulfilment of what is contained in these texts. If one advocates such a spiritual conception of Christianity at the present time one finds oneself at odds with a great deal of theological and historical research, and contemporary theologians in particular will tend to regard such a conception as historically without foundation. It is thought to be fairly clear that in the first century, or at any rate in the first two-thirds of the first century, the Gospels did not play any particular part. There are even Christian theologians who doubt whether there is any evidence that in the first century of the Christian era people of consequence thought of, or more to the point believed in, the person of Christ Jesus.

Now it will become increasingly apparent that if the seemingly so careful research of the present day would but expand its horizons and become not merely precise but also much broader in its scope, many of its reservations will fall away. One can of course draw all sorts of conclusions today from questions arising from, for example, certain contradictions between Christian and Jewish records. But these conclusions fail to acknowledge that the apocryphal Gospels, that is to say, those records not officially recognized as Christian, are very little known and are virtually ignored, especially by Christian theologians. A large part of this lack of recognition derives from the fact that Christianity—and specifically the Mystery of Golgotha—has not been understood in a sufficiently spiritual way, and that no real relationship has been formed with the Pauline distinction between the soul and the spiritual aspects of man's being. Just consider our very simple division of man into body, soul and spirit. The fact is that Paul, who was familiar with the atavistic nature of the truths of the ancient mysteries, envisaged with his distinction between the psychic and the spiritual aspects of man something very similar to what we mean when we speak of the soul and the spirit as two parts of human nature. But it is precisely this distinction between psyche and pneuma, or between soul and spirit, that has more or less completely disappeared in the West. However, it is not possible to understand the real nature of the Mystery of Golgotha without some concept of man's spiritual nature as distinct from his soul.

I should like first of all to refer to something that I have already mentioned in previous years, something that can show you that there is much in the received historical record that is actually incorrect, especially as regards recent research into the life of Jesus. As I have said, the conventional view is that the Gospels came into being relatively late. This can be challenged on purely historical grounds. It can, for example, be countered by the fact that in the year AD 70 the Rabbi Gamaliel II was involved in a legal case.[3] He was the son of Rabbi Simeon, who was the son of that Gamaliel of whom Paul was a pupil; and the aforesaid Gamaliel II had a sister with whom he was involved in a lawsuit over inheritance. They were led before the judge, who was a Roman—and perhaps also a Jew, although that is difficult to confirm—sympathetic to Christianity. Gamaliel pleaded that he was the sole heir, because according to Mosaic law daughters cannot inherit. The judge raised the objection: 'Since you Jews have lost your country the law [Torah] of Moses is no longer valid. What matters now is the Gospel, and according to the Gospel a sister can also inherit.' There was at first no straightforward solution. So what happened? Gamaliel II, who was not only keen to acquire his inheritance but also cunning, requested an adjournment of the case, which was granted. In the course of the adjournment he stood before the judge whom he had bribed, who now gave a different verdict and said that he had made a mistake at the original hearing. The Gospel was indeed applicable to such cases, but in the Gospel it states that Mosaic law [the Torah of Moses] is not annulled by the Gospel. As confirmation of this he quoted the verse in St Matthew's Gospel (chapter 5, verse 17) that relates to this in the version that we have today, of course with the minor differences between the Greek language and the language in which the Gospel was written when the judge's verdict was given in AD 70.[4] In his ruling the judge simply referred to St Matthew's Gospel, while the Talmud, where this story is related,[5] accepts this statement from St Matthew's Gospel without question.

Through a broadening of the scope of research even of a purely historical nature, much could therefore be adduced to show that one does not stand on solid ground if one refuses to assign an early date to the origin of the Gospels. Historical research will one day fully confirm the research emanating from completely different, spiritual sources which forms the foundation of my book *Christianity as Mystical Fact*.

Now everything that has a relationship to the Mystery of Golgotha has within it very deep mysteries which can be penetrated if spiritual-scientific faculties of perception are developed to an increasing degree. There is much to indicate that these questions are not as simple as people very often imagine them to be today. Thus, for example, little attention is paid to the relationship of Judaism to the way that Christ Jesus was perceived in the first century of our era. There are theologians who study certain Jewish writings in order to find evidence for their various theories. However, one can easily demonstrate that these Jewish writings on which so much reliance is placed did not exist in the first century AD. One thing does, nevertheless, seem to be very clear historically, namely that in the first century—and especially in the second third of that century—there was a relatively good relationship between Judaism and Christianity , if one can use this word in the context of the period concerned, and that it frequently happened that when certain enlightened Jews of that time entered into discussions with followers of Christ Jesus, it was not so very difficult to reach an agreement. One needs only to recall such instances as the following, when the famous Rabbi Elieser became acquainted around the middle of the first century with a certain Jacob (as he calls him), who acknowledged himself to be a pupil of Jesus and who healed in His name. The famous Rabbi Elieser[6] conversed with this Jacob, and said in the course of the conversation that there was absolutely nothing against the true spirit of Judaism in what he had said or, quite especially, in that he healed the sick in the name of Jesus.

One can then see that this more or less easy harmony that existed in this earlier period disappeared towards the end of the first century; that in other words even enlightened Jews became fierce opponents, implacable enemies of everything of a Christian nature. It also happened that when the Jewish texts that are considered to be important today were composed in the second century AD, an altogether different mood with respect to Christianity entered into their composition than was the case within Judaism in the first century. One can witness the development of a hatred for Christianity growing from decade to decade especially within Judaism. This went hand in hand with a transformation of Judaism itself. Although modern Jewish scholars do of course know the Old Testament in their own way, they do not know what was still living within Judaism in other respects at the time of the Mystery of Golgotha; and they are also largely unaware of the major issues with which a truly historical investigation of this period is concerned. It is necessary to realize that the Old Testament was read completely differently in the first century AD from the way that the most learned Jewish Rabbis can read it today. Especially since the nineteenth century the capacity to interpret ancient texts has more or less disappeared. Certain things which even in the eighteenth century still existed as a secret tradition in the form of truths derived from old atavistic clairvoyance could no longer be imagined by people in the nineteenth century; and the only conception that people have of them today is that those who speak about them—even if they belong to an earlier time—must be a bit crazy!

In the previous lecture I drew your attention to an important book called *Des erreurs et de la vérité* by Saint-Martin. This book is undoubtedly a late example of its kind, inasmuch as it contains insights deriving from ancient traditions which have now become veiled in obscurity, while nevertheless faithfully reflecting these traditions. I have recently quoted extracts from this book which people today would understand only with the greatest difficulty. But if we allow ourselves to be guided by Saint-Martin's views, we shall see that he was expressing thoughts which a modern person would either regard as pure fantasy (and virtually everything of this nature is regarded as such today) or consider to be utterly absurd. Saint-Martin indicates that the human race as it is now has fallen into its present condition from primeval heights. Many people today who have not become wedded to the materialistic conception of the world are willing to tolerate the idea that the present human race can be traced back to former times when with a part of its being, as it were, it was at a higher level. Despite the materialistic character of Darwinism, which assumes that man has evolved purely from animals, there are other people who are of the opinion that man descended from a lofty origin of some kind where he was inspired by ancient traditions of a divine nature. But when one goes beyond such an abstract picture and approaches the sort of concrete assertions that Saint-Martin makes (and which he can only make because these assertions are associated with ancient traditions from the primal epoch of clairvoyance), it is beyond the wit of modern man to make anything of such things.

How is a person of today who knows his chemistry, his geology, his biology, physiology and so on with absolute thoroughness, and who has also assimilated that strange artefact that goes by the name of philosophy nowadays—how is such a person to respond when Saint-Martin says that the human race became as it is now only after the Fall, and that it was originally very different? In those former times man had a certain kind of impenetrable armour, which he has now lost. It originally formed part of his organism, and had enabled him to withstand the struggles that he had to endure in these ancient times. He was also armed with a lance of bronze which could inflict wounds in the way that fire does; and with this lance he was able to be equal to the battle against beings of a different nature to human beings which faced him at that time. And in the place where he originally dwelt he had seven trees at his disposal. Each of these trees had 16 roots and 490 branches. He then left this place and fell from these lofty origins.[7]

I doubt that one would be thought of as being in one's right mind if one were to do what Saint-Martin undoubtedly did, namely to insist that his views were no less real than the beautiful constructions that geologists form about primeval times. If one were to come up with abstract allegories or symbols, this would make it all a bit more acceptable. But Saint-Martin was not speaking symbolically; he was speaking of realities that had really existed. It was of course necessary for Saint-Martin to choose imaginative pictures for certain things that existed when the Earth in its primal state was more spiritual than in later times. However, such imaginative pictures represent realities; they should not be interpreted symbolically but must be accepted in the imaginative form in which they are presented. I wanted to mention this not in order to enter deeply into this theme but merely to show you how fundamentally different the language of the eighteenth century—the language in which a book such as *Des erreurs et de la vérité* is written— was from the language that is now regarded as the only one that passes muster today. The kind of writing that one still finds in Saint-Martin has completely died out.

But as the Old Testament, for example, can only be read in its full depth if one is either still or is again possessed of certain knowledge associated with imaginative perceptions, you can understand that by the time of the nineteenth century in particular it had become impossible to read the Old Testament with any real understanding. But the further back one goes, the more does one find that at the time when the Mystery of Golgotha took place the world of Judaism encompassed not only the exoteric documents of the Old Testament but also an esoteric teaching, a true mystery wisdom; and it was an important aspect of this mystery wisdom that it gave one the possibility of reading the Old Testament in the right way. It is simply not possible to read the Testament in the right way unless one views what it says against a background of spiritual realities.

At the time of the Mystery of Golgotha the strongest aversion to the particular qualities of Jewish occult teachings derived from Rome. Indeed, one might say that there has possibly never in the whole of earthly evolution been a greater contrast than that between the spirit of Rome and the mystery wisdom guarded by the initiates in Palestine. One should, of course, not simply view this mystery wisdom in the way that it lived at that time in Palestine, for one would not find Christianity in it but only a kind of prophetic anticipation of it. On the other hand, however, one can only comprehend what was fermenting within Christianity if one views it against the historical background of the mystery teaching living in Palestine. This mystery teaching was full of hidden knowledge about the spiritual being of man; it was full of indications for a path of human cognition extending into the spiritual world. Ramifications of what lived in this occult teaching were also to be found in the Greek mysteries. There was, however, little trace of it in the Roman mysteries. Rome had no place for the dynamic thrust that underlay the Palestinian mysteries, for it had developed a particular kind of human community, a particular form of social life, which could exist only if one disregarded the spiritual dimension of man's being. The essential quality of Roman history was that a human community was to be established which would more or less exclude man as a spiritual being. A society was to be brought into being where it would be meaningless to speak of man as a threefold being with a body, soul and spirit. The further back one goes into history the more one realizes that the way that the Mystery of Golgotha was understood in ancient times was based on this division of the totality of man's being into body, soul and spirit, just as Paul still spoke consistently of psyche and pneuma, of the soul and the spirit.[8] But this was highly offensive to all the sensibilities that were natural to Romans, and this was the reason for much that happened subsequently.

As you are aware, that body of wisdom which can no longer be applied today but at the time in question sought to rescue the threefold picture of man and the cosmos was Gnosticism. In later centuries it was more or less completely eliminated and repressed, with the result that it totally disappeared. I am certainly not suggesting that it ought to have survived; I wish merely to state the historical fact that Gnosticism still had a spiritual conception of the Mystery of Golgotha and was repressed. Events now developed in a very strange way, for what happened was that Christianity increasingly became part of the Roman world. But this process of increasing amalgamation was not matched by any understanding on the part of this Roman world for the relationship of Christianity to the spiritual aspect of man's being. It gave more and more offence that some Gnostic Christians continued to speak of body, soul and spirit. In those circles where Christianity had become the official religion, there were increasing efforts to suppress the spirit, the very idea of the spirit. People felt that one should not make any reference to the spirit, for it was thought that this could lead to all the old ideas of a division of man into body, soul and spirit reviving once more.

Historical development continued along these lines. If we make an exact study of the early Christian centuries, we find that much that is generally explained in a different way is seen in its true light if one becomes aware that it was increasingly the aim of the growing Roman character of Christianity to cause the idea of the spirit to disappear altogether. Innumerable questions of conscience and epistemology can be seen for what they are only if one becomes truly aware of this need of European-led Christianity to get rid of the spirit. This development eventually led to a formula or dogma being laid down at the Eighth Ecumenical Council of 869 in Constantinople which, while not being so explicit in its wording, was later interpreted as meaning that it is contrary to Christianity to speak of body, soul and spirit, and that the only truly Christian thing to say is that man consists of a body and a soul.[9] The Eighth Ecumenical Council initially stated that man had an intellectual soul and a spiritual soul. This formula was phrased in such a way as to avoid having to speak of the spirit as a distinct entity. Nevertheless, it amounted to an ousting of all knowledge of the spirit.

There is much connected with this of which people are unaware. Our modern philosophers embark on their studies in such a way that they investigate the body on the one hand and the soul on the other. If you were to ask these people—for example, Wundt[10] or others like him—what is the basis for making this distinction, they would of course affirm that it rests on purely factual foundations, on the actual observation that it makes no sense to speak of body, soul and spirit but only of a body that is related to the outside world and a soul that is related to one's inner world. Someone such as Wundt would say that this is perfectly obvious! He has no idea that all this is the consequence of what the Eighth Ecumenical Council had decreed. Even today, modern philosophers do not speak about the spirit, for they follow the dogma of the Eighth Ecumenical Council. Precisely why—even though not explicitly—modern philosophers deny the spirit they have no more idea than the Roman cardinals knew what they were actually swearing when they made the vow to protect a fund that no longer existed.[11] People generally tend to pay very little attention to the truly seminal aspects of history, the real forces underlying it. Thus anyone who rejects the view of 'unprejudiced' or 'objective' science, as it is called, that man consists only of a body and a soul, may well be regarded as an ignoramus, simply because those who perpetuate this 'objective' science are unaware that their assumptions are based on the decrees of the Eighth Ecumenical Council in 869. And so it is with many other things. It is fair to say that this Eighth Council is an important window through which one can gain insight into a good part of the evolution of western thought.

You are aware that a deep rift runs through the cultural development of the West with respect to the schism between those different forms of religious worship which live on today in, respectively, the Russian Orthodox Church and the Roman Catholic Church or have evolved from them. From a purely doctrinal point of view (and there are of course many more far-reaching impulses lying behind the actual dogmas themselves), the difference between them revolves, as you know, around the famous 'filioque' clause. According to the later Council (the Russian Church recognizes only the first seven Councils),[12] the Roman Catholic Church recognizes the wording that states that the Holy Spirit proceeds 'from the Father and the Son'; not only from the Father but also from the Son. This was declared heretical by Constantinople (i.e. the Eastern Church); for the Russian Church—as has been said, many deeper impulses lie behind these doctrinal issues but it is enough for today merely to state that this is so—recognizes that the Holy Spirit proceeds from the Father. The great confusion with respect to this dogma could only arise because there was a general confusion about the notion of the spirit, in that the very idea of the spirit was gradually becoming completely lost. This is undoubtedly connected with the fact that as the fifth post-Atlantean cultural period approached man had for a while to be denied all perception of the spirit. Compared with this underlying truth, what actually took place is, I would say, merely a surface reflection. But it is necessary to penetrate beyond this reflection if one wants to arrive at a valid point of view that is rooted in reality.

Now the period of evolution which played an important part in the establishment of this dogma that there is no spirit, that man consists only of a body and a soul, has not come to an end. The Christian theologians of the Middle Ages, who still lived in the midst of ongoing traditions (for it was only orthodox Church doctrine that maintained that man consists of a body and a soul, whereas alchemists and those other people who still had confidence in the old traditions knew perfectly well that man has a body, a soul and a spirit), knew how difficult it was to hold orthodox opinions, on the one hand, while on the other to have to acknowledge that behind the heretical teachings of body, soul and spirit which surrounded them everywhere a kernel of truth lay hidden. We see everywhere Christian theologians making frantic but vain attempts to avoid what they referred to as the trichotomy—the division of man into three parts. Anyone who does not make himself aware of the difficulties that theologians had in avoiding the trichotomy can have no real understanding of medieval Christian theology.

Indeed, this evolutionary period has not finished by a long way, for it corresponds to a very important impulse in the cultural development of the West; and because so much will take place in the twentieth century that one will need to be aware of if one wants to understand our present age, I shall need to speak further about this century. Originally (if what has come about in relatively recent times may be referred to in this way) man was divided into body, soul and spirit. Evolution had advanced to the point that by the ninth century the spirit could be abolished. But matters did not rest there. People do not follow these processes properly today because they fail to consider important matters such as the complete transformation of thinking by Saint-Martin, to mention one example. Things proceed further, and not only is the spirit being abolished but there is a growing tendency towards abolishing the soul. Hitherto only certain preliminary steps have been taken in this direction, but the time is now ripe for the abolition of the soul as well. But people fail to recognize these important tendencies that are living among us now. We are already witnessing powerful evolutionary impulses that are preparing for the abolition of the soul. It is not a matter of organizing Councils as in the ninth century, for things take a different course today. I must repeat that I am not criticizing these phenomena but am merely making you aware of certain facts.

There is evidence for the preliminary stages in abolishing the soul in all manner of different areas. Thus in the nineteenth century there emerged dialectical materialism, which has become the view of history that underlies modern [German] social democracy. If we regard Engels[13] and Marx[14] as the major 'prophets'—it might perhaps be regarded as inappropriate to use such a traditional word, but it may suffice for our present purposes—of dialectical materialism, they are also the direct descendants (in historical terms) of the Church Fathers of the Eighth Ecumenical Council. There is an unbroken line of development between the two. What the Church Fathers set in motion by abolishing the spirit has been carried forward by Marx and Engels in their already well-advanced plans to abolish the soul. After all, according to this view soul, or inner, impulses will no longer be of any significance; for the sole driving forces of history are material impulses, the struggle for material possessions. Moreover, the soul is conceived of as being merely a superstructure added to the solid foundation of a purely material process. But it is really important to recognize the true Catholic nature of Marx and Engels; for it is essential that one views these aspirations of the nineteenth century as the next stage in the development of what occurred in connection with the abolition of the spirit.

The development of the modern scientific outlook is another factor contributing to the abolition of the soul. The scientific view of the world—I am referring not to experimental science itself but to the theories which attribute reality only to physical phenomena and regard everything of a soul nature merely as an illusion, as something that has no existence independent of our corporeal nature—is a direct continuation of those developments that we have perceived in the important impulses enshrined in the Eighth Ecumenical Council. However, a large part of humanity will probably not take this seriously until the abolition of the soul will acquire legal force from certain focal points of earthly evolution. It will not be long before laws are drafted in a number of countries which will lead to anyone speaking in all seriousness about a soul being declared as not in his right mind, while the only people who are regarded as sane will be those who recognize the 'truth' that thinking, feeling and will arise from certain bodily functions out of pure necessity. Various steps have already been taken in this direction, but so long as these initial steps are only of a theoretical nature they will not have any great, deeply influential effect or significance. This will only happen when they become part of the social order, of social life in general. The first half of this century will barely be over before something happens in this realm which for someone with the requisite insight will be a terrible spectacle: a desolation in the soul realm akin to that which afflicted the spirit in the ninth century.

It is worth saying again and again that what matters is to have insight into such things, insight into the impulses that have governed human life over the course of history. For it all too easily happens that, through their education which is governed by a purely materialistic view of the world, people in the present time have a tendency towards a soporific state of being. The materialistic world-view to a certain extent prevents a person from thinking properly, from perceiving reality in a really healthy way, lulls them to sleep when it comes to the important aspects of historical developments. And so even those who have a real longing to follow a path of spiritual knowledge do not have the strength of will to kindle an awareness of certain impulses that are inherent in our evolution and to make a real effort to perceive things as they really are.

Thus there was in Palestine a kind of occult teaching which was a preparation for the Mystery of Golgotha, a teaching with respect to which the Mystery of Golgotha represented a fulfilment. I have expressed this by saying that the Mystery of Golgotha was the greatest mystery ever to have been enacted on the stage of world history. If this is so, one can pose the question as to why such a strong antipathy developed in the Roman world to what emerged through the Mystery of Golgotha in the form of Christianity, and why this antipathy led specifically to the abolition of the spirit.

These things are far more closely related than one might think if one merely looks at them superficially. Few people today would want to consider the idea that Marx and Engels are like Church Fathers, though this does not represent the full truth of the matter. One begins to understand it at a deeper level if one considers the following. At the court of justice where Christ Jesus was condemned, those referred to as the Sadducees played a leading part. What was their role when the Mystery of Golgotha took place? Who were the people who have rightly been called the Sadducees? They were those who wanted to make everything deriving from the mysteries vanish away, disappear into oblivion. The Sadducees had a fear, a terror, an absolute dread of any form of mystery cult; but they were also the people who had responsibility for the courts and likewise for the administration in Palestine. They were, however, wholly under the influence of the Roman state. Indeed, they were the slaves of the Roman state, as was outwardly apparent that they purchased their positions with enormous sums of money, and then in turn extracted vast amounts of money from the population of Palestine. It was they who—because of the way that their ahrimanic materialism had sharpened their perception—were particularly aware that the Roman world would be seriously threatened if the notion that everything associated with Christ was in harmony with the essence of the mysteries came to be generally accepted. They had an instinctive sense that something was flowing from Christianity which would gradually overthrow the authority of Rome. This is also the real reason why in the course of the first century and also in later centuries those terrible wars of extermination, which really were quite terrible, were waged with the underlying idea that once the Jews were slaughtered all those who knew something of the reality and traditions of the mysteries would also be eradicated. Everything related to the mysteries specifically in Palestine was to be wiped out root and branch.

This process of eradication also strongly entailed creating a barrier, a wall that made it virtually impossible to perceive the spiritual aspect of man's being or to find a path to it. It would have been dangerous for those who later sought to abolish the spirit on behalf of Rome, of Roman Christendom, if many of those from the ancient mystery schools of Palestine who still knew something about the paths to the spirit, those who could still have borne witness to the fact that man consists of body, soul and spirit, had still survived; for the impulse of the Roman world was that an outward social order had to be established where the spirit had no place. A stream of development was to be introduced that would exclude all spiritual impulses. This would not have happened if too many people had known something about the interpretation of the Mystery of Golgotha that lived in the mysteries. It was instinctively felt that what was to evolve out of the Roman state could have nothing of a spiritual nature. The Church and the Roman state entered into a marriage; and from this union jurisprudence, in particular, was born. In all this the spirit was not allowed to utter a word. This was important.

However, it is equally important that it is seen that we are now living at a time when the spirit must again be invoked, it must be summoned so that it may participate in human affairs. You can imagine how difficult this will be, since things have fallen to so deep a level. I believe that it will be a long time before it is recognized that the materialistic interpretation of history is a true continuation of the Eighth Ecumenical Council. I also believe that it will be a long time before people understand what lies in the few letters that distinguish the Eastern aspect of European Christianity from the Western aspect. It is sufficient today to speak about these matters in a superficial way and to pass only superficial judgements. Much will have to live on the level of feelings, and feelings can be a reliable guide if one thing is borne in mind. The feeling to which I refer and with which I shall conclude for today is as follows.

If one studies the history of Europe since the emergence of Christianity and is not satisfied with that *fable convenue* which is the travesty of history that is taught today and is the hidden cause of so much mischief, if one has a sense for the real study of history and has the courage to reject with sufficient strength that awful parody of history that passes for history today, one will—specifically in connection with the development of Christianity—arrive at a feeling which can be a leit-motif, a guiding principle, in one's endeavour to understand the present. One finds that nothing has met with so many obstacles, so much incomprehension and misrepresentation as the development of Christianity; and nothing has been so difficult as the fact that Christianity has spread. A further feeling that arises from this is that if one is speaking of miracles, there is no greater miracle than that Christianity has survived, that it exists. But it does not merely exist; for we live today at a time when Christianity will have to prevail not only against the abolition of the spirit but also against the abolition of the soul—and yet it will indeed prevail! Christianity will develop its greatest power precisely at the time of the greatest opposition! And through the resistance that must be developed against the abolition of the soul, the strength will also be found to recognize the spirit once more. When out of the spirit—please forgive the inappropriate use of the word in this context—that rules our present-age laws will be promulgated whereby those people who regard the soul as a reality will be declared as not being in their right mind (of course the laws will not specifically state that someone who recognizes the existence of the soul will be declared as not being in his right mind, but laws of this nature will nevertheless be enacted under the brutal impact of the scientific world-view), when, that is, this modern metamorphosis of the Eighth Ecumenical Council manifests itself, the time will have come to restore the spirit to its rightful place.

We shall then have to recognize that vague ideas are of no use unless one is aware of the deeper sources, the deep-seated feelings underlying these nebulous concepts. For behind such concepts is often hidden what modern man is most unwilling to acknowledge but to which has nevertheless succumbed. It is because he does not want to admit this and does not recognize it openly that it is manifested in his thinking as a punishment. Nevertheless, as Saint-Martin says in the more important passages in his book: 'These things cannot be spoken of.'[15] It is true that there are certain things that it will not be possible to speak about for a long time, but many things would have to be inscribed on stone tablets if people are to be made aware of what is actually going on. And in a not too distant future such a clear inscription will make manifest the hidden tendencies whence the materialistic interpretation of Darwinism has arisen, the perverse, sense-bound tendencies out of which the materialistically oriented theory of Darwinism has sprung.

However, I do not want to depress your spirits with something that could well disturb your sleep, so I shall not continue in this vein but simply allow you to ponder these questions. The next time we meet I shall try to present a framework for the building stones that I wanted to lay down as a foundation for a special study of the Mystery of Golgotha.

LECTURE 9

ON this occasion the Mystery of Golgotha will be the focus of our studies, which have been prepared by what I have presented in the previous lecture.

Let us recall the most important points that relate to this theme. Last time I mentioned that an essential part of any true and inwardly satisfying knowledge of the world is the insight that both the various aspects of the cosmos and the various elements of man's being need to be studied in the light of the three principles of body, soul and spirit. This is something that must urgently be recognized at present, especially in our anthroposophical domain. I should therefore like to point out that this threefold conception forms the central theme of my book *Theosophy* from its first edition onwards. You will all have read *Theosophy* and will know that the structure of the whole book is based on this idea, as is enshrined especially in these words:

> The spirit is eternal; the body is subject to birth and death in accordance with the laws of the physical world; the soul-life which is subject to destiny mediates the connection between these two during earthly life.

When I wrote these words I considered it to be necessary to refer to this threefold principle as clearly as possible. For only by emphasizing this idea as one of special and even central importance is one in a position to understand, or to endeavour to understand, the cosmos as a whole and, in particular, the central event of our earthly evolution—the Mystery of Golgotha.

In the previous lecture I explained to you the extent of the forces of resistance when the effort is made in our time to study both the world and man in such a way that the threefold principle of body, soul and spirit is not merely of secondary importance but is the central theme. I indicated the opposition to this in the cultural development of the West and showed that the idea of the spirit was lost in the course of this development. I mentioned that through the Eighth Ecumenical Council at Constantinople the spirit, together with the very idea of the spirit, was eliminated from western thought, and that this exclusion of the idea of the spirit has not merely influenced the development of religious ideas and feelings but has had a profound effect on all the thinking of modern times, so that among the officially recognized schools of philosophy today there are none that are able to distinguish between soul and spirit with any discernment. And even amongst those who would consider that they think in a completely different way, one encounters everywhere the rigid assumption—the sole source of which is the Eighth Ecumenical Council—that man consists of a body and a soul. Anyone who has any real knowledge of the intellectual life of the West—not only in the way that it is reflected in the more superficial realms of philosophy but as it has implanted itself in the thoughts and feelings of everyone, even those who would not even think of devoting any time to philosophical ideas—is struck by the all-pervasive effects of the elimination of the idea of the spirit. And when in recent times a tendency developed to draw upon certain elements of eastern wisdom, what was adopted was presented in such a light that it would be most unlikely to occur to anyone that the world and humanity had a threefold foundation of body, soul and spirit. For in the division of man's being derived purely from astral observation into a dense body, an etheric body, an astral body, sthula sharira, linga sharira (prâna as it was then called), kâma, kâma-manas and the other divisions which are an arbitrary collection of seven principles[1] there is no sign of what should be regarded as of the greatest importance, namely that our conception of the world should be founded on the threefold idea of body, soul and spirit.

One can therefore justly say that this idea of man's threefold nature has been suppressed. It is true that much is said about the spirit today, but it is nothing but mere words. The problem is that people in our time are no longer able to distinguish between mere words and realities. It is for this reason that serious attention is given to explanations and analyses which are really nothing but kaleidoscopic combinations of words, as for example the philosophy of Eucken.[2]

The essential nature of the Mystery of Golgotha cannot be understood if one is determined to reject the threefold idea of body, soul and spirit. As I explained in the previous lecture, the rejection of the spirit was enshrined as a dogma with the Eighth Ecumenical Council; but it had long been undergoing preparation. That this came about is fundamentally connected with a necessary development in the intellectual life of the West. The simplest way to gain some idea of how one may approach the Mystery of Golgotha from the standpoint of the threefold principle of body, soul and spirit is to form a picture of how Aristotle,[3] who stood at the summit of Greek thought, envisaged the soul. For Aristotle was at the same time the leading philosopher of the whole of the Middle Ages, and modern thought continues to be sustained by medieval concepts, however little people may want to admit this. Moreover, we can see that what was developing over the course of human history manifested itself in Aristotle a few centuries before the Mystery of Golgotha, and that efforts were subsequently made by the leading intellectual figures of the Middle Ages to understand the Mystery of Golgotha with the help of Aristotle's ideas. There is something of such great significance in these sequences of events that one really needs to take the trouble to investigate them in an unprejudiced way.

What is Aristotle's conception of the human soul? I should like to express in a few very simple words Aristotle's view of the human soul and, hence, what the Greeks had to say about it through the mind of this enlightened figure. Aristotle—and we have here the views of the most influential European living a few centuries before the Mystery of Golgotha—thought in the following way about the soul. When a human being comes into the world, when someone enters into incarnation through birth or, rather, through conception, he owes his physical existence initially to his father and mother. But, says Aristotle, only his bodily existence can come from his father and mother; the whole person could never arise as a result of the union of father and mother. Thus according to Aristotle the whole human being cannot originate from this union, for this individual has a soul. One part of this soul—for we need to be well aware that Aristotle distinguishes two parts of the soul—is completely bound up with the body, expresses itself through the body and receives its impressions of the outside world through the sensory activity of the body. This part of the soul arises as a necessary by-product through the person's material inheritance, which derives from the father and mother. This is not the case with the spiritual part of the soul, which participates through thinking in the general spiritual life of the world, in the 'nous', in the thinking of the world. This part of the soul is regarded by Aristotle as non-material; and it could never come into being from what is inherited from the father and mother but it can only arise from the participation of God—or, rather, 'the divine', to use the Aristotelian expression—in human procreation by father and mother.

This is how man, the whole human being, comes into the world. It is very important that one recognizes that Aristotle says explicitly that the whole human being originates through the collaboration of God with the father and mother. Man receives his spiritual, or as Aristotle calls it his reasoning or intellectual soul, from God. This intellectual part of the soul, which comes into being through God, through divine collaboration, with each incarnation of an individual, physical human being, is in a process of development between birth and death. When a person crosses the threshold of death, the bodily portion of his being is given over to the Earth, and with the body also that part of the soul that is bound to the organs of the body; whereas the spiritual part of the soul continues in existence. This spiritual part of the soul, says Aristotle, lives on in such a way that it is transported into a different world from the one with which it was connected through the bodily organs and continues to live an immortal existence. This immortal existence, according to Aristotle, is such that if the person concerned performed good deeds while he was in his body during his lifetime he is able to look back on these good deeds that he has contributed to the cosmic order but cannot change anything in this cosmic order in which he is placed. Indeed, we understand Aristotle rightly only if we interpret his ideas as meaning that the soul after death has to look for all eternity back at whatever good or evil deeds it may have performed.

In the nineteenth century in particular, the greatest possible efforts were made from various sides to understand what Aristotle meant by this idea, for it is often difficult to understand him because of the way that he expressed himself. It can be said that Franz Brentano, who died recently,[4] has in his controversy with Eduard Zeller[5] endeavoured throughout his life to gather together all the various elements which can enable one to gain a clear idea of what Aristotle thought about the relationship of the spiritual part of the human soul to the whole human being. And it must be emphasized that the way that Aristotle thought about this matter was passed on to the philosophy that was taught throughout the Middle Ages into modern times, and is still taught in certain ecclesiastical circles. Franz Brentano, who studied these ideas with a genuine intensity inasmuch as they derive from Aristotle, came to the following conclusion.

He made it clear that Aristotle was a figure whose inherent intellectual discipline enabled him to transcend materialism and therefore was in no danger of succumbing to the belief that the spiritual part of the soul evolves out of what a person receives through his father and mother. There were, thought Brentano, only two possible ways for Aristotle to envisage the spiritual part of the soul. One possibility was this: that the spiritual part of the soul arises through a direct creation by God in collaboration with what comes from the father and mother, so that it comes into being through the influence of God upon the human embryo; and that this spiritual part of the soul does not perish at death but embarks upon a path of everlasting life when the human individual passes through the portal of death. What other possibility would have been open to Aristotle, says Brentano, if he had not developed this idea? Brentano regards it as perfectly justified that Aristotle accepted it. There was only one other possibility, as a third one does not exist, according to Brentano. This second possibility is to accept the pre-existence of the soul—thus not merely its post-existence but also its pre-existence, its existence in the spiritual world before birth or before conception. But

Brentano very clearly recognizes that as soon as one even begins to admit that the soul exists before conception in some way or other, there is no alternative but to accept that it does not only experience a single incarnation but reappears again and again in successive earthly lives. There is no other possibility. And since, indicates Brentano, Aristotle in his later years rejected palingenesis (i.e. reincarnation), he had no option but to accept creationism, the notion that the human soul is created completely anew every time that a human embryo is created, which is not at variance with post-existence but denies pre-existence. Franz Brentano had originally been a priest and was, I would say, one of the last of those who represented the positive side of Aristotelian scholastic philosophy. It therefore appears to him eminently reasonable that Aristotle rejected the doctrine of repeated earthly lives and recognized only creationism and the post-existence of the soul.

This view, in all its various aspects, forms the basis of all Christian philosophy, in so far as this philosophy rejects the idea of repeated earthly lives. It is a strange phenomenon, both utterly tragic but also deeply endearing, that such an eminently capable thinker as Franz Brentano, who had resigned from the ministry, makes endless efforts to clarify his ideas about creationism and yet is completely unable to bridge the gulf that separated him from the doctrine of repeated earthly lives. Why is this? The reason is that, despite the depth of his convictions and the energy and sharpness of his mind, the very idea of the spirit was closed to him and he was never able to formulate an idea of the spirit as distinct from an idea of the soul. It is impossible to arrive at an idea of the spirit without acknowledging the idea of repeated earthly lives. The notion of repeated earthly lives can be lost only if one loses the idea of the spirit altogether. By the time of Aristotle the idea of the spirit had begun to be increasingly vague. From certain key passages in Aristotle's writings one can observe how he always becomes obscure when he is speaking about the pre-existence of the soul. In such instances his clarity always forsakes him.

All this is connected with something immensely significant and profound, namely with the actual course of human evolution. For during the centuries before the Mystery of Golgotha mankind had entered a stage of evolution when something of the nature of mist enshrouded the soul when there was any mention of the spirit. This phenomenon was not so marked then as it is now when there is any reference to the spirit, but the whole process of the corruption of thinking with respect to the spirit was already starting to manifest itself at that time. And this, my dear friends, is connected with the fact that the evolution that mankind had undergone had led over the course of time to the soul becoming different from what it had been in the earliest period of human evolution on Earth. In these primeval times there was a direct experience of the spirit because of the atavistic clairvoyance that existed then. It was not possible to doubt the reality of the spirit. Indeed, it was no more possible to do so than to doubt the existence of the sense-perceptible world. It was merely a question of the degree of spiritual perception that people were able to attain. But in these former times no one had the slightest doubt about any of this. And this conviction which was founded on an immediate awareness of the spirit came to expression everywhere in the mysteries wherever they were cultivated. It is striking that one of the earliest of the Greek philosophers, Heraclitus,[6] speaks of the mysteries in such a way that one can see that he is aware that in earlier times they were of immense significance to mankind but that they had already declined from their former greatness. Thus enlightened Greeks were even in these very early times already speaking of the decline of the mysteries.

There were various different aspects to these mysteries. However, only the central idea of the mysteries is of particular interest to us today. We shall dwell for a moment on this central idea of the mysteries as they were practised until the time of the Mystery of Golgotha and as late as the reign of Emperor Julian the Apostate.[7] In recent times certain aspects of the cultivation of these mysteries have been cited as having an anti-Christian quality. It has been pointed out that what is known as the 'Easter legend', as the Mystery of Golgotha, hence the central legend of the suffering, death and Resurrection of Christ was known everywhere in the mysteries. From this the conclusion has been drawn that the Christian Easter mystery was merely a transference of ancient pagan mystery practices and customs to the figure of Jesus. Thus many people seemed to think that, although they did not doubt the truth of the idea, there was such a common identity between the two that they needed to say: 'What the Christians say about the God called Christ, that He suffered, was crucified and was resurrected, that His Resurrection brings with it a hope and a longing for salvation extended to all human beings—indeed, everything that Christians have made of ideas such as this—is to be found in the mysteries, in all the different cults of the mysteries. Pagan customs have been brought together and fused into the Easter legend, and transferred to the individual figure of Jesus of Nazareth.'

In more recent times this tendency has been taken even further, curiously in official Christian circles, in that—for example in the case of certain Protestant groups in Bremen[8]—the historical existence of Jesus of Nazareth becomes a matter of indifference. People start saying that the various mystery legends and cults were brought together through a purely social process and had been centralized, and that in the early Christian community the legend of Christ had been created out of these old pagan legends. In the course of a discussion that took place here in Berlin some years ago[9] (during the tragic history of recent years all previous events have almost acquired mythical status and seem to be a distant memory, but the discussion was indeed only a few years ago), one could see that the official representatives of Christianity were declaring that there could be no question of attaching any real importance to a historical Jesus but only to an 'idea of Christ' which arose as an idea in the early Christian community through all manner of social impulses.

As one studies the pagan mystery cults it is very tempting to compare them with what emerged in the form of the Christian Easter mystery. This can be illustrated by a faithful description of the Phrygian Easter festivals. Other festivals could also be cited in addition to the Phrygian festivals, for there were a large number of such festivals. Firmicus,[10] for example, gives an account of the Phrygian Easter festival in a letter to the sons of Constantine. The image of Attis, hence of a certain god (we do not need to investigate any further which god this was) was bound to the trunk of a tree and solemnly carried round in a procession in the course of a midnight ritual, and the sufferings of the god were then celebrated. During this time a lamb was placed beside the tree. At dawn the resurrection of the god was proclaimed. And whereas on the previous day, when the god was bound to the tree and had therefore seemingly been consigned to death, there was a ritualistic outpouring of the most terrible lamentations, these cries were on the following day suddenly transformed into exuberant joy when the resurrection of the god was celebrated. Firmicus relates that the image of the god Attis was buried elsewhere. At night, when the sorrow had reached its climax, a light was suddenly kindled, the tomb was opened; the god had risen. And the priest spoke the words: 'Take comfort, devout people, for the god has been saved, and you may be sure that you too will be saved'.

No one could deny that these ritualistic festivals that were celebrated everywhere for centuries and centuries before the Mystery of Golgotha took place have a great similarity with what was enacted as the Christian mystery of Easter. Because it was so appealing to think in this way some people even believed that these widespread images and conceptions of the god who suffered, died and resurrected had in a certain sense been formed into a unity through Christian influence and transferred to Jesus of Nazareth.

Now it is important to understand the real source of all these pagan, pre-Christian rites. They can be traced far, far back to those times when the mysteries were developed from very deep, ancient insights about the being of man and his relationship with the world, as revealed to atavistic clairvoyance. At the time when the Phrygian festivals were celebrated, people only knew roughly as much about the real meaning of these rites as is known today in certain Freemasonic temples about the ceremonies that take place there. Nevertheless this can all be traced back to an originally grand vista of knowledge of the world and man which is very difficult to comprehend today. For you need to consider that man does not merely live in his surroundings by virtue of his physical body and depend on his surroundings with respect to this body but that his soul and spirit are also part of this environment. He derives his ideas and mental pictures from this outward environment, they become familiar to him and he makes them his own, and for various reasons he cannot free himself from them. Therefore even with the best will in the world it can be difficult to understand certain things, which for these and other reasons have been lost to the spiritual evolution of mankind.

Modern natural science—I do not need to reiterate at every opportunity that I admire it, for I do indeed despite my reservations—is concerned only with things at their most superficial level and leads to no more than the most minimal understanding of their true nature. It is true that science has made considerable progress in certain areas, but this notion of 'considerable progress' only means that one has understood something or other. To be sure, one cannot but have admiration for a science that has developed wireless telegraphy, together with much that plays a considerable role in modern life. But one may legitimately ask: how would it be if we had not arrived at this situation? If we were to pursue this question, we would firmly come up against something that it is forbidden to speak about today. Modern science regards the wisdom of which the last corrupted vestiges survived in the mystery rituals to which I have referred as pure nonsense, as sheer foolishness. This may be so. But as Paul said, what human beings regard as foolishness may often be wisdom in the eyes of God.[11]

True insight into the nature of humanity and the world yields among many other things (and today I want to emphasize those aspects that are of importance for an understanding of the Mystery of Golgotha) a particular view of the human organism that does of course seem completely crazy to modern scientists. For the human organism has very significant differences from the organism of animals. (I have already mentioned several differences, and today I specifically want to refer to one that relates particularly to the Mystery of Golgotha.) The human organism, as I have said, differs in significant ways from that of animals, for the animal organism—if one really studies it through spiritual-scientific means—has within it the seeds of death. To put it another way, if you make a serious study of the animal organism in the light of spiritual science, you can see from the way that it is constituted that it has to pass through death in its particular manner, that it disintegrates and is given over to the elements of the Earth. The death of an animal has nothing mysterious about it; it is no less understandable then that one can clearly perceive from studying an animal organism that the animal needs to eat and drink. That an animal has to die is apparent from the nature of its organism.

This is not the case with the human organism. Of course, we are touching upon an area that must inevitably be totally incomprehensible to modern science. If you study the human organism with all the means of spiritual science, there is nothing, absolutely nothing in the human organism itself which explains the necessity for death. We have to accept death simply as something that man experiences; but we cannot explain why it is that people die. Man was not originally born in order to die; not even his outward organism was made for death. That death occurs in a person through an inner process cannot be explained from the being of man itself. It cannot be explained from the way that man's being itself is constituted.

I know very well that this will be regarded today as perfectly crazy by all those who want to rise to scientific heights. Indeed, it is in general very difficult to discuss such matters, for they are actually connected with certain very deep mysteries. Even today anyone wanting to form a relationship to such questions encounters something that can only really be expressed in the way that Saint-Martin, of whom I spoke here recently, writes in his book *Des erreurs et de la vérité*. Thus in an important passage where he is speaking about the consequences for human evolution that ensued from the event that took place in the spiritual world before man incarnated for the first time on the physical plane, he wrote the following words about this event in the super-earthly domain which anyone who is intimately familiar with such matters will understand:[12]

> However much I may want to do as I am asked, the obligations that I have undertaken do not allow me to give any explanation whatsoever about this subject; and, moreover, I for my part would rather blush for man's transgressions than to speak of them.

In this context Saint-Martin is being asked to speak about an offence committed by man before his first incarnation on Earth. This he cannot do. Today it is possible for certain reasons to say much that Saint-Martin was not yet able to say—not because people have become better since his time but for many other reasons. But if one wished to discuss a truth such as that man was not born in order to die in connection with everything else of relevance to this question, this would necessarily raise certain issues that modern ears are not as yet able to hear. Man is not born to die and yet he dies! These words express something that is indeed an absurdity as far as modern scientists are concerned, but for someone who wants to arrive at a real understanding of the world this is one of life's deepest mysteries. Man is not born in order to die, nevertheless he dies.

This awareness that man is not born to die and yet dies flows as a hidden impulse through those ancient mysteries to which I have referred as the Attis mysteries. A possible way of understanding this enigma that man is not born in order to die and yet dies was sought in these mysteries; and they were expected to give an answer to this riddle. But why were these mysteries celebrated? They were celebrated in order that people might be able to hear something every year anew, something that they wanted to hear, wanted to feel, wanted to experience in their souls. What they wanted to be reminded of was that the time had not yet come when they had seriously to face the inexplicable problem of their death. So what did someone with such beliefs expect from the priest of the Attis mysteries? He had the instinctive certainty that the time would one day dawn on the Earth when the enigma of death would have to be confronted in all seriousness. But this time had yet to come. And as the priest celebrated the sufferings and resurrection of the god, this act of celebration brought the comforting message that the time had not yet come when he had to grapple seriously with the mystery of death.

It was common knowledge in these ancient times that the event described in what we may call a 'symbolic' way in the Bible at the beginning of the Old Testament referred to a reality. The people of these ancient times knew this instinctively. It was only through modern materialism that this instinctive feeling that the description of the temptation by Lucifer refers to an actual event was lost. There can be no doubt that the intellectual crudities displayed in the materialistic interpretation of Darwinism are to a very considerable degree at variance with what should be regarded as the actual truth of this matter. For these crude, perverted ideas would have us believe that in former times there were animals of a certain kind which gradually evolved into the human beings of today. The story of the temptation in paradise does of course have no place in the materialistic interpretation of Darwinism; for only a very degenerate form of intellect could conceive of the idea that a primeval ape of whatever gender could have been seduced by Lucifer.

Thus there was an instinctive certainty that behind the story that is told at the beginning of the Old Testament a previous actual event or fact was concealed. And how was this fact experienced? It was felt that the nature of man's original physical organism was such that he was not mortal, but that through this fact something was added to his original organism which corrupted it and thereby also implanted within it an impulse of mortality. Man became mortal as the result of a moral process, through what is generally—and we will return to this later—called original sin. Man did not become mortal in the way that the other beings of nature became mortal; he did not become mortal through natural or material processes but, rather, through a moral process. His mortality originated from the soul.

The animal soul as the soul of a species is immortal. It is embodied in the separate individual animal, which by virtue of its organs is immortal. The soul of a species departs from the dead animal as it had been embodied in it. But the organism of an animal as an individual organism is inherently constituted for death. This does not apply to the human organism to the same extent. The species soul or human group-soul that lies at the foundation of the human organism has the inherent capacity to come to expression in the individual human being and endow him with immortality as an independent human organism. Man could only become mortal through a moral act originating in the soul. In a certain sense man has to be endowed with a soul before he can become mortal. For as long as these ideas are regarded as abstract concepts, it is impossible to understand what is going on. Only if one makes the effort to grasp these phenomena as they actually are is it possible to comprehend them.

Now in ancient times—and also shortly before the Mystery of Golgotha, when these mysteries were being celebrated—people were very clearly aware that man's soul causes him to die. The human soul is in a constant process of development over the ages. Of what does this development consist? It is a process whereby the soul increasingly corrupts the organism and plays an ever more prominent part in the corruption which is the effect of its destructive influence upon the organism. People looked back to ancient times and said to themselves: a moral event has taken place which has led to the soul becoming such that when it comes to dwell in the body through birth it corrupts it, with the result that it does not live between birth and death as it would do if this corruption had not occurred. This situation has become worse and worse over the centuries and millennia. The soul has been increasingly corrupting the body! This is what they said. Because of this it is more and more difficult for the soul to find its way back to the spirit. As human evolution proceeds, it corrupts the body more and more; and because of this the body is impregnated ever more deeply with the seeds of death. And a time must come when human souls will, once they have spent so much of their existence between birth and death, no longer be able to find their way back to the spiritual world.

In ancient times this moment was awaited with fear and dread. The worry was that, with succeeding generations, the generation would eventually arise that had souls that had corrupted their bodies to such a degree and had impregnated them so intensively with death that it would no longer be possible to find the path back to the divine world. This generation will indeed come, they said to themselves. And they wanted to be reassured whether such a moment was nearer or further away. This was the purpose of the Attis rites and similar customs. The aim was to find out whether there was still enough of a divine nature in human souls that the time had not yet come when they had eradicated all trace of their divine heritage and could no longer find their way back to the Gods. It was therefore of immense significance when the priest said: 'Take comfort, devout people; for the god has been saved, and you may be sure that you too will be saved.' With these words the priest wanted to say: 'See, the god still has influence on the world, human souls have not come to the point of completely breaking off their connection from the god, whose resurrection is ever renewed!' This is what the priest wanted to tell them; it was a message of comfort that the priest sought to impart. 'The god is still within you!,' he said.

When we speak of these matters, we are unearthing feelings and emotions from former periods of human evolution of such infinite depth that people in our time, whose interests have become completely externalized, no longer have the slightest idea what those who were living then had to contend with. Although they may have known nothing of what is called culture nowadays and may also have been completely illiterate, they nevertheless had such feelings. And in the mystery schools where the last traditions deriving from ancient clairvoyant wisdom were preserved the pupils who were being initiated were told that, if evolution were to continue in the way that it has been progressing under the influence of that moral event at the beginning of earthly evolution, one would need to be prepared for the time when human souls would turn from God to the world that they themselves create when they bring death to the human organism through their ever-intensifying corruption of the physical body. Souls would unite with the Earth and, through the Earth, with what is called the underworld; and as a result they would be lost. But since these schools still preserved the wisdom of the spirit, there was the awareness that man consists of body, soul and spirit. What I have been telling you now relates to the soul, not to the spirit. For the spirit is eternal and has its own laws. From their spiritual insight people were enabled to say that souls will disappear into the underworld, but the human spirit will appear again in ever-repeated earthly lives. A future scenario of earthly evolution is approaching when human spirits would incarnate again, but they would look back upon all these soul qualities that had formerly existed here on Earth. Souls would be lost, and there would no longer be any souls. Spirits would reincarnate which would cause the human body to be activated after the fashion of an automaton, without the way that they activate the human body being felt and experienced by the soul.

What, on the other hand, were the feelings of those who were drawn to the Christian Easter mystery? Their feeling was that if nothing were to happen on the Earth other than what had already done so, human beings would in future reincarnate without souls. They therefore awaited something else, something that could not arise from within earthly evolution but was to enter earthly life from without, namely the Mystery of Golgotha. Their expectation was that a Being would enter earthly evolution who would rescue the soul, rescue it from death. There was no need to save the spirit from death, but it was essential that this happened for the soul. This Being who now forged a connection with earthly evolution from without through the body of Jesus of Nazareth was experienced as the Christ, who had appeared for the salvation of souls. Thus Christ is that Being with whom man can unite his soul, so that through its union with Christ it loses its power to corrupt the body and all that had been lost can gradually be restored once more. That is why the Mystery of Golgotha is in the middle of earthly evolution. From the beginning of earthly evolution until the Mystery of Golgotha more and more is lost as a corrupting influence increasingly takes hold of the soul, with the object of making people automata of the spirit; while from the Mystery of Golgotha until the end of earthly existence is the time when what had been lost before the Mystery of Golgotha is again gradually brought together. Thus when the Earth has reached the end of its evolution, human spirits will incarnate for the last time in bodies which will once again be immortal! This is how the Easter mystery was experienced.

For this to happen it was, however, necessary for the power that had caused the moral corruption of the soul to be overcome. This was achieved through what is recognized by Christianity as the event of Golgotha. There were some important words heard by the original Christians who were familiar with these matters. They were expecting an event deriving from wider spheres that would bring the possibility that the corrupting influence on the soul would be brought to an end. The words of Christ on the Cross, 'It is finished', rang out to them as a sign that now the time had come when the corrupting power of the soul had lost its force.

It was an extraordinary event, an event that encompasses vast, unfathomed mysteries; for vast questions appear when we survey the Mystery of Golgotha. We shall see as we pursue our studies further that the Mystery of Golgotha cannot be conceived of without the Risen Christ. The Risen Christ—that is the essence of the Mystery of Golgotha! Paul's words strike to the heart of the matter: 'And if Christ did not rise again, then our proclamation is without content, and the power of faith in your hearts is an illusion.'[13] The Risen Christ is unique to Christianity; and without the Risen Christ Christianity has no reality. The death of Christ is also an integral part of it. But how is this event portrayed? And how must it be portrayed? An innocent man was put to death, He suffered and died. Those who put Him to death clearly bear a heavy burden of guilt. After all, it was an innocent person who was put to death, and His tormentors bear a weighty responsibility. But what does this guilt represent for mankind? Salvation! For if Christ had not died, mankind would not have been saved. As one beholds this unique event of Golgotha, one is led to the realization that the killing of Christ is at once the greatest healing deed that has taken place for humanity and the greatest guilt that it must necessarily bear. Thus the greatest benefit coincides here with the weightiest burden of guilt.

A superficial way of thinking may well, of course, fail to see this. But for those who do not dwell merely on the surface of things this represents a profound riddle. The most momentous murder in the whole of human evolution has turned out to be for the salvation of mankind! Let this riddle reverberate through your feelings. If one really wants to understand the Mystery of Golgotha, it is also necessary at least to try to make sense of this riddle. A powerful key to solving it can be found in the paradigmatic words spoken by Christ from the Cross: 'Forgive them, Father, for they know not what they do.'[14] We shall see that the answer to the momentous question as to why the most appalling murder has become the source of mankind's salvation lies in the right understanding of these words.

If you reflect on all of this you will begin to understand that one has to approach the Mystery of Golgotha with the threefold conception of body, soul and spirit. For Christ died for the souls of human beings. He restores these souls to the spiritual world from which they would have been completely cut off if He had not come. Morality would have disappeared from the world. In a body that behaves like an automaton the spirit would be impelled by a necessity devoid of all morality, and nothing would be experienced on a soul level. Christ had the task of redeeming human souls. Should one be surprised if three centuries before the Mystery of Golgotha the most enlightened of Greeks, Aristotle, did not speak accurately about the soul and its connection with the spirit in view of the crisis that loomed before the human soul? Is it surprising that what he said about the soul was incorrect if human souls were confronted by this crisis and Aristotle did not know that the Saviour of souls was at hand? One should surely not be surprised at this! Another explanation will be necessary to explain why Aristotle's erroneous explanation of the relationship between the soul and the spirit persisted for so long. Christ's significance for the human soul is manifested to us in the light that enables us to discern man in his threefold being of body, soul and spirit, and in the inner relationship that exists between objectively real events and moral events—a relationship which will never be recognized for what it is unless we acknowledge man's threefold being of body, soul and spirit.

I have today merely been able to give you a preparation for explaining how deeply one needs to penetrate into the human soul if one is even to some small degree to be able to understand the Mystery of Golgotha. I believe that it is of very deep concern to us specifically in our time—and we may perhaps take advantage of the present Easter festive period—to enter more deeply into these matters, in so far as this is possible today. Much can perhaps be addressed initially on a feeling level which can be a seed that will mature in future periods of human evolution. For there are many respects in which we must realize that we shall only gradually become fully awake, that we are living in a time when there is much that we do not fully comprehend, whatever the particular theme may be. This is evident from the difficulty that people have today in forming a clear conception of events that are approaching us in a fully conscious way. Unfortunately it is impossible to indicate even in bare outline how the grievous event[15] of which the people of Europe or at any rate of Central Europe have recently heard should be understood in a clearly conscious way. Matters of this nature are for the most part experienced as though in a state of sleep; but it is not possible to speak further about them here.

My purpose today was merely to evoke some questions in order to use them as a basis for speaking next time about the Mystery of Golgotha.

LECTURE 10

BERLIN, 10 APRIL 1917

I should like to begin today by pointing out that it can be very easy in our time to misunderstand the essential nature of the Mystery of Golgotha, inasmuch as one does not realize how difficult it is to form a relationship of any real depth to the Mystery of Golgotha with the cognitive faculties that we generally possess today. It is very easy to believe, for example, that through mystical contemplation and by seeking God on an inner mystical path you will find the Christ. The majority of people who think in this way at present and for some time prior to it do not find the Christ. One will not find the Christ if one maintains, as do many theosophists, that if one can but be aware of the divine that dwells within one's own inner being the Christ will appear to one. This is not so. What may most likely appear and manifest itself as an inner light can never, if we understand it rightly, be called the Christ but could only be referred to as a divine being in general terms. And because people are not accustomed today to distinguish between different phenomena even if only in a theoretical way, many mystics believe that they can find Christ through what is usually called mysticism, through a mysticism that is relatively undisciplined. This is also not the case. It is important to bear this in mind, just as it is important to be aware that the philosophies of the late nineteenth century until our own time have developed philosophies of religion as subsidiary branches of their discipline, and that these philosophies are frequently deemed capable of speaking about Christ. The fact is that their research—and therefore also what they actually discover—is confined to what may be referred to as divinity in general but not as the Christ. Consider, for example, the philosopher Lotze, who was on a search for such a path.[1] If you read his philosophy of religion you will find that he is speaking of a divine being in general terms, but he does not speak in such a way that this divine being of whom he is thinking or meditating could be called the Christ. It is even less possible to discover anything about the essential nature of the Mystery of Golgotha through the mystical path or the paths pursued by such philosophies. In order to gain a closer insight into our theme we shall focus upon certain aspects of ideas about the Mystery of Golgotha, initially as pure expressions of opinion.

If the Mystery of Golgotha is to fulfil what is necessary for humanity in its historical path of earthly evolution, it is an essential part of its nature that the Being—that is, the Christ Being—who passed through the Mystery of Golgotha achieved something by doing so which has a relationship to the whole cosmic order. If we regard the Being who passed through the Mystery of Golgotha as separate from the world as a whole, we no longer have this Being in view; and although we may be speaking of some kind of divine being it is not possible that we are speaking of the Christ Being.

Among the many things that need to be understood there are some that I propose to speak about today. Thus a further question that must be considered if we are to approach the Mystery of Golgotha in the right way is this: what did Christ Jesus Himself mean by faith or trust? People today have a far too theoretical, a far too abstract conception of faith. Consider for a moment what is very often imagined by faith when one speaks of the antithesis between faith and knowledge. Knowledge is thought of as that which can be proved in some way, whereas faith is that which cannot be proved and is yet considered to be true. It is a question of the particular way in which one knows or understands something. When one refers to a particular aspect of knowledge or insight in terms of faith, one is thinking of it as something that cannot be fully proved.

Compare even in a quite rudimentary way this notion of faith with the idea of it that Christ Jesus presents. I shall refer you to the passage in the Gospel where Christ says: 'If you have the power of faith ... you will be able to say to this mountain: rise up and throw yourself into the sea, and it will be so!'[2] What a gulf there is between the modern notion of faith, which is really merely a pale substitute for knowledge, and this conception of faith that is expressed in this paradoxical and yet radical way in these words of Christ! A little reflection can enable one to discern the essential nature of Christ's conception of faith. What, then, is faith? It is an active force which brings something about. It is not merely an idea, something to awaken knowledge; for if one has such faith something will happen as a result. You can see this from the Gospels. Wherever you find the words 'faith' or 'trust', you will see that they are being used in this active sense, that one is to have a power that enables something to be achieved so that a tangible result occurs. This is of the greatest importance.

I should also like to mention something else of importance. There are many references in the Gospels to the mysteries of the Kingdom of God or the Kingdom of Heaven. In what sense are these references to mysteries to be understood? What is meant by these references to the Kingdom of God or the Kingdom of Heaven? It is difficult to form a clear answer. But anyone who has made a thorough study of the Gospels from an occult standpoint increasingly comes to realize that every sentence in the Gospels is as though cast in stone and that not even the fine details are a matter of indifference but are of immense importance. Any criticism that one might well understand if it originates from a scrutiny of the Gospels themselves is reduced to silence if one studies them ever more deeply from a spiritual-scientific point of view. In order that I may be able to speak about this mystery of the Kingdom of Heaven, I want to draw your attention to something that is highly characteristic.

In previous lectures on the Gospels I referred to that important passage which relates to the healing or, as one might call it, the raising of the twelve-year-old daughter of Jairus.[3] Since we can speak openly here, I can mention the deeper medical knowledge of an occult nature which becomes available to anyone who studies this miracle in a spiritual-scientific way. The daughter was twelve years old. Christ went up to her—you can read about the immediate circumstances in the Gospels—when she was already thought to be dead in order to heal her. It should be noted that one can never arrive at an understanding of matters such as this if one does not relate a passage of this nature to what precedes it and also to what comes after it. There is a strong tendency to wrench individual parts of the Gospel from their context and read them in isolation from one another, whereas they are linked together. As you will recall, immediately before this miracle took place, there is that passage in the Gospel when as Christ was on His way to the twelve-year-old daughter of Jairus He was touched on the hem of His garment by the woman with an issue of blood, who had had this condition for twelve years. As she touched His garment she was healed; and He felt that a power had gone out of Him. The words that He then speaks can only be comprehended if one rightly understands the idea of faith referred to above: 'Your trust, your faith has made you well.' There is a deep significance when the Gospel says here that she had the condition for twelve years; while the daughter is twelve years old, she has lived for twelve years here on the physical Earth. What was the matter with Jairus's daughter, what was the nature of her illness? She was unable to develop sexual maturity; she was unable to acquire what the woman had had too much of for twelve years. When He healed the woman who had suffered a surfeit for twelve years, He felt power streaming forth from Him. He then transferred this power to the twelve-year-old girl, thus giving her the possibility of developing sexual maturity, that is to say: He awakened within her a power without which she would have wasted away and thereby restored her to life. What is going on here? Nothing less than that Christ in the entirety of His Being is not living purely within Himself but is dwelling in His whole surroundings and is able to transfer the powers that He radiates self-lessly around Him from one person to another. He is able to reach out from Himself in an active way. This resides in the power that He feels arising within Him when the woman touches His garment in the fullness of her trust and faith.

This is connected with something that He often said to the disciples. 'To you who are my pupils it has been given to know the mysteries of the Kingdom of Heaven, the Kingdom of God; but those who are without are not to know these things.' Let us assume that the mystery of which I have just spoken—I do not simply mean the theoretical description but what had to be done in order to bring about this transformation—was imparted by Him to the Scribes and Pharisees. What would have happened if they had been able to transform powers that were related to one particular person? They would not always have done so correctly. It is apparent if one reads the Gospels that Christ did not always expect this of the Pharisees, and still less so of the Sadducees and others. They would not always have used the powers in order to transfer them appropriately from one person to another but they would have caused untold harm; for that was characteristic of their attitude. This mystery therefore had to be confined to initiates, as He indicated. I wanted to elucidate this point by means of a particularly explicit example.

There are three significant factors that we especially need to consider. I could mention many others. The day after tomorrow I shall say more about this, but for the moment I simply want to focus on the most important aspect. So there are three factors that we need to characterize if we are speaking about the supreme significance for the world of the Mystery of Golgotha. It will be necessary this evening for me to present something of a more aphoristic nature as a contribution to our theme.

We need to develop a clear idea of what is meant by the expression the mystery of the Kingdom of Heaven. It has a very definite meaning, as I was able to show by means of an example. Now when John the Baptist was about to baptize Jesus, he said: 'The Kingdom of Heaven (or the Kingdom of God) is at hand.' We can envisage this happening. What did John the Baptist do? It is clear from the whole context that, because the Kingdom of Heaven, the Kingdom of God was nigh, he baptized with water, as he himself indicates. He baptized with water for the forgiveness of sins; and before indicating this he said that one was coming who will baptize with the Holy Spirit. What is the difference between the baptism performed by John and the baptism of which he says that it is a baptism with the Holy Spirit?

We cannot understand what is meant by baptism with water or what it alludes to (and I have often spoken to you about the way in which the ceremony was performed) if we do not make some attempt to investigate it with the help of spiritual science. I have for many years been trying to elucidate this mystery with the help of those means that spiritual science makes available. It suddenly became clear to me that the whole way in which John the Baptist appears before us in the Gospels has something very, very significant about it. What, ultimately, was the water with which John was baptizing? Outwardly, of course, it was the water of the Jordan. But we know that the candidates for baptism were completely immersed, so that as they were submerged their ether body was loosened from their physical body and they were momentarily able to behold themselves clairvoyantly. This is the real significance of the baptism by John and of similar baptisms. But when John spoke of baptism with water he did not only have this in mind but he was referring quite particularly to that passage in the Old Testament where it says that 'the spirit of God moved upon the face of the waters'. For what was the purpose of the baptism with water in the Jordan? What was intended to happen was that through the loosening of the ether body and the experiences associated with it those who were being baptized should feel themselves transported in their consciousness to the time before the Fall. Everything that had taken place since the Fall was to be completely erased from their consciousness; they were to be transported back to the primal state of innocence in order that they might see what man's condition had been before the Fall. It was made clear to them that through the Fall man had taken a false path, and that if he were to continue further on this path it would not bode well for him. He had to return to the beginning, he had to cleanse his soul from everything that had entered his soul as a result of this aberration.

It was characteristic of many people at that time—historical accounts are somewhat vague on this point—to transport themselves back to the age of innocence, to wipe away the effects of these aberrations and as it were to begin earthly life afresh from the beginning before original sin took its toll, in preference to experiencing what had been enacted and legally formulated in the social order and national life since the Fall and until the time of the Roman Empire or the time of Herod, when John the Baptist himself was living. People such as this, who were of the view that it was necessary to extricate themselves from what the world had become since the Fall, therefore withdrew into the wilderness and solitude to lead the lives of hermits. This is very precisely described in the case of John the Baptist, in that he is depicted as living in the desert and feeding on honey and such animals as can be found in the desert and clothed with a coat of camel's hair.

Compare this with a widespread movement of that time which reflected in various ways what is indicated in the Gospel of St John. People were saying that one must renounce the world and develop oneself spiritually. This wish to withdraw from the world still had its most spiritual echo in Gnosticism; and it comes to expression in monasticism. But what is the reason for this? Why did this powerful impulse of the Baptist, which was a relatively recent development, become so widespread? The answer is to be found in the words: 'The Kingdom of Heaven, or the Kingdom of God, is at hand.'

At this point we need to call to mind what was said in the previous lecture about human souls, which have progressively deteriorated since the Fall and have been less and less able to fulfil the function that they need to perform for the human body because of their increasingly corrupted state. This progressive decline could continue for a certain period of earthly evolution, but it would eventually have to come to an end; and this will happen when the course of earthly evolution comes to be governed by an impulse deriving from the heavenly world. People such as John had a prophetic vision of this: he saw that the time had now come when human souls would perish altogether unless something else were to intervene. Human souls must either withdraw from life as it has been since the Fall, which has been the cause of their corrupted state—in which case earthly evolution would all have been for nothing—or something else must happen! This is what John the Baptist had in mind when he said: 'One will come after me who will baptize with the Holy Spirit.' John could rescue people from the consequences of the Fall only by facilitating their withdrawal from the world. Christ Jesus wished to save them in a different way; he wanted them to remain in the world and yet find salvation. He did not want them to return to the time before the Fall; rather did He want them to experience the further stages of earthly evolution and yet also participate in the Kingdom of Heaven.

A further aspect that needs to be understood is this: what was Christ's real intention? There is evidence of this throughout the Gospels, but it must be experienced with the deepest possible intensity of feeling.

As you well know, there are the four Gospels. Despite a number of apparent contradictions, each of these four Gospels contains a certain core of facts and truths which were enacted or proclaimed by Christ Jesus, but in the case of each Gospel this common nucleus is pervaded by a quite particular mood. Here one needs to bear in mind what I mentioned to you when I was speaking about Richard Rothe,[4] namely that the Gospels have to be read differently from the way they are read today, that they must be read in the spirit that indwells them, in that distinctive mood with which they are pervaded. People read the Gospels today in such a way that they endow them with what they regard as a universal human ideal. In the age of the Enlightenment they saw Christ Jesus as an enlightened human being; whereas certain Protestant groups have created an image of Jesus where He becomes a typical nineteenth-century Protestant. Ernst Haeckel[5] even managed to turn Jesus into a proper monist in his own mould. These are attitudes that mankind must learn to outgrow. What really matters is to feel what lives in the Gospels amidst the atmosphere of their own time. It is important to gain some kind of experience of this.

Let us first consider the Gospel of St Matthew. It would be legitimate to ask: what is the purpose of this Gospel, what was its intention? It is very easy to be misled by all kinds of things that one readily accepts in these Gospels but which are actually erroneous interpretations. In spite (or perhaps precisely because of) the statement that 'no jot or tittle of the law shall be changed',[6] the Gospel of St Matthew was written by its author with the intention of generating total opposition to traditional Judaism. It is a polemic against traditional Judaism. The author of this Gospel places a challenge before the world of traditional Judaism and explains that it was the will of Christ Jesus to bring it to an end.

The Gospel of St Mark, on the other hand, was written for the Romans, and was directed against everything that had been built up in the Roman Empire, in 'the kingdom of the world'. It was an attack upon the legal structures and the social order of the Roman Empire; it was altogether a polemic against Rome. The Jews realized full well what they meant or, rather, what they felt when they said: we must kill Him, otherwise our people will follow Him and the Romans will come and take our land and our kingdom. The Gospels of St Matthew and Mark, respectively, were written against Judaism and the world of Rome. These documents directed the full seriousness of their opposition not, of course, towards the essential nature of either Judaism or Rome but against what they had at that time outwardly become as kingdoms of the world, as distinct from Kingdoms of Heaven or of God. Along with similar phenomena, these characteristics are not taken today with the degree of seriousness that they warrant; and there is, indeed, not even an awareness of this lack. A few years before the war the Tsar, who has now been deposed, wrote the following words in his own hand on one of his decrees: 'It is my firm belief that intellectual giants and giants of action will appear, and they will bring salvation and well-being to Russia!' As you may well imagine, if these giants of thought and deed in whom the Tsar had placed his trust had indeed materialized, he would have imprisoned them in the Peter and Paul Fortress or packed them off to Siberia! This is the degree of seriousness that we attach to words today. With such an attitude it is impossible to fathom the real meaning of the Gospels.

And what about the third Gospel, that of St Luke? Its real intention becomes apparent if one considers the passage where Jesus went into the synagogue and was handed the book of the prophet Isaiah, and proceeded to speak words from a passage that He found there: 'The spirit of the Lord is upon me. He anoints me to bring the message of the spirit to the poor; he sends me to proclaim liberation to the captives and new sight to all the blind. I am to lead on the way of salvation those who have been crushed.'

He then explained what Isaiah actually meant or, rather, the full depth of what he meant, by these words. And in the course of His explanation He contrasted what lives in these words with what He found around Him. He wanted to speak out of the Kingdom of Heaven in contrast to the kingdoms of the world and characterized this difference by speaking about the worldly kingdom of the Jews and by doing so in the synagogue. He said: 'You will respond to me with the proverb: Physician, first heal yourself! The deeds which we hear you have done in Capernaum, do here also in your home town.' And He said, 'Yes, I tell you, no prophet is accepted in his home town. It is the truth I tell you: At the time of Elijah, when the sky was closed up for three and a half years and there was a great famine in all the earth, there were many widows in Israel; and yet Elijah was sent to none of them. Rather, he was sent to the widow of Zarephath in the land of Sidon. And there were also many lepers in Israel at the time of the prophet Elisha, and none of them was healed, only Naaman the Syrian.'

None of the Jews was healed either by Elijah or by Elisha but only non-Jews or Gentiles. This was the interpretation that Jesus gave to His words in order to characterize the world around Him in contrast to the Kingdom of Heaven. And what happened?

'At these words, all in the synagogue became furious. They sprang up, pushed Him out of the town and led Him to the brow of the hill on which their town was built. They wanted to throw Him over the precipice, but He went through the midst of their ranks and disappeared.'[7]

You see, this is what St Luke's Gospel is directed against. No longer is it merely against the Jews, as in St Matthew's Gospel, nor against the Romans, as in that of St Mark, but it presents a challenge to the passions and emotions of all those who were in the vicinity of Christ Jesus. We must therefore take heed of the powerful and highly expressive impulse behind Christ Jesus's words, an impulse that did not have a worldly source but was derived from the Kingdom of Heaven.

The impulse of St John's Gospel goes even further. In this Gospel the challenge is directed not merely towards a small nation like the Jews or a large one like the Romans or even the whole of humanity with respect to the qualities that it has developed since the Fall; in St John's Gospel the focus is upon the spirits behind the physical world in so far as they have gone astray from their true path. The Gospel of St John can be rightly understood only if one realizes that, just as the Gospel of St Matthew is concerned with the Jews, that of Mark with the Romans and that of Luke with fallen humanity as a whole, its concern is with the spirits of human beings and with those spirits associated with humanity who have also fallen with it. Christ Jesus likewise calls the spirit-world itself to account. It is very easy for our materialistic age to conclude that anyone who speaks in this way is a fanatic. One has to put up with such criticisms, but what I am saying is nevertheless true! And the more one studies these matters, the more obvious it becomes that this is so.

This powerful impulse which comes to expression in this fourfold way makes it plain that Christ brought something into the world which did not previously exist there. The world did not appreciate this, nor would it have done at any time. But new impulses do need to be given at various times. It is made abundantly clear to us in the Gospels that we can only understand what they mean if we see this meaning in the context of the whole cosmos, if we consider its relationship to cosmic events. This is most clearly apparent—I shall use the Gospel of St Mark as an example, as it is the shortest and the most concise—if you turn to St Mark's Gospel for an answer to the question: Who was the first to recognize that through Christ Jesus a sublime impulse of the kind that has just been described was given to the world? Who recognized this? One might say John the Baptist. But it would be truer to say that he had a presentiment of it; this is particularly apparent in the description of the meeting of Christ Jesus with John in St John's Gospel. But who were the first to recognize Him? The demons in those who were possessed, whom Christ Jesus heals. It is they who are the first to cry out, 'You are the Holy One of God,' or, 'You are the Son of God,' or something of this kind. It was the demons. Christ had initially to forbid the demons to betray Him.[8] Spiritual beings were the first to recognize Him. So you see that the first indication that we have is of a relationship of the word of Christ to the spiritual world. Before human beings had even the slightest inkling of what was living in the world through Christ, the demons gave expression to this out of their supersensible knowledge. They knew this from the fact that He was able to cast them out.

Let us now relate what I previously characterized through one particular instance to the mysteries of the Kingdom of Heaven whence Christ Jesus derived His healing impulses. You see, if in accordance with the methods of modern research we ask about the source of the particular supernatural power through which Christ Jesus worked, we will not arrive at any answer with the means that modern historical research generally employs; for times have changed to a far greater degree than one might suppose. People assume today that two or even four thousand years ago human beings were much the same as they are now, that although they have now become far cleverer they have hardly changed at all. These calculations are then extended even further back in time to millions of years ago. I recently spoke in a public lecture[9] about predictions extending millions of years into the future and arriving at the end of the world. People have carefully worked out what certain substances will be like then: milk will be solid but luminous (I wonder how this milk will be produced, but we won't go into that now), albumen will be used to paint walls because of its phosphorescent qualities, so it will be possible to read the newspaper in its light. Dewar[10] put forward this idea a few years ago in a lecture before the Royal Institution when he discussed the end of the world as envisaged by physicists. At the time I spoke of these calculations of physicists in the light of the following comparison: that it is as though someone were to observe the changes in the human stomach or the human heart over two or three years and then multiply and work out what changes will have taken place in two hundred years and, hence, what the human body will be like in two hundred years. This is all very ingenious; but in two hundred years' time the person will have been long since dead. It is similar where our Earth is concerned. Although the wonderful calculations that physicists make regarding what will happen after millions of years may be very accurately done, the physical aspect of earthly humanity will have perished long before this. And when geologists work out in accordance with the same methods what the conditions of the Earth were like millions of years ago, this is comparable to trying to deduce from the condition of a seven-year-old child's stomach what the child's organism was like 75 years earlier. People simply do not realize what havoc their thoughts cause, for in those times to which geologists go back in their calculations mankind did not exist as a physical entity. Because powerful remedies are necessary to combat many errors of our time which are put forward with a considerable weight of authority, one should not be afraid of counteracting such ideas with strong medicines for those who need them. One could say to such people: you are calculating what a human organism will be like in two hundred years in accordance with the changes taking place in it now; but it will of course no longer be alive as a human organism in two hundred years! Or one can make them aware that, as is evident from the occult research that I have undertaken (I realize of course that modern science regards this as nonsense, but it is nevertheless true), humanity as it is now will in four thousand years from now[11] no longer exist, no more than someone who is 20 years old at present will still be living after two hundred years. For one may learn through occult research that during the sixth millennium women as they are constituted today will become barren and will no longer bear children. Completely different arrangements will come into effect in the sixth millennium! This is demonstrated through occult research. I know that to someone who thinks in accordance with modern science it will seem totally absurd to say such a thing; but this is what will eventually happen. In our modern materialistic age people have very confused ideas as to the historical course of earthly evolution. This is why we no longer understand such subtle allusions to differently formed soul constitutions in relatively recent times as are transmitted to us even purely outwardly by history.

There is a very beautiful passage in the writings of the Church Father Tertullian,[12] who lived at the turn of the second century AD (150– c. 220), a little over two centuries after the Mystery of Golgotha. He writes that he had himself still seen the pulpits of the apostles where in a variety of places their successors read aloud from the letters that were still in the apostles' handwriting. Tertullian indicates that as the letters were being read, the voices of the apostles seemed to become audible again; and that when one looked at the letters the figures of the apostles themselves became visible to spiritual sight. These are not mere empty words for someone who perceives these phenomena clairvoyantly. The faithful sat before these pulpits in such a way that they heard the sound of the apostles' voices sounding forth from the timbre that they detected in the voices of their successors, and distinguished the features of the apostles from their handwriting. Thus at the beginning of the third century it was still possible to form a living image of the apostles and hear their voices replicated in this way. Clemens I,[13] the Roman Pope, who occupied the papal see from AD 92 until 101, also knew these pupils of the apostles personally and knew some who had still seen Christ Jesus. There was a strong ongoing tradition at this time! Something radiates through this passage which can be investigated clairvoyantly. Those pupils of the apostles who listened to the apostles could hear from the sound of their words something of the manner and the tonal quality of Christ Jesus's speech. This is something of immense significance. For it is particularly important to reflect on this sound, this quite distinctive quality of the way that Christ Jesus spoke if one is seeking to understand why those who heard Him said that a special magical power resided in His words. A kind of elemental power took hold of His listeners; His words possessed an elemental power that had never been known in anyone else. Why was this? Exactly why was this so?

I have already spoken to you about Saint-Martin. He was one of those who understood what was expressed through the words of the Christ Spirit. One can see that he understood this, in contrast to nineteenth-century Freemasons. What Saint-Martin understood was the power expressed in those words, the power of that language which was once the common property of all human beings and of earthly beings in general, a language that came to be differentiated into several separate languages but was closely related to the inner word.[14] Outwardly, of course, Christ Jesus had to express Himself in the language of those who listened to Him; but the inner word which lived in His soul differed from the way that ordinary speech was formed and was imbued with the lost power of the word, the power that language once possessed before it was differentiated into separate languages. Unless we are able to form an idea of this power which is independent of these separate languages and which lives in someone who is fully inspired by the word, we cannot understand the power that lived in Christ, nor the significance of what is actually meant when Christ is referred to as 'the Word' (with which He wholly identified Himself) through which He worked and performed His acts of healing and expulsions of evil spirits. This 'word' had to be lost; for this has formed part of human evolution since the Mystery of Golgotha. It must be sought once again. But we are for the present in a phase of evolution where there seems to be little prospect of finding a way of recovering it.

I would like to remind you about one thing. A significant fact runs throughout the Gospels that needs to be very strongly emphasized, namely that Christ Jesus never wrote anything down. Scholars have even argued over whether He was able to write, and those claiming that He could write can only refer to the passage about the adulteress, when he wrote with His finger in the earth. But apart from this there is no evidence that He could write. Nevertheless quite apart from this, He did not write His teachings down in the way that other founders of religions have done. This is not fortuitous, and is intimately connected with the immeasurable power of the word.

It is important to focus in this respect only upon Christ Jesus, for there is otherwise a tendency to view His situation from the vantage-point of our own times. You see, if Christ Jesus had written His words down and had translated them into the symbols that formed the basis of the language of that time, an ahrimanic quality would have entered into them; for anything that is fixed in whatever way has an ahrimanic tendency. Words that are written down have a different effect from when there is a gathering of a group of pupils whose attention is solely focused upon the power of the spirit. It should not be imagined that the writer of St John's Gospel was sitting next to Christ as He was speaking and recording His words in shorthand as these experts here are doing.[15] It is of immense significance that this did not happen. We only realize the full significance of this when we have learnt from the Akashic Record what really lies behind those words that Christ Jesus directed against the Scribes, who derived their wisdom from documents. His objection towards them was that because their knowledge was gleaned from documents they were not inwardly connected with the source whence the living word flows. He saw that this must necessarily lead to the debasement of the living word.

But we fail to understand the full significance of this if we imagine that the memory of those who lived at the time of the Mystery of Golgotha was the same kind of psychic sieve that people refer to as memory today. Those who heard the words of Christ Jesus kept them faithfully in their hearts and knew every word. For the power of memory was totally different from what it is today; but then so also was the constitution of the soul. It was a time when considerable changes had taken place over a relatively brief period. We are not so aware of this today. We tend to overlook the fact that the history of the East was written in such a way that people either implanted into it what they saw around them or took over certain elements from Greek history. Greek history unfolded in such a way that it had a great similarity to that of the Jews; but the course of oriental history was very different, that is to say, the soul faculties in the East were altogether different. Hence people really have no idea of the great changes that happened over a brief period or of how that enormous faculty of memory that existed in this twilight condition of the old atavistic clairvoyance was lost relatively quickly, so that it became necessary for the words of Jesus to be recorded in writing. As a result these words of Jesus suffered the same fate as Christ Jesus discerned in the Scribes whom He opposed. I leave you to ponder what would happen if a pupil of Christ Jesus who faintly resembled Him were to appear today and were to speak with the same impulse with which He spoke at that time. I shall let you judge whether those who call themselves Christians today would behave differently from the high priests.

With this in mind we need to consider somewhat more closely the mystery of the incarnation of Christ in Jesus. What we need to be aware of is that it is important that we in a certain sense retrace the path that has been followed since the Eighth Council of 869 and rediscover the threefold picture of body, soul and spirit as the three aspects of man's being.

First, let us consider the human body. It manifests itself to us only as an outward phenomenon. And when we consider our own body, we also only observe it from without. Perception of the outside world is made possible through our body. Moreover, the concern of science—or what we call science—is with the body.

In turning to the soul, I tried to indicate its nature when I referred you to Aristotle.[16] When we are speaking of the soul, we should be aware that Aristotle's ideas are not so far removed from the truth; for what concerns the soul or the inner life more or less arises with each individual human being. However, Aristotle lived at a time when he was no longer fully able to perceive the soul's relationship with the cosmos. He therefore says that with the birth of a human being the soul enters into existence together with the body. He was an advocate of what one may call creationism, but he accepts that the soul lives on in a certain way after death. Aristotle does not say any more about this, because the knowledge of the soul had already become obscured. The nature of the soul's continuing existence after death is bound up with what people now more or less symbolically call original sin (or whatever one wants to call it, the precise term does not matter in the least); for original sin has had a considerable influence upon the life of the soul. And the effect of this was that, around the time when the Mystery of Golgotha came about, human souls were in danger of being corrupted to the point where they were deeply connected with earthly existence and with what the Earth was destined to become. The life of the soul therefore follows its own path, as will be characterized in the forthcoming lectures.

The third aspect of man's being is that of the spirit. The bodily aspect comes to expression in the link between father and son. The son in his turn becomes a father, his son likewise becomes a father and so on, and particular qualities are passed on from generation to generation. The soul as such is created when a person is born and continues to exist after death. Its destiny is determined by the extent to which the soul has an affinity with the Kingdom of Heaven. The third aspect is the spirit. The spirit lives through repeated earthly lives, and for the spirit everything depends on which bodies it finds for its earthly incarnations. On the one hand there is the physical line of descent, in which the spirit is of course involved, but the line of descent is pervaded by physically inherited qualities. The qualities that spirits find in the course of their successive incarnations are dependent upon the extent to which mankind has advanced or regressed. Bodies cannot be created by the spirit to suit its purposes. One has to choose those which are relatively best suited to the spirit that wants to incarnate; but they cannot be made in the way one wishes.

This is what I wanted to say in my book *Theosophy*, in the section that I recently read to you about the three paths of spirit, soul and body. There is something here that must be clearly understood. For if one follows the path of outward observation to its logical conclusion by studying the physical organism, one arrives at the idea of a universal divinity, an idea which represents the limit of the knowledge of the mysticism—and the associated philosophy—to which I referred at the beginning of this lecture. If, however, one wants to study the soul, one needs to follow the path to that Being whom we call the Christ, who is not to be found in nature, although He has a relationship to it; rather must He be found in history as a historical being. A path of self-observation is related to the spirit and to its repeated earthly incarnations.

A study of the cosmos and of nature leads to the universal divinity that underlies the process of our birth: Ex Deo nascimur.

The study of a true historical record leads to a knowledge of Christ Jesus, provided that it can be pursued sufficiently far—to the knowledge that we need if we want to know about the destiny of the soul: In Christo morimur.

Inward contemplation, spiritual experience, leads to a knowledge of the spirit in repeated earthly lives and—provided that a connection is found with the spiritual environment in which it dwells—leads to an intuitive knowledge of the Holy Spirit: Per Spiritum Sanctum reviviscimus.

Not only is the trichotomy of body, soul and spirit fundamental to an understanding of man's being but it is also the basis of the paths that we must follow if we really want to nurture a fruitful relationship with the world. You see, our age which is so chaotic in its thinking does not easily relate to these matters and for the most part prefers not to address them at all. As you well know, there are atheists, those who deny the existence of God; there are also those who deny the spirit. It is really only possible to become an atheist if one has no inclination clearly to observe the processes inherent in the natural world and in man's bodily nature. This can, however, only happen if one's bodily forces have lost their vibrancy. For unless one's physical senses have become dulled, one cannot really become atheist; for one will be constantly experiencing the presence of God. Atheism is a sickness of the soul. To deny Jesus Christ is not a sickness, for He has to be found in the whole course of human evolution. If one does not find Him, one will fail to find that power that rescues the soul from death. This is a misfortune of the soul. To be an atheist is a sickness of the soul, of the human self. To deny Jesus, to deny Christ is a misfortune of the human soul. Note the difference. To deny the Spirit is to be guilty of self-deception.

It is important to think these three ideas through and meditate on them: to be an atheist is a sickness of the soul; to deny the existence of Jesus is a misfortune of the soul; to deny the Spirit is self-deception. These are the three main aberrations of the human soul.

All this is necessary in order to form a basis upon which to approach the Mystery of Golgotha, for it is essential to become familiar with the relationship of Christ Jesus to the human soul. To this end the destiny of the human soul itself over the course of earthly evolution must be carefully studied. Similarly, there is a need to consider the effect upon the human soul of that impulse that extends to it from Christ.

In order that we can all reflect somewhat further about these matters, I should like to offer you by way of a conclusion the following thoughts, which may serve as a preparation for the ensuing deeper study of the Mystery of Golgotha.

A person today studies nature in the light of his education. This natural world is governed by its own laws. People think about the earliest beginnings, the maturity and ultimate state of the Earth in accordance with these natural laws. In addition to this there is the moral world-order. Kantians, in particular, feel subject to the categorical imperative, and there is a general sense of being an integral part of the moral order of the world. But just consider how feeble the idea has become in our time that this moral world-order has in itself an objective reality in the way that nature does. After all, even Haeckel,[17] even Arrhenius[18] and others like them, for all their materialism, were convinced that the Earth was moving towards a new Ice Age, or towards entropy or some such condition. But their idea was that the little idols that they call atoms will disperse and will be conserved—hence the conservation of matter! This fits in pretty well with the present view of the world. But these ideas about matter fail to take into account the problem of what becomes of the moral world-order if the Earth becomes iced up or enters into a state of total entropy. It has no place in earthly conditions of this nature! What becomes of the moral order once the human race has disappeared? In other words, the moral ideas to which people feel themselves bound through the urging of their conscience seem to be highly necessary; but if one is perfectly honest they have no connection with the natural order, with what natural science regards as fundamental realities! Ideas in general have become enfeebled. They are strong enough to provide the structure for our deeds and the stimulus for our conscience; but they are not sufficiently strong to enable us to think that our cogitations about moral ideas represent a real effective force in the world. Something more is needed for this to happen. What is it that transforms what lives in our moral ideas into a real effective force? It is the Christ! This is one aspect of the Christ Being!

If we allow that everything that lives in stone, plant, animals and the human body, all that lives in the elements of warmth and air, will go the way that scientific research predicts, that all human bodies will perish at the end of time, according to scientific research all our moral aspirations would—if that is not putting it too strongly—vanish into oblivion; whereas according to the Christian view there lives in the Christ Being the power which takes hold of our ideas and forms a new world out of them: 'Heaven and Earth will pass away, but my words will not pass away.'[19] It is the power that will convey the moral qualities of the earthly world to Jupiter.

If you picture the Earth as physical nature, in the way that you conceive of a plant, the moral order as the seed of the plant and the power of Christ as that which enables the seed to sprout up as the future Earth, as Jupiter, you have the whole imagination of the Gospels as it can be restored from spiritual-scientific research!

But how can this be? How can that which—according to a materialist—lives only in the realm of thought and is a mere idea to which one feels a moral obligation, how can this be transported into a reality such as that which burns in coal or flies through the air with a bullet? How can so tenuous a moral idea become a solid reality? A new impulse is needed for this. This moral idea needs to be taken hold of by something else. What is the nature of this impulse? Recall what we said previously: faith should not merely be a substitute for knowledge but needs to bring something about. Its task is to make our moral ideas a reality, to transform them into the basis for a new world. What matters is that our articles of faith are not merely unproven knowledge, something that people believe because they do not know it, but that our faith has the power to transform the seed of morality into a cosmic reality. This power had to be introduced into earthly evolution through the Mystery of Golgotha. It had to be implanted in the souls of the disciples through their being told about the loss suffered by those who possessed only the written records. What matters is the power of faith. And if we do not understand what Christ means when He so often uses the words 'faith' or 'belief', we do not understand what entered into earthly evolution at the time of the Mystery of Golgotha.

You can now also see that the Mystery of Golgotha has a cosmic significance. For the natural order is subject to the laws of nature. But just as at a certain stage of development the plant brings its seed to fruition, so did the Mystery of Golgotha manifest itself as a new seed which will be available for the future Jupiter evolution in which the reincarnating human being will participate.

Thus from our study of the unique nature of the Christ Being, I have indicated how this Being is related to the cosmos as a whole and how, at a certain point in earthly evolution, this evolution was revitalized with a youthful energy. This comes very clearly to manifestation from time to time, though only for those who can perceive it in imaginative consciousness. The author of St Mark's Gospel gives us an example of this. When Christ was taken prisoner as a result of Judas's betrayal of Him, the author of the Gospel perceived through his spiritual perception of this scene that among those fleeing there was a youth clothed only with a linen shirt. This garment was torn from him but he wrenched himself free and escaped. This is the same youth who, according to the same Gospel, was sitting beside the tomb clothed in a long white garment announcing that Christ had risen. Such is the way that St Mark's Gospel describes this event through imaginative perception. In this scene the body of Christ Jesus deriving from ancient times and the seed of a new world-order encounter one another in this clairvoyantly perceived vision.

Try to feel this—and I shall conclude today's lecture with this thought—in connection with what I said recently, namely that the human body was not originally ordained for death but for immortality. Ponder this together with the truth that the organism of animals is inherently mortal, whereas man's organism is not. He is mortal only because his soul has been corrupted, a state of being that has been redeemed by Christ. If you bear this in mind, you will understand that the living power that will stream into earthly evolution through the Mystery of Golgotha will indeed have an influence upon the human body. At the end of earthly evolution the power that was lost through the Fall and which brings about the disintegration of the human body will be regained, will be restored through the power of Christ, and human bodies will be seen in their true physical form. If one recognizes the trichotomy of body, soul and spirit, the 'resurrection of the body' also acquires its full significance. Otherwise it remains a mystery. A modern rationalist will of course regard this as a thoroughly reactionary idea, but anyone who understands repeated earthly lives from a wellspring of truth is also aware of the real significance of the resurrection of human bodies at the end of Earth existence. And when Paul rightly says, 'And if Christ did not rise again, then our proclamation is without content, and the power of faith in your hearts is an illusion,'[20] we know from our spiritual-scientific studies that this is a testimony of the truth. But if this is true, it is equally true to say that if earthly evolution were not to lead to the conserving of the form that man has the potential to develop over the course of earthly evolution in his bodily nature, if this form were to perish and if man were to be unable to resurrect through the power of Christ,[21] the Mystery of Golgotha would have been in vain and the faith that it inspired would have been equally devoid of fulfilment. This is the necessary implication of Paul's words.

LECTURE 11

BERLIN, 12 APRIL 1917

The more that one studies the Mystery of Golgotha in accordance with spiritual-scientific principles, one comes to recognize that future ages will need to penetrate this mystery to an ever greater degree. Moreover, in many respects one will come to realize that what has been understood of the Mystery of Golgotha hitherto and also what is known of it today is merely a preparation for the understanding that needs to be developed of this mystery and, quite especially, for what needs to be enacted by earthly humanity as a result of it. There can be absolutely no doubt that it will eventually be possible that what we are today obliged to explain within the anthroposophical movement in a somewhat involved way and in a manner that many people would probably regard as difficult to understand will be imparted to humanity in a few simple words. We may well anticipate that this will be so. But the deepest truths cannot always readily be conveyed in simple formulations. We must therefore accept it as the karma of our time that there is much that we need to bring together today in order to make ourselves aware of the full gravity and importance of the Mystery of Golgotha.

In today's discussion, which is again of a somewhat aphoristic nature, I should like to begin by saying how necessary it is that we attach great importance to the ideas of 'faith' and 'trust' which we have been considering recently.

We need to be clearly aware that the conventional materialistic view of the world, if we may refer to it as such, is in the process of excluding moral considerations from its understanding of the world. I have explained on a number of occasions the extent to which this aim is striven for not only in academic circles but also in the everyday thinking of ordinary people. The impression that one may have today is that people are interested only in which physical and chemical laws could have given rise to earthly existence out of a primal nebula at the dawn of earthly time, and the endeavour is to understand how these physical laws will determine that in due course the world as we know it will come to an end. To a certain extent we acquire our moral ideas in conjunction with these physical notions of reality; and as I have already pointed out, they are not sufficiently strong to be a force of reality in themselves. We have to accept that this is the situation today. Moreover, this situation will continue to deteriorate. After all, for anyone who is firmly grounded in the scientific outlook it is of course pure fantasy, even a form of superstition, to suggest that a deed or event with a moral foundation, such as the biblical story of the Fall, stands at the beginning of our earthly existence. It is also the case that the minds of people today are incapable of envisaging a moral development extending from our present time to the end of earthly existence, with the result that the physical and chemical processes at work in earthly substance would be uplifted through a moral development to another planetary existence, to a Jupiter existence. Scientific ideas about physical realities and moral ideas exist alongside one another, but they cannot, so to speak, 'tolerate' one another. Science endeavours to exclude everything to do with morality from its methods of observation, while morality is, I would say, beginning to be resigned to the idea that it does not have the forces that are capable of grounding it in the physical world. And the dogmatism of certain religions serves to reinforce ideas which perpetuate the cleavage with natural science, in that the scientist emphasizes that morality needs to be very clearly separated from interpretations arising from disciplines such as physics, chemistry and geology.

I want to begin my lecture today with something that apparently has no connection with our subject, but it will lead directly to the theme of our studies. I should first like to point out that not all those who have devoted themselves to studying the world in one way or another have been disposed to exclude all moral judgements from their studies of natural phenomena and the processes associated with them. It would not occur to a modern botanist to apply moral concepts to a study of the laws underlying the growth of plants. He would even regard it as childish to attribute moral standards to the vegetation of plants or to consult plants about their moral life. Just imagine how someone who even suggested such an idea would be regarded. But not all people were like this. Indeed, I should like to give you a characteristic example of a person who was not, someone whom many people would not regard as a Christian but who was more Christian in his outlook on the world than many others. If you refer to studies of Goethe, especially by Catholic authors, you will find the view that—and because he was a person of a certain stature he is sometimes treated indulgently—he did not take Christianity seriously. (This is emphasized particularly strongly in Catholic studies on Goethe.) However, there was something deeply Christian about Goethe's whole disposition and attitude, far more so than many so-called Christians who at every opportunity have the words 'Lord, Lord' on their lips. Goethe did not constantly invoke the Lord, but his view of the world had a deeply Christian quality. I should now like to draw your attention to something about Goethe that is not so generally recognized.

As we know, in his theory of metamorphosis Goethe tried to gain insight into the growth of plants. I have often spoken of how he arrived at the ideas underlying this theory in a conversation with Schiller[1] after they had both heard a lecture by Professor Batsch[2] in Jena. Schiller did not greatly appreciate the way Batsch spoke about plants, saying that all this analysing and classifying was unnecessary and that it should be possible to think of a completely different approach. Goethe then made a simple sketch of his idea of the metamorphosis of plants in order to show how one might conceive of a spiritual link between the separate phenomena of the plant world. Schiller replied: 'That is not an experience; it is an idea.' Goethe did not really understand this objection, and then said: 'I am very glad that I have ideas without knowing it and that I can even perceive them with my eyes.' Thus he did not understand how something that is derived from reality, like a sound or a colour, could be described as an idea. He maintained that he saw his ideas with his eyes. This makes it apparent that Goethe was trying to perceive the spiritual aspect of plant growth in this particular case.

Now Goethe was well aware that he was only able to a certain extent to impart what he wanted to say to his contemporaries, and that for certain things the time had not yet come. It then turned out that others who specialized in the field of natural history had been stimulated by Goethe's theory of metamorphosis—for example, the botanists Schelver[3] and Henschel.[4] Schelver and Henschel wrote some remarkable things about the growth of plants, some quite remarkable things, of which Goethe strongly approved. For modern botanists the whole history of this collaboration between Goethe, Schelver and Henschel is utter nonsense. However, in such an instance one always has to recall the words of Paul, where he says that what is foolishness in the sight of men may be the greatest wisdom in the eyes of God. Goethe wrote some aphoristic thoughts about the impressions that he received from the way that Schelver presented his ideas.

I shall now say a few words about what Schelver wanted to establish. The whole way in which people, and botanists in particular, studied plants was anathema to him. In broad outline, what he said was this. The generally accepted view of plants is that the blossom develops on the one hand the seed vessel and on the other hand the stamens. The seed vessel or ovary is fertilized by the stamens and a new plant arises. To Schelver this was totally wrong, and he said that such an idea is not appropriate for the plant kingdom. Every plant, he thought, has an integrity of its own simply by virtue of being a plant, and it can also reproduce its own kind. He regarded the need for fertilization as a more or less secondary phenomenon which he actually considered to be inherently wrong, as an aberration of nature. According to Schelver, the truly natural course would be for every plant to bring forth a further plant out of itself without the seed vessels needing to be pollinated by the wind in order to ensure the continuity of the plant world.

Goethe, who had always studied such phenomena as the transformation of the leaf into the blossom very attentively, regarded it as self-evident that the whole plant is able to bring forth a new plant through a process of metamorphosis; and he liked Schelver's idea. He now in all seriousness penned an aphorism which is extraordinarily interesting but which—for all its utter seriousness for him—is of course utterly non-

186 ✳ BUILDING STONES FOR AN UNDERSTANDING...

sensical to modern botanists. Thus for example he wrote the following in his article about Schelver:

> This new theory of pollination would be highly welcome and most becoming when lecturing to young men and women; for a teacher who wants to approach the subject in a personal way has hitherto been in a state of considerable embarrassment. Thus when such innocent souls have consulted botanical texts in order to further their own studies, they have been unable to conceal the fact that their moral sensibilities have been offended; these perpetual weddings where there is no freedom, and where the monogamy on which our morals, laws and religion are founded is dissolved into a vague lasciviousness, are completely intolerable to the pure in heart.

You see, then, that Goethe casts his eye over the plant kingdom and finds it intolerable that perpetual weddings are being celebrated, that constant fertilization is going on, and that he finds it—as he so delicately puts it—more becoming if one would no longer have to speak about it but were able to say that plants bring forth their own kind out of themselves. And he then goes on to say:

> Scholars have often, and not without reason, been reproached for in some way compensating for the unattractive dryness of their endeavours by enthusiastically dwelling more and more upon certain somewhat improper and frivolous passages in the works of ancient authors than is warranted. In the same way some naturalists, on discovering certain aspects of nakedness in good Mother Nature, have also had some ambiguous pleasure at her expense, as was the case with old Baubo.[5] Indeed, we remember having seen arabesques where the sexual relationships within the calyx of a flower were depicted highly realistically, after the manner of antiquity.

Goethe therefore considers it to be an excellent idea that this study of sexual behaviour with respect to the plant world should cease to be a preoccupation. This was, of course, regarded as a crazy idea even in his time; while today, in the age of psychoanalysis, when the aim is to explain everything in sexual terms, it is an ever greater folly to say that it would be beneficial to the study of nature if this immoral intermingling of the sexual principle could be done away with. Goethe expressly says: 'Just as extreme tendencies—both liberal and royalist in nature—can be observed today on every side, so was Schelver an extreme proponent of the theory of metamorphosis; he broke through the last limitation that kept it imprisoned within the former circle.' But he does not say that he lacks appreciation for these extreme views but on the contrary welcomes them with great joy.

One has to look somewhat more deeply into Goethe's soul— Goethe's Christian soul, if I may say—in order to discern what lies behind all this. After all, someone who studies nature as it is from the standpoint of modern science does not know what to make of ideas of this sort, for certain presuppositions are necessary to make sense of them. It needs to be borne in mind that plants as they are now are at variance with the way that they were originally conceived to be. Those who make a thorough study of the plant world are obliged to acknowledge that, when they study the original structure of plant growth, the whole way in which the pollen flies around and brings about fertilization does not correspond to the original structure of plants. It needs to be done differently! This makes us aware that the entire plant kingdom as it is spread out around us has descended from a different, original form to the form that it has now, and that the kind of observation of nature that Goethe undertook in plants as they are today was still capable of discerning an intimation of what the plant kingdom was like, shall we say, before the Fall, to use this symbolic expression. Indeed, we cannot understand Goethe's theory of metamorphosis unless we understand its innocence, its childlike quality, unless we understand that, with his theory of metamorphosis, Goethe wanted to indicate that what takes place now in the plant kingdom is not what was originally intended but arose only after earthly evolution had fallen from a certain lofty sphere down to its present level.

On this basis, you will also be able to conceive of the idea—the details of which I cannot enter into at present but will do so at some later point[6]—that originally the mineral kingdom was likewise not as it is now. And someone who studies these matters in a really scientific way will also come to realize that what I have said can also be applied to the animal kingdom in so far as one is speaking of the cold-blooded animals, but not the warm-blooded animals. Thus the mineral kingdom, the plant kingdom and the kingdom of the cold-blooded animals, which lack an inner warmth in their bodies that constantly exceeds the temperature of the external environment, these three kingdoms are not as they were originally intended to be. They have descended from one sphere into another, with the result that their situation is such that the sexual principle necessarily governs them today. These kingdoms have not developed the potential that they have within them to the full but need to be helped. Plants originally possessed a capacity not only to metamorphose leaves into blossoms but also to bring forth a new plant. But they now lack the forces to do this; and they need an external stimulus, because the region where the plant kingdom was has been abandoned. The mineral kingdom and the kingdom of the cold-blooded animals were also intended to be different from what they are now. These beings are, so to speak, condemned to come to a halt midway through their evolution.

Let us now consider the other aspect of nature: the kingdom of the warm-blooded animals, the kingdom of those plants with a ligneous quality, the trees (for the plants of which I have been speaking, those that have a regular pattern of metamorphosis, are the herbaceous plants that produce green leaves and stems in contrast to the ligneous plants); and we may include in our consideration of the warm-blooded animals also the human kingdom. In my previous lecture I pointed out that physical man, as he is presently constituted, does not fulfil the potential that his body has for immortality. But this insight has further implications. Not only has physical man lost the potential for immortality that resides within him but in addition these other beings, the ligneous plants and the warm-blooded animals, bear the seeds of death within them. They are not as they were originally, not as if they were created as immortal beings; they have fallen from what they originally were. Because of this, however, another situation has arisen for them. As I have said, the beings of the warm-blooded animal kingdom, the ligneous plants (those that form bark and a wooden core) and the human kingdom, do not manifest their original state in the form in which they are at present. Thus the former have not arrived at the end of their evolution; they need another influence. The beings to which I have referred as the second group, the ligneous plants, the warm-blooded animals and human beings, belie their origins through the way they are now; they do not manifest their original potential. The former are not reaching the end of their development, and the latter's present state is such that one cannot discern their original potential in it.

If you accept this as a foundation you can more or less predict the direction that the study of nature will need to take in the future. It will have to make a very clear distinction between what beings have the potential to become and what they are now.

The question now arises: what is the reason that all this has come about? All around us we have a natural world which, even if investigated scientifically, is not as it was intended to be. Why has this happened? How can we account for this? The answer is that man is to blame for this! And this blame arises from the fact that he succumbed to the luciferic temptation, as I have always referred to it, to what is called in the opening chapter of the Bible the Fall or original sin. For spiritual science this is an absolutely true fact, but it is one whose consequences have not only been played out in man but, because man was still so powerful and so strong, have—while initially influencing man himself—extended their influence over the whole of the rest of nature. Man involved the evolution of plants in his fall, so that they have been unable to reach the end of their development and need a further impetus. He also brought it about that, alongside the cold-blooded animals, the warm-blooded animals were also affected, that is, animals capable of suffering and pain similar to his. Thus man drew the warm-blooded animals into the sphere into which he has himself fallen through succumbing to the luciferic temptation.

People always tend to imagine that man has always been related to the world as he is today, that he has no creative involvement with the rest of nature, that animals and plants enter into existence alongside him apparently without any influence on his part. However, this was not always so. For before the present order of nature arose man was a mighty being who did not merely himself participate in the luciferic temptation but drew the rest of earthly nature into it; and this eventually culminated in the moral order being completely divorced from the natural order.

If one says something like this today, one is of course expressing something that is not to the slightest degree comprehensible to someone who thinks in a scientific way. Nevertheless, it will need to be understood in the future! Modern science is merely an episode. Despite all the services that it has rendered, despite all its achievements, it is an episode. It will be replaced by another science, which will recognize once more that there is a higher picture of the world within which the natural order and the moral order are two aspects of the same essential reality. However, one cannot arrive at such a picture through pantheistic vagueness; rather does one have to look very concretely at how outward existence unmistakably shows that it was differently constituted from what is manifested in the natural order today. One must therefore have the courage to apply moral criteria also to the life of outward nature. The materialistic monism of today, which takes pride in excluding morality at every opportunity, does this out of cowardice, out of intellectual cowardice, because it does not want to probe with sufficient depth to the point where, as was the case with Goethe (within certain limits which I have indicated), it becomes necessary to apply moral criteria, just as for a study of outward phenomena purely scientific criteria are required.

However, this possibility that I am speaking about, the possibility of once again thinking of the world as being imbued with morality, would have been lost to man if the Mystery of Golgotha had not intervened. We have seen that essentially everything that belongs to the purely natural order has in a certain sense been corrupted, that it has fallen from another region into the one where it is now and must again recover this exalted state. Our view of the world must likewise rise above its present level. Our thinking itself, too, is an integral part of this present view of nature. And when du Bois-Reymond and others like him[7] maintain that our thinking cannot penetrate to reality, when they assert their 'ignorabimus', that we can never know, this is in a certain sense true. But why is it true? Because our thinking has forsaken the realm originally ordained for it and must find its way back again. Everything is dominated by the influence of the decline of thinking. One can therefore say that those who assert that thinking cannot penetrate the essence of reality are to a certain extent perfectly correct; this thinking has been corrupted together with other beings and it must again be raised to a higher level. The impulse for redeeming this thinking lies in the Mystery of Golgotha, that is, in the new impulse which the Mystery of Golgotha brought to mankind. Even our thinking itself is subject to original sin and must be redeemed if it is to penetrate the true nature of reality. And our present natural science, with its obligatory amoral outlook, is simply a product of this thinking which has been corrupted, has fallen from its original state. If we do not have the courage to acknowledge this we will inevitably be standing not within but wholly outside reality.

It will become particularly clear what it is about the Mystery of Golgotha that is able to restore and revive what has fallen from a higher to a lower region if one asks oneself the question: What would have happened to an earthly evolution which has been drawn down to the level of the natural order (I say this not as the expression of some sort of crazy idea but as the result of spiritual-scientific research, whose findings are as exact as those of natural science), what would have happened to earthly evolution after it had been drawn down into the depths through the actions of human beings if the Mystery of Golgotha had not brought a new impulse? Just as a plant cannot fulfil its development if the ovary is removed, so the Earth would not have been able to discover its future path of evolution if the Mystery of Golgotha had not taken place.

Today we are in the early stages of the fifth post-Atlantean epoch. The Mystery of Golgotha took place in the fourth epoch, after roughly one-third of it had elapsed. There is evidence everywhere of the descending stream, and anyone who is not blind can evaluate this for himself. It is obvious that the kind of thinking that can penetrate into the essence of things has suffered a serious decline! Any real thinking or feeling about things that matter has deteriorated to a quite abysmal extent. Copernican cosmology and similar phenomena are, to be sure, valuable contributions to knowledge on a superficial level, but they do not address what lies beyond the surface; and indeed, they are the outcome of an ongoing failure to penetrate to the essence of things. This tendency will become more and more pronounced. Even today one could cite definite instances (at the risk of being accused of weaving fantasies) of what is likely to arise if this trend, which is already to some extent endemic, were to continue unimpeded; and the only way to bring it to a halt is for the impulse of the Mystery of Golgotha to become an ever mightier force.

I ask that you look with me for a few moments through a window into the possibilities for future evolution, and forget what I have to say as far as the outside world is concerned lest you are exposed to ridicule for describing plain facts; for to state anything of this kind will be likely to provoke a hellish degree of derisive laughter. If the beliefs that are currently dominant in, for example, purely academic science continue to prevail, if they were to spread and especially develop ever more strongly in intensity—and we are now living in the early stages of the fifth post-Atlantean epoch, which will be followed by a sixth and then a seventh age—certain phenomena will acquire some very strange characteristics unless there is a deeper understanding of the Mystery of Golgotha. Now if one speaks today about a new scientific view of the Fall in the way that I have done here, and, moreover, outside a circle of people who have been prepared over a number of years by acquiring ideas that provide proof that such matters can be scientifically demonstrated, one would of course be regarded as a complete fool at the beginning of our fifth post-Atlantean epoch; one would be laughed at and subjected to derision. If anyone belonging to the materialistic, non-Christian world were to notice that someone held such views he would have very little confidence in such a person. In the sixth post-Atlantean epoch, however, the situation will be quite different and specifically in one portion of humanity; and bitter struggles will take place in order to implement the Christ impulse.

The general attitude today towards someone who tries to speak the truth out of spiritual-scientific insights is to improve on him by wielding a rod of scorn or mockery or, as it is frequently called, criticism. In the sixth epoch such people will be treated medically! That is to say, by that time medicaments will have been discovered which will be forcibly administered to those who claim that there are such realities as good and evil, that good and evil have any existence outside legal statutes. A time will come when people will say: 'What is all this talk about good and evil? The state deals with all of that. What the law declares to be good is good; what the law says we should refrain from is evil. If you say that good and evil exist as moral values, you must be ill!' And they will be given medicines and be cured. This is the growing tendency. It is no exaggeration to say such things. I am simply enabling you to look through a window to where things are heading. As for what would follow in the seventh post-Atlantean epoch, I shall refrain from saying anything about that just now. But it is true nonetheless. A time will come—for one cannot reverse the developments that have taken place in human nature—when it will gradually come about in this sort of way that such people will be regarded by those holding conventional scientific views as being ill, and attempts will be made to bring about the necessary healing. This is not fantasy. Even the most sober awareness of what is going on now will confirm what I am saying. Anyone with eyes to see and ears to hear can see the first signs of this everywhere.

It is important to be fully aware of—and gradually translate into action in one's life—the reality that the human ether body is, quite crucially, not as it was originally intended to be. Among the various kinds of ether that it originally contained (and it originally had all manner of etheric forces present in their full vitality), the human ether body has today the quality of warmth. Thus man possesses warm blood, in common with the animals which he dragged down with him through his Fall. He therefore has the possibility of transforming the warmth ether in a quite particular way. But this is not the case with the light ether. Man does indeed assimilate the light ether, but he radiates it in such a way that only a certain lower degree of clairvoyance is available to perceive the etheric colours in the human aura. They are indeed present there. But man was additionally intended to have his own particular tone; he was endowed with his own tone amidst the harmony of the spheres and with a primordial life, so that it would always have been possible for the ether body to maintain the immortality of the physical body if it—that is, the ether body—had retained its original vitality. What then ensued would not have come about; for if the ether body had continued to exist in its original form, man would have remained in the higher region whence he has fallen. He would not have succumbed to the luciferic temptation; and altogether different circumstances would have prevailed in these higher realms. They did indeed formerly exist. Such individuals as Saint-Martin still had a certain awareness that circumstances of this nature once prevailed. They therefore speak of such conditions in terms of an erstwhile reality.

Let us call one of these circumstances to mind. People could not have spoken in the way we do now, because speech had not been differentiated into different languages; for this differentiation depended on a quality of permanence entering speech. But language was never intended to have such a quality but had an altogether different purpose. You need to develop a living picture of what man was intended to become. If even a glimmer of Goethe's way of looking at the world[8]—I am referring not merely to his ideas but to the way he implemented them—were to manifest itself amongst mankind, one would be able to see what is meant by such a statement also from the standpoint of a Goethean view of the world. Suppose that man still had the original attributes that he was intended to have. He would have looked out upon a world from which he was able to receive outward impressions. But not only would he be aware of colours and sounds, of what is transmitted to him through outward impressions, but spirit would also emanate everywhere from phenomena: with the colour red he would see the spirit of red, with the colour green the spirit of green, and so on. On every hand he would behold the spirit of which Goethe merely had an inkling when he said: if this archetypal plant is merely an idea, I can see my ideas, they are outward realities in the way that colours are. Such a way of thinking has a prescient quality. I would ask you to form for yourselves a fully substantial and utterly real imagination that spirit is indeed streaming towards us in a living way. If, however, outward impressions were to come towards us with such a vital energy as this, our breathing processes would respond to every outward impression that we receive (for our breathing always responds to the impressions that we receive through our head by way of our senses). Thus, for example, the impression of red comes from without; our breathing responds to this impression from within, but with a tonal quality. With each individual impression a sound would be elicited from man. Instead of there being a language with the quality of permanence, each thing, each impression would immediately be answered by a sound from

within. The word would be wholly at one with the outward reality.
What has developed in the form of speech or language is but the earthly
projection, the fallen or residual nature of this living, fluid language.
The expression 'the lost word', which is so little understood today,
captures something of this original language that is spoken together
with the entire world. The words 'In the beginning was the Word, and
the Word was with God and the Word was a divine Being' are remi-
niscent of this living communion with the primal spirit, when man did
not only have eyes to see but had eyes to perceive the spirit, and when he
responded to visual impressions with a tonal gesture from within his
breathing processes. The opening words of St John's Gospel speak of
this communion with the spiritual world.

   That is the one aspect. The other is as follows. In the process of
respiration (in so far as it extends to the head), as we breathe in and out
there is not merely an interaction with the outside world but a pulsation
is brought about within our entire organism. The breathing process in
the head responds to the impressions that we receive from without. But
the respiratory process also responds to what is going on in the meta-
bolism in the lower part of our organism. If man still possessed the
original vitality of his ether body something totally different would be
associated with our breathing than is connected with it today. For the
metabolic process is not so totally independent from the breathing
process, but the nature of its dependence is concealed; it is of an occult
nature. It would, however, be on a completely different level if man had
retained his ether body with its original vitality, if its life had not been
subdued to a certain extent. For it is this loss of vitality, not only
through the outward sheath of the physical body but also from within,
that is the cause of death. If man had retained his original potential, he
would have had a digestion of such a kind that something of a substantial nature would have been produced by him. This substantial
element would have been the one aspect. Man would not merely have
produced secretions but something of the nature of substance. The other
aspect would be the air breathed out by man, which would have been
taken hold of by the formative forces of what he had breathed out. This
would have brought forth in his environment the animal kingdom as it
was originally intended to be; for the animal kingdom is a secretion of

man, and it was intended to be of such a nature that man could extend his dominion over it. This is how we should think of animals; and this is the conclusion that we can draw from what I have put before you.

Natural science today is somewhat more inclined to the view that animals were originally far more closely related to man, as I have already said—not in the way that a crude materialistic Darwinism imagines, that man has ascended the ladder of evolution, but that animals have descended. Today it is no longer possible to see the original spirit underlying the whole relationship of man with the animal world. Just as the plant world is unable to reach the ultimate end of its evolution, so does the animal world not manifest its origin. Animals exist alongside man. Naturalists ponder how they may have evolved. The reason why they exist in proximity to man can be traced back to the realm whence man has descended. It cannot be found where Darwin and his materialistic interpreters look for it; it lies in the mighty events of prehistoric times.

You need to bear in mind the fact that I mentioned to you recently, that it is clear to anyone who engages in spiritual-scientific research that in the sixth or seventh millennium mankind will begin to become barren as this is understood today. Women will, as I have said, become infertile. Humanity will cease to be able to reproduce in the present way. A metamorphosis has to be undergone whereby a connection is sought with a higher world. In order that this can take place, and that the world does not merely fall into the decadent state where all beliefs and opinions as to what is good or evil are 'healed' or treated medically; in order that good and evil, all personal determination of what is good and evil, is not viewed as merely a matter of government regulation or legal statutes; in order that this decadent state has not come to prevail at the time when the present order of nature within the human race ceases to be able to maintain its continuation (for just as women cease to be fertile at a certain age, so is it no less inevitable that at a certain stage of earthly evolution human beings will cease to be able to reproduce as they have done hitherto)—in order to forestall this the Christ impulse came into the world.

With this you have a picture of the Christ impulse in the context of earthly evolution as a whole. I doubt if there is anyone who really believes that the Christ impulse loses anything of its majesty and sub-limity when one places it in the context of the entire cosmic order, when, in other words, one restores the Christ impulse to its rightful position in the cosmos, and when there is the awareness that both at the beginning and the end of earthly evolution there lies an order that is different from the natural order and from a moral order that is devoid of any relationship to physical reality. The Christ impulse had to come in order that the end of earthly evolution might be worthy of what lies at its beginning. This is how the Christ impulse may be viewed in the whole context of our earthly evolution. And those who understand the words of the Gospels not merely in an outward sense but who also summon forth the true faith demanded by Christ can find in the Gospels all that is necessary to foster an ever greater understanding of the Christ impulse, an understanding that can be equal to the demands of outward scrutiny and can once again relate the Christ impulse to the entire cosmic order.

Certain things in the Bible can only be understood if one approaches them with the help of spiritual-scientific research. Thus it is written in the Bible: 'Not a jot, not a tittle of the law will lose its validity.'[9] Many commentators interpret these words as implying that Christ wished to leave Judaism as it was and that He merely wanted to add a con-tribution of His own. In their view the meaning of this passage is that He did not want to attack Judaism in any way but simply wanted to supplement it. This is not what this passage means, and, moreover, no passage in the Gospel should be separated from its context but the relationship to this context in the Gospel needs to be identified. Anyone who studies this relationship (I cannot at the moment go into all the details that compel one to accept what I am about to say) will find the following. When He was speaking about jots and tittles of the law, Christ was saying that in olden times, when the law was brought into existence, man still possessed his ancient inheritance of earthly wisdom and had not descended to the point where he was now, when the Kingdom of Heaven was at hand, when he had to change his whole mental attitude. In olden times there were still prophets or seers who were able to discover the law out of the spirit. 'But you, who are now living here in the kingdom of this world, you are no longer capable of adding to or changing anything in the law. Not a jot or tittle should be changed if the law is to remain true. For now is no longer the time to make alterations in the law; it must remain as it is. On the other hand, it is necessary to try to rediscover the original meaning through the new powers that have been achieved. You are the Scribes, but you are not capable of understanding anything in the Scriptures; for you would have to rediscover the spirit out of which they were originally written. You are out there in the kingdom of the world, whence no new laws can originate. Those who dwell in the spirit are they to whom is granted the impulse of the living power' (which, as I said recently, had to be given in such a way that it was not recorded in writing by Christ). 'As for you, you have to take into account something quite different that cannot be written into the law, something that must live without the mitigation of words. You must begin to judge the world as something other than a purely outward sensory phenomenon.'

Thus was the first great impulse given to mankind to view the world as something other than a purely outward sensory phenomenon. This is something to which one can only slowly and gradually accustom oneself. Every now and then someone feels moved to speak from this Christian standpoint, and he is subjected to ridicule. Schelling and Hegel, although they are not regarded as proper Christians, especially by Catholics, have sometimes allowed themselves to say something genuinely Christian.[10] But they were sharply reprimanded for doing so. People have objected by saying: 'Nature is not as you describe it!' And Schelling and Hegel were induced to reply: 'So much the worse for nature!' This is not very scientific in the modern sense, but it is Christian in spirit, just as it is a Christian sentiment when Christ Jesus Himself says that however much the Scribes may speak about laws, that is not the real law. Not only have a jot and a tittle changed from the law but much else besides; for the Scribes speak from the kingdom of this world, from the point of view of the ordinary world, not from the Kingdom of God. Anyone who speaks from the Kingdom of God speaks of a cosmic order of which the natural order is but a subordinate part. To this one must reply: 'So much the worse for nature!' Moreover, if people had objected to Goethe's claim that the plant world is not determined by sexual reproduction on the grounds that if one studies the plant world one finds that seed vessels or ovaries are everywhere fertilized by windblown pollen, he would have said, if he had given his honest opinion: 'So much the worse for the plant kingdom if it is so bound up with the natural order!'

On the other hand, great minds such as these will always emphasize that something must flow from the human mind and be nurtured in man's feeling life in such a way that people are able to think, feel and experience that what a person speaks—the spoken word—will again be able to become a reality (and this needs to be so until the sixth or seventh millennium), and that this is able to have the same creative power with respect to the outside world as the seed has today. The word must regain its power; for what has become abstract today must acquire the creative power of the 'Word' which was 'in the very beginning'. And those who lack the courage to add to the opening words of St John's Gospel 'In the very beginning was the Word, and the Word was God, and the Word was a divine Being' the following words deriving from spiritual-scientific sources 'The Word will one day live again!' are not speaking in the sense that Christ Jesus meant. For Christ Jesus framed His words in such a way that they are strongly at variance with the outside—or 'this'—world. He has, of course, given the impulse. It is nevertheless true that there has meanwhile been a rapid decline, and an ever greater effort needs to be devoted to the Christ impulse in order to instil an upward movement to earthly realities. In a certain respect we have taken a step upwards since the Mystery of Golgotha, but for the most part this has happened without any intellectual awareness. Nevertheless, people must also learn to collaborate in a conscious way with cosmic processes. They must learn not merely to believe that 'when I think, something is happening in my brain' but, rather, learn to recognize that 'when I think, something is happening in the cosmos!' And they must learn to think in such a way that, to the extent that their thinking is entrusted to the cosmos, their whole humanity may likewise once again be united with the cosmos.

The changes that need to take place in our outward lives in order that the Christ impulse can really play a part in social life are not addressed by those people who already have some knowledge of this today; for there are particular reasons for this reticence. It is possible to speak about it only under certain prior conditions. I can only give some idea of the reasons for this. You may recall my speaking about a future time when people who acknowledge something beyond mere government regulations will be given medical treatment. Let us imagine this time! By the time it arrives a reaction will have been generated. One part of humanity will indeed be advocating such measures, but another part will be carrying the Christ impulse into the future and, hence, will bring about a reaction to them. A battle will then ensue between these declining and uplifting forces; and the Christ impulse will withstand this battle. When the etheric Christ appears in our present century, the Christ impulse will become such a vital force that it will be able to engender such energies in the human soul as will gradually make it impossible for governments to be founded on ambition, vanity, prejudices or error of any kind. It is possible to discover principles of government that exclude vanity, the quest for personal glory, prejudice and even rashness and error; but such a potential can be realized only through a true and well-grounded understanding of the Christ impulse. Parliaments will not make decrees about these impulses; they will come into the world in another way. This tendency already exists. A momentum has already been generated out of the longing not merely to understand the place of Christ in world evolution but to incorporate Christ into the social evolution of mankind. This requires thinking afresh about a number of things. It will require a certain strength of mind to take seriously the sort of things that I have been saying about the Christ. When He said what He had to say, there were those who were so incensed that they wanted to cast Him down from the mountain. One should not imagine that the course of world evolution runs smoothly. We have to realize that those who have the right things to say in a number of areas will already have met with the sort of attitude that Christ encountered in those who sought to cast Him down from the mountain.

All these preparations are being made at a time when people are anxious not to step out of line or give offence, to develop a reputation of some sort or stir up rebellion in one area or another; and there is probably good reason why this is so. Everything is being prepared beneath the surface of consciousness, but there is little evidence of it on the surface. On the surface of things there reigns the unchristian principle of opportunism—that unchristian principle which can never withstand the accusation levelled by Christ against the Scribes and Pharisees: 'The Kingdom of God is not for you.' We need to understand what is the modern equivalent of the Scribes and Pharisees whom Christ indicted at that time. There are many examples of people who apologize for or explain away things that Christ Jesus has said. There is in our time a preacher,[11] not one who is allied to a particularly dynamic religious community, who has said many wonderful things about Christ Jesus but he was not able to refrain from adding that, in his view, Christ was clearly not a practical person, for he advised people to live like the birds of the air, which 'do not sow, nor reap, nor do they gather into barns'; and this would not get you very far today. This preacher has not tried particularly hard to understand what the Gospels are saying. And it is true that there are some passages which present difficulties, such as this one: 'To him who strikes you on the cheek, offer the other also. From him who takes your coat do not withhold your cloak either. Give to everyone who asks you; and do not ask for the return of what is taken from you.'

When we read all that has been said in extenuation of this somewhat unpopular passage it has to be said that humanity today has made some progress towards excusing Christ Jesus for having occasionally said such strange things. Much has to be excused in order that one can retain at least one's own version of the Gospels. Nevertheless, it is far more important to understand what is being said—even though this is difficult because all these things are interrelated. All the same, one can glimpse something of the connection if one continues reading from the sentence: 'Give to everyone who asks you, and do not ask for the return of what is taken from you.' This is how it is expressed in St Luke's Gospel, but in St Matthew's Gospel it is even clearer:[12] 'Everything which you want men to become able to do, that you should first do to them yourselves.' These latter words do, of course, relate to the previous passage. Christ is here calling upon the power of faith and trust.

If Christ Jesus had formulated only those ideas which exist easily on the surface in the wider world He would never have been able to say: 'From him who takes your coat do not withhold your cloak either.' But

He is not speaking here of what governs outer life, for that is the concern of the Scribes and High Priests; He is speaking of the Kingdom of Heaven, and in this passage He is wanting to make it particularly clear that in this context different laws prevail from those in the ordinary world. And if you compare this passage with the way that it appears in St Matthew's Gospel—and much depends upon a correct translation—you will see that Christ Jesus wants to say something that awakens faith in man, which would in turn render all the laws and statutes concerning the stealing of coats and cloaks unnecessary. For, He wants to say, if you simply tell people, 'You shall not steal,' nothing is achieved. You recall that He says, 'Not one jot of the law will lose its validity,' but in the way that these words were originally understood they have no impulse for the present epoch. We must develop within ourselves the power under circumstances that are such that someone can take our coat to offer him our cloak as well; for if one cherishes the conviction that one should not treat others in a way that one would not want to be treated by them, if one firmly believes that this is a principle that everyone can share, no one would take one's coat. But this condition will only apply if the person whose coat is to be taken really has the inner conviction to say: 'If someone takes my coat, I shall give him my cloak as well.'

If there was a social order of this nature, there would be no stealing. This is what Christ wishes to say, because the Kingdom of God is in total contrast to the kingdom of this world. In a world governed by the principle that if I give someone my coat he can also take my cloak, there would be no stealing. But we must develop the power of faith, that is to say, morality must rest upon this inner power of faith and, hence, must be a miracle. Every moral deed must be a miracle; it should not merely be a fact of nature but a miracle. Man must be capable of performing miracles. Because the primordial world-order has descended from its lofty heights to a lower region, the purely natural order must be replaced by a supernatural moral order which does more than merely comply with the natural order. It is not enough merely to abide by the old commandments which were given under certain conditions, not even if they are transformed. It is necessary to become accustomed to a different order, one where if someone takes my coat I have in mind that I shall also give him my cloak, that I shall not take him to court. In the Gospel of St Matthew it states that Christ Jesus wanted to do away with the courts. But there would have been no sense in directly following the passage [in the Gospel of St Luke] about coats and cloaks with the words 'As you want men to treat you, do so to them' (Luke 6:31) unless Christ's remarks were aimed at another kingdom, a kingdom where miracles take place. For Christ performed signs or miracles out of His vast powers of faith deriving from a realm beyond the Earth. No one who regards man merely as a being of nature is able to do what Christ did. What Christ demands is that, at any rate in the moral sphere, there should be more living in our ideas than what resides in ordinary outward reality. In ordinary life what happens is that if someone takes your coat you take it back again! But on the basis of this principle it is not possible to establish a social order along the lines of the Christ principle. There must be more substance in one's ideas than what corresponds purely to the outside world, to ordinary reality. Otherwise there would be a strange degree of inconsistency between these sentences. For consider the whole sequence in question: 'To him who strikes you on the cheek, offer the other also. From him who takes your coat do not withhold your cloak either. Give to everyone who asks you; and do not ask for the return of what is taken from you.' And then: 'As you want men to treat you, do so to them' (Luke 6:29–31). And contrast this with the following sequence: 'If you strike someone on one cheek, see to it that he offers you the other one as well, so that you can also experience the satisfaction for a second time; if you take someone's coat, do not hesitate to take his cloak as well; if you want something from someone, see to it that he gives it to you' and so on. This would be the negation of the principle contained in the following sentence: 'As you want men to treat you, do so to them.'

From an earthly point of view Christ's principles are meaningless. They are simply a meaningless sequence of statements. They only acquire meaning if one presupposes that those who would participate in the redemption of the world initiated by the Christ impulse, whereby the world will be raised up once again to higher realms, must start from principles that transcend those of the outer world; for what will then happen is that moral ideas, moral concepts will again acquire physical force in the practical realm.

It requires an inner courage to understand the Gospels in the light of the Mystery of Golgotha; and human beings need to foster this today. To this end we need above all to take seriously all that Christ Jesus said about the Kingdom of Heaven, which must be added to, and opposed to, the kingdom of this world that has gradually been formed under the influence of the descending stream of human evolution. Indeed, those who in times such as the present are experiencing Easter may feel a growing longing to understand the Mystery of Golgotha with the necessary courage and, through this courage, to unite themselves with it; for throughout the Gospels there runs this theme of courage, the challenge implicitly to follow that impulse which Christ Jesus has implanted into earthly evolution.

Through such a description I wanted today to enable you to have a clearer insight into the Mystery of Golgotha, emphasizing that aspect which shows how the Mystery of Golgotha must again be incorporated into the whole cosmic order and can be understood only if one is aware that the Gospels are pervaded with a higher form of speech and not merely the language of human beings. In the development of theology in the nineteenth century, when theology paraded itself as an academic pursuit, the endeavour was to draw the Gospels down to the level of human speech. Our immediate task is to read the Gospels once more from the standpoint of the Word of God. Spiritual science will in this respect be able to contribute much to an understanding of the Gospels.

LECTURE 12

BERLIN, 14 APRIL 1917

I have frequently mentioned the name of Herman Grimm in various contexts in the course of discussing the intellectual history of modern times. I should like to link what I have to say today to one of the numerous instinctive (if I may say) remarks that Herman Grimm[1] made about the needs of recent cultural history, although he was unable to translate his instinctive sense for truth into actual insight; and I want to make a connection with one of the many observations that he made in this respect. It concerns a certain oppositional tendency which characterized Herman Grimm's relationship to the whole modern approach to historical research, in that he had the understandable feeling that this method of studying history unconsciously—and of course instinctively—set out to exclude the Christ event from the whole study of human history, to study history in such a way that no account is taken of the fact that the Christ event plays an utterly decisive part in the course of human evolution. Herman Grimm, on the contrary, wanted a method of historical research where Christ was regarded as a significant factor in the historical development of mankind, so that through such a study of history the significance of the impulse that entered human evolution through the Mystery of Golgotha would become apparent. As I have said, Herman Grimm had an instinctive understanding of Goethe's conception of the world, but because he lacked insight into the spiritual worlds this remained an instinctive feeling, an intuitive sense that he was unable to translate into intellectual concepts.

It may seem paradoxical to say that a method of historical research makes a primary aim of totally eradicating the Christ event from historical enquiry. Nevertheless, this is indeed so. It is a point of view which is so firmly rooted in the assumptions underlying the modern view of the world that many people do much at this very basic level to prevent the deep significance of the Christ event from being seen as part of the historical course of human events. One aspect of this instinctive attitude that lives so strongly in people's souls is that in the general consciousness of humanity there is almost total ignorance about these centuries that came before and after the Mystery of Golgotha. It is not merely that no attempt is made to undertake a proper study of the Mystery of Golgotha from a historical point of view (a tendency which is understandable for a number of reasons, which we have been able to adduce in the course of our spiritual-scientific investigations), but they viewed what happened both before and after with the same preconceptions, with the result that they were unable to perceive what actually occurred during these centuries around the time of the Mystery of Golgotha. One might say that people set about studying the history of these centuries in such a way as not to notice how powerfully the Mystery of Golgotha impacted upon the events of these centuries. When one bears in mind that our age, which claims to be free from all authority, is so very dependent on a belief in authority, one can also judge how thoroughly it has succeeded in suppressing virtually all knowledge of what occurred in the evolution of humanity during those centuries. And when an individual such as Goethe appears (and in the previous lecture I gave a particular example of his way of studying nature, which led directly to a conception of the world which views morality and nature as one), the attempt is made—albeit instinctively—to do everything possible to weaken the effect of or reject altogether that which in such a personality, if it was understood in the right way, would lead in an altogether amazing way to a spiritual-scientific view of the world.

One can then experience something very remarkable. As I have already indicated, Goethe was not satisfied with conventional botany; he wanted a spiritualized botany. As a result of his investigations he was able to discover the spirit as it is manifested in the plant kingdom, that spirit which the plant kingdom in its present form is unable to reach on the grounds that it is unable fully to develop its inherent possibilities (as I explained in the previous lecture). Goethe therefore tried to probe further into the inherent potential of the plant kingdom (and also of the mineral kingdom), more deeply than mere sense-perception permits; for sense-perception can only perceive what the plant kingdom has become. Hence it was particularly inopportune for Goethe that Haller's view of nature should manifest itself in his time, a view which Haller[2] beautifully summed up in these words:

> No created spirit reaches
> Nature's inner heart,
> Blessed are they t'whom she reveals
> Her outer shell alone.

To which Goethe replied:

> This have I heard for sixty years,
> I curse and swear, yet furtively;
> Nature richly shares her all,
> This I know a thousandfold.
> Nature has neither kernel
> Nor shell;
> Come test yourself if you but will—
> Are you kernel or are you shell?'

Thus one can say that Goethe was very strongly opposed to the view that a created spirit cannot penetrate to the inner essence, the inner kernel of nature. Why was this so? It was because there was a vast spiritual background to Goethe's instinctive knowledge which the nineteenth century did its best to bury under mountains of rubble. A scientist or philosopher of the nineteenth century would have been familiar with Schopenhauer's maxims 'The world is my idea', 'Without the eye there can be no colour, no light'.[3] Goethe opposes this with the logically consistent argument that it is of course true that light cannot be perceived without the eye; it is true that without our eyes the world would be dark and silent! (I have often referred—also in public lectures—to this characteristic nineteenth-century view.[4]) But Goethe goes on to argue that without light there would be no eye, for the light has formed the eye for the light. The light, said Goethe, has conjured the eye into existence out of undefined organs! If one goes deeper into this whole question, something quite extraordinary emerges.[5]

According to the indications that I gave in the previous lecture, the plant kingdom was intended to bring forth its own kind spontaneously, without fertilization, through metamorphosis. Fertilization would have had a completely different significance than it has now for the plant kingdom. Goethe had an inkling of this. That is why he took such great delight in Schelver's explanation of the fertilization process, and he had the courage to bring moral values into the study of plants. He had this courage. The plant kingdom therefore lives in a different sphere from the one in which it would have evolved purely through metamorphosis. This was the result of that great event of the luciferic temptation, whereby mankind fell from a higher sphere into a lower one. But the forces that would be active in plants if they had been able to bring the process of metamorphosis to full expression—if, that is, a new plant were simply to grow from the existing one without a sexual process of reproduction—have become spiritual, they live spiritually in our environment; and they are responsible for the fact that man has the sense organs that he has today. The words of Lucifer, 'Your eyes will be opened', signified that in this sphere plants were unable to reach their full potential, while human eyes were opened. The influence of the light was such that it could indeed open the eyes of human beings in the sense suggested by Goethe. But of course this opening of the eyes was in another respect a loss of vision. For through human beings' capacity to direct their eyes and their senses in general to the outer, sense-perceptible world the spirit dwelling in that world could not enter into them. These eyes of theirs were closed to the revelation of the spirit. As a result there arose that strange view, which developed with a furious intensity especially in the nineteenth century, which asserted that man beholds only the outer sense-perceptible world and that he cannot see behind this world. 'No created spirit reaches nature's inner heart. Blessed are they t'whom she reveals her outer shell alone.' This means that man cannot penetrate to nature's innermost essence. But with a heightened, purified consciousness he can do so, and Goethe knew this. That strange—I might even say dark—notion arose which asserts that man sees only what his senses can perceive. This notion, which in the realm of natural science is merely pernicious but is nevertheless useful by virtue of its corrupting influence, would in the field of art—were the artist to accept a view of this sort and were he not to work or, rather, create in defiance of it—lead to the destruction of his creative imagination. For this view would be tantamount to saying that Goethe's *Faust* exists only in books. We can see the letters, but *Faust* is more than the mere printed words. No one reaches 'the inner heart' of these letters; blessed are they to whom the letters reveal only their 'outer shell', their superficial meaning! Now there are certain philologists who admit that they are perfectly content with this, that what they see in *Faust* is only the printed letters. These letters must be there, of course, but if one is to understand *Faust* one has to see through them, one cannot dwell on them alone. They have to be there, but such people do not try to interpret them. There is a real lack of awareness of the extent to which what we have become habitually accustomed to in our materialistic age contradicts the most everyday realities of life.

We would, however, arrive at a different view if we were able to develop a certain sympathy for what Goethe was expressing in these words:

> This have I heard for sixty years,
> I curse and swear, yet furtively . . .
> Nature has neither kernel
> Nor shell;
> Come, test yourself if you but will—
> Are you kernel or are you shell?

One of the mysteries of human evolution is that if one distances oneself from this view of Goethe's and becomes wedded to that of Haller, one can study the historical periods before and after the Mystery of Golgotha in such a way that one altogether fails to see the real significance of the Mystery of Golgotha. This may seem paradoxical at first, but it is really the case. If one contemplates the course of history from the anti-Goethean point of view, one understands the pre-Christian period in such a way that one comes to recognize that some kind of historical event took place at the beginning of our Christian era, but the whole powerful impulse of the Mystery of Golgotha must necessarily be shifted to that 'inner realm' where 'no created spirit can penetrate'. One will then fail to see that, whereas historical events are clearly moving in a certain direction as the Mystery of Golgotha approaches, something then intervenes which represents a real turning point and indeed the greatest turning point in the evolution of earthly humanity; and equally, as one considers the early Christian period, one fails to recognize the repercussions of this turning point that lie hidden there. This is why there is an instinctive need surreptitiously to cause Goethe's view of the world to vanish from the purview of modern thought, so as to prevent it from becoming too significant a presence.

People sometimes give themselves away when adopting this instinctive attitude. I have no intention of levelling any moral accusation against anyone, for I am of course well aware of the objection that can be made, namely that someone who politely dismisses Goethe's views from the realm of modern academic study has the best of intentions! After all, there are the familiar words that Mark Antony repeats as a kind of litany in *Julius Caesar*: 'So are they all, all honourable men.' I admit all of this from the outset, of course; but what matters is not what one may say about a person's intelligence but what is the effect of what he says and what influence it may have upon human evolution. And one can sometimes, as it were, apprehend people as, in their well-intentioned way, they politely dismiss the Christ event by refusing to allow Goethe's views to have a place in their methods of study, views which if accepted today would lead directly to spiritual science. In this connection I recently came across a pamphlet which has had a considerable influence at the present time, where there are some reflections about history in so far as it relates to Christ Jesus. In this pamphlet any possibility of evaluating the Mystery of Golgotha as the greatest turning point in earthly evolution is instinctively dismissed from the study of history. The author can do this only if he views the whole of history from the perspective that one cannot penetrate to the 'inner essence' of history but can dwell only upon its 'outer shell', that is, look at it superficially; and that one's response to the most important event of all must be to say that one cannot penetrate to history's inner core. What is the author trying to do? I shall read to you some of his actual words, for they are most interesting.

> It is necessary to be aware quite especially of the fragmentary nature of even the most complete historical knowledge. The wealth of events, the historical reality of the past, is in its extent and content infinitely greater than our knowledge of it will ever be, even if we were to research into it for thousands of years. For out of the vast mass of events only certain aspects can be accessible to the historian, only what has been handed down to him through source material and records. Everything else that has not been transmitted and could not be transmitted, because it belongs to the inner life of the spirit, the unfathomable domain of the soul life and the inner motivations of the personal life, cannot be 'known' by the historian but can at best be surmised. And this 'surmising' will, however precise and conscientious our investigations may be, in all circumstances be marred by imperfections and subjective factors. When Goethe says, 'No creative spirit reaches nature's inner heart,' we must add, 'No one can penetrate into the inner core of history.'[6]

As I have said, I do not want to pass any moral judgements, but I shall merely state quite objectively: this is how Goethe is misrepresented after so short a time! This is how even Goethe is misrepresented! What he says is distorted so that it says the opposite, the result is communicated to the general public—who do not even notice! This extract is taken from a pamphlet called 'Christianity in the Ideological Struggle of Today', which was written in order to show the place of Christianity in the ideological debates of our present time. But the whole spirit that pervades this document is the same as that which characterizes this way of understanding Goethe. You have here a solid instance which betrays the sense of truth of those who have a large following today. I recently told you[7] that this same man gave some lectures not so long ago which clearly demonstrate that his thinking is always inconclusive and incoherent, totally corrupted with inconsistencies; and that he never even tries to penetrate beneath the surface of things. Because I had to read the book in question in Dornach (since one cannot always be carting everything from one place to another), I had promised to obtain a copy of it again here in order to read to you a few examples which would confirm the discontinuity and corrupt nature of his thinking, just as the passage I have quoted is evidence of the complete unreliability of his view of Goethe. I was unable to purchase a copy; it is so much in demand that it is temporarily out of print and therefore unobtainable.

You see, this is how things stand when one is trying to ascertain what is really true today. It is therefore both necessary and justified to indicate in a few words what is really needed, and to make you aware that behind words such as 'change your attitude of mind' there lies something of great profundity which can also be understood historically if one has a mind to do so. The Baptist's words 'change your attitude of mind' are not only connected with what one can derive from a spiritual-scientific study of human evolution but they are also related to what one can glean from history in general, provided that one works out of a Goethean view of the world that is not tailored to suit the whims of a modern philistine but is, rather, made a living reality. For it then becomes a powerful impulse towards really understanding Christianity and leads directly to spiritual science.

It will be easiest for us to develop some real clarity regarding the essential issues in human evolution if we recall certain things that I have often explained to you in some detail. Thus I have indicated that in pre-Christian times there were certain mysteries. I tried to show something of the purpose of these mysteries in my book *Christianity as Mystical Fact*,[8] in which I quoted what Plato said about these mysteries. Today, of course, one can look upon the following sayings of Plato with a sort of regal smile (though it really has more of the nature of materialism and philistinism): 'Those who are initiated into the mysteries participate in eternal life. The others sink into the mire.'[9] When I was writing *Christianity as Mystical Fact* I made a special point of referring to these words of Plato, for they bear some weighty evidence of what Plato had to say about the mysteries.

The great secret that was imparted to the pupils of the mysteries in pre-Christian times through a special discipline actually consisted in being granted insight into what mineral and plant nature would have become if they had been able to develop their inherent potential in an uninterrupted way. For by this means they would have acquired a knowledge of humanity which would have enabled them to say that, had the mineral and the plant kingdom been able to develop in accordance with their full potential, man would manifest his true nature in the sphere in which he would then be dwelling. When the pupils of the mysteries were led in this way into the inner heart of nature and when they were enabled to see what man was originally intended to be, they underwent a total transformation. For then these pupils of the mysteries also saw how the warm-blooded animals, the ligneous plants and man as a physical being do not now manifest their true origin but represent something of a riddle, because they do not bear within them any direct evidence of their origin. Thus whereas plants and minerals do not fully develop their potential, human beings and animals do not reach back to their origin.

It was necessary in pre-Christian times—and this was an essential part of the existence of the mysteries—to initiate certain individuals. In times of great antiquity this was the atavistic knowledge of all human beings, but in later times, when atavistic knowledge had receded, it was necessary to initiate particular individuals. It was therefore necessary to initiate individual human beings into the mysteries of outer nature, of the mineral and plant kingdoms, in order to see man as he really is. Similarly, it is necessary in our time once again to refer to man's origin, to come to know him from the other side, so that he again reveals his origin (I attempted, in my cumbersome way, to do this in *An Outline of Occult Science*,[10] in so far as it is possible in our time), so that man is once again integrated into everything that is. Just as the mysteries undertook this task for pre-Christian times, so does spiritual science fulfil it for the time in which we are now living, in the aftermath of the Mystery of Golgotha. And this will become clear to us provided that the times around the Mystery of Golgotha are not obscured for us by the prejudice with which anti-Goetheanism befogs our perception, but that we study them in the way that Herman Grimm would have wished but which he was unable to accomplish for himself.

The leaders of the mysteries in olden times knew full well why they called for a special discipline in those whom they initiated. Until a certain time they insisted very strictly that no one was initiated into the mysteries who had not undergone this training. Especially in ancient Greece, great emphasis was placed upon not initiating anyone into the mysteries who had not fulfilled these strict demands. The neophytes learnt to make the right use in daily life of the mystery wisdom imparted to them; and much weight was attached to this especially in Greece. Moreover, it was strictly laid down that the mysteries should not be betrayed to the unworthy, just as Christ Jesus did not disclose the mysteries of the Kingdom of God to the Scribes and Pharisees but only to those whom He had chosen as His disciples.

Although the leaders of the mysteries did not bear the slightest blame for this, at the time when the event of Golgotha was approaching it was no longer possible to keep the mysteries secret as had formerly been appropriate. The time for this was past. And why was this so? As I have said, irrespective of any blame on the part of the leaders of the mysteries the time for this was over. The leaders of the mysteries, the hierophants, were not responsible for this. It was the Imperium Romanum, Roman imperialism, that unjustifiably unveiled the secrets of the mysteries. It was impossible for the leaders of the mysteries to withstand the orders specifically of the Roman emperors; and this overpowering of spiritual life by the Roman emperors is reflected in all the events of that time. A man such as John the Baptist had a prophetic vision of this in all its details; for those who want to see can discern with absolute clarity what is about to happen. But those who do not want to see are unable to discern it. This comes to expression in the words of people such as John the Baptist, which for all their ambiguity are true in all their various meanings. In the words 'Change your attitude of mind, for the Kingdom of Heaven is at hand' there is also an underlying meaning which could be rendered as follows: 'Behold, the wisdom of the mysteries which has brought healing to mankind is no more. It has been appropriated by Rome, which has also taken Judaism—an intimate part of your own world—under its wing. So change your attitude of mind! Do not look any longer for salvation in what emanates from Rome, but seek it in what is not of this Earth. Receive the baptism which loosens your ether body, so that you see what is to come, and what will inspire new mysteries; for the old mysteries have been forcibly appropriated.'

What happened was that the Roman emperors demanded by

imperial edict to be initiated into the mysteries, a step which Augustus,[11] who did not abuse them in any way, was the first to take. This then became the general custom. It was especially this that John the Baptist was protesting against, in that he sought to rescue those who wanted to receive baptism from these developments so that they did not see the salvation of human evolution as lying in what emanated from Rome.

One of the emperors who was most fully initiated into the secrets of the mysteries was Caligula,[12] and later on, Nero.[13] It is one of the enigmas of history that Caligula and Nero acted as initiates in such a way that they forcibly demanded knowledge of the secrets of the mysteries. Imagine the state of mind of those who knew that all this was coming, and who at the same time were able to sense what it signified. Just imagine what it must have been like for these people. They could of course say that what must, and will, come is the Kingdom of Heaven, and that this is where the sacred mysteries must henceforth be sought, not in the realm of human beings! History often speaks through symbols. As a Greek philosopher, Diogenes[14] went about the marketplace in Athens with a lantern looking for 'man' who was lost, who had lost his spiritual vision. Why was he lost? Not because this 'man' was unknown, or because the time was approaching when people no longer sought what could be communicated in the mysteries about the secrets of evolution. People like Caligula and Nero were fundamentally aware of this, but for this very reason it was veiled in obscurity. Like John the Baptist, Diogenes felt in his own way that the time was coming when, precisely because the secrets of the mysteries were known to have been betrayed by man, 'man' would be plunged into darkness and would have to be sought with a lantern.

Caligula had received instruction as to how rightly to live in esoteric circles in accordance with the teachings of the old mysteries. He therefore understood how to order his consciousness between going to sleep and waking up in such a way that he could be fully engaged with everything in the spiritual world that was known in the ancient mysteries of the lunar gods, the gods of the Moon. From the old mysteries he understood the art of conducting dialogues during sleep with the spirits of the Moon. It was part of the secrets of the mysteries to learn to know what lies behind ordinary consciousness, and to discover how, by modifying this ordinary waking consciousness, one learns the secrets of this other consciousness during sleep. For by knowing where his individuality is when it is in the spiritual world between going to sleep and waking up, the person concerned realizes that his individuality is not only incarnated here on Earth as a being of nature but that it—this individuality—is related to the spiritual world, to everything that lives amongst the spiritual hierarchies. If, therefore, a person knows the mysteries of the Moon gods, this also changes his relationship to the Sun gods, to the gods who are not perceived in the surrounding world by the waking consciousness that has been dulled by Lucifer but who are now perceived clairvoyantly [during sleep]. When someone like Caligula knows from his own experience that the human individuality lives in the spiritual world between the time of going to sleep and waking up, he is also aware that during the time of waking consciousness this individuality does not merely inhabit the outward shell of external nature but also dwells amongst the spirits of the Sun, that it does not only live amidst the rays of the physical Sun but also amongst the spirits of the Sun.

But Caligula had not, of course, had the necessary training. His knowledge was restricted to conversing with the Moon gods in sleep; and what this brought about was that by day he addressed Jupiter, whom the ancient gods had, in a quite different sphere, looked upon as Zeus, as 'brother Jupiter'. This was Caligula's habitual form of address, to speak of 'brother Jupiter', for he clearly felt himself to be a citizen of the spiritual world where Jupiter dwelt. Caligula knew himself to be living amidst a world of spiritual beings; and he therefore bore himself in such a way that this was manifested by his appearance and demeanour. At certain times he appeared in a Bacchus costume with a thyrsus staff in his hand and with a garland of oak leaves on his head, and invited homage to Bacchus. At other times he appeared in a similar vein as Hercules with a club and a lion skin. Or he would appear as Apollo with a radiant crown on his head and a bow in his hand, inviting homage from a choir that surrounded him singing appropriate songs in his honour. He appeared as the god Mercury with a winged head and a herald staff, and also as Jupiter. A tragic poet who was regarded as an expert in these matters and had been asked to decide who was the greater, Caligula or Jupiter (a statue of whom Caligula had had placed beside him for this purpose), was scourged because he did not venture to accept Caligula as the greater.

What, then, are we to make of Caligula? It is relevant to note that when Lucifer tempted man and he said, 'Your eyes shall be opened and you shall be like gods,' he ended by saying: '. . . and you shall distinguish between good and evil.' But this distinction between good and evil was implanted into mankind by a spirit involved in human evolution who was able to participate in human evolution only up till a certain time. This time was now over. It came to an end when John the Baptist first proclaimed the words 'The Kingdom of Heaven is at hand'; but he did not add what was technically the case, namely 'and the kingdom of Lucifer is at an end'. He was of course speaking only of the Kingdom of Heaven. We can see especially in our judgement of Caligula the extent to which Lucifer's kingdom had come to an end. For when a judicial error had occurred under the reign of Caligula—an innocent person had been condemned to death and was about to be killed, because he had been mistaken for the person who was guilty—Caligula said it did not matter, since the innocent man was just as guilty as the guilty one! And when Petronius was condemned to death, Caligula said that those who had condemned him could equally well be condemned themselves, for they are just as guilty as the person they have condemned. You can see that the power to distinguish between good and evil had ceased to exist. It no longer functioned in the time of which I am speaking. We can ascertain when it ceased to do so if we really study the events of history.

Nero was an initiate of a similar kind. He was actually a psychoanalyst—not so much of a philistine as many of our modern psychoanalysts are but, rather, one in the more grandiose, heroic mould. He could even be thought of as the first psychoanalyst, for he was the first to venture the idea that everything in man is determined by the libido, by sexual drives; and this is a doctrine which has been revived in a more philistine fashion by psychoanalysts in our own time. But Professor Sigmund Freud[15] is no Nero. He lacks not the inner attitude but the stature.

But what John the Baptist knew was also known by Nero. For Nero also knew—and in this respect Nero differs from Caligula—from his initiation into the mysteries that man is confronted by the dilemma that the truths underlying the real impulses of the mysteries were fading from view and had lost their power, and that they could therefore be perpetuated only by outward force. It was not only John the Baptist who said that the old world-order had come to an end (though he also added, 'The Kingdom of Heaven is at hand, change your attitude of mind!') but Nero also knew that the kingdoms of the ancient world were spent, that a decisive turning point in earthly evolution had now been reached. However, Nero had a diabolic consciousness, he had all the devilish impulses that an unworthy initiate can possibly possess residing within him. He therefore, just as John the Baptist, just as Christ Jesus, foresaw that the world was coming to an end. If one rightly understands what John the Baptist and Christ Jesus say about the end of the world, one has no need to explain in ponderous detail that it will happen at this or that particular time, but that it will happen as the Bible says it will. But you already have an intuitive sense—and in my next lecture I shall say more about this—that the Parousia, the Second Coming, is a reality, if it is rightly understood. Nero knew that a whole new order was coming, but it was not to his liking, it did not suit him. It was therefore characteristic of him to say that there was nothing that would please him more than to participate in the destruction of the world. It was particularly typical of him to say: 'If the world goes up in flames, I shall take a special delight in it!' This was his distinctive obsession—the longing to see the world go up in flames. Although one may well doubt this from a historical point of view, it is nevertheless true that, because of this obsession of his, he caused Rome to be set alight; for in his madness he imagined that from the burning of Rome the fire would spread to the extent that the whole world would be engulfed in flames.

I have given a few indications which are intended to characterize how the world was in a certain sense coming to an end and had to begin anew. But the realities of outer life are such that one thing always flows into another, that the old order continues to persist even when the new has already manifested its first impulses. And although since the Mystery of Golgotha the Kingdom of Heaven has been amongst us, the

Imperium Romanum continues to exist alongside it in a state of decline, in a decadent phase of evolution. This has led present-day scholars with all manner of good and evil intentions constantly to emphasize that it is the spirit of the old Imperium Romanum, the spirit of Roman imperialism, that lives amongst us today and also pervaded the early manifestations of Christianity. One would come upon some strange facts if one were to continue in this vein. To begin with, it would become clear that the legal concepts that appeared later can all be traced back to Roman law, and that Roman law, which has an anti-Christian quality, has had a very widespread influence. One would need to touch upon many other areas of life if one wished to consider the continuing presence of Roman imperialism down to our own time, and especially if one was wanting to discuss everything associated with the progressive decline of Rome.

There is something instinctive in the way that Roman history is taught in schools and in the way that historians—and especially the most learned ones—who write the *fable convenue* that people call history today convey to mankind a consciousness of Rome that excludes the spirit that lives within it. One thing that one can be quite sure to achieve by these means, my dear friends, is that the far-reaching consequences of the moment when the Cross was erected on Golgotha are not brought to the general consciousness of mankind. There was an instinctive endeavour to obscure the full significance of the events that took place then; for there is little evidence of the courage that is required to reach from the outer shell, or surface, of history to its inner heart or kernel. And we see authors with a considerable public readership who go so far as to misrepresent Goethe in order to encourage people to think that even Goethe's views were such as to advocate studying history as if it were merely an outer husk. Such influences affect wide areas of our inner lives, and the point is not so much whether one's understanding of a particular issue is correct but that our whole life is influenced, coloured by such a tendency. An impulse of this nature dominates the whole of life, which is then unerringly led in the direction of this same impulse. People like Goethe therefore continue to be preachers in the wilderness, and they are, moreover, slandered through views being ascribed to them which are the opposite of the ones they actually held.

We can also see where such impulses are leading. There is much that comes towards us through karma, also when we are looking for something to round off what we are wanting to say to our fellow human beings. And so it was that yesterday I came across some remarks expressed by one of our contemporaries. Although this occurred only yesterday, these observations have a close connection with the inner impulse that has been flowing through these discussions about the Mystery of Golgotha. This contemporary of ours has gone through many changes. Finally he has found his way to Christianity in the form of Catholicism and is now active in propagating it. Thus we have a remarkable instance of a freethinker who publicly bears witness to Christ and, moreover, from a Catholic standpoint. He has now expressed his Christian beliefs in the particular way that he has come to represent them. This testimony is very typical; it is very much a document of the present. I shall now read to you this testimony of a modern witness to Christ:

> It is totally futile to seek the after-life. It probably does not even exist, and no matter how we approach this problem we are never any the wiser. Let us leave any form of occultism to initiates and charlatans; whatever form mysticism may take, it is totally irrational. Rather let us submit to the authority of the Church ... because it has formulated the rules of ethics in which nations and children need to be instructed with the authority of centuries and with great practical experience [the Church, if you please!]; and finally because, far from delivering us into the hands of mysticism, it directly defends us against it, silences the voices of the mystic groves [this is how he refers to anything that might derive from the spiritual world], explains the Gospels and tailors the magnanimous anarchism of the Saviour to the needs of society.[16]

Here we have the confession of a man who has converted to Christianity from modern materialism, who turned to Christianity in so far as his ideal was to be able to convert to a Christianity where the sublime impulses that Christ bequeathed to the world were adapted or sacrificed to the needs of modern society. However, there is a large audience for what such a witness of Christ has to say, much larger than one might think; for there is an enormous need to make Christ appear in a way that pleases people today, in a way that they find acceptable. And there is a strong instinctive tendency to prevent people from being aware of the truth that the death of Jesus was a totally natural, inevitable event which was predicated by the fact that Christianity and the Roman Empire were mutually incompatible and that the death of Christ was the only possible consequence of their coexistence. It follows from this that if we really want to find the light instead of continuing to wander about in the shadows we need to discover how much there is in modern life that has a relationship to a true understanding of Christianity, and that we must gradually summon up that righteous anger that Christ Himself had when He had to reply to the Scribes and Pharisees.

I wanted today to give you a picture of what lived in the centuries into which Christianity was born, and I wanted to draw your attention to the need for historical research to focus quite particularly on that moment of history when the Mystery of Golgotha took place; for this is possible even if one dwells purely on historical study alone. But it is also important to acquire a sense for assessing the importance of particular historical events, a sense for what is significant and characteristic of the time and for what is less so. One also needs to gain a sense for what lives on from the various streams of the past, and where these traces can still be found.

LECTURE 13

THERE is much about events taking place now and in the way that they will come to be shaped in the immediate future which can be understood in its true essence if one sees these events as a continuation of what took place in the early years of the Christian era. This may sound somewhat paradoxical today. And yet the reason why it is difficult for many people today to understand how certain forces which were implanted into the evolution of humanity and the Earth during the spread of Christianity could still be exerting an influence now is that the view that prevails among our contemporaries is that one should not consider the deeper impulses, the deep forces that underlie contemporary events, but merely look at what is happening on the surface. The deeper spiritual forces are inaccessible to people today because they do not want to consider them. On the other hand, anyone who wishes to penetrate even to a small extent to what lies beneath the surface of events in our time will, in many a document that is currently published amidst wide acclaim—often by individuals who are unaware of the motives that determine their actions—become aware of impulses that are often a continuation and even a reappearance of certain impulses that were manifested especially in the early centuries of the Christian era. It is not even possible to characterize the most significant 'revivals' (as one might call them) of former impulses in our time because people cannot tolerate such characterizations. But those who study the early Christian centuries from a certain standpoint will be able to detect the forces that are actively at work and making a reappearance. It is

therefore my aim to draw your attention to certain phenomena associated with the spread of Christianity in the early centuries of the
Christian era, because through the appropriate use of the ideas that can
be arrived at as a result you will be able quite naturally to understand
much that is taking place today.

Today I want to contribute something that arises out of our recent
studies which may serve as a basis for what we will consider afterwards
and will enable these subsequent investigations to be fruitful.

I have often spoken to you about this strange and remarkable fact
that the first Roman emperors had acquired their initiation by forcible
means. I have also pointed out that many of their actions arose from the
fact that they had forced their way into initiation and therefore knew
certain things associated with cosmic events and the impulses relating to
them, while nevertheless—as we saw last time—using the secrets
derived from the mysteries to their own advantage.

The first thing to be aware of when considering these matters is that
the appearance of the Christ impulse on the stage of human history was
not merely an outward event on the physical plane, which one can
understand by considering the historical facts available, but that it was a
truly spiritual event. I have already pointed out the profound significance of the fact that Christ was first recognized by demonic beings.
We are told that Christ performed miracles of healing which are
described in the Gospels as the casting out of demonic spirits. We are,
moreover, constantly made aware on the one hand that the demonic
beings who had resided in people knew who Christ was; and on the
other hand it is pointed out to us that Christ Himself said to the demons
that the time had not yet come to speak about Him and that they
should not say who He was.[2] Thus one can say that the appearance of
Christ was not only accompanied by the judgements of human beings.
It might well have been the case that human beings did not at first have
the slightest idea what lay behind the appearance of Christ. But the
demonic beings, spirits who were to be thought of as belonging to a
supersensible world, recognized Him. It was therefore an event whose
recognition involved the spiritual world. The more knowledgeable
leaders of the early Christians were very clearly aware that the coming of
Christianity was not merely an earthly event, that what had taken place

was not an event of the earthly world alone, but that it was something that concerned the spiritual world and had in a certain sense brought about a radical change in the spiritual world. This was the firm conviction of these leaders and inspirers of the early Church.

Now it is a curious phenomenon that the Roman emperors, who were aware of certain mysteries of the spiritual world because of having forced their way into initiation, had to one degree or another an intuitive sense of the whole far-reaching significance of the Christ impulse. There were of course some of these Roman emperors who, despite having forced their way into initiation, understood little about the mysteries; but there were also some who understood to the point where they were able to divine something of the power and potential influence of the Christ mystery. And it was these more gifted and perceptive among these initiated emperors who began to adopt a certain policy towards the growing movement of Christianity. The first emperor after Augustus, Tiberius,[3] already started working in this way. One could object that Christianity had not spread by this time, but such an objection would not be valid. For Tiberius, through having been initiated into the ancient mysteries to a certain degree, was well aware that something significant was going on when he learned of Christ's birth in Palestine. Thus we need to consider for a moment how the policy that the initiated Roman emperors were to follow towards Christianity began already under Tiberius, who announced his intention to acknowledge Christ as one of the Roman gods.

The Roman Empire had a quite specific policy towards worship of the gods. Essentially, this policy was that when the Romans conquered a people they received the gods of the conquered race into their Olympic fold. That is to say, they declared that these gods were worthy of veneration, and they were added to the gods already recognized by Rome, with the result that the family of Roman gods gradually grew in number. This policy was followed by the Roman rulers in order to take over those whom they conquered not only on a material level but also in spirit and in soul. Moreover, the initiated emperors were very far from seeing in these gods merely the outward images or, indeed, what the ordinary people saw; they knew that behind what was manifested in the images of the gods truly spiritual powers were present from the various hierarchies. This policy was therefore totally understandable and made perfect sense; for the power inherent in the principles of Roman rule was to be augmented by the power that resided in the acknowledging and assimilation of the gods. And, as a rule, not only was the religion associated with these gods taken over in an outward and exoteric sense but the secrets of the associated mysteries were also received into the Roman mystery centres and connected with the mystery cult of the ancient Roman Empire. Since at that time there was the prevailing view that it was neither right nor possible to govern without the support of spiritual powers such as were represented by the gods, such a policy was adopted as a matter of course.

The aim of Tiberius was therefore simply to integrate the power of Christ, as he imagined it, with the impulses that emanated from the divine forces recognized by him and those whom he governed. The Roman Senate thwarted his intentions, and nothing came of them. But the initiated emperors constantly made such attempts—as did Hadrian, for example.[4] Again and again, however, this was resisted by the dignitaries who wielded a certain influence against this policy of the initiated emperors. Now if we examine that objections were actually raised against this policy, we can form a good idea of what was really going on at this highly significant turning point of human and earthly evolution.

What we behold is a remarkable interplay of forces. On innumerable occasions Roman writers, influential Roman individuals and, in their wake, large sections of the Roman public expressed their opposition to the Christians, who as they increased in number were becoming more conspicuous, accusing them of profaning what others held sacred, and of regarding as sacred what others considered to be profane. That is to say, the Romans repeatedly asserted and emphasized that these Christians differed radically in their thoughts and feelings from not only Romans but also all other people; for the other peoples, together with their gods, had more or less been absorbed by the Romans. You can see, therefore, that it was already the case that everyone looked upon Christians as different, as people with different, even opposite, feelings and sensibilities. One could simply dismiss such views by regarding them as slander. After all, it is easy to make such accusations if one takes a superficial view of history. But one will not regard it as slander if one realizes that much of what entered into Christian teaching was derived more or less verbatim—I am aware that one should not attach too much value to the way things are worded, but precisely because we do not do so it is worth emphasizing—from the opinions of earlier times and contemporary opinions with regard to the Mystery of Golgotha. Expressing the same thing more clearly one could say: the Christians expressed their feelings with words that could already be found amongst their contemporaries. One of those who expressed more of less to the letter what can be found among the Christians was Philo of Alexandria,[5] a figure to whom I have often referred and who was a contemporary of Christ. Philo of Alexandria makes the following remarkable statement: 'According to traditional teachings I must hate what others love' (he is referring to the Romans) 'and love what others hate' (again he means the Romans). If you consider this statement and then consult the Gospels, you will find plenty of echoes—especially in St Matthew—of what Philo is saying here. Thus one can say that Christianity grew out of a spiritual milieu that required people to say: 'We love what others hate.' That is to say, the Christians—and this statement often featured in the early Christian communities and was even one of the main principles of instruction in Christian life—themselves expressed what others reproached them with. So it was not simply an instance of slander, for it accorded with what the Romans said: 'The Christians love what we hate, and hate what we love.' But the Christians, on the other hand, said exactly the same with respect to the Romans.

You can see from this that something immeasurably different from what had preceded it was now entering human evolution; for it would not otherwise have been able to make so marked an impression. Of course, if one wishes to judge this whole situation one needs to realize that what had manifested itself had indeed come from the spiritual worlds and that many who were, like Philo, contemporaries of the Mystery of Golgotha caught fleeting glimpses of it and then gave expression to them in their own way. And so many passages from the Bible which are interpreted in such a variety of ways today—as in the case of M. Barrès whose words I quoted at the end of the previous lecture—and in such a manner that they fit in with people's opportunism will only be seen in their true light if one does not insist on the standpoint of interpreting them in whatever way one pleases but if the interpretation is forged out of the whole spirit of the times. There are some strange statements in the Gospels; and they are sometimes interpreted today in very curious ways. But much that Philo says is in harmony with the Gospels. I should therefore like to share with you a sentence from Philo, from which you will see that, merely because he was not so inspired as the Evangelists were to be subsequently, he wrote in a somewhat different way from them. Because he was a professional writer his way of expressing what he had to say did not make such demands on the reader as was necessary in order to understand the Evangelists. In this striking sentence Philo gave expression to much that was living in people's hearts and heads: 'Do not worry about genealogical records or the documents of despots, take no thought for bodily concerns; do not ascribe civil rights and freedoms to the citizen, or a lack of freedom to those of humble origin or to slaves obtained through purchase, but give heed only to the ancestry of the soul!' If you read the Gospels with understanding, you will not fail to recognize that, albeit raised to a higher level, something of this same mental attitude pervades the Gospels, and that therefore it is very possible for a modern opportunist to say the sort of things that I read to you in my previous lecture. It is worth our while to take careful note of what he has to say, and I shall therefore read this passage again:

> It is totally futile to seek the after-life. It probably does not even exist, and no matter how we approach the problem we are never any the wiser. Let us leave any form of occultism to initiates and charlatans; whatever form mysticism may take it is totally irrational. Rather let us submit to the authority of the Church ... because it has formulated the rules of ethics in which nations and children need to be instructed with the authority of centuries and with great practical experience; and finally because, far from delivering us into the hands of mysticism, it directly defends us against it, silences the voices of the mystic groves, explains the

Gospels and tailors the magnanimous anarchism of the Saviour to the needs of society.

In a statement of the kind that I quoted to you from Philo you can see, since it is echoed again and again in the Bible, in the New Testament, what really lies behind this whole movement. And when Philo speaks of the ancestry of the soul, he means—among many other things—something that rises up against all the prevailing ideas in the Roman Empire. For the Roman Empire was interested only in the ancestry of the body in its various forms; and the whole social order was based on this. And then suddenly someone said: 'Take no thought of bodily concerns, but give heed only to the ancestry of the soul!' It would be difficult to imagine anything so radically at variance with the principles of the Roman Empire; a greater contrast could hardly be conceived of. And this contrast was raised to a higher level with the appearance of Christ Jesus—the world was indeed awaiting it—and was vigorously opposed to the world-order prevailing at that time.

It could be said that the Roman emperors might have found it right to include Christ into the pantheon of their gods as a new god to join their other gods, even though what was appearing through Him negated the very essence of their social structures; and in this way the Christ God who—to put it mildly—embodies a far deeper reality would have become one of their own gods. But these initiated emperors were bound to see that they would not have an easy time with what had descended to them from spiritual heights. When initiation forces are having so strong an outward influence as they must be having once it had become mandatory for the emperors to be initiated, as was the case in Rome after Augustus, anything that the emperors did outwardly was of course imbued with significant additional forces, including the measures and impulses through which the social order was shaped. The aims and intentions of the initiated emperors were manifested more forcefully than those of an ordinary initiate. For let us suppose that one of the emperors who had been affected by initiation had said—well now, let us imagine a hypothetical situation, where the Baptist is baptizing with water. Ether bodies were loosened through this baptism with water (and of course the initiated emperors knew this), as a result of which those being baptized acquired insight into the inner structure of the spiritual world; and they knew first and foremost that a decisive turning point in world evolution had been reached. This was what those being baptized knew through complete immersion in water. And let us now suppose that one of these initiated emperors might have said, 'I want to do battle'—such things occurred within the mysteries—'against what has intervened at this turning point in world history!' The autocratic self-will of these emperors was really quite a phenomenon. It never occurred to them that they might be powerless against the will of the gods, but they resolved—and this was why they had insisted on being initiated—to take on the challenge represented by these spiritual world-impulses by in a certain sense stemming the tide of world evolution. Something of the kind has also occurred at other times, and it is happening again today. But people do not notice this, they are completely unaware of it.

The following incident has a bearing on the hypothesis that I have put forward. Licinius,[6] who in the age of Constantine[7] ruled over the other part of the Empire, had something of this sense of challenging the gods. He wanted to perform a sign, for such cultic acts or ritualistic performances symbolized the battle against the spiritual powers. He wanted to perform a cultic ceremony in order that he might demonstrate in the public domain that he was taking up this battle. In other words—for it was baptism that had made known to the whole world that the turning point in world history had come—he wanted to ridicule baptism before those around him, and thereby combat Christianity and blunt the strength of its impulse. A special festival was organized for this purpose, a spectacle at Heliopolis. It was arranged that a Thespian by name of Gelasinus[8] was to be submerged in warm water dressed in a white baptismal robe. This was to be a real spectacle, and the intention was to mock the Christian baptism. Gelasinus was therefore dressed in a white priestly garment, was immersed in warm water and pulled out again, and everyone was supposed to laugh at him. And what happened? Well, he said: 'Now I am a Christian and will remain so with every fibre of my being!' This was Licinius's answer from the spiritual world: instead of a mockery of baptism the effects of baptism became manifest to him. He recognized that a turning point in world history had come. Such an initiated emperor as Licinius was had taken upon himself to consult the gods and even challenge them and had received a dismissive answer.

It would be difficult for us in our time to form a clear idea of the significance that such an answer has. It was at that time a fully valid answer for all people, including the heathen; an answer that had to be reckoned with. Something had entered from another source into the consciousness of those who were at that time familiar with the mysteries of world events which gave them confidence in the thoughts that arose through the spread of Christianity. All manner of different customs, all of which had an occult significance, had been transmitted from ancient times. In the Antonine age the Sibyls spoke, or people heard and took advice from them, from the Sibylline oracles. One important oracle from the Antonine age had expressly stated that Rome was doomed to destruction; ancient Rome would not survive! Well, oracles speak in such a way that their meaning is ambiguous but can be understood perfectly well. This oracle spoke in a strange way. It said that 'Rome will perish, and in the place where ancient Rome once stood foxes and wolves will roam and exercise their dominion there'. This was also something that people took seriously. Of course they sought a deeper meaning behind this; but they felt that a turning point in world history had come. They knew that what had come to wield such power in Rome would fade. Foxes and wolves will be everywhere and will take charge. Naturally, oracles are often ambiguous; and from time to time, even in those days, the aura of initiation was transmitted through an ordinary, uninitiated sage, so that he sometimes said remarkable things which can only be understood as having a connection with the time of the turning point in world history.

In my previous lecture I spoke to you about Nero, and about what this initiated emperor actually thought. He wanted to set the world on fire so that he might be there to see its end. So if the end of Rome, that is to say Rome's sovereignty over the globe, was going to come about he wanted to have some degree of control over it. Seneca[9] once gave him a warning in a remarkable statement, which can be understood only if one knows that the Roman emperors who were in possession of the principle of initiation believed that they had the omnipotent powers of gods, a degree of veneration which the Christians were not willing to offer them. Seneca, who knew of no other way of telling this man with absolute authority what he needed to impart to him, said to Nero: 'You have great power, you can even have these people killed who you think might be able to contribute something to the world-order that will emerge after the downfall of Rome. But there is,' said Seneca, 'one thing that no despot can do: he cannot bring about the murder of his successor.' These were deeply meaningful words. They should not of course be understood as referring to a successor as yet to be determined but to the actual successor. Seneca wanted to indicate to him that death set a limit to his power. Thus the idea of Rome's downfall was already playing a significant part in the cultural circles of Rome.

It is striking that the Christians had a radically different view of this idea from the Romans. This is really quite a paradox: when they were amongst themselves the Christians advocated the notion that Rome would not perish but that the dominion of Rome would last until the end, that is to say until the end of the particular era in question. Thus it was the Christians who championed the idea that Roman sovereignty would endure and that it would survive the wolves and foxes. It was not that the Christians would have denied—to speak somewhat in terms of the oracle—that wolves and foxes would make Rome their natural habitat; but they nevertheless maintained that the dominion of Rome will continue.

We need to keep all these different moods and attitudes in mind. Much of their substance has even become a reality. Thus, for example, Alexander Severus's[10] mother, who was a pupil of Origen[11]—who despite being suspected of heresy was nevertheless regarded as a kind of Church Father—had managed to set up a sort of pantheon of devotion for her private use; for in her private chamber she venerated Abraham, Orpheus, Apollonius of Tyana[12] and Christ at one and the same time, and was convinced that bestowing reverence upon these four was both necessary and right for her own salvation. Moreover, as a good pupil of Origen she found that such a practice was in no sense at variance with his teaching.

Now if we consider these shades of opinion which I have tried to characterize in brief outline, we find that they reflect the attitudes of the early centuries of the Christian era up till the fourth century. Again and again we find initiated emperors who endeavoured to amalgamate Christianity with their religious systems coming to terms with Christianity. This is indeed the case right through until the fourth century, despite the persecutions of Christians recorded by history.

In the fourth century, as you know, a remarkable personality appeared in the figure of the Emperor Constantine, the contemporary of Licinius. He was an outstanding personality, both in an outward sense but also spiritually; and I have indicated on other occasions[13] how spiritual forces were at work in the figure of Constantine in his complex task of guiding the destiny of the Western Empire. We shall consider him today from another point of view.

Although he was a figure of such stature also in a spiritual sense, his spiritual affinities were such that he was unable to have a real relationship to the old initiation. He recoiled in a certain sense from what his predecessors and contemporaries did not forbear to do, namely forcibly initiating themselves into the old mysteries. He was also burdened in his soul by the Sibylline oracles and by all the other things that were known about the downfall of the Roman Empire and so forth. But he knew in addition that the Christians held the idea that Rome would last until the end of the world. He knew about all these things. But he had a dread of being initiated in the old mysteries; he had a dread of having, in a certain sense, to engage in a battle with Christianity in the realm of the mysteries. This is of great significance.

What history relates about the Emperor Constantine is extraordinarily interesting and shows that Constantine tried to acquire a relationship to Christianity in a different way, in that he emerged as the great protector of Christianity, in the sense that he wholly incorporated Christianity—in the way that he understood it—into the Roman Empire. But he was unable to connect this Christianity with the old principle of initiation. There was a great difficulty in this, because the Christians themselves and their leaders had very strongly resisted such an attitude on the grounds that they had a feeling—and indeed an insight—that through Christianity the old mysteries, which were veiled in secrecy in the temples of the mysteries, should be made outwardly visible on the stage of world history and thus placed before the whole world. They wanted to present the truths of the mysteries before the whole world instead of restricting them solely to the temples. The initiated emperors, on the other hand, had a fundamental desire that Christianity should be withdrawn from the world into the temples of the mysteries. People would then be initiated into Christianity in the same way as they had been initiated into the secrets of the ancient pagan mysteries. But it was also difficult for Constantine to achieve what he sought in the face of what the Christians were aspiring towards; for the way that the Christians understood the impulse which was in their opinion to become a force in the world at this turning point in world history was as a wholly spiritual impulse. This notion is reflected with particular clarity in the occult teachings of the early Christians. By saying that the Roman Empire would endure they were at that time already indicating something that has actually happened. I recently pointed out to you that the deeper impulse of the Imperium Romanum has not ceased but lives on, and not only in the realm of jurisprudence. The significant point here is that many things have appeared in various domains which those who do not look beneath the surface regard as new, whereas nothing has actually been added to what has emanated from Rome. There has simply been a prolongation, an extension of the impulses of the Imperium Romanum. Although the ancient Roman Empire no longer exists, its spirit lives on and is present in our world on a very broad scale and at a deep level.

Certain people who are aware of the mysteries speak of how the ghost of the old Roman Empire continues to live amongst us as a spectre that haunts our world and will continue to do so. This is a constant adage expressed even today by those who know about such things and is something that one will always hear. The Christians wanted to indicate something similar. But at the same time they wanted to say that in Christianity there will always be something that is antagonistic to Rome. The supersensible element in Christianity will always be at odds with the Roman preoccupation with the sense-perceptible world. Thus the idea about Rome promoted by the Christians was prophetic.

You will also understand more clearly why the Roman senators and emperors were worried; for they inevitably related the decline of Rome to the outward empire, and they saw it gradually disintegrating under the influence of Christianity. A man such as the Emperor Constantine was strongly influenced by such a picture. Despite not being initiated, the Emperor Constantine was well aware of the existence of an ancient wisdom, when in olden times human beings possessed an atavistic clairvoyance. This ancient wisdom was then transmitted to later ages, was preserved by the priests and was gradually corrupted; but it certainly existed. We Romans, Constantine said to himself, also have something in our social order that is associated with the institutions engendered by this primal wisdom, although we have buried it beneath the social order of an empire founded upon materialistic principles. This was expressed in an important symbol which is an imagination— although it is not merely an imagination but a cultic act arising from world history, in the way that these imaginations very often came to expression in cultic acts. This was because there was an awareness that wisdom was in earlier times not thought out by human beings but was a revelation from the spiritual world. Thus the priests who were the earliest ancestors of our own epoch lived not in Rome but in Ilion and in Troy. This comes to expression in the legend of the Palladium,[14] the image of Pallas Athene that bears this name which fell from heaven in Troy and was preserved in a sanctuary, and then came to Rome and was buried under a porphyry pillar which was erected over it. As they sensed what was associated with this imaginative cultic act people had the feeling that they were tracing their own culture back to the ancient primal wisdom that descended from the worlds of spirit, but that they were unable to perceive the sublime form which this primal wisdom had had in ancient Troy.

Constantine was aware of such feelings. He therefore also felt that even if he had been initiated into the later mysteries they would not be of much help to him; they would not lead him to the Palladium, to the ancient primal wisdom. He therefore decided to challenge the cosmic powers in his own way by doing something to, in a certain sense, rescue the principle of the Imperium Romanum. Of course he was not so foolish as to believe that this could be achieved in any way other than in accordance with certain cosmic impulses. He knew that it would have to be done in accordance with certain cultic acts which are enacted over a wide historical period. He therefore initially decided to transfer the imperial capital of Rome to Troy, to have the Palladium dug up and brought back again to Troy. These plans were frustrated. Instead of establishing a new Rome in Troy, another plan arose to found Constantinople and to transfer to this city the power to save the waning power of Rome for the future. He believed that by these means he would be able to forestall the turning point in world history. He was quite willing for foxes and wolves to take over Rome as the Sibylline oracle had foretold, but he wished to transplant the hidden impulses of Rome to another site and in a certain sense to bring them back to their source. And so he conceived the great plan of founding Constantinople, and the building work was completed in 326. You can see that he conceived of this founding deed in conjunction with the events of the great turning point of time purely through the fact that for the laying of the foundation stone he chose the time when the Sun stood in the sign of the Archer and the Crab ruled over the hour of the day. Thus what he did was governed by the cosmic signs. But he also wanted Constantinople to have something quite special about it. He wanted the enduring impulse of eternal Rome to be transferred to Constantinople. He therefore had the porphyry pillar transported to Constantinople (it was later destroyed by storms); and he ordered the Palladium to be dug up and placed beneath this porphyry pillar. He had in his possession some remnants of the Cross of Golgotha and the remainder of the nails with which it was put together. He used the remnants of the Cross to make a kind of frame for a particularly valuable statue of Apollo, and the nails of the Cross were arranged to form a nimbus around Apollo. This was placed on the porphyry pillar which was subsequently destroyed, and an inscription was engraved on it which said approximately: 'What radiates from this place radiates like the Sun, and it shall proclaim the power of its founder Constantine for all eternity!' These things must of course be understood in a more or less imaginative way, but with the qualification that, while they are to be understood in this way, they refer to very definite historical events.

This whole story has passed over into legend and lives on in a metamorphosed form in the legend which can be expressed approximately as follows. The Palladium, which is of course a symbol for a quite particular centre of ancient wisdom, once resided in the secret mystery

centres of the initiated priests of Troy who kept it hidden. It then came
to light for the first time when by way of certain circuitous routes it was
transported from Troy to Rome; it then appeared for a second time
when it was brought to Constantinople by Constantine. And those who
acknowledge the truth of the legend add that it will see the light of day
for a third time when it is taken from Constantinople to a Slavic city.
This legend lives on at a deep unconscious level in all manner of ways.
There are many things in our time which are manifested in aspects of a
purely physical nature which, however, are merely the outer surface of
what lies hidden behind them.

Constantine therefore wanted directly to counteract the decline of the
Imperium Romanum despite his firm belief in the Sibylline oracle. He
sought to remove Rome from the place of its own downfall.

Now in everything that I have told you, you need to be aware of
impulses living in the soul of the Emperor Constantine, who was a
personality of world-historical dimensions, which had significant and
far-reaching effects. And if you also bear in mind what the first
Christians and their leaders had said, 'No, the Imperium Romanum will
not come to an end, it will survive, and the impulse that we have
received will also come to fulfilment, it will be an enduring presence,'
you have something of significance which has a bearing on a number of
different elements which have played a part in the cultural development
of the West. It will above all be possible for you to form a picture of how
people in the early Christian centuries right up to the time of the
Emperor Constantine thought about Rome and about the Imperium
Romanum, and how there were radically diverging views as to the way
that people thought about the future. And you will perhaps find clues to
enable you to see many of the events that were to come later in their
true light. Many of these later events can be rightly evaluated only if one
answers the following question: How does what has been happening
hitherto accord with what was intended, and what needs to happen if it
is to be more in harmony with these original intentions?

It will, furthermore, be essential that we focus upon an even more
important moment in evolution with respect to the expansion of
Christianity, when an initiated Roman emperor called Julian the
Apostate encountered the developments that were taking place within

Christianity. Finally, we may conclude this historically based study by considering the question: How can we approach Christ as His etheric presence becomes a reality in the world in this century? How can we prepare our souls so as to discover how we may draw near to Him in our time?

Next time I should like to discuss the situation surrounding the initiated emperor Julian the Apostate and to give some indications about the relationship of our present age to Christ, in so far as this theme can be addressed today.

LECTURE 14

J ULIAN, called the Apostate (or 'renegade') and one of Constantine's successors, who in the year 363 was assassinated during a campaign against the Persians, was one of the greatest figures in world history. In Julian the Apostate we have before us an individual who occupies a very special place in the history of the West; for he was a person who demonstrated how opposing forces need to be at work if world evolution is to be able to unfold in the appropriate way. We saw in Constantine a personality who needed in a certain sense to terminate the old ruling principle of the Roman emperors which had applied to the majority of them, namely that they were granted access as of right to the secrets of the mysteries. Instead, Constantine did everything he could to endow Christianity with an exoteric status, as I indicated yesterday.

Even from his very earliest childhood Julian was viewed in the worst possible light by the imperial family and those associated with them. At the time of which we are speaking, the birth of such an individual was preceded by all sorts of prophecies and predictions. His family had been led to believe as a result of various Sibylline prophecies that he would grow to oppose the impulse that had lived in Constantine; and from the very outset they tried to prevent Julian from becoming emperor. Efforts were made to have him killed. All manner of preparations were made to have him murdered along with his brother. There was a kind of aura around Julian which inspired terror in those around him. It is apparent from the stories that gathered around the figure of Julian that he was viewed by those who had the attitude indicated as having something uncanny about him. When he was taking part in a military campaign in Galilee when he was still a young man, a somnambulist cried out as the army passed by: 'There is the one who will restore the old gods and their images!'[1]

Thus there is something deeply meaningful, something spiritually determined, about the appearance of Julian. As very often happens in such cases, he was allowed to live for fear that an even greater disaster might ensue from his murder than from his life being spared. People talked themselves into believing that any initiatives that he might take to counteract the policies inaugurated by Constantine could be frozen in their tracks and speedily aborted; and every possible precaution was made to render ineffectual the tendencies arising from Julian's particular disposition. The primary aim was to give him a thoroughly Christian upbringing in accordance with the orientation of the ideas of Constantine. However, this had little effect on him and met with complete resistance on his part; and wherever he was able to apprehend anything deriving from ancient Hellenic traditions his soul was fired with enthusiasm. Because where powerful forces are at work they will ultimately win through, it so happened that as a result of the very efforts that were made to keep him away from dangerous places he was driven into the hands of all sorts of Hellenic tutors, became familiar with Hellenism and with the traditions of Hellenism; and then, when he grew older and had learned how the work of the neoplatonic philosophers was imbued with the spirit of Hellenism and ancient Greek culture, it eventually came about that he was initiated into the mysteries of Eleusis. Thus after the principle of initiation had already been erased from the sphere of influence of the Roman emperors, Julian embodied this principle as an initiate on the imperial throne when he eventually came to occupy it.

Everything that Julian did and what history has, it has to be said, been at such pains to distort in every respect must be viewed utterly in the light of the Eleusinian mysteries; and one can only rightly evaluate a figure such as Julian if one is prepared to take the effects of this initiation very seriously. What, after all, did Julian derive in terms of soul development from having undergone initiation into the Eleusinian mysteries? He had learnt through direct inner perception the essential truths of cosmic and world evolution; he had learnt about the spiritual origin of the world, and how these primal spiritual forces find expression in the planetary and solar systems. He had learnt to understand certain things which were completely beyond the comprehension of his contemporaries, with the exception of a few Greek initiates, and specifically the relationship of the influence and essential being of the Sun to the ancient Logos referred to by Hermes. This was something that lived strongly in his soul. He had in a certain sense understood the meaning of the words of Pythagoras, 'You shall never speak against the Sun!,'[2] by which, of course, he does not mean the outer physical Sun but that Spirit which is concealed behind the Sun. Thus he had come to know that it is in harmony with ancient sacred traditions to ascribe the spiritual foundations of the world to the soul-spiritual essence underlying the Sun, and to see that it is of primary importance for man to form a relationship to it if he wants to arrive at the source of his existence.

So you need to be aware that Julian had an inner experience of the whole of the ancient Sun mystery, of the truth that this physical Sun which appears before our physical eyes is merely the outward aspect of a spiritual Sun which can be reawakened in the human soul through initiation; and once it has been awakened it can reveal to the soul the intimate connection between the expanses of the cosmos and the historical life of man. It was made clear to Julian that nothing can ever be instituted here on Earth that emanates purely from human reason and is bound up with the human brain, that only someone who is able to conduct a dialogue with the Sun Logos has any right to have a say in the way that the institutions of the world are organized; for he was obliged to recognize a common law in the movement of the heavenly bodies and in what takes place here on the Earth amongst human beings, in the great historical movements of mankind.

Even a Church Father such as St Chrysostom[3] was fully aware of the existence of an ancient Sun mystery, a spiritual Sun mystery, since he went so far as to declare that the outward physical Sun dazzles human beings on the Earth to the point where they are unable to perceive the spiritual Sun. But if one beholds everything that lived in the surroundings of a man like St Chrysostom, in whose soul a ray of the wisdom of ancient times continued to shine, one can see that there was barely more than a last vestige of understanding for that method of awakening the soul to the secrets of the universe as they had been communicated through the old mysteries and as they were indeed communicated to Julian the Apostate, who was one of the last to be a recipient of them. The situation was, therefore, that Julian the Apostate was completely surrounded by adherents of Constantine, by those who thought entirely as Constantine did. It is true that every now and then in the period until the end of the ninth century a few outstanding figures appeared in the West, also among the popes, who continued to be inspired by the old mysteries. But the impulse that emanated from Rome was aimed at nullifying the efforts of such individuals, and a quite definite policy was pursued towards the traditions of the old mysteries which I shall speak briefly about shortly. Julian was indeed utterly surrounded by a thoroughly exoteric form of Christianity.

Through complicated processes that are difficult to describe in their full psychological details, he arrived at the idea of envisaging how it would be if he were to utilize the last vestiges of the old initiation that had come down to him in order to bring about their continuing development in human evolution. I must emphasize that Julian was far from being an opponent of Christianity; he was simply committed to the continuing development of Hellenism. One sees him for what he really was if one understands him more as an advocate of Hellenism then as an opponent of Christianity; for all the fiery enthusiasm and energy at his command was devoted to the cause of preventing Hellenism from dying out, from being eradicated, and to furthering its ongoing development, so that a legacy might be bequeathed to subsequent generations. He was opposed to an abrupt break in continuity, to any sudden change; and he was indeed a personality of considerable stature. Since he had been initiated in the Eleusinian mysteries he knew that the kind of things that he wanted to achieve would not be feasible unless one were closely linked with the spiritual forces that are at work in the sense-perceptible world. He knew that if one seeks to introduce impulses into world evolution merely out of what lives in the physical world of the senses and in outer historical events, one is, as Pythagoras put it, 'speaking against the Sun'. He did not want this; and indeed, he wanted the opposite.

He actually took up one of the greatest challenges that it is possible to imagine.

Now we must not forget that there was already active opposition in Rome to such a campaign, as indeed there was in the entire south of Europe. Do not forget that up to the century of Constantine last remnants of ancient spiritual rituals continued to exist in their abundance among broad sections of the population. Indeed, the whole question of miracles represents a particular problem, a real burden for those seeking to interpret the Gospels today, because there is a great reluctance to read the Gospels out of the background of the time when they were written. For the contemporaries of the Evangelists the miracles did not present any problem whatsoever, for everyone knew perfectly well that there were rituals where forces were derived from the spiritual world which people were able to control.

While Christianity was being introduced in an outward political sense, a process that culminated in the deed accomplished by Constantine, a similar degree of energy was devoted to suppressing the old spiritual rituals; one law after another was enacted in Rome with the object of ensuring that no rituals should be celebrated which derived forces from the spiritual world. This was outwardly presented as an attempt to stamp out old superstitions! It was declared that no one should engage in ritualistic ceremonies in order to cause harm to anyone; no one was allowed to communicate with the dead, and so forth. Such laws were brought into force. But behind these laws was the endeavour to eradicate every last trace of such spiritual realities as had remained from ancient times. It is true that history tries wherever possible to hush up or conceal what was really going on. But our modern scientific approach to history, which claims to be 'unprejudiced and not subject to any kind of authority', does not take into account that the initial attempts at writing historical accounts and records were undertaken in monasteries by priests and monks; and there was in such places an absolute commitment to obliterating the true character of antiquity and to preventing anything of significance from being passed on to the future.

And so Julian saw the vanishing world of antiquity in a completely different light from those who preceded Constantine. And he knew from his initiation that the human soul has a connection with the spiritual world. Of that he was sure. He could only hope to succeed in the task that he had undertaken—to use the forces of the ancient principles of initiation to contribute to a continuing process of development in human evolution—by in a certain sense counteracting that trend in evolution which dominated the world in which he lived. And indeed, Julian's initiation had led him to become a man with a very deep love of truth, with a sense for truth that people such as the Emperor Constantine had not even the slightest inkling. It can indeed be said that the serious respect for truth that emanated from Julian has barely any parallel in the subsequent history of the West. With his profound sense for truth engendered through his initiation, he assessed what was going on in the schools and institutions for higher learning of his day. Since Constantine Christian dogma had been introduced into schools in the form in which it had been disseminated by that time. On the basis of this Christian dogma, the teachers gave their interpretations of the old Hellenistic writers, those authors whose works included significant elements about the gods of antiquity: Zeus, Apollo, Pallas Athene, Aphrodite, Hermes (Mercury) and so on. The idea now arose in Julian's mind: 'What do these teachers think they are doing? Are they not the most mendacious sophists imaginable? How can they presume to expound ancient writings whose whole foundation is that those who wrote them had the inner feeling that the gods are living forces in the world? Can such teachers, who because of their dogmas must necessarily deny in the most fundamental way the very existence of the gods, presume to be able to interpret such writers?' Julian's instinct for truth was outraged. He therefore forbade all those who, on account of their Christian dogmas, were inherently unable to believe in the ancient gods from giving interpretations of the Hellenistic writers in the schools. If one were to proceed today in accordance with the same honesty of purpose as Julian displayed, one may well imagine the extent of what would not any longer be taught in our schools! But you need to be aware of the deep sense for truth that did indeed reside in Julian.

Julian wanted to be equal to the challenges of his time, which were from another point of view nonetheless very necessary. He was thoroughly aware of the Gospels, which had arisen in a completely different way from what had been imparted to him through the Eleusinian mysteries. He could not reconcile himself to the way that the Gospels had arisen. He said to himself: 'If what has derived from Christ is a principle of initiation, it must be possible to discover it in the mysteries, for it would have to be able to live in the depths of the mysteries.' He also wanted to ascertain whether it would be possible to continue the ancient mystery teachings. What he knew of Christianity was initially only what it had become in his time. He wanted to make a great experiment and to do so over a particular issue, though not the sort of experiment that reckons only with human issues (which he would have considered childish); he wanted to perform a deed that would have significance for events in the spiritual world itself. He therefore said to himself: 'The Christians prophesized that the temple in Jerusalem will be destroyed so that no one stone will rest upon another.[4] This,' he said, 'has happened. But Christianity will not come to fulfilment if this prophecy were to be discredited, if it were to be countered by something else!' He then resolved, with great capital expenditure, to rebuild the temple at Jerusalem in accordance with the conditions at that time; and it indeed came about that a number of workmen gathered together in order to rebuild the temple in Jerusalem. Now this whole affair must be regarded from a spiritual viewpoint—for Julian wanted to challenge not only human beings but also the gods! And it is an undoubted fact that can even be proved historically—in so far as historical facts can be outwardly demonstrated, for from an inner point of view it is absolutely certain—that each of the workmen who had started to rebuild the temple had a vision of tongues of flame flaring over the place where he was working, and they all had to withdraw. The enterprise was abandoned. Nevertheless, you can see the scale of Julian's ideas.

After this scheme had failed, after this grandiose attempt before the whole world to discredit the prophecy of the destruction of the temple has come to nothing, Julian sought to achieve his object in another way. And what he now attempted was no less ambitious. The time had not yet come for evolutionary developments in Europe to be affected by that wave of change which owed its origin to the fact that one of the greatest teachers of the Church, Augustine, was unable to raise his sights to a certain idea because he lacked the spiritual maturity necessary to do so.

You probably know from your historical studies that Augustine (and I have spoken about this on various occasions, among others when discussing the legend of Faust[5]) had originally been an adherent of Manichaeism, that teaching which had arisen in Persia and claimed to be able to understand Christ Jesus better than Rome and Constantinople. This Manichaean doctrine (whose ultimate secrets it is, unfortunately, not yet possible to speak about today, even in our circles) filtered through in a variety of ways and also, in later times, into the West and had—in a somewhat degenerate form—more or less disappeared from view by the time that the Faust legend was first written down in the sixteenth century. Through an intuition of genius the revival of the Faust legend by Goethe was also in a certain sense a revival of Manichaeism. Julian thought in broad perspectives; he had ideas that embraced humanity as a whole. In a person such as Julian it becomes especially clear how insignificant ordinary human thoughts actually are. Thus the doctrine of the 'Son of Man' had to take on its various forms depending on people's capacity to form ideas about man, about the essential being of man. It was, of course, inevitable that the ideas that were formed about the Son of Man depended on people's conception of man, for the one follows from the other. People differed very widely in this respect, very, very widely; and we have at present only a very slight understanding of such matters.

In Sanskrit the word for man is 'manushya'. This word expresses the basic feeling that a large number of people associated with the idea of humanity. What is one referring to if one gives man the name manushya, thus if one uses this word-stem to designate man? One is referring to the spiritual aspect of man; one is evaluating man above all as a spiritual being. If we wish to express the idea that man is spirit and his physical aspect is only the expression, the revelation of the spirit—if, that is, we are attaching a primary value to man as spirit—we use the word 'manushya'.

In accordance with what was said earlier, one can study man from another angle by focusing one's attention particularly upon the soul. One will then pay less attention to the fact that man is spirit and focus more upon man as soul, while the outward, physical aspect and everything associated with it will remain more in the background. One will then characterize a person primarily from the way that his inner qualities are manifested in his eyes and from the erect gesture of his head. If one examines the derivation of the Greek word 'anthropos', one finds that this is what it means. Hence those who characterize man with the word manushya or with a word with a similar sounding root are viewing man primarily in terms of the spirit that descends from the spiritual world, while those who characterize him with a word that sounds like the Greek word anthropos (and this applies especially to the Greeks themselves) are giving expression to man's soul nature.

There is, however, also a third possibility. It is possible that one concentrates mainly upon the outward, earthly aspect of man, the bodily nature that is engendered by physical means. One will then characterize man with a word that essentially refers to a procreating being or to what has been procreated. If one considers the derivation of the word 'homo' one finds something of what has been described.

Thus we have a quite remarkable threefold conception of man. But you will be able to discern from this threefold picture that a person like Julian, who knew something about these matters, was very understandably guided by an instinct to search for a spiritual interpretation of the 'Son of Man'. The thought arose in his mind: 'You have been initiated into the Eleusinian mysteries. Is it perhaps possible for you to force your way into the Persian mysteries and to have yourself initiated into the mysteries lying behind the teachings of the Manichaeans? You may perhaps gain from there the possibility of furthering the continuing development which is your aim.' This was a momentous idea. But just as the campaign of Alexander had more to it than the purely trivial purpose of making conquests in Asia, so was there more involved here than the conquest of Persia; for he wanted to see whether the Persian mysteries could enable him to make further progress with his objective.

The best way for us to understand what is involved here is to ask: What was it about Manichaeism that Augustine[6] did not comprehend? As I have said, this does not involve speaking about the ultimate aims of Manichaeism; but it is possible to give a few indications. In his youth Augustine was greatly preoccupied with Manichaean teachings—they made a considerable impression upon him. He then exchanged the teachings of Manichaeism for Roman Catholicism. What did he not understand about Manichaeism? What was it that was beyond his grasp?

The Manichaeans did not develop abstract concepts, they did not develop the sort of concepts that separate thoughts from the rest of reality. To foster ideas of this nature was impossible in Manichaean terms, as it was for initiates of the Eleusinian mysteries. I have tried to indicate the difference between purely logical ideas and those with some bearing on reality. The basic principle of Manichaeism was to cultivate ideas that are not simply logical but are grounded in reality. Not that unreal ideas do not also have a part to play in life. They do, unfortunately, play a big part, especially in our time—but the part that they play is also what you might expect! And so one of the features of Manichaean teaching is to form ideas which are not mere thoughts but which are powerful enough to take hold of the outer world of nature and to play an active part in that world. The sort of idea that was fairly widely formed about Christ Jesus at that time would have been inconceivable from the Manichaean point of view. So what was the commonly held picture of Christ Jesus? The somewhat nebulous idea had arisen of Christ having incarnated in Jesus, and that through him something had occurred in earthly evolution. These ideas became very obscure, especially in the nineteenth century.

If, however, one were to ask whether what is ascribed to Christ and His potential influence in Christian dogma can really lead to something (if one asks insistently, honestly and sincerely), it is impossible to answer in the affirmative. For if human ideas are not powerful enough to envisage an Earth that is not the grave of humanity but one that enables mankind to undergo a transformation, if one does not have the capacity to think of earthly evolution other than how modern scientists describe it (which is to the effect that the Earth will cease to support life and the human race will become extinct), no idea about Christ Jesus will be of the slightest help. For even if He has had a certain influence upon the Earth, the conception that is generally formed of this is not powerful enough to raise matter to the point where it can be envisaged as being capable of being transmuted from its present earthly condition to a future state. Far more powerful ideas are needed than have hitherto been formed in

order that the Earth may be embraced through such ideas and translated to a new existence.

I recently said in the course of a public lecture[7] that natural science
thinks—or rather calculates—that if the forces of nature as they are
today were to persist for millions of years a state of affairs would arise (I
described this to you in connection with a lecture before the Royal
Institution[8]) where one will be able to paint walls with albumen and
read the newspaper in phosphorescent light. I also referred to the
scientist who claims that in the distant future milk will be solid and emit
a blue light, and so forth. These ideas arise from nebulous conceptions of
reality which are not powerful enough to lay hold of reality. For this
obsession that science has with calculations is equivalent to studying the
changes in the human stomach over four years and then reckoning what
it will be like after 250 years (the idea being that if I simply extend the
number of years I shall know how things will be). In the same way that
the scientist calculates what the Earth will be like in a million years, so
can I work out what the condition of a person's stomach will be like
after 250 years—only the person concerned will be dead by then! Just as
geologists calculate how the Earth looked millions of years ago, so could
one calculate, on the basis of the changes in a child's inner organs in a
week or in a fortnight's time, their condition 250 years ago—when of
course the child was not yet alive. These concepts are not capable of
fathoming the full reality of the situation. They have a limited validity
encompassing the millennia surrounding our time, extending roughly
from 6000–7000 BC to AD 6000–7000, but not any further.

However, man's being cannot be limited to such narrow time-scales;
and the Christ Being has an essential place in such a wider evolutionary
framework. It was for this reason that I said that[9] there is a difference
between what was referred to in the Middle Ages as a 'mystical wedding' and what Christian Rosenkreutz called the 'chymical wedding'.
The mystical wedding is only an inner process. As many theosophists
have previously said (and perhaps still say now): if one looks deeply into
one's inner being, one finds an identity with the Divinity! This was
depicted in such graphic colours that those who had heard one of these
hour-long lectures left with the conviction that if they zealously pursued
an inner quest they would feel as if they were themselves some kind of

god! The chymical wedding of Christian Rosenkreutz, on the other hand, conceives of these forces as being active within man in such a way that they take hold of the whole of his being, so that—when matter has been reduced to ashes—it is able to make the transition to the ages of Jupiter, Venus and Vulcan.

An important aspect of Manichaeism was the conquest of evil, the victory over matter through thought. The challenge to understand the questions of the Fall, of evil in general and—in association with them— the question of Christ Jesus at a deeper level was what confronted Julian; and he hoped to derive some illumination regarding these questions from his Persian initiation which he could then bring back to Europe. It can also be verified historically that he was assassinated by an adherent of Constantine, or rather of the Christians who adhered to his policies. Thus you can see that the principle of maintaining some kind of continuity was, I would say, tragically led into a blind alley through the premature death of Julian the Apostate.

As a result the Augustinian principle—that ideas that are in accordance with the Manichaean principle of uniting material conceptions with a spiritual thinking should be forbidden—became the generally accepted view. The West was therefore driven towards a process of abstraction, which with a certain inevitability permeated the whole of western Europe. Only certain significant individuals rebelled against this tendency. One of these was Goethe, whose whole way of thinking led him to do so; whereas one of those whose thinking was most fully in tune with this abstract idea was Kant. If you open up his *Critique of Pure Reason*—and I am well aware that I am saying something thoroughly heretical here, but it is true nonetheless—and read its main propositions, and then transform each one of its propositions into its opposite, you will arrive at the truth. This is especially the case with his most important statements enshrined in his theory of space and time. One can methodically transform every proposition into its opposite and say no where he says yes and yes where he says no, and you more or less arrive at something that is tenable in the spiritual worlds. You can gather from this why people have such an incentive to misrepresent Goethe, the great antithesis to Kant, in the way that this was done by the person I told you about recently, who put words into his mouth that mean the opposite of what he wanted to say: 'No created spirit reaches nature's inner heart.'

If we bear all this in mind, we shall also be able to appreciate the full value of what Julian wrote, which was directed specifically against Pauline Christianity.[10] It is a remarkable document—not so much because of what it contains but because of its similarity to much that was published in the nineteenth century. This may seem paradoxical; but the fact of the matter is that if you read Julian the Apostate's polemic against Christianity you find that all conceivable arguments are advanced against Christianity, against the historical Jesus and against certain Christian dogmas, and with an intense sincerity of feeling—not with a false emotionalism but with utter sincerity, with a strong inner conviction. And if we compare these arguments with what liberal theologians of the nineteenth century and their successors in people like Drews[11] and those people who, on the basis of this liberal historical research, have denied the historical existence of Christ Jesus—if we consider what is presented in all the relevant literature, which had its origins in the eighteenth century and then leads in the nineteenth century to the most meticulous, painstaking and thorough philological studies imaginable (and there are a great number of repetitions, so that one has to consult whole libraries), we find that we can draw together certain guiding principles. Many of the criticisms had their origin in the discovery that a comparative study of the Gospels reveals discrepancies of one kind or another. (I have often spoken about this and there is no need to repeat myself here.[12]) But if we make a list of these guiding principles and statements, we can find all of them already expressed in what Julian writes. Nothing really new was said in the nineteenth century; it had already been said by Julian the Apostate. Moreover, he expressed it with a certain creative originality, whereas in the nineteenth century it was stated with enormous industry and great theological erudition, and with an equal degree of theological sophistry.

Julian the Apostate had therefore taken on a battle of titanic proportions. His ultimate aim was to achieve continuity in the development of the mysteries by giving a fresh impetus to Manichaeism. Just imagine what it would have meant for really enlightened people such as Goethe, who had an instinctive urge to bring the spirit of ancient Greece to life within his own being, if Julian the Apostate had been successful in his aims! There was, however, quite another reason why there was an inevitability about the fact that he failed. But one will not understand his failure if one is insensitive to his greatness, if one is blind to his stature as a titanic figure who fought for a human understanding of cosmic relationships that can really penetrate earthly realities. In our present time it is particularly important to recall such great impulses in the historical evolution of the West. For we are living at a time from which we will not emerge in a healthy way if we do not consider the aims of someone of the magnitude of Julian the Apostate in a fresh light. It was not possible at his time—and this was his great tragedy— to reconcile the old principle of initiation with the deepest essence of Christianity. In our time this has become possible, and we must make use of this opportunity to translate it into reality if the Earth is not to enter an evolutionary decline and mankind is not to enter a downward cycle of development. We need to envisage the importance of regeneration in all spheres of life; and it is especially crucial to restore communication with the spiritual world.

We must to begin with form a clear picture of what is trying to frustrate these aims. People today are afraid of clarity of this nature, they dread such penetrating insights. Although there is plenty of physical courage in our time, there is a conspicuous absence of intellectual courage! This is what above all is lacking! There is a real unwillingness to face realities; and this is what is so abundantly necessary in our time. For if it is not to descend into oblivion, our age must learn to understand one thing especially: it must learn to understand the principle of the creative mind; it must learn to understand the significance of the fact that when the mind is engaged in a creative process it is working with the same forces as live in the instincts, except that whereas our instincts work in the darkness the mind that has become creative works in the light of the Sun, that is to say, of the spiritual Sun. This is what our age needs to understand; and there is much in our time that is actively engaged in directly opposing this.

Cato, the Roman statesman, whose main policy was to establish a strong framework for the Roman state, regarded it as a necessary precondition for the achievement of this purpose to exile those who were engaged in Greek or Hellenistic philosophy; for, he said, 'they only chatter, and this undermines the decrees of our authority'.[13] Machiavelli,[14] the great Renaissance figure from Florence, agreed with this, and especially praised Cato for banishing those who interfered with government decrees from the standpoint of spiritual knowledge. Machiavelli also fully appreciated the fact that in Rome the death penalty was at certain times used as a tool to make people submissive to the social order.

Having anything to do with the spiritual world was something utterly abhorrent to Rome and to its successors in Europe. Efforts were therefore made in a great number of areas to create as much uncertainty as possible regarding such matters and to cover them with a veil of secrecy. It is nevertheless the case that if a conception of the Mystery of Golgotha that is of the fully uncompromising nature that such a conception really needs to have makes its presence felt in the world, these mists of uncertainty and unawareness will evaporate rather as snow in sunlight. This has thoroughly uncomfortable consequences. But it must happen. And what needs to happen most of all is to arrive at a true understanding of the Being of Christ. In the next lecture I shall discuss how the human soul can directly approach the Christ Being in our time.

However, much can be gained in this respect if we focus our attention, on the one hand, on a figure who, I would say, inaugurated the exoteric aspect of western cultural development and, on the other hand, on the figure of Julian the Apostate, who tried in a way that proved impossible at the time to take up the struggle against this exoteric aspect of western evolution. But what is curious about all of this is that if someone today with only a little knowledge—I am not even saying a little knowledge of occult facts but merely a little knowledge of such facts as is still contained in certain ancient writings—makes a study of Christian dogma, some remarkable things emerge. And if such a person considers something like the Mass—again, not with occult knowledge but with the insights recorded in ancient writings that derived originally from these occult sources—some equally surprising results arise from such a study as they do in the case of dogma. One then begins to ask oneself: what lies behind this dogma and these cultic rituals? Not only I but countless writers who have studied these questions from the standpoint referred to have come to the conclusion that in both dogma and ritual there is such an enormous amount of ancient paganism present in a revived or reconstituted form that one can make the attempt—like, for example, the French writer Drach,[15] who was well familiar with ancient Hebrew—to demonstrate that everything in the dogmas and rituals of the Catholic Church is simply a revival of paganism. And other authors have attempted to show that certain people went to great lengths to hide this fact, so that it should not become generally known that the dogmas and rituals of the Church are imbued with paganism.

It would be a strange phenomenon if paganism were indeed to be living on in this very unconscious way, and the question might well arise: what would the survival of paganism have contributed to the survival of the Imperium Romanum? And how would things stand, then, with Julian the Apostate? Indeed, if many recent writers are correct in saying that, for example, the Catholic Mass is to all intents and purposes an ancient pagan sacrifice, and Julian expended all his energy on preventing the decline of ancient pagan customs and trying to perpetuate them, he did to a certain extent achieve something after all. Innumerable highly intractable problems—as Nietzsche says, 'problems with horns'—arise from a study of the great contrast between Julian the Apostate and Constantine. Problems of this nature which are fraught with fateful consequences for us today urgently need to become the issues of our time.

I shall take up this theme again next time.

LECTURE 15

BERLIN, 24 APRIL 1917

It has become clear from the previous lectures that it is important for the present and will be even more so for the future to realize that our understanding of Christ Jesus and of everything connected with the Mystery of Golgotha cannot rely solely upon the kind of outward observation as is characteristic of the ordinary scientific approach to the study of history today; and that sources other than historical study in the modern sense need to be tapped in order to arrive at a knowledge of Christ and the Mystery of Golgotha that is convincing and can be demonstrated as being true, even when these sources are the Gospels themselves. I have often stated—and anyone who makes himself familiar with the relevant literature can confirm this—that the most assiduous, diligent and painstaking research has been devoted to critical study of the Gospels in the nineteenth century. And it can indeed be said that, purely as an outward historical phenomenon, this Gospel criticism has yielded only negative results which have served more to destroy and dissipate the ideas that one may have of the Mystery of Golgotha than to affirm and substantiate them. We know that a large number of people today—not out of a spirit of opposition but because they do not see what else they can do—acknowledge that from their historical research they have arrived at the conclusion that there is no justification on purely historical grounds for saying that it is possible to prove that Christ Jesus actually existed at the beginning of our era. Of course it cannot be disproved either, but that is of no particular consequence.

I shall now address the question how it is possible to discover other sources for a knowledge of the Mystery of Golgotha than are available from historical sources. I shall approach this question by first considering certain aspects of occult history that I have already touched upon in earlier lectures.

If one studies the first centuries of the development of Christianity with the awareness that this evolutionary journey is really only comprehensible if one intensifies a purely historical study by means of research of a spiritual-scientific nature and if, therefore, one initially grants at least a hypothetical validity to such a spiritual-scientific study of this period, a very remarkable picture emerges. As one casts one's eye over these early Christian centuries one comes to the conclusion that the Mystery of Golgotha did not occur only once, as an isolated occasion on Golgotha itself, but that it was in a sense replicated on a second occasion in the whole panorama of historical development. There is, indeed, much that is remarkable about this whole period of history.

The established, traditional view is that there is a history of the Catholic Church which begins with the founding of Christianity, and then proceeds from the early Church Fathers and teachers of the first Christian centuries to the teachers and philosophers of the following centuries, the formulation of particular dogmas by the Councils and infallible popes and so forth. History is seen as a kind of unbroken thread which is described as though it was unfolding with the same character. Much criticism is levelled against the early Church Fathers, but by and large people are afraid to reject them completely because one would then be interrupting the ongoing process of development that links up with the Council of Constantinople in 869 of which I have already spoken. As I have said, the picture is given of a continuous historical process. But if there is a radical gap anywhere in an apparently continuous process, it is in this seemingly consistent line of historical development. If one really looks at the essence of what is going on, it would be scarcely possible to imagine a greater contrast between the spirit of the early Church Fathers and that of the later teachers of the Christian Church and the decrees of the Councils. A radical difference can be discerned here which, because of the prevalence of certain interests, has been equally radically blurred. It has therefore been possible to maintain an ignorance amongst people today of the early Christian centuries and of what actually happened then. There is, for example, hardly any real idea even amongst scholars of the way that Gnosticism was eradicated. Similarly, there is a considerable lack of clarity as to the real intentions of people like Clement of Alexandria, his pupil Origen and others, including Tertullian,[1] because a large part of the fragmentary information that has come down to us consists of the writings of those who opposed them. And because of all the extraordinary theories that have been constructed on the basis of these fragments it is well-nigh impossible to arrive at a reliable picture of these early Church Fathers and teachers.

In order to arrive at a clear understanding of these matters we need to look more closely at the reasons for this obscurity, and specifically to what in a certain sense led the Mystery of Golgotha to be enacted for a second time in history.

When the Mystery of Golgotha had taken place, ancient pagan rituals were still being practised on a very wide scale. Their prominence was such that, as we saw from the previous lecture, a figure such as Julian the Apostate was initiated into the Eleusinian mysteries; and it was also the case that, albeit in a somewhat irregular way, a large number of Roman emperors had undergone an initiation of some sort. Furthermore, everything connected with the ancient pagan rituals still existed, although this is usually dismissed today with a few words in a way that does not do justice to history. Everything that occurred is related in a highly superficial way. But even these superficial descriptions may be sufficient for many people to be able to speak of a second Mystery of Golgotha, even though they do not have any real understanding of the inner meaning of these events.

If one looks at the outward phenomena, one can say that in the early centuries of the Christian era there were pagan temples of every kind scattered over a very wide area which had a splendour and magnificence that is barely conceivable today; and these temples had idols which in the very details of their formation were an artistic reflection of what had lived in the old mysteries. Not only was there no town or landscape without an abundance of artistic representations of the mysteries in these far-off times, but out in the fields where the peasants grew cereals there were little isolated shrines, each with its idol. No agricultural work was done without a living connection being established with those forces which, the peasants believed, streamed down from the universe with the help of the magic powers which resided in these images. The Roman emperors, in conjunction with the bishops and priests, did all they could in the course of these centuries utterly to destroy all these temples and shrines with their images and idols—a process that we can follow until the reign of the Emperor Justinian in the sixth century through a steady succession of edicts ordering their ruthless destruction. A massive wave of destruction swept over the world during these centuries that is without comparison in the whole of human evolution, especially if one bears in mind *what* was being destroyed. This period, when one of the most important tasks of the Roman emperors who had formed Christianity in their own mould since the time of Constantine was to destroy what remained from ancient times, culminated in the event when St Benedict[2] with his own hands and the support of his workmen levelled the temple of Apollo on Monte Cassino to the ground in order to found a monastery dedicated to the Benedictine Order, and—more generally—in the time of the Emperor Justinian.[3] There were also edicts which were seemingly intended to stop this work of destruction. However, if one reads them one receives a curious impression. One emperor, for example, issued a decree which stated that not all the pagan temples should be destroyed at once, as that would incite the people to rebellion, and that everything should be done very gradually so that they would allow it to happen and not engage in insurrectionary activity.

All the terrible measures associated with this destructive work are very often glossed over like many other things. But this should not happen; for where the truth is sullied in any way the path to Christ Jesus is also obscured and cannot be found. Some special discoveries can be made regarding this earnest love of truth, my dear friends. I should like to recount a minor incident that occurred in my own life, which I mention because I experienced it in my early childhood. One never forgets such things. Now unless one has been thoroughly blocking one's ears one will have heard from the history of the Roman emperors that this Constantine of whom we have been speaking was no model of virtue. Indeed, if he had been a person of real virtue he would not have unjustifiably accused his own stepson of having a liaison with his own mother (the accusation was false and was fabricated in order to supply a reason for his murder) and then had his stepson murdered for this fabricated reason followed by the stepmother. These were by no means the worst of Constantine's deeds. But since the Church was very deeply indebted to him, official Church history is ashamed of presenting Constantine as he really was. I should like to read you a passage about Constantine from my school textbook on the history of religion![4] 'Constantine manifested his religious convictions also in his private life' (and I have already told you how things really stood!). 'Although he was reproached for his domineering nature and irascibility, one needs to bear in mind that faith is no protection against every indiscretion and that Christianity could not manifest its full sanctifying power through him because to the end of his life he eschewed participation in the holy sacrament.'

Justifications of this kind are very widespread, and you can glean much from them about the degree to which a love of truth has been a common phenomenon in history. The situation with respect to recent history is little better; but because other interests are playing in one does not so easily notice that the problems relate to different points of view.

When these edicts are discussed it is also mentioned that the Roman emperors were particularly opposed to blood sacrifices, or the sacrifice of animals, which are said to have been made in such temples (together with other, similar practices). My intention here is neither to engage in criticism nor to gloss over anything but simply to relate what actually occurred. The point to bear in mind is that when reference is made to opposition to animal sacrifice (from the entrails of which future events were said to have been predicted), what is being spoken of was indeed a decadent form of sacrifice. However, it was not the trivial pursuit that history often implies, but it was a profound scientific endeavour (albeit very different from the science of today). It is difficult to speak about these matters today because they are regarded as utterly repulsive, and it is only possible to characterize them in general terms; but the object of such animal sacrifices was to stimulate something that was no longer directly available at this time, because the age of the old atavistic clairvoyance was past. It was a way—one way among others—of reviving the ancient clairvoyant powers within certain circles of the pagan priesthood. A more satisfactory method of cultivating this ancient clairvoyant power in order to penetrate to primeval times was to revive the particular form of sacrifice practised in the Mithras mysteries, which was the most spiritual form of that time. In the priestly mysteries of Egypt and the Egyptian temples the practices were more brutal and bloody. If one studies the Mithras mysteries with occult means one realizes that they represented a way of gaining insight into the mysteries of the forces at work in the universe through sacrificial rites which went beyond what one associates with sacrificial rites today; for they yielded a far deeper insight into the mysteries of nature than modern autopsies and dissection of corpses, which do not delve into secrets of any sort but merely dabble on the surface. Anyone who had performed these sacrifices in the right way developed a certain clairvoyance for particular forces that are present in the mysteries of nature. It was for this reason that the true foundations of the ritual sacrifices were surrounded in secrecy and that access to them was granted only to those who were adequately prepared.

Now when we study the Mithras mysteries we find that they all go back to the third post-Atlantean epoch and that they were therefore at the time in question in a decadent phase of their development, in that in their pure form they were suited to the third epoch. In their most elevated phase in the third post-Atlantean period they represented a way of entering deeply into the mysteries of nature (albeit one that was enshrouded in danger and secrecy), in that the rites that were performed had the power to bring this about. In the presence of the pupils the priests performed certain rituals associated with the separating out of the elements of natural substances in order to arrive at a knowledge of the constituent parts of natural processes. Through the way in which this occurred—how in the course of these rituals the water present in the organisms interacted with fire and how this interaction represented a stimulus for the one who was present at the sacrifice—a special path was opened up to the pupil which led him to a self-knowledge that reached to the innermost fibres of his being and, hence, to a knowledge of the world.

Hence these sacrifices were a path leading to self-knowledge and knowledge of the world. People experienced themselves differently from their experience of themselves in ordinary life when they were present at such sacrifices. But this experience was to a high degree tailored to man's weakness; for self-knowledge is extremely difficult to acquire, and these sacrifices lessened the burden of acquiring it. Through these sacrifices people were led to feel and experience themselves inwardly, though far more intensely than through mere intellectual or conceptual processes. One might say that they strove for a self-knowledge that penetrated to their bodily organism, to their physical form, a self-knowledge that can be discerned in the minds of the great artists of antiquity, who in a sense owed their sense of form to their experience of the forms and movements of nature in their own organism. For the further back we go in the history of art, the more do we arrive at a time when it would have been completely incomprehensible to create from a model, to have a model in front of one which one proceeded to copy. We become increasingly aware that people had a living reality within themselves which they embodied in their creations. Everything has inwardly become so inert nowadays that it hardly bears speaking about, because words are inadequate as a means of expressing what we mean by them. It is quite extraordinary how times have changed.

Now the Greek mysteries of Eleusis were a direct continuation of these mysteries which were widely disseminated at the time of the Mystery of Golgotha. They represented a continuation but also a different aspect of these mysteries. Whereas in the Mithras mysteries there was an emphasis upon experiencing oneself through the instrument of the body, in the mysteries of Eleusis everything revolved around experiencing oneself outwardly rather than inwardly. The rituals in the Eleusinian mysteries were quite different from those of the Mithras mysteries, where the neophyte was drawn deeply into himself; whereas in the Eleusinian mysteries he was lifted out of himself, so that he experienced the mystery-laden impulses of the creative activity of nature and the spirit outside the body. If we ask ourselves what a person derived from these mysteries—both the Mithras mysteries, which by then were decadent, and those of Eleusis, which were not decadent then but had, even, been at the peak of their development a few centuries before the beginning of the Christian era and specifically in the fourth century BC—the answer would be couched in terms of the great injunction of the Delphic oracle: 'Know thyself!' Everything was oriented around self-knowledge and, moreover, self-knowledge in two different forms. On the one hand this occurred through the person becoming totally immersed in himself, so that the etheric and astral bodies were compressed and he was thrust inwardly into himself, with the result that the inner impact of his soul upon his bodily nature led him to experience: 'You are what you perceive when you reach down inwardly into yourself and encounter what is there.' This happened through the Mithras mysteries. Through the Eleusinian mysteries, on the other hand, a person arrived at self-knowledge through the soul being lifted out of the body by means of various rituals which will not be described further here, and the person concerned entered into connection outside the body with the mysterious influences of the Sun upon the Earth, with the forces of the Moon that irradiate it together with the impulses of the stars and of elemental forces such as warmth, air, fire and so forth. These external forces, this outward existence, pervaded the human soul which was thus lifted out of the body, and through this encounter with the outer world self-knowledge was attained. Those who understood the essential meaning of the mysteries knew that they had access to every kind of soul experience; but it was not possible for them to arrive at a real idea of the ego unless it derived directly from the mysteries. For the ego otherwise continued to be a wholly abstract phenomenon at that time. People were able to experience anything else of a soul-spiritual nature, but the ego had to be nurtured through the mysteries and required this strong external stimulus. The essential point is that this was known to be the case at this time.

What came about then was, as you know, a fusion between Christianity as it was then evolving and the impulse of Rome. I have already described how this arose; and as it did so there was a growing desire to wipe out all trace of what remained of the past, to prevent any real legacy of this world from being bequeathed to posterity, and specifically what people had been doing in the early centuries of the Christian era to form a connection—whether in or outside the body—with those divine forces that bring man his ego-consciousness. If we wish to enter more deeply into a study of the development of Christianity, we will need to consider not merely the continuing development of dogmas but most especially the development of cults and rituals. From certain points of view the ongoing development of ritual is far more important than the history of dogma. For dogmas bring arguments. In a certain sense they are like the phoenix bird, in that they rise again from their own ashes; and however much dogmas may have been eradicated, some crank will always come along favouring what has become outmoded. It is far easier to wipe out all trace of rituals. And the intention behind eradicating these ancient rituals, which were the outward signs, the visible external symbols, of what was taking place in the mysteries, was to make it impossible for anyone to discern from the continuing existence of the rituals how people had endeavoured to enter into a relationship with divine-spiritual forces.

In order to delve more deeply into these matters we need to turn our attention to the Christian rituals, for example the chief sacrament of the Mass, the Catholic Mass. What, fundamentally, is the inner significance of the Catholic Mass? What is it? The Mass, together with everything associated with it, is a continuing development of the Mithras mysteries combined, in a certain sense, with elements from the Eleusinian mysteries. It is none other than the continuation of ancient rituals, though developed further in a certain way. Especially the bloody character that the Mithras mysteries had gradually assumed has been distinctly reduced in its intensity. However, anyone who is able to appreciate certain details can only be aware of the considerable similarity of the spirit underlying these rituals: for example, the priest—together with anyone who is receiving communion—receives the body of the Lord after he has not eaten anything for a certain while; thus a period of fasting is far more important for understanding what is going on here than a great deal of what people argued about so furiously in the Middle Ages. And if a priest—as may well happen—neglects to honour this commitment to perform the transubstantiation and communion after a period of fasting, the Mass does not have the significance or the effect that it should have. It does in any case not have the required effect for the most part because the communicants have not been appropriately instructed; for there can only be an influence if people have been told about what is experienced immediately after receiving the bloodless body of the Lord. But you are probably aware of how little attention is paid to these details today, how little people realize that they should be having an experience that represents a certain inner residuum, a kind of modern renewal of what was imparted through the Mithras mysteries. Thus there are great mysteries hidden behind these rituals. The Church similarly sought to establish a certain continuity of the ancient principle of initiation through ordination, except that it has largely forgotten that the principle of initiation lay in giving specific teachings as to how to understand what is being experienced.

Now Julian's avowed intention was to discover how the Eleusinian mysteries, into which he had been initiated, were related to the mysteries of the third post-Atlantean age. But what was he able to learn of this from these mysteries? History has virtually nothing to say on this point. But if you were really to engage in a study of how people such as Clement of Alexandria, his pupil Origen, Tertullian and even Irenaeus,[5] to say nothing of the still earlier Church Fathers, were themselves largely rooted in the pagan principle of initiation and then in their own way made the transition to Christianity, if you were to glimpse into the minds of these great individuals you would find that their ideas and concepts were imbued with a quite particular quality of inner mobility, that a completely different spirit lived in them from that which was later to dwell amongst mankind. If we want to develop a closer understanding of the Mystery of Golgotha, it is really important that we gain something of an inkling of the spirit that lived in these early Fathers.

The fact is that people are so very much asleep—and I mean this quite literally—with respect to the wider dimensions of culture. They view the world as if they were in dreamland. We can see this in our own time. I have often spoken to you about Herman Grimm. I must confess that it is quite different for me now to be speaking about Herman Grimm from when I spoke about him four or five years ago. If one is attentive to these matters, what we have now been experiencing in the three years of this war makes what immediately preceded it and the decades leading up to this time seem like a kind of fairy-tale world which could well be centuries ago. Things have changed to such an extent that one has the feeling that events took place longer ago than they really did. In a similar way, much that is important in the world is experienced by people in a state of sleep.

If one tries to understand ancient writers with ordinary faculties of comprehension today—and of course, a university professor will be able to understand everything that has been transmitted to posterity—one may, even without being a person with such an enlightened mind, arrive at the conclusion that the ancient Greek philosophers such as Thales, Heraclitus and Anaxagoras, who did after all live not so very long ago, cannot really be understood unless one is able to study them with occult means. Even if one reads them in Greek, the fact is that they speak a different language from the one that is generally available for ordinary human discourse. This even applies to Plato, for example. I have often said that Hebbel was aware of this when, in a sketch for a play that he jotted down in his diary, he had the idea of depicting the reincarnated Plato as a grammar school pupil who has to study Plato with his teacher and who, despite having a clever teacher, is completely unable to cope with Plato, even though he is the reincarnation of him.[6] Hebbel wanted to make a drama out of this idea. He never got round to it, but he did indeed write in his diary how it would turn out if the reincarnated Plato was a modern grammar school pupil and found that he could not understand a word of what Plato had written. Thus it was Hebbel's view that not even Plato can readily be understood. Understanding in the sense of a precise grasping of concepts is something in human intellectual life that really begins only with Aristotle. It does not go further back; it begins with Aristotle in the fourth century BC. What preceded Aristotle cannot be understood with ordinary powers of reason. People have therefore been constantly trying to understand Aristotle, for on the one hand he can be understood, while on the other hand with respect to certain of his thought-forms no further advances have been made beyond Aristotle, for the reason that his way of thinking belonged very much to his time. After all, trying to think in the way that another age has thought is essentially the same as the situation of a man of 56 who wants to be 26 years old for a quarter of an hour in order to experience what it is like to be 26. A certain way of thinking is appropriate only for a quite specific time; the particular character of thinking is constantly changing from age to age. It is, nevertheless, interesting to note that in the Middle Ages Aristotle dominated the intellectual scene; and that he again reappears in the work of Franz Brentano, to whom I have often referred in a very recent publication. For in 1911 Franz Brentano wrote a very fine book about Aristotle where he has elucidated those ideas that are particularly suited for our present time.[7] It is very timely that Franz Brentano should have just now written a comprehensive book about Aristotle, which everyone who values keeping in touch with a certain quality of thinking should read. This book by Brentano about Aristotle is, moreover, very readable.

It was, however, Aristotle's fate that his work was indirectly mutilated not so much by Christianity but by the Church, and that some important parts of his writings have been lost. Thus what has come down to us in a mutilated form needs to be supplemented by occult means. The most important omissions relate to the human soul. And I find a certain link with respect to the challenge of responding to people today when they ask: how can I direct my meditative life, as described for example in the book *Knowledge of the Higher Worlds*, in such a way that through inner soul experiences I can find a sure path to discerning within myself the sources of the Mystery of Golgotha? For Aristotle tries in his own way to bring that inner experience to life within himself which anyone asking this question would have to replicate. But according to his commentators, whenever Aristotle is about to describe his own meditative path he stops short and says no more. However, this apparent taciturnity does not necessarily imply that Aristotle did not write about these matters but, rather, that those who came after him did not copy it, with the result that it has not come down to us. Aristotle had already opened up a quite distinctive inner or even mystical path. He wanted to discover that quality in the soul that endows it with the inner certainty that the soul is immortal.

Now if a person honestly and sincerely engages in inner meditative work and practises an inner discipline, he will have an inner experience of the soul's immortality through this being inwardly revealed to him. It was completely and utterly clear to Aristotle that it is inwardly possible to experience something that is independent of the body and which, therefore, has nothing to do with the death of the body. This was totally clear to Aristotle. But he goes further, and tries to experience with full intensity within himself that which one can experience with absolute certainty as not belonging to the body. And then he experiences with full clarity—though the relevant passage is corrupt or has been mutilated[8]—what one must have experienced in order to come to an understanding of the Mystery of Golgotha: inner solitude. Solitude! Mystical experience inevitably leads one to such a solitude, to suffering the grief of solitude. And if this feeling of solitude has grown in intensity to the point where one asks, 'What have I forsaken that I have become lonely?' one will be obliged to answer, 'I have with the best part of my being forsaken father, mother, brothers, sisters and the rest of the familiar world in my soul.' This was what Aristotle was aware of. This inner experience is something that one can have; it can be invoked. One is well aware in this sense of solitude that there is something within one that transcends death but that this is not connected with anything except one's own ego and it has no relationship to the outside world. One comes to realize what Aristotle also realized: that one's contact with the outer world is mediated through the organs of the body. There are other ways in which one can experience oneself; but one needs the organs of the body in order to experience the outer world. Hence the solitude that becomes a feature of our experience. And now Aristotle said to himself, as everyone who follows in his wake must also realize: 'I have therefore experienced the soul, I have experienced my immortal soul which death cannot destroy. But at the same time everything that brings me in touch with the outside world has gone. I am confined within myself. I cannot make any further progress with understanding immortality,' he said, 'beyond realizing that after death I shall experience myself in utter solitude, with nothing before me for all eternity other than the good and evil deeds that I have performed. This is what I shall behold for all eternity; and it is this that lies in my power to achieve. If I want to know anything else about the spiritual world, I cannot rely on my own forces alone but must either follow a path of initiation or listen to what the initiates can tell me.'

All this was stated in Aristotle's writings, but it was not passed on by his successors. And because Aristotle perceived this, he became a kind of prophet, he became the prophet for that different quality of perception that lay beyond the possibilities of his time and which is different today from how it was then. But there is no need to make a historical survey to discover this; for we know that it is so from personal experience.

Let us consider once more this experience of total solitude which belongs to modern life, this mystical experience which is completely different from the way that mystical experiences are very often described. For they are very often described in a self-satisfied way as if to say: 'I experience God within my inner being.' But this is not the full mystical experience. The full mystical experience is to say that one experiences God in complete and utter solitude, that one experiences oneself alone with God. And then it is only a question of having the necessary strength and endurance to continue living in this solitude. For this experience of solitude is a potent force! If one does not let oneself be oppressed by it but allows it to live within one as a source of strength, one meets with another experience—these are, of course, mere descriptions, but everyone can have these experiences—in the form of the inner certainty: 'This solitude that you are experiencing is of your own making, you have brought it about yourself. It was not born with you. You were born of the God whom you experience, but this solitude was not born with you, it originates from you. You are responsible for this solitude.' That is the second experience.

This experience leads directly to a feeling of shared responsibility for the killing of what has been born of God. At this point, when the solitude of the soul has been exerting an influence for a sufficient time, it becomes clear that something happened at the time when the divine element within man was killed off by the human element (for this has not always been the case, otherwise no evolution would have taken place; there must have been a time when this feeling did not exist). If I had time I would be able to explain more fully what is meant by the killing of the Son of God. Mystical experience should not be something isolated, vague or indeterminate but unfolds in stages. It is possible for us to experience the death of Christ.

And once this experience has been intensified, then (and I can express it in no other way) the Christ, the Risen One, becomes a living presence within us! For the Risen One, He who passed through death, is initially present as an inner mystical experience. We also experience what motivated His death in the manner described.

Thus one can have a threefold mystical experience. But then it is perhaps still not sufficient to find the path to the sources of the Mystery of Golgotha; for something else needs to be added which has been strongly misrepresented today, and even concealed. The only person who has pointed out with a sufficient degree of force what has with the greatest ingenuity been hidden from mankind through nineteenth-century education and culture was Friedrich Nietzsche, specifically in his treatise *On the Uses and Abuses of History*. For nothing has contributed more thoroughly to obliterating our knowledge of Christ than what passes for history today; and no single factor, therefore, has so thoroughly negated the Mystery of Golgotha as the objective historians of the nineteenth century. Of course I am well aware that anyone who criticizes these objective historians today is regarded as a fool, and there is no question of belittling the painstaking philological and scholarly efforts that have been devoted to historical research. But however scholarly and exact this history may be, it is a desert for the soul; and history is the surest way to create such a barren wasteland. It has no understanding of the things in human life that really matter.

I may perhaps be allowed to speak personally in this realm, for I have certain personal associations in this regard. I have studied Goethe's work since my eighteenth or nineteenth year, but I have never felt tempted to write an objective historical account of him or his use of language for the simple reason that from the very outset the idea that inspired me was that what is most important is that Goethe is alive! The point here is not to focus upon Goethe as a physical human being, who was born in 1749 and died in 1832; what really matters is that since Goethe died in 1832, his spirit has been living on not only within him as an individuality but also all around us in our whole intellectual and cultural environment, and not only in what people say and write about him (and in any case nothing very illuminating is said about Goethe today). We are indeed surrounded by a spiritual mantle that did not exist for the people of ancient times. The ether body is separated from the soul after death like a kind of second corpse, but through the residual effects of the Christ impulse that have remained from the Mystery of Golgotha it is now conserved to a certain extent and does not completely dissolve. And if we have the faith—I am now using the word 'faith' in the way that I defined it at the beginning of these lectures—that Goethe has resurrected in terms of his ether body, and on this basis make a study of his work, his ideas and insights will then become alive and we will not describe him as he was but as he is now. We will then have brought the idea of the resurrection to life, in such a way that we can believe in it. We can then say that we do not merely believe in dead ideas but in the living influence of ideas. This is connected with a deep mystery of modern times. No matter what we may think (this is not true of our feeling and will, but what I am saying is true as far as our thinking and perception are concerned), for as long as we are in the physical body there are impediments to giving full expression to one's ideas in the right way. However great Goethe may have been, his ideas were even greater than he was himself; for his physical body has to bear responsibility for the fact that they were not able to attain a greater stature than they actually did. The moment when they could become separate from the body (and I am now referring to the ideas which in a certain way live on in his ether body, not to his feeling and will) and can be developed further by someone who lovingly embraces them and continues to ponder them, they become something beyond what they were and acquire new life. You need to have faith that the first form in which ideas may arise is on no account the final form that these ideas may have; you need to believe in a resurrection of ideas! Believe so firmly in this that you gladly form a connection not merely with your ancestral blood-relations but with your spiritual ancestors, and that you indeed find them. They do not have to be Goethes and might well be called Smith or Jones. Fulfil Christ's injunction not only to relate to bodies through blood but to connect with souls through the spirit; and you will then transform the idea of resurrection into a living reality. For what really matters is not to be forever saying 'Lord, Lord!' but that Christianity can be understood in its living essence and that its most crucial idea of the resurrection is regarded as a living force. Anyone who in this sense derives a certain support from the past is learning to experience the continuing existence of the past. And then it is only a question of time when the moment arrives when Christ is there among you. Everything depends on keeping faith with the Risen One and the

Resurrection and saying: 'We are surrounded by a spiritual world, and the Resurrection has become a reality in our midst!'

You may well say that this is purely hypothetical. Well then, let it be a hypothesis! If ever you have the experience of forming a connection with a thought of someone who has died and whose physical body has been assimilated by the Earth, and the thought or idea lives on in you, the time will come when you will say to yourself: 'This thought that has become revitalized within me has been made alive by Christ, and it could never have been brought to life in this way before Christ was on the Earth.'

There is a path to the Mystery of Golgotha which can be followed inwardly. But it really is quite essential to part company with so-called objective history which, because it dwells only on the outer surface and blots out all reference to the spirit, is actually thoroughly subjective. As you can see, many biographies of Goethe have been written. These biographies of Goethe by and large set out to portray his life as faithfully as possible. Every time this is done something is maimed within the person who is doing it; for the thoughts that Goethe had in the way that he conceived them at the time have passed through death and live on in a different form. It is important that we should understand Christianity in this same way, out of a spiritual perception.

In short, it is possible to understand the Mystery of Golgotha in a mystical way (in the true sense of the word); but one should not remain content with abstractions but, rather, undergo the sort of inner experiences that have just been described. And if anyone asks, 'How can I myself approach Christ?', he needs to be aware that he must reach out to the Risen Christ and that, provided that he has the patience and endurance to follow the path that has just been described, he will approach Christ at the right moment and can be sure of meeting Him. It is, however, important to be aware of not allowing the most crucial aspects of this encounter to pass one by.

I said that Aristotle was in a sense a prophet, and that Julian the Apostate had something of this same prophetic spirit. But because of the form that the Eleusinian mysteries had adopted at that time he could no longer discover what he sought; and he endeavoured to establish a connection with the Mithras mysteries—hence his Persian campaign. He wanted to discover the whole continuity in the mysteries and to understand the connections between them. This could not be allowed; and he was therefore assassinated.

However, the early Church Fathers also sought to experience Christ after the fashion of the Eleusinian mysteries. And irrespective of whether we refer to them as Gnostics or not (the real Gnostics were banned from the Church, though one could well describe Clement of Alexandria as a Gnostic), because they endeavoured to approach Christ through the Eleusinian mysteries they related to Christ in a totally different way from their successors. Their relationship with Him was such that first and foremost they acknowledged Him as a cosmic Being. For example, the question would often be asked: 'How does the Logos work purely in the spiritual world?' And: 'What were the essential characteristics of that being whom man encountered in paradise? What was this being's connection with the Logos?' These people concerned themselves with questions of this nature, which have to be answered purely in terms of spiritual conceptions. And the fact is that if one studies the Eleusinian and Mithras mysteries, which were being remorselessly eradicated, in the early centuries after the Mystery of Golgotha the Risen One was Himself associated with the mysteries seeking to reform them. Thus there is a deep truth in the statement that Julian the Apostate was probably a better Christian than Constantine. Constantine was, to begin with, not even initiated, and then his way of accepting Christianity was very superficial. But Julian had an intuitive understanding of the idea that if Christ is to be sought he can only be found through the mysteries, and that once He has been found He can endow one with the ego to which human beings could not yet be afforded access at the time of Aristotle.

There was, of course, a deep historical necessity involved in the mysteries being so totally eradicated, instead of their being a means whereby the path to Christ could be sought. However, the path to the world of ancient Greece needs to be rediscovered, though without the aid of old records and documents. This world must be revived, though not of course as it was, otherwise one gets into these absurdities such as the aping of the Olympic Games. The point is not to mimic ancient Greece, and I certainly do not have that in mind. Ancient Greece needs to be revived from within, and this will surely happen; for people must find the path into the mysteries, albeit in a very inward way. They will, by the same token, also find the Christ.

However, just as the first Mystery of Golgotha took place in Palestine, so was the second enacted by the impulse brought by Constantine; for the eradicating of the mysteries led to Christ, as a historical reality, being crucified, killed for a second time. The terrible destruction that spread over several centuries was not merely a destruction of artistic and mystic treasures (though this should not be underestimated) but the destruction of vast swathes of human experience. But there was no understanding of what had actually been destroyed and had disappeared, because any real depth of understanding had been lost. When the temples of Serapis and Zeus were destroyed together with their magnificent sculptures, the people said: 'Yes, those who are destroying these temples are right; for ancient legends have predicted that if the temple of Serapis is destroyed the vaults of heaven will collapse and the Earth will be reduced to chaos. But none of this has happened, even though the Roman Christians have levelled the temple of Serapis to the ground.' It is true that the stars have not fallen in an outward, physical way, and the Earth has not descended into chaos; but what was formerly known to human experience through Sun initiation has disappeared. The whole vast wisdom that, in the view of the ancients, arched more mightily into the celestial regions than the physical sky, fell together with the temple of Serapis. This ancient wisdom, of which Julian the Apostate still felt an echo in the Eleusinian mysteries, where the spiritual Sun and the spiritual Moon hovered over him raying down their impulses, disappeared without trace. All that the ancients experienced in the Mithras mysteries and in the mysteries of Egypt, where through sacrificial worship they inwardly experienced the mysteries of the Moon and the mysteries of the Earth as they were manifested within man when, to use the somewhat banal expression I employed earlier, he arrived at self-knowledge within his inner being through the inner compression of his soul, was reduced to chaos. The spiritual situation was such that the vaults of heaven collapsed and the Earth was reduced to chaos; for what disappeared in the course of these centuries was comparable to what would be lost if we were suddenly to be deprived of our senses, when at any rate for us the sky would no longer be above us and the Earth were no longer to be beneath our feet. The vanishing of the ancient world was not the trifling episode that it is made out to be, but had far-reaching dimensions. If we do not want to accept that what has been lost has disappeared altogether, we need to believe in the Resurrection. But this asks of us that the ideas that we formulate should be powerful and courageous; and above all else it is necessary that people today recognize the need for that impulse to which reference has been made so often in these lectures.

Human beings have, through a necessary requirement of world karma (although of course it is only a necessity from a certain point of view), had to have a sense of having lived for centuries in a somewhat empty and purposeless way, so that out of a strong inner urge for freedom the Christ impulse can again be found in the fullest sense. However, they must rid themselves of the self-satisfaction in which so many tend to indulge at present.

Sometimes this sense of self-satisfaction acquires remarkable dimensions. A Benedictine father by the name of Knauer gave some lectures in Vienna in the 1880s. I should like to read you a passage from these lectures. The lecture from which I should like to read you a short extract is about the Stoics. The most important representatives of the Stoics were Zeno (342–270), Cleanthes, who lived two centuries before Christ, and Chrysippus (282–209); thus the members of this school lived several centuries before the Mystery of Golgotha. What can an expert on the Stoics tell us about them (bearing in mind that they lived some centuries before the Mystery of Golgotha)?

> Finally I should like to say something in praise of the Stoics, in that they had an aspiration towards a league of nations embracing the whole of the human race, which would be potentially able to end all racial hatred and war. I need hardly say that the Stoics were in this respect at a far higher level than the often inhuman prejudices of their time and even those of later generations.[9]

A league of nations! I had to read the lecture again, because it occurred to me that I might not have been hearing aright when I heard Wilson and the other statesmen of our present time speaking about a league of nations, because I was hearing the voice of the ancient Stoics from the third century BC! For they said it much better. They said it much better because they had the power of the ancient mysteries behind them. They said it with an inner power which has now disappeared, and nothing but the empty husk remains. Only those historians who are not historians in the ordinary somewhat trivial sense see historical phenomena in a different light.

And Knauer continues (I do not need to take back anything that I said about Immanuel Kant; nevertheless, it is remarkable that a good philosopher like Knauer said the following words about the Stoics in the 1880s): 'This idea'—he means the idea of the league of nations—'has been revived again and declared feasible by no less a figure among modern philosophers than Immanuel Kant[10] in his treatise *On Perpetual Peace. A Philosophical Outline*, which is far too little known. Kant's basic idea is in any event right and practical. He says that eternal peace must surely arise when the most powerful countries of the world have a constitution that is truly representative.' Well, this is now referred to, more vaguely, as a reorientation. Kant's term is already pretty innocuous, but now people talk about a reorientation. But in his further study of Kant, Knauer comes up with these additional details:

> Under such a system the owners of property and the educated classes, who have been most adversely affected by war, will be in a position to take decisions about war and peace. Kant does not, however, consider our constitutions which are modelled on those of England to be constitutions that are truly representative. They are mostly dominated by partisanship and sectional interests, which are fostered by an electoral system founded almost entirely on arithmetical and statistical principles. However, the crux of the argument is this: 'International law should be based upon a federation of free and independent states.'

Are we hearing Kant or the voice of reorientation? With Kant the arguments are more forcefully expressed and more firmly grounded. I do not want to carry on reading what follows; for dear old Kant might otherwise incur the displeasure of the censor.

What I have been discussing has been used by a writer whom I have often mentioned, the American author Brooks Adams, as a means of studying the course of human evolution.[11] His aim has been to investigate the significance of the fact that former aspects of human history have from time to time been revived by certain peoples, as, for example, the way in which the Germanic peoples restored the idea of the Imperium Romanum. As he surveys the present epoch Brooks Adams finds many similarities with the Imperium Romanum; but nowhere does he find indications of anything that might regenerate it. He does not consider that the Americans can do this (he was writing in America), and there are good reasons for that. For such a revival cannot come from outside; it must come from within, through an enlivening of the spirit. A revival cannot come from bodies; it can only be engendered by souls. However, this is only possible if the Christ impulse is understood in all its living essence. All the stupid empty phrases that one hears so much of nowadays have to do with the past but not with the present and future; it is meaningless simply to quote proverbs, such as 'Minerva's owl can only spread its wings in the twilight'. This was valid for former times; for when these peoples had reached a certain maturity they founded schools of philosophy, they looked back in spirit to what they had come to know through instinct. In future things will be quite different. This instinctive knowledge will not return; rather must the spirit itself become instinctive, so that out of the spirit itself the possibility for new creativity can emerge.

These are quite momentous thoughts. You need to reflect on these words: new creative possibilities must emerge from the spirit! The power of the spirit must become instinctive! And this all depends on the idea of the Resurrection. What has been crucified must arise again. This will not come about through waiting on events; it will only be possible if we make the creative powers of the spirit truly alive within us.

This is what I wanted to say to you at this time on the subject of the Mystery of Golgotha.

LECTURE 16

BERLIN, 1 MAY 1917

In these lectures I have been speaking about some of the earliest events in the development of western civilization. As you have seen, however, my purpose in doing so was to discover from such thoughts as may emerge from these studies of antiquity what is of importance for the present. My intention today is to develop this line of enquiry in a similar direction.

Our present time, as one can see from a cursory glance, is an age where the only thoughts that have real influence are those which have been derived from the mysteries underlying human evolution. In order to sense the full implications of such a statement, we need—quite apart from being awake to many other things—to be acutely aware of the needs and shortcomings of present-day thinking, feeling and willing. It is evident from this that our present age has need of new thoughts, impulses and ideas and, moreover, of such a kind that spring from the very foundations of the spiritual life which is the object of spiritual-scientific research.

There is much about our present times that must be viewed with a certain sadness, although this sadness should never be something that makes us despondent but, on the contrary, can prepare us adequately for work and new endeavours in our time. In recent weeks a book appeared, and if I may say so when I acquired it I had the feeling that it would give me the greatest pleasure. It has been written by a man who is one of the few who have been able to show an interest in our spiritual-scientific endeavours, and I might have wished that he could have included some aspects of this research in his own creative work. I am referring to the book *The State as Organism* by Rudolf Kjellén, the Swedish political economist.[1] When I had read the book I have to say that it left me with a sense of melancholy, because I could see the extent to which this person who, as I have said, could be interested in spiritual science is removed in his thinking from those thoughts which are so clearly needed today and which need to be clearly formulated if they are to be able to influence the way that our modern age is developing. Kjellén endeavours to study the state, and one has the feeling that at no point does he possess the necessary ideas or insights to enable him to have even the most remote possibility of solving his problem or to come anywhere near to doing so. It is a melancholy experience—which, as I have said, should not make one despondent but should, on the contrary, reinforce one's determination to meet the challenges of one's time—to have to make such discoveries again and again.

Before I elaborate further about matters such as this, I should first like to focus your attention once again upon aspects of early history and specifically upon that which, as you can easily imagine from the indications that I recently gave you about the destructive element in the Christian Church, is made only very dimly apparent through ordinary historical research and which must therefore be illuminated through spiritual science. In my previous lecture I mentioned the incredible fury that accompanied the destruction of ancient works of art by the Christian Church as it expanded its sphere of influence in the early Christian centuries, and how much this growing Christian world erased from earthly existence. It is not possible to take an impartial view of Christianity without being prepared to consider this other aspect of what was going on with complete objectivity. And you need to be aware, moreover, that you are bound to receive a certain picture from the various books that have been written on this subject. Everyone who has received even the minimum of education will have been given a picture of the cultural development of the ancient world, of that world that preceded Christianity. But just imagine how different this picture that people receive today would have been if Archbishop Theophilus of Alexandria[2] had not in AD 391 burnt seven hundred thousand rolls containing highly important cultural documents about Roman, Egyptian, Indian and Greek literature and their cultural life! Consider for a moment how different the accounts in the books would be if these seven hundred thousand rolls had not gone up in flames! From this you will be able to form a picture of what a history of the past that relies entirely upon documents actually is and, equally, what it is not.

Let us now take up the train of thought that I outlined last time. I made it clear that in many respects the ritualistic life of Christianity derived its inspiration from ancient symbols and ceremonies of the mysteries, while on the other hand the Church ensured that the forms of these rituals and symbols were to all intents and purposes completely eradicated. The Church made a clean sweep of these ancient forms of worship, so that people had no knowledge of what had preceded their time and therefore devoted themselves solely to what the Church offered. This was indeed the course that human evolution followed; and we must be prepared to acknowledge without dwelling on such pessimistic feelings as we may have that it is not always a path of straightforward progress.

In my previous lecture I also drew your attention to the fact that much that formed part of the rituals [of the Roman Church] goes back on the one hand to the Eleusinian mysteries, which were, however, interrupted in their development because, as I indicated, Julian the Apostate did not receive the recognition that he desired and was unable to fulfil his intentions; but to an even greater extent what came to be manifested in later times flowed from the Mithras mysteries. However, the spirit of the Mithras mysteries, that which justified their existence and was the source of their essential spiritual substance, can no longer be investigated in the ordinary way because there was a determination to wipe away all traces of their existence. Some insight into their true nature can therefore only be gained if one endeavours to form some conception of it through spiritual-scientific research. Today I want to give you some idea of just one particular aspect of the Mithras mysteries. There is of course far, far more to say about these Mithras mysteries than I can possibly say today, but it is best to approach an understanding of such matters by becoming familiar with some particular details.

In order that we may understand the Mithras mysteries, which continued to have a considerable influence extending right into western

Europe in the first centuries of the Christian era, in their essential nature, we need to be aware that they were founded wholly upon a basic view that was entirely right and appropriate in the ancient world prior to the Mystery of Golgotha. This basic view was that the human community or individual human communities such as folk communities or other communities within particular peoples or ethnic groups do not merely consist of the separate atoms that one can call human beings but that, if what was going on was to be rooted in reality, a group spirit or community spirit of supersensible origin must be living in the community concerned. A community did not simply consist of the number of heads that could be counted in it but it represented for these people the outward manifestation, even the incarnation (if I may use such a word here), of the actual community spirit concerned. Moreover, the aim of those who were received into these mysteries was to live in community with this spirit, to share in its thoughts; and it was regarded as essential that no single human being should remain isolated with his own obstinately egotistic thoughts, feelings and will impulses but that each one should live in such a way as to be receptive to the thoughts of the group spirit. Specifically in the Mithras mysteries there was the awareness that this aim cannot be achieved if one views a wider human community merely in terms of those who presently constitute it; for through the purely contemporary aspect what resides within the community spirit is significantly obscured. For—it was said—the dead are also part of present realities, and the more that one can live with those who have long been dead, the better and more rightly one will live in the present. Indeed, the longer the people concerned had been dead, the more beneficial it was found to be to live with their spirit. What was best of all was to be able to live in community with the spirit of the ancestor of a tribe, a folk community or a race by forming a connection with his soul; for the assumption was that this soul achieves a further development once it has passed through the portal of death, and that it has a deeper insight into what is to occur here on the Earth than those who are living on this Earth incarnated in a physical body. Thus the whole purpose of these mysteries lay in establishing ceremonies and rituals that could bring the neophyte in contact with the spirits who had for the most part died long, or even very long, ago.

Those who had been admitted to these mysteries had to undergo a first stage of initiation, which was usually referred to by means of an expression derived from the bird world; they were called 'Ravens'. A Raven was someone who was at the first level of initiation. Through particular mystery rituals, powerful symbols and richly artistic dramatic ceremonies, he learnt to be aware not only of what one sees with one's physical eyes in the surrounding world or what one learns from one's fellow human beings but what the dead are thinking. He acquired a certain capacity to remember the dead and the ability to develop this capacity further. Such a Raven had an obligation, namely that he was strictly required to be thoroughly awake to the present moment and to observe everything around him with open, clearly focused eyes, to acquaint himself with human needs and familiarize himself with the natural world. Anyone who daydreams and has no feeling for what is living in man and in nature was not regarded as suitable for being received into the mysteries; for only a person who actively observed life in the world around him was equipped for the task that he had to fulfil in the mysteries. His task was that he had to try as hard as he could to become involved in all the various situations of life in the outer world in order to deepen his experience, to share in the joys and sorrows of the events taking place around him. Someone who was unresponsive to current events was not a suitable candidate; for his first task within the mysteries was to re-enact what he had experienced in the world around him in the environment of the mysteries. In this way these experiences provided information for the dead, for those whose advice was being sought. You might well ask whether an initiate at a higher level would not have been more suitable for this. This was actually not so; first-degree initiates were particularly suitable because they possessed all the feelings, all the sympathies and antipathies that enabled them to relate directly to the outer world, whereas those at a higher level had more or less divested themselves of such trappings. So these first-degree initiates were particularly suited to experience life in the present in the way that an ordinary person experiences it and to offer it up to the mysteries. It was therefore the special task of the Ravens to mediate between the outer world and those who had long been dead. An echo of this had been preserved in legends, which as I have often pointed out by and large rested on deep foundations. Thus when it is asserted in a legend that Friedrich Barbarossa long after his death is instructed in his castle by ravens, or that Charlemagne is taught in 'Salzburg-amidst-the-mountains' by ravens[3] in order to tell him what is going on in the outside world, these are echoes of ancient mysteries and specifically of the Mithras mysteries.

When someone was ready for the second level, he was referred to as an 'Occultist' or a pupil of the mysteries. He thereby became able not only to bring the outer world to the world of the mysteries but also, in the way that information is received from the dead, to hear about the impulses which the supersensible world in which the dead reside had to impart to the outer world. And only when he was fully integrated into spiritual life as a whole, in its interrelationship between the super-sensible and sense-perceptible worlds, was he deemed ready for the third level of initiation, when he was given the possibility of applying in the outside world the impulses that he had received in the mysteries. He was now elected to become a 'Warrior' for those supersensible impulses that must be made manifest in the world of the senses.

Now you may well ask whether there was not a deep injustice in the fact that the people as a whole were left in ignorance about matters of the greatest importance and only certain individuals were initiated. You will, however, only have a proper idea of what lies behind this if you start from the premiss that I stated at the outset, namely that there was a group spirit, or group soul, involved in this situation. It was perfectly acceptable if certain individuals acted on behalf of the whole group of people. They did not feel themselves as individuals but as members of the group. It was therefore only possible to act in this way at the time when the group-soul element, the selfless feeling of belonging to the group, was a living reality.

And then, when the initiate had been a Warrior for the supersensible world for a certain time, he was considered suitable for establishing smaller groups within the large group, smaller communities that proved to be necessary within larger groups. In those ancient times there would have been no point in anyone simply setting up an association on his own initiative as is done today, for nothing would have come of it. In order to establish such a society or association it was necessary in the

Mithras mysteries to be a 'Lion', for that was the fourth level of initiation. Such a person must have consolidated his life in the supersensible worlds through his connection with those impulses which were not confined to the living but which united the living with the dead.

From this fourth level the initiate was enabled through certain measures to rise to take over the leadership of an already existing group or folk community, which included the dead. If we go back to the eighth, ninth and tenth centuries before the Mystery of Golgotha we find ourselves in totally different times from today. It would not have occurred to anyone then to claim the right to choose who would do a particular thing, for anyone doing something on behalf of the community had to be initiated to the fifth level. And then at the next level the initiate was able to gain access to that knowledge which the Sun mystery (of which he had received intimations) had implanted in the human soul; and thereafter his path led to the seventh level. I do not need to elaborate on this any further, for what I wanted to do was simply to indicate the nature of the course of development of a person who had to acquire from the spiritual world his capacity to take an active part in community life.

As you well know, it was of course a necessary part of the evolution of the human race that the whole phenomenon of group souls gradually receded into the background. The situation was such that at the time of the Mystery of Golgotha human souls developed a consciousness of their ego or 'I'. This had been prepared for many hundreds of years, but the time of the Mystery of Golgotha represented a culmination or critical moment in this respect. It would no longer be possible to make the assumption that the individual had the power to carry the whole community with him and to pass on his feelings and impulses selflessly to the whole community.

It would be foolish to believe that the course of history might have been different than the one that it has actually followed. But sometimes it might prove fruitful to consider, for example, what would have happened if at the time when Christianity was beginning to make its mark upon human evolution not absolutely everything had been totally eradicated but if a certain knowledge—of the kind that those who only believe in documents would have had access to—had been transmitted historically to posterity. But Christianity [in the form of the Church] did not want this to happen. I shall speak on some future occasion about the reasons why it was opposed to this, but today I shall simply state this as a fact. This Christianity was confronted by a totally different kind of humanity, which was not related to the old group spirits in the way that was formerly the case; a humanity where the approach to the individual was totally different than in ancient times, when the individual was not taken into account to any real degree and when people related to the group spirit and acted out of it. By destroying all documentary evidence of this ancient time for outward perception, Christianity fostered—and even consciously created—a certain obscurity with respect to that age when it first began to develop. It incorporated what it needed into its traditions, its dogmas and especially into its rituals, and then wiped away all trace of the sources of these rituals. There is an immense amount residing within these rituals, but everything has been given a different interpretation and has been differently formulated. The outward trappings still existed for people to see them, but they were not to know with what ancient wisdom they were connected.

Take, for example, the bishop's mitre from the eighth century. This eighth century mitre has clear symbols, but all these symbols are similar (though different in detail), and they are all swastikas. The swastika is embroidered in various different ways on these bishop's mitres. This symbol goes back to the earliest times of the mysteries and can be traced back to those ancient times when people could observe the activity of the lotus flowers in the human etheric and astral organisms, how what lives in these so-called lotus flowers is one of the most important aspects of etheric and astral forces. But it became a dead symbol. The bishop bore it as a symbol of his authority, and it became a dead symbol through all traces of its origin being effaced. Even what is said in cultural history about the origin of such things has nothing living about it. Only through spiritual science can the living quality in such phenomena be rediscovered.

I said earlier that a certain degree of obscurity was created. However, something must again emerge from this darkness. And I think that I have over the years said more than enough to make it clearly understood that it is of quite particular importance in our time to have ears for these things that can really hear and eyes that can really see. For our time is one when the darkness that inevitably had to hold sway has run its course, and when a new light, the light of spiritual life, must shine forth. The hope initially would be that many people would in their hearts and souls feel with all the seriousness at their command that this is a necessity for our time, and that what is going on around us and calls forth such sorrow in our time is connected with all these questions. It is already becoming clear that it is not enough to look at things only on the surface, that it is inadequate to speak about the causes of what is going on at present on the basis of superficial observations. For as long as people speak only about what lies on the surface, they will not find the thoughts or be able to develop the impulses that have the potency to lead forth from the obscurity which has been the cause of everything that is happening now.

Although I must emphasize once more that we should not become despondent or critical but simply fulfil the necessary task of observing and interpreting what is going on today, it is indeed remarkable that people in our time are unwilling to look at wider perspectives of evolution because, for the most part, they do not as yet manage to see what needs to be done. It is heartbreaking to see how an individual who suffered deeply from the confusion and chaos of the second half of the nineteenth century to the point of becoming seriously ill experienced the darkness and turmoil that prevails in our time. There is much more to Friedrich Nietzsche than merely to regard him as someone whom one enthusiastically follows, as so many have done. To such people he himself addressed these cautionary words:

> The house in which I dwell's mine own,
> Allegiance bear to me alone,
> And every master ridicule
> Who cannot sometimes play the fool.[4]

This is also the underlying mood of the whole of his *Thus Spoke Zarathustra*. But this has not prevented large numbers of people from following him. This is the one extreme. This extreme is not one that can be fruitful for the present. But the other extreme is certainly not fruitful either (and between these two extremes there are all manner of shades of opinion), where the view is expressed that, although Nietzsche exhibited many flashes of genius, he eventually went mad and is best ignored. Friedrich Nietzsche is a strange phenomenon who does not deserve anyone's slavish devotion; but in the years of his illness he experienced with an acute sensitivity the darkness and chaos of our present time. Indeed I would say that we can create a very good foundation for studying the difficulties of our own time if we take account of what Nietzsche writes about the sorrow that afflicted him. I want to read you two passages from Nietzsche's posthumous book entitled *Versuch einer Unwertung aller Werte* (The Will to Power; the Revaluation of all Values), which was written when he was already mentally ill but which could also have been written today with a completely different intention in mind from that of its author and could have been written with the object of giving expression to the deeper underlying causes of the symptoms of our present time. Nietzsche writes as follows:

> What I am relating is the history of the next two centuries. I am describing what is about to happen and what cannot be avoided: *the arrival of nihilism*. This history can already be written now, for necessity is at work here. The future already cries out in a hundred signs, this destiny announces its presence everywhere; all ears are already pricked for this music of the future. The whole of our European culture has long been inexorably moving towards catastrophe in an agony of suspense which increases from decade to decade: restlessly, violently, precipitously, like a river that surges towards the ocean without any longer pausing to reflect and even has a dread of doing so.

Much of what you can experience in the present can be judged by these words of a sensitive human being who wrote them at the end of the 1880s; and they can be compared with another passage that I want to read to you, which vividly portrays the depths to which each of us can plunge in our experience.

> My friends, we had a hard time when we were young: we suffered in our youth as if from a serious illness. This is owing to the time into which we have been cast—an age of great internal decay and

disintegration which, with all its weakness and even with the best of its strength, is opposed to the spirit of youth. The disintegration, and hence the uncertainty, is peculiar to this age: nothing is based on a firm foundation and solid beliefs. People live for tomorrow, for anything beyond that is uncertain. Our path is slippery and full of danger, and the ice that bears us has become so thin: we all feel the ominous breath of a thawing wind. Within a short time no one will be able to walk where we are still able to tread!

There can be no doubt that these sentiments have been expressed out of a deep grasp of the realities of the present. Anyone who wishes to understand the age in which we live and especially the task that any individual who wants to think beyond the confines of everyday life can envisage for himself will have a similar feeling to what is expressed in these passages, and he will perhaps say that, while Nietzsche may have been prevented by the onset of his mental derangement from adopting a critical attitude to the ideas that he had, these ideas arose out of an acute sensitivity to the immediate realities of the present. Perhaps one day such a sensitivity to the present will be compared with what is said by those 'experts' who do not even touch the fringe of the causes that underlie the difficult times in which we live. There will then be a very different attitude regarding the necessity for spiritual science today; for at present it is simply not the case that people want to hear about it. Not that I want to attribute any blame to anyone for this. As I have said, I am very far from wanting to reproach anyone in particular. Those of whom I speak are mostly people whom I regard very highly and whom I would consider the most likely to be receptive to spiritual science. But I need to point out how difficult it is for any individual to be inwardly open to spiritual science if he is up to his ears in what will come his way if he succumbs entirely to the superficial trends that dominate all areas of modern thought.

I have now come to the point where I can say a few words about Kjellén's book, *The State as Organism*. This book is really rather curious, because although its author makes every possible effort to give a clear answer to the question as to what the state really is, he has no trust in the power of human beings to generate any ideas or conceptions which could really deal with this question or problem. To be sure, he says many fine things which, as I have seen, have been greatly admired by modern critics; but he has not the slightest idea of what needs to be known to furnish a solution to humanity's present predicament. I can only mention a certain aspect of what he says. Kjellén begins by asking what is the relationship of the human individual to the state. As he sets out to tackle this question he enters immediately into a quandary. He wants to conceive of the state as something real, as an integrated whole, as something living—thus as an organism. Many people have thought of the state as an organism, in which case they always have to find a way of dealing with the question of the cells of which an organism consists: what are the cells of this state? These are the human individuals! And so Kjellén's line of thought is as follows: the state is an organism; and just as the human organism consists of individual cells, so is the state made up of individual cells, of human beings—they are its cells.

It would be impossible to conceive of a more misguided or misleading analogy than this! For if one builds up a line of thought on this analogy, one can never do man justice. Never! Why is this so? You see, the cells in the human organism are juxtaposed to one another, and this has a particular significance. The whole organization of the human organism depends on this juxtaposition. The human individuals in the state are not in direct contact with one another as are the individual cells. That is certainly not the case. The human personality is very far from being related to the totality of the state as are the cells to the organism. And even if one feels obliged to compare the state with an organism, one needs to be quite clear that one will be sorely mistaken—and the same can be said of the whole of political science—if one overlooks the fact that the individual human being is not a cell; for whereas cells together form the organism and collectively make it what it is, the human individual is the productive or creative element that is able to sustain the state. Thus when the group spirit is no longer present in the way that it was in former times, the modern state is only able to progress if its functions are carried by the single human individual. This can, however, never be compared with the task of cells. By and large it is a matter of indifference what one compares something with, but if a comparison is being made it needs to be appropriate; and comparisons do as a general rule have a certain validity, but they cannot be so far-fetched as Kjellén's analogy. He can perfectly well compare the state with an organism, he could also compare it with a machine (there would be no harm in that) or with something like a penknife, provided that some points in common could be found; but if one is consistently making a comparison it must be appropriately done. But people are not sufficiently familiar with the basic structure of thinking to be able to perceive something of this kind.

So Kjellén is fully entitled to compare the state with an organism. But then he must look for the right cells; and the problem is that, if one really wants to compare the state with an organism, the right cells cannot be found. It quite simply has no cells! If one thinks about this matter in a realistic way the idea simply does not add up. I need to put it quite plainly that only if one thinks as abstractly as Kjellén does the idea make any kind of sense; whereas as soon as one thinks in a realistic way one comes to grief, because the idea has no basis in reality. The cells cannot be found; there are no cells. On the other hand, one finds something completely different. One discovers that individual states can more or less be compared with cells; and the aggregate of all states on Earth can then be compared with an organism. One then arrives at a fruitful idea, although it is first necessary to answer the question as to what kind of an organism this is. Where can we find something similar in nature, where cells interact in a manner similar to the way that the cells representing individual states function with regard to the entire organism of the Earth? If we pursue this idea we find that we can only compare the whole Earth with a plant organism, not with an animal organism and still less with a human organism. Whereas natural science is concerned with the inorganic realm, with the mineral kingdom, we need to think of the plant kingdom if we want to give a firm foundation to political science. We are not involved here with the animal kingdom, and certainly not with the human world, but we need to free ourselves from a purely mineralized thinking. But political scientists are unable to do this; they remain firmly wedded to the mineralized thinking that governs natural science. They cannot rise in their thinking to the plant kingdom but apply the laws that have been found in the mineral kingdom to the state and call it political science.

In order to arrive at the kind of fruitful idea referred to above all our thinking must be rooted in spiritual science. We will then also come to the point of realizing that in the entirety of his being man is, by virtue of his individuality, far superior to the state; he reaches up to the spiritual world, where the state is unable to penetrate. Thus if you want to compare the state with an organism and the human individual with cells, you would—if you are thinking realistically—arrive at the idea of a strange organism, an organism that consists of individual cells, but the cells would be growing all over the skin. You would have an organism extending beyond its skin; the cells would be developing wholly on their own, independently of the organism. You would therefore have to picture the organism as if living bristles which feel themselves to be individuals were growing all over the skin. Thus you can see how living thinking brings us in touch with reality, how it shows us the impossibilities that we are bound to encounter if we want to understand an idea that is to be fruitful. It is therefore no surprise that ideas that have not been fructified by spiritual science do not have the capacity to address the needs of the real world. For how can there be any hope of organizing earthly affairs if one has no idea what is going on there? No matter how many Wilsonian proclamations are made about all manner of international associations and other similar initiatives, they are nothing but empty talk unless they are rooted in reality. Hence many of the proposals being put forward today are nothing but hot air.

Here you have an instance where you can see how vitally necessary it is that the impulses of spiritual science can be truly influential in our present age. It is the misfortune of our time that it is powerless to formulate ideas that could possibly regulate anything of an organic, living nature. Hence everything slides into a state of chaos. But you can now see where the deeper causes lie. It is therefore no surprise if books like Kjellén's *The State as Organism* conclude in so strange a way. Just consider that we are now living at a time when everyone is wondering what to do to enable people to live in harmony with one another on the Earth in the light of the fact that as every week goes by they are increasingly determined to kill one another rather than live together.

How are they to be able to live in harmony once more? But the science that is concerned with how people may live together again within the state offers only the following conclusion, as expressed in Kjellén's words:

> This must be our final word in this study of the state as an organism. We have seen that the modern state has for compelling reasons made very little progress in this direction and has not as yet become properly conscious of a task of this nature. Nevertheless we believe in a higher form of state which enables a rational purpose to be more clearly discerned and which will strive towards this goal with ever greater confidence.

This is how the book ends. We do not know anything, we have no idea what will come of everything! This is the net result of a strenuous, dedicated intellectual effort, the concluding summary of a thinker who is so completely identified with present trends of thought that he cannot be receptive to what is really needed. One must recognize such phenomena for what they are; for the impulse to gain insight into these issues only arises if one is quite matter-of-fact about them, if one knows what the driving forces in our time really are.

Without even looking very far, one finds that there is a characteristic longing today for a certain social process—not, I would say, for socialism but for a socialization of the earthly organism. But because such an endeavour must be conscious in its origin and not arise from unconsciousness, as was the situation for two thousand years, socialization, reorientation or reorganization is only possible if one acquires a knowledge of man; for this was also what the ancient mysteries sought to achieve for former times. Socialization applies to the physical plane; but it is impossible to establish a social order if one is completely unaware that here on the physical plane there are not only physical human beings but people with a soul and a spirit. Nothing can be accomplished, nothing can be achieved if one thinks of man only in outward, physical terms. However much you may try to create social structures along the lines of present-day thinking, everything will descend into chaos again if you disregard the fact that man is not merely the being that natural science acknowledges but is endowed with a soul and a spirit. For the soul and the spirit exert real influence; although they may not figure in our ideas and conceptions, they cannot be abolished. But if the soul is to be able to inhabit a body which is part of an outward structure appropriate for our time, it must as a matter of priority have freedom of thought, the right to make up one's own mind. No social process can dispense with freedom of thought; and no socialization or freedom of thought is conceivable unless the spirit is firmly established within the spiritual world itself.

Freedom of thought as an attitude of mind, together with pneumatology, spiritual wisdom, spiritual science as a scientific basis for all social arrangements—these aspects are inseparably linked with one another. However, we can only discover through spiritual-scientific study how they relate to man and how they can be manifested as an outward social reality. Freedom of thought, that is, an attitude of mind towards one's fellow human beings that truly recognizes the other person's freedom of thought in the fullest sense of the word cannot become a reality unless one's perception of the other is based upon the idea of repeated earthly lives; for otherwise one will be looking upon the other person as an abstraction. One will never be able to see him as he really is unless one views him as the result of former earthly lives. The whole question of reincarnation must be considered in connection with that of freedom of opinion, or freedom of thought. It will in future become impossible to function in the real world if the individual is not inwardly rooted within the life of the spirit. I am not implying that he must become clairvoyant (although some people certainly will); I am simply stating that there needs to be a firm grounding in spiritual life. I have often explained that this is perfectly possible without being clairvoyant. If we look about us we shall realize where the major obstacles lie and where we need to look in order to find the sources of these obstacles. For it is not the case that people are unwilling to search for the truth—as I have said, I do not want to reprove or criticize unduly; but the impediments obstructing the soul's progress in this regard are indeed very considerable.

There may sometimes be an isolated instance that is so illuminating that it is possible to understand many contemporary phenomena from such symptoms. It is, for example, quite remarkable how people who are otherwise so brave and courageous become terribly anxious when they hear that spiritual knowledge may acquire some degree of credibility. They really cannot cope with this. I have often told you that I have met several people who have heard one or two of my lectures and then they are never seen again. When I meet them in the street I ask them why they did not return. 'I could not,' said one, 'I feared lest I became convinced!' Someone who speaks like that finds the idea of being convinced highly problematic and thoroughly disagreeable, and he does not have the strength or courage to take responsibility for this. There are many other experiences that I could cite in this connection, but I would rather mention symptoms from public life.

I spoke a short while ago about Hermann Bahr, who recently gave a lecture in Berlin called 'The Ideas of 1914'.[5] I pointed out how this man—and you need only read his last novel *Himmelfahrt* [Ascension]—does not only try to approach spiritual science to some extent but has even tried in his later years to familiarize himself with Goethe and, hence, follow the path that I would also recommend for anyone who wants to find a good foundation for spiritual science. Many people today have a strong wish to speak once again of the spirit, and they would welcome the opportunity to do so. I do not want to sound like a schoolmaster, and certainly not with a person whom I like as much as Hermann Bahr. But however reluctant I may be to pontificate about such matters, the influence of such an intellectual outlook on the corruption of thought, even to the point of leading thoughts into what could be said to be a kind of original sin, is sometimes clearly apparent in some strange way.

Now in his recent lecture here in Berlin about ideas relating to 1914, Hermann Bahr expressed all sorts of fine sentiments; but there are a number of strange discoveries to be made. Thus he began by saying that this war has taught us something completely new. It has taught us to find a right way of integrating the individual once more into the whole; it has taught us to overcome individualism and egotism and to serve the whole community; it has taught us to get rid of old ideas and to replace them with something entirely new. And he went on to characterize and define all the many new things that this war has brought us. I do not want to criticize him for this, indeed quite the contrary. But it is very strange if, after long discussions about how the war has transformed us all and how we are becoming very different because of it, we hear these concluding words: 'Man always hopes for better times, but in himself he remains incorrigible. However, the war will hardly be likely to change anything very much.' As I say, I do not want to sermonize, but I simply cannot help being aware of such things. All the same, such people are full of good intentions; they would like to make contact with the spiritual domain. Bahr therefore emphasizes that we have based everything for too long upon the individual; we have become obsessed with the idea of individualism. We must learn once again to form a whole. He believes that people who belong to a particular nation have learned to feel themselves as belonging to the totality of a nation and, hence, to limit the exclusivity of individualism. But nations, he thinks, are themselves also individualities; and a greater whole needs to emerge out of them. It sometimes becomes apparent—and in this lecture it does so in a remarkable way—that Bahr pursues particular paths in order to find the spirit. He sometimes does this rather vaguely, but these indications nevertheless give quite a lot away. The old is finished with, he says. The Enlightenment wanted to ensure that people base everything upon reason; but this did not come to anything and we are now in a state of chaos. We must once more find something that brings us in touch with the absolute rather than with chaos. And then he makes some very noteworthy remarks:

> Perhaps nations would then have learnt something that is very difficult for them (as it is for individuals), namely to grant the right to a particular nature that each demands for itself also to others; and it is, moreover, the case that the particular nature of others is ultimately the precondition of one's own. For if all were alike, there would be no distinctive qualities. And they would have learnt that just as each individual citizen with his distinctive gifts is necessary in his own particular area in order to make his contribution to what the nation is able to achieve and thus find self-fulfilment while at the same time serving the whole, so does the universal cathedral of mankind, whose spire reaches up to God, arise from the nations as an overarching dome.

This is a hint, albeit not a blatant one but nevertheless a pretty clear hint. What is expressed here is an aspiration to gain access to God, to the spiritual world, but there is a reluctance to do so in the way that is appropriate for our time. And so a different avenue is sought which does indeed exist, but it does not occur to the author that this avenue was effective until 1914 and that in order to overcome what it brought about he is advocating that we return to it!

However, the symptoms that I am presenting to you here are worth some quiet investigation; for these are not only the views of a single individual but a considerable number of people think and—especially— feel in this way. A book recently appeared by Max Scheler with the title *The Genius of the War and the German War*.[6] I think highly of it, it is a good book. Bahr also admires it. Bahr is a man of good taste and well informed, and has every reason to like the book. But he wants his praise to be made public; in other words, he wants to write a really favourable review of it. He thinks to himself: 'I want to write a really good review to give Scheler a good boost. But how shall I do this? I could do it in such a way that people feel offended. But it is not good to cause them offence. I must find some other way of approaching them. But how?' Now Hermann Bahr is a very upright, honest person, and he explains pretty candidly what he would do in such a case. Thus at the beginning of the article that he has written about Scheler[7] he says that Scheler has written many articles and many other things to indicate how we can extricate ourselves from our present misery, and that what he wrote caught the attention of many. But people today, according to Bahr, do not appreciate being directed towards a particular individual. And so Hermann Bahr characterizes Scheler by saying: 'People were curious about him and were somewhat mistrustful of him; Germans want first and foremost to know where they stand in relation to an author; they do not like imprecision of any kind.'

But where can we find precision? Not by reading books and following their reasoning; something else is needed for this. People do not like imprecision. Again Bahr gives a hint of what he really wants to say:

> Similarly in the Catholic world there was a tendency to withhold judgement to avoid being disappointed. Here too it was his idiom

that alienated people. For in every intellectual atmosphere a distinctive idiom emerges in the course of time which creates a particular vernacular out of words in common usage; through this one recognizes who the author is, with the result that one ultimately pays less attention to what is said than to how it is said.

Now what has Hermann Bahr actually decided to do? He has resolved to announce Scheler with a good fanfare. Scheler is, in his words, rather like Bahr himself in that he proclaims these distinctively Catholic aspirations with—perhaps a few matches, though not quite with torches. Now according to Bahr, Scheler does not speak like a dyed-in-the-wool Catholic. But Catholics do, after all, want to know how they stand in relation to Scheler, and I myself—Hermann Bahr is speaking personally here—am exemplifying this tendency through the great fanfare I am making on Scheler's behalf in the Catholic journal *Hochland*, on the grounds that people really need to know that Scheler can be recommended to Catholics. They do not like imprecision, they want to have clarity.

So this is what it is all about: a clear picture is being created to show people that Catholics are perfectly safe with Scheler! It is of no consequence if he is also a highly intelligent man, for Catholics won't have any problem with that. Bahr, however, wants to portray Scheler as a really great man, so that he can tootle his fanfare; but at the same time he does not want to offend anyone. To begin with he bewails the fact that people have become so shallow, that they have lost their connection with the spirit and that they need to recover it again. I shall quote a few passages from what Hermann Bahr writes about Scheler:

> Reason severed itself from the Church on the basis of the presumption that it can of itself understand, determine, order, control, direct and shape life.

Hermann Bahr does not have the courage to say that reason must now seek the spiritual world, or something of the kind! So he says that reason must again look to the Church for guidance.

> Reason severed itself from the Church on the basis of the presumption that it can of itself understand, determine, order, con-

trol, direct and shape life. It had hardly begun to attempt to do these things when it became fearful, when it lost confidence in itself. This consciousness of reason in its own right, this awareness of its limitations, of the extent of its own powers when set loose from God, begins with Kant. Kant recognized that reason out of itself cannot achieve what it is constantly required to do out of its own forces. He called a halt precisely when something might have come of this endeavour. He denied its right to find its wings, but his pupils exceeded the boundaries that he set and tried to outdo each other in the process. Nothing remained for godless reason other than to renounce its claims. It finally realized that it cannot know anything. It searched for truth until it found that none exists, whether because this is inherently the case or simply that man is not capable of discovering it.

Well, this does abundant justice to the way people feel nowadays; for all those fine sentiments about the 'limits to knowledge' are very clearly expressed.

Since then we have lived without truth, believing that we know that there is no truth, and yet we continued to live as if truth must nevertheless exist. In order to live we had to live in defiance of our reason. We therefore preferred to abandon reason altogether. Man's head was amputated from his body. He soon came to be regarded as consisting only of desires. He became an animal and gloried in the fact. The consequence of this was—1914.

Thus Hermann Bahr paints a picture of what Scheler resolves through his Catholic impulse. He then somewhat abuses Goethe by making an extended effort to present him as a dyed-in-the-wool Catholic, and he goes on to say:

The modern 'man of science' renounced this belief in being an honourable part of the spiritual world. Science abandoned all presuppositions. Reason ceased to derive the 'impulse' wherewith alone it is able to function from God. Where else can it come from? Only from desires. There were no other possibilities. Thus bereft of all established values man lost the ground from under his feet. And the result was—1914.

If we are to build everything up again, it must be done from the foundations. It would be presumptuous to try to rebuild Europe in a cultural sense immediately. We must begin quietly from below. Man must first be restored to himself in his lost innocence, he must once again become conscious of himself of being an integral part of the spiritual world. Freedom, individuality, dignity, morality, science and art have vanished since faith, hope and love have lost their central focus. Only faith, hope and love can restore him. We have no other choice: the end of the world or *omnia instaurare in Christo* [to renew everything through Christ].

However, this *omnia instaurare in Christo* does not imply reaching towards the spirit, an endeavour to explore and study the spiritual world, but, rather, encompassing all nations within the orb of the Catholic Church. But how do we achieve this, says Bahr. How is it possible for people to be able to think and yet become good Catholics? We must look to those who are suited to the challenges of our present time. Here Scheler is right, for he does not compromise himself by speaking of an evolution into the spiritual world or of a particular aspect of spiritual teaching. He does not compromise himself by venturing to say more than that one can speak in this way about the spirit and then find everything else if you enter the Church and, moreover, the Catholic Church. For this view which seeks to satisfy everyone on an international scale is what is upheld by both Bahr and Scheler. In this way everyone can be brought under one roof, or under the one umbrella of the Church. Nevertheless, people today still want to think for themselves, and Scheler is quite happy to adapt himself to the way they want to think. Indeed, says Bahr, he does well to think in the way that people want:

> Scheler does not raise his voice or gesticulate, but he attracts attention by these very means; for people ask involuntarily who can it be who seems to be so sure of the effect that he is having that he does not consider it necessary to make a lot of noise. It is a

proven device of experienced speakers to begin with a quiet voice and thus compel the audience to be quiet and attentive, though they must also have the power to captivate them. Scheler is a master in this respect. A listener who does not notice where he is being led is guided firmly towards a goal that he had no intention of aiming for. Scheler's art of persuasion, beginning from wholly innocuous propositions in response to which the reader or listener allows himself without argument to be forced imperceptibly into conclusions which, had he had the slightest warning, he would have resisted with all his might, is quite unparalleled. He is a born teacher; I know of no one who is able to guide our troubled age to the truth with a hand that is at once so gentle and yet so firm.

It is indeed a special art if one can take people by surprise in this way: first one tells them things that are perfectly innocuous, and then the argument gradually unfolds until one leads them to a conclusion that they would have actively resisted if one had presented them with it from the start. How is one to account for this, Bahr asks, and what must one do in order that it happens in the right way. He is very sincere, very honest, and so in this review about Scheler he tries to address this issue in what he has to say:

> The question now is whether the average German has learnt to grasp the enormity of the present moment. With the best will in the world he still imagines that modern man has lost all belief, that faith of any kind has been scientifically refuted. It does not enter his head that in the meantime this science of unbelief has itself long been scientifically refuted. He knows nothing of the quiet preparatory work undertaken by the great German thinkers of our time—Lotze, Franz Brentano, Eucken and Husserl.

And now I beg you to pay special attention to the following words:

> In the ears of the average person there can constantly be heard the fading echo of the latest aberration which has already been overcome. Amidst the numbing confusion that he feels, a calm, clear voice will most likely be heard which does not arouse any suspicion of having fallen prey to the rapturous enthusiasm, romanticism

and mysticism of which the average German has a terrible dread. Precisely because Scheler upholds the cause of reverting to the spirit in such a non-effusive and unemotional way and in the familiar jargon of 'modern culture', he is the man we need today.

So now we have it! You now see exactly what Bahr likes about Scheler: he cannot be accused of being a dreamer or a mystic, for 'the average German' has 'a terrible dread' of such qualities. And, by God, one really needs to respect this fear; for if it were to occur to anyone to try to get rid of it, if someone came to regard it as necessary to combat it, not even all the courage that could possibly be devoted to such an undertaking would be adequate to the task.

Because I have a high opinion of Hermann Bahr and am also very fond of him, I would like to show how characteristic he is of those who find it difficult to accept something that is so necessary for our time. The only way to find a way forward out of this situation is that we cease to be paralysed by this terrible dread, and that we pluck up the courage to acknowledge that spiritual science is not some kind of effusive fantasy but that a considerable degree of clarity of thought is necessary if we are to do justice to it. For clarity of thought is not exactly a prominent feature of the few examples that I have given you in today's lecture of passages from the work of Hermann Bahr and other contemporary writers. However, a certain degree of courage on the intellectual plane is required if we want to find ideas with penetrating power and resilience. We should not follow Nietzsche beyond a certain point, nor do we need to agree with everything that he says in a passage which may attract our attention; but we must be able to accompany this sensitive spirit when, perhaps prompted by his illness, he gives expression to thoughts of so courageous a nature. Similarly, we should not be governed by a fear of being misunderstood. It would be the most awful thing that could happen today if we were to have a dread of being misunderstood by someone or other; for it is sometimes necessary to pass judgements such as the following one made by Nietzsche, even though it is not necessarily justified in every detail (and that is not of any great importance). Nietzsche writes the following words in his treatise *On the History of Christianity*:

One should not confuse Christianity as *a historical reality* with that one root to which its name is linked: the other roots out of which it has grown have been far more dominant. It is an unparalleled abuse of a word if such decadent structures and monstrosities as the 'Christian Church', 'Christian belief' and 'Christian life' are associated with that holy Name. What did Christ *deny*? Everything that is called Christian today!

Even though this is perhaps taken to an extreme, Nietzsche has touched upon something that has a certain validity, even if he expresses it rather radically. There is some truth in the suggestion that if Christ were to appear in our midst today He would in all probability be most strongly opposed to what is generally referred to as 'Christian' today, together with much else besides which I shall speak about at another opportunity.

We will take up these threads again next Tuesday.

LECTURE 17

BERLIN, 8 MAY 1917

It might well seem as though in the period following the Mystery of Golgotha no rays of spiritual enlightenment were streaming towards mankind; and there could be every reason to think that a situation of this kind was the generally prevailing condition of humanity, and increasingly so as we come closer to our own times. This is actually not the case; and if we want to have a clear oversight of these matters we need to make a distinction between what is common to all mankind and what takes place in particular pockets of human life and in such a way that it can be discerned in the most diverse areas of life. It would be discouraging for many people today if they were obliged to be constantly saying to themselves: yes, we are being told about a spiritual world, but the paths to this spiritual world are closed to people today. There are many at this present time who come to this discouraging conclusion. But such a conclusion arises from the fact that they do not have the greater courage to make an unqualified commitment where clear paths open up into the spiritual world; and they also lack the courage to make an objective judgement in this domain. It may therefore seem—and I emphasize that this is only apparently so—that we are today very far removed from those times when the spiritual world was to a certain extent open to the whole of mankind through atavistic clairvoyance or from those later times when it could be opened up to individuals through initiation into the mysteries. We need to draw together certain threads which connect former periods of human evolution with the present if we are to be able to arrive at a full understanding of the mysteries of human existence and, in particular, of such phenomena as we have been speaking about in these lectures in connection with the nature of the mysteries. I would therefore like to take an example from recent times which is accessible to everyone and which can help to give us the courage to make the resolve to seek paths leading to the spiritual world. Out of the plenitude of examples that I could have chosen, I should like to select one where we can see immediately how phenomena such as these are misjudged from a materialistic standpoint in our present age and, I am aware, will continue to be so misjudged.

You will all have heard something about the poet Otto Ludwig,[1] who was born in the same year as Hebbel and Richard Wagner (1813). Otto Ludwig was not only a poet (and one may even be of the opinion that he wasn't a very good poet, although that is of no importance in the present context) but he was a man who had been much concerned with self-observation, who sought self-knowledge and who also succeeded in penetrating beyond the veil that for the majority of people in our time enshrouds their inner life. Otto Ludwig describes very beautifully what he observes when he is writing poems of his own or when he is reading other people's poetry and is relishing its effect. He concludes that he does not read or compose in the way that other people do but that something very powerful begins to stir within him both when he is engaged in composition and when he is reading and allowing the effect of other poetry to work upon him. He describes this very beautifully. I want to read you this passage, because you can discern in it a piece of self-knowledge of a thoroughly contemporary man who died only in the second half of the nineteenth century and who, as he imparts the self-knowledge that he has acquired, speaks of things that our present materialistic age regards as the wildest fantasy. But Otto Ludwig was no dreamer. He did have a tendency to brood; but anyone who experiences the effect of his poetry will be aware that there was something thoroughly sane and balanced about this man. This is how he describes his inner experiences when he is either composing his own poems or reading the poetry of others:

> The first thing that I experience is a musical mood which becomes a colour, then I see figures, one or several, adopting particular

positions and gestures either on their own or facing one another, rather like a copperplate engraving on paper of the particular colour in question, or to be more precise like a marble statue or sculptural group on which the Sun falls through a veil of that same colour. I also experience this phenomenon of colour when I have read poetry that has made a deep impression on me; if I awaken the mood that is evoked by Goethe's poems I see a deep golden yellow that extends into golden brown, whereas with Schiller I see a radiant crimson and with Shakespeare every scene is a nuance of the particular colour that I associate with the whole play. Curiously enough the image or group that I discern is not normally associated with the dénouement, and sometimes there is only a characteristic figure in a melodramatic position which is immediately joined by a whole series of other figures. To begin with, I am ignorant of the plot or the content of the story, but from the situation that I initially envisage until the end a whole series of ever new three-dimensional miming figures and groups flit before me, until I see the whole play in all its scenes. All this happens at great speed and is quite a strain to take in; and a kind of physical anxiety takes hold of my hands. I am then able to reproduce at will the content of individual scenes in their sequence; but it is impossible for me to summarize the content of the story in a short narrative. The gestures then begin to be accompanied by speech. I write down what I can, but if the mood forsakes me what I have written down is nothing but a dead letter. Now I set about filling in the gaps in the dialogue; but in order to do this I need to view what I have already written with a critical eye.

Thus we have a remarkable person who, to the great distress of a modern materialistically thinking person, experiences crimson red when reading Schiller's plays and golden yellow or golden brown when he reads Goethe's plays or poems; while with every play by Shakespeare he experiences a particular colour and with every scene a nuance of this colour sensation. Moreover, when he composes or reads a poem he sees figures that are like copperplate engravings set against a background of a particular colour, or even three-dimensional miming figures illuminated by the Sun through a veil which diffuses the light that is for him evocative of the overall mood.

A phenomenon of this nature needs to be understood in the right way. It is not quite clairvoyant, but it represents a path to spiritual vision. A right way of understanding this mood through spiritual science would be to say that Otto Ludwig certainly knows about spiritual vision. For were he to continue on this path, he would not only have such moods but, just as physical objects appear before the outward physical eye, spiritual beings would come before his spiritual eye and would be encompassed within his inner experience. Just as we see flashes of light that seemingly radiates from our eyes and fills the room, so is it with Otto Ludwig. His soul radiated a certain inner atmosphere consisting of moods of colour and tone. As he rightly says, he experiences them first in the musical realm, as tonal moods. He does not use them to arrive at spiritual perceptions; but we can see that he has the inner capacity to find a path to the spiritual world.

It would therefore not be right to say that there are no people in modern times who are aware that what we may call the eye of the soul, what was revealed to the pupils of the mysteries in the way that I have recounted in the previous lectures, is indeed a reality. For the real purpose of these ceremonies was primarily to make the eye of the soul perceptible and to enable the human soul to be aware of its presence. That the phenomena which I have just described are not appreciated for what they really are can be seen from the observations that Gustav Freytag makes about Otto Ludwig. This is what he says:

> The work of this writer, and indeed his whole being, was some-
> what like that of an epic poet from the time when, in the early
> dawn of history, figures imbued with sound and colour hovered as
> living imaginations around the head of the poet.[2]

What he says is absolutely correct, except that it does not have anything to do with writing poems. For what Otto Ludwig experienced was not only experienced in ancient times by poets but by everyone, and in later times by those who were initiated into the mysteries, irrespective of whether they were poets or not. Thus it has nothing to do with poetic inspiration. What Otto Ludwig describes can be found enshrouded within the souls not only of poets but of all human beings, in a place where the eyes of present-day materialists are not able to penetrate. That Otto Ludwig was a poet has nothing to do with this phenomenon, but it is a fact that exists alongside it. One might be a far greater poet than Otto Ludwig and what one is able to describe may remain entirely in the subconscious. It will certainly be present in the depths of the subconscious, but will not necessarily emerge. For the art of poetry, and indeed art of any kind, amounts today to something quite other than the conscious assimilating of clairvoyant impressions.

Thus I wanted to mention Otto Ludwig in order to give you an example of a man—and people of this kind are by no means rare but are actually quite frequently encountered—who is without doubt on a path to the spiritual world. If one practises the exercises described in *Knowledge of the Higher Worlds*, it is not a matter of bringing something new into being but of raising what already exists in the soul to consciousness so that one learns to use it or apply it consciously. This is what needs to be emphasized. The problem is not so much that it is difficult to gain access today to what lives unconsciously within the soul but, rather, that people are unable to summon up the courage to become involved with a quest of this nature; and that for the most part those who would willingly do so because of their cognitive and emotional needs and longings feel a certain pressure to confine their somewhat bashful acknowledgement of this to their own intimate circle and to say nothing whatever about it when they are amongst modern intellectuals. There is, however, something to be said for the idea that what we should characterize today as the right path in this realm, perhaps because we are living since the year 1879,[3] does not need to be followed in the same way everywhere; and if we consider the recent past we can be aware of a high level of clairvoyant forces in many people which, on the one hand, do not need to be fully recognized and accepted unreservedly or, on the other hand, regarded as something dangerous and undesirable.

There are in any event many factors that have for some time undermined the courage to acknowledge clairvoyance, and it is for this reason that Swedenborg,[4] who has often been mentioned in your circle, has met with so strong a reception. Many people could also view him as someone who penetrated the veil enshrouding the spiritual world. Swedenborg had developed faculties of imaginative cognition to a high level. Anyone wishing to gain insight into the spiritual world needs to avail himself of these faculties. Although they were indispensable to him, they essentially represented a transitional stage to higher faculties of knowledge. Swedenborg's clairvoyance was strongly linked to imaginative cognition. It was only because this imaginative cognition was so powerful a force within him that he was able to make statements about the relationship of the spiritual world to the outward physical world that are highly relevant to those seeking to gain clarity about clairvoyance through particular examples. As one example of what I am referring to, I should like to indicate how Swedenborg arrived at his convictions, how he thought and felt in order to maintain his inner connection with the spiritual world. He was not prompted by egoistic motives to gain insight into the spiritual world. He was already 55 years old when the spiritual world became open to him. Thus he was a thoroughly mature man by then, and he was well grounded in an active scientific career. Swedenborg's most important scientific works are only now being published by the Stockholm Academy of Sciences in several volumes, and they contain indications that will point the way ahead for scientific endeavours for quite some time to come. But with a person such as Swedenborg, who was one of the most eminent scientists of his time, people have learnt the trick of recognizing him in so far as they agree with him and dismissing him as a fool where they do not. They perform this trick with the greatest dexterity. They are oblivious to the fact that someone like Swedenborg, whose achievements in his scientific endeavours were not only on a par with all his peers (which is no mean feat) but who stood head and shoulders above all his contemporaries as a scientist, bore witness from the age of 55 onwards to the reality of the spiritual world.

One question that was of particular interest to Swedenborg was that of the interrelationship between the soul and the body. After his spiritual enlightenment he wrote a very fine treatise on this theme.[5] What he said was approximately as follows. There are only three possible ways in which one can think about the interrelationship between soul and body. One view is that the body is the decisive factor; the body is the source of sense impressions, sense impressions influence the soul, which receives these influences from the body. The soul is therefore dependent upon the body. A second view is possible, according to Swedenborg, namely that the body is dependent upon the soul; for the soul is the source of spiritual impulses. It fashions the body and makes use of it in the course of life. One should not speak of a physical influence but of a psychic influence. The third possibility, says Swedenborg, is that both body and soul work alongside one another but not on one another, so that a higher power brings about a harmony or correspondence between them in the way that there is an agreement between two clocks, neither of which influences the other as to what is the right time. A higher influence brings about a harmony. Thus when an outward impression is made upon my senses, the soul is led to develop thoughts; but these processes are mutually independent of one another, in that a corresponding impression is made upon the soul through the senses from without. Swedenborg explains that for those who are able to perceive the spiritual world the first and third views are impossible, as it is evident to those who are spiritually enlightened that the soul is by virtue of its inner forces related to a spiritual Sun, just as the body is related to the physical Sun, but that everything of a physical nature is dependent on soul and spiritual factors. He is therefore speaking in his own particular way about that mystery which we referred to, when speaking of the mysteries, as that of the Sun as a spiritual being. It was this in particular that made him an opponent of Christianity, because the Christianity of his time wanted to deny Christ's relationship to the Sun. Swedenborg restored the Sun mystery through imaginative cognition, to the extent that this was possible for his time.

Now I have presented you with these thoughts because I wanted to give you an idea of what was living in Swedenborg's soul as he was on the path towards attaining spiritual knowledge. He embodied the thoughts that he had formed in relation to the question to which I have briefly referred in a kind of philosophical treatise such as is written by someone who has real insights into the spiritual world, as opposed to what might be written by a modern academic philosopher who has no insight into the spiritual world. At the end of this treatise Swedenborg speaks of what he calls a 'vision'. By this he does not mean something that he has thought out but something that he has actually perceived and which he has beheld with his spiritual vision. Swedenborg is not shy of speaking about his spiritual visions. Thus he recounts what a particular angel said to him because he knows that this was so; he knows it just as well as someone else knows that a certain physical human being has said something or other. This is what he said: 'I once had a vision: three advocates of the view of physical influence, three scholastics, Aristotelians, disciples of Aristotle, appeared before me, thus adherents of that doctrine which says that everything streams into the soul from without through physical influence. They were on one side. On the other side there appeared three disciples of Descartes,[6] who spoke about spiritual influences on the soul, albeit in a somewhat incoherent way. And behind them appeared disciples of Leibniz,[7] who spoke of pre-established harmony, of the independence of body and soul and a state of harmony created from without. Nine figures surrounded me,' he said. This is what Swedenborg saw. And the radiant leaders of each group of three figures were Leibniz, Descartes and Aristotle. The way that he describes this vision is as if he were recounting something from everyday life. He goes on to describe how a guardian spirit rose out of the abyss with a torch in his right hand. And as he swung this torch in front of the figures they immediately started arguing. The Aristotelians asserted the primacy of the physical influence from their particular standpoint, the followers of Descartes stood up for spiritual impulses in their particular way and the adherents of Leibniz likewise defended their master's views. (Visions of this nature have a way of going into minute details.) Swedenborg goes on to say that Leibniz appeared clad in a sort of toga, the lappets were held by his disciple Wolff.[8] (Such details always appear in these visions, of which these features are very characteristic.) They began disputing amongst themselves. The reasons were all good, for everything in the world can be defended. Then after some time the guardian spirit reappeared, but he had the torch in his left hand and lit up the backs of their heads. Then the battle really began in earnest. They said: 'Now neither our body nor our soul can distinguish which is right.' Then they agreed to cast three slips of paper into a box. On one was written 'physical influence', on the second 'spiritual influence' and on the third 'pre-established harmony'. Then they picked out one of them and it was that which said 'spiritual influence'; and they said that they would agree to accept this. Then an angel descended from the higher worlds and said: 'It was not purely fortuitous that you drew out the slip of paper saying "spiritual influence". This choice had been anticipated by the wise spirits who guide the world, because it is the truth.'

This is the substance of Swedenborg's vision. Of course, anyone is at liberty to belittle its significance or perhaps even consider it naive; but what matters is not whether it is naive but simply that this is what he experienced. Sometimes the simplest things are also the most profound; for what seems arbitrary in the physical world, the result of fortuitous circumstances, is when viewed from a spiritual perspective the symbol of something altogether different. It is difficult to arrive at an under-standing of chance, because chance is merely the shadow picture of higher necessities. But Swedenborg wants to indicate something quite specific, or rather not he but 'it' wants to be indicated through him. He creates this picture because 'it' wants this to happen within him. This is an exact description of the way in which he arrived at his truths, an exact description of the spirit out of which this treatise was written. What did the Cartesians do? They wanted to demonstrate the idea of spiritual influence on the basis of human reason, on intellectual grounds. It is possible to arrive at the truth by these means; but it is rather like a blind hen looking for a grain of corn. The Aristotelians are no less intelligent than the Cartesians; they defended the idea of physical influence, again on human grounds. The followers of Leibniz were certainly no dafter than the other two, but they stood for the idea of pre-established harmony. These were not the paths that Swedenborg followed to the spirit, but he used all his skill to prepare himself for receiving the truth; and his way of expressing this receiving of the truth—not establishing the truth for himself but being the recipient of it—was through this process of drawing slips of paper from a box. That is the important thing to bear in mind.

We do not appreciate the true value of matters of this nature if we approach them intellectually. We only appreciate them for what they are if we view them pictorially, even if intelligent people may regard this picture-language as naive; for the effect of an image or symbol is dif-

ferent from that of an intellectual concept, in that it prepares us
inwardly to receive the truth from the spiritual world. This is the
essential point. And if we give proper attention to these things we shall
gradually develop a familiarity with ideas and concepts that are essential
for people today, ideas which they really need to develop and which only
appear to be inaccessible because of an antipathy deriving from
materialism and from no other source.

The main focus of our studies today has been to study human evolution as leading initially to a certain turning point in which the
Mystery of Golgotha falls. History then continues. Both these two
phases of evolution are radically different from one another, and I
have already made it sufficiently clear in what respects this is so. But
it is worth considering the following in order to have a clear picture
of this difference. In ancient times it was always possible that, without making any particular inner preparation associated with the
activity concerned (for in the mysteries this was associated with outer
ceremonies and ritualistic acts), people became convinced through
these outward ceremonies of the reality of the spiritual world and,
hence, also of their own immortality, because this was still an integral
part of their bodily nature before the Mystery of Golgotha. By the
time of the Mystery of Golgotha it was no longer possible for the
human body to exude a conviction of immortality. The body could
no longer as it were impregnate the air around it with a living experience of this kind. This had been prepared in the centuries before the
Mystery of Golgotha, and it is really extraordinarily interesting to see
the way in which that giant of thinkers, Aristotle, made every effort
before the Mystery of Golgotha to understand the immortality of the
soul, but the idea of immortality that he was able to arrive at was a
very strange one. For Aristotle, man is only fully man if he has his
body. And Franz Brentano, one of the best Aristotelians of recent
times, says in his study of Aristotle that man is not complete if he
lacks any part of his being; how can he be fully a human being if he
lacks his whole body? Thus for Aristotle, when the soul passes
through the gate of death it is of lesser stature than when it was in
the body. This represents an incapacity to perceive the true nature of
the soul, and it can be contrasted with the former capacity to per-

ceive the soul in its immortal aspect. But the curious thing is that Aristotle was the leading philosopher throughout the Middle Ages. In the opinion of the scholastics, whatever can be known was known by Aristotle, and as philosophers we cannot do other than rely on Aristotle and follow in his footsteps. There was no wish amongst them to develop spiritual faculties or spiritual forces that go beyond what was laid down by Aristotelianism. This is highly significant; and it gives some very clear insight into the fact that Julian the Apostate rejected the Christianity that had come to be practised in the Church at the time of Constantine. Matters such as this need to be viewed in a higher light. I have also become acquainted with someone who, apart from Franz Brentano, was one of the leading Aristotelians of our present age, Vincenz Knauer, who was a Benedictine monk and whose relationship as a Catholic to Aristotle was similar to that of the scholastics. Thus when he spoke about Aristotle, he always sought to consider what could be known about the immortality of the soul through human knowledge. Vincenz Knauer summarized his opinion in the following way; and there is much of interest in this:

> The soul, that is, the departed human spirit [hence, the departed human spirit that has passed through death] is according to Aristotle not in a more perfect state but in a highly imperfect state that does not accord with its destiny. The image that is often used for the soul—of a butterfly that after shedding its chrysalis soars into the blue ether of the sky—is by no means appropriate. It is far more like a butterfly whose wings have been torn from it by a cruel hand and now crawls helplessly in the dust in the form of a miserable worm.[9]

It is highly significant that those who are well familiar with Aristotle readily admit that human knowledge cannot do other than arrive at a recognition of this kind. One can therefore see that a certain effort needs to be made to resist what has arisen from this line of development. For as I have often pointed out, modern materialism is unwittingly wholly under the influence of the abolition of the spirit which came about through the Council of Constantinople in 869, when there was no longer a wish to view man as consisting of body, soul and spirit but when, with the abolition of the spirit, man was left with a residue of a body and a soul.

Modern materialism is now going beyond this; for it is also abolishing the soul. But this is a closely related process. A certain strength and courage are therefore needed in order to find our way back again and, moreover, in the right way. Now Julian the Apostate, who was initiated into the Eleusinian mysteries, was aware that through a certain measure of soul development it would be possible to come to a recognition of the immortal nature of the soul. He had a knowledge of this Sun mystery. And now from this source he perceived something that filled him with dread. He was unable to understand that what was for him so fearful an experience was a necessity. What did he actually see? When he looked back to ancient times he saw that human beings were either directly or indirectly through the mysteries under the guidance of super-earthly powers, beings and forces. He saw that what was ordained by spiritual spheres was enacted here on Earth through the knowledge that human beings derive from these same spheres. And then he saw that, through the impulse of Constantine, Christianity had taken on that form which the old principles of the Imperium Romanum had applied to its organization and to Christian society, that Christianity had adopted what the Imperium Romanum had developed purely for the outward social order. He could see this. In a certain sense he saw the divine-spiritual world harnessed to the yoke of Rome. This was what he found so terrible. He was unable to accept that—if he could but see this—such a situation was necessary for a while, and this was the basis of his opposition to what was going on in the historical circumstances in which he lived. As I have already emphasized, we need to be fully aware of the great period of the early stages of Christianity before the age of Constantine; for powerful impulses were at work at this time which were obscured through the free human quest for knowledge under the influence of the Christ impulse being harnessed to the decrees of the Councils.

If we go back to Origen or Clement of Alexandria we find that these teachers were open-minded and had something of a Greek spirit; and yet they also had an awareness of the greatness of what had taken place through the Mystery of Golgotha. But the way that they speak about the Mystery of Golgotha and about what has occurred as a result of it is regarded as heretical today by all Christian denominations. The great Church Fathers of the period before Constantine are really regarded as the most outrageous heretics—even though they are recognized by the Church. For however much they were aware of the great significance of the Mystery of Golgotha for earthly evolution, they had no intention of wanting to eradicate all traces of the path to the Mystery of Golgotha, the path of the mysteries and ancient clairvoyance , as the Christianity of Constantine was determined to do (as we have seen). Especially in the case of Clement of Alexandria we can see how his writings are irradiated with great mysteries whose occult nature is such that it is difficult for someone today to make any sense of them. Clement of Alexandria speaks, for example, about the Logos, about the wisdom that streams and surges through the world. He conceives of this Logos as a music of the spheres that is deeply imbued with meaning. He imagines this in a very living way. And the way that he thinks of the outwardly visible world is that it is in a certain sense the expression of the music of the spheres, just as the visible vibration of the strings of a musical instrument is the outward manifestation of the oscillation of sound waves. Thus for Clement of Alexandria the human form is a visible likeness of the Logos. We see, then, that as Clement of Alexandria looks up to the Logos, the human form becomes for him a confluence of tones from the music of the spheres. Man, he says, is an image of the Logos. And in many of Clement's utterances we find traces of a sublime wisdom that dwelt within him, a wisdom that was irradiated by what flows from the Mystery of Golgotha. If you compare what Clement of Alexandria says with the things that are generally said today, you will become strongly aware of the need to recognize a person such as Clement of Alexandria even if you do not understand him.

When it is said that spiritual science seeks to live wholly within the stream of Christianity and that it is necessary for our time that it blossoms forth from this foundation as a new flowering, many people come and say (and I well know that this is so) that it is a revival of the ancient gnosis. And at the very mention of this word, many professing Christians today cross themselves as if the devil himself were at large. The modern form of gnosis is indeed spiritual science, though this modern gnosis is different from the gnosis that Clement of Alexandria was familiar with. But what does Clement of Alexandria say from his vantage-point in the second half of the second century AD? He says that faith is the basis from which we proceed. A modern Churchgoer does not want to go beyond this. Clement, however, goes on to say that, while faith is already knowledge, the concise knowledge of what is needed, the gnosis confirms and reinforces what has been received through faith; it is founded upon faith through our Lord's teachings and develops this faith to the point of scientific irrefutability and clarity. Clement expresses in his own way for his time what needs to become a reality today. A demand of Christianity is here being expressed that gnosis in the form of modern spiritual science must contribute actively to the development of Christianity. The conventional view today is that on the one side there is science, which is confined to outer facts, and faith on the other. Clement of Alexandria says that to faith is added gnosis, to gnosis love and to love the kingdom or the divine inheritance. This is one of the most profound things that have been said by anyone, because it testifies to a deep bond with the life of the spirit. We begin with faith; but gnosis, that is, knowledge or understanding, is added to it. And out of a living knowledge, that is, from entering deeply into actual realities, there emanates a genuine love, and this love is the bearer of our divine inheritance. The divine world can only stream through humanity in the way that it did in ancient times if gnosis is added to faith, love to gnosis and the Kingdom, our divine inheritance, to love. Such utterances as these need to be viewed in such a way that one can see them as a testimony to the profundity of a thinker such as Clement.

Although on the one hand it is difficult, it is on the other hand necessary to make the true form of Christian life accessible once more to human beings; for if certain phenomena are described in the right way, the real source of our present afflictions will become apparent. It is the case with afflictions of this nature that one does not normally perceive what lies at the bottom of them. Thus when an Alpine village is buried beneath an avalanche, everyone sees the avalanche plunge down to the village; but anyone looking for what caused the avalanche may need to examine what was going on far above in a tiny snow crystal. It is easy to observe the destruction of the village by the avalanche; it is not so easy to state that in purely physical terms it may perhaps have been caused by a crystal of snow. We have a comparable situation with the great events of world history! We can see perfectly well that we are caught up in a terrible catastrophe, which is like an avalanche that has descended upon us. Its origins are to be sought in a place equivalent to where the crystal began to move. We shall need to look for several different crystals; but we tend not to pursue our investigations to the point where a potential cause develops into an actual one. We are reluctant today to see certain things for what they really are.

Let us suppose that someone wants to form a judgement as to what constitutes science in a particular field. How, generally speaking, is this done? He relies on the judgement of an expert in that subject. Why is this judgement authoritative? Because the person concerned has the title of Professor at this or that university. That is generally the reason why something or other is recognized today as being scientific. But let us take an actual instance. I know very well that people do not appreciate it if one speaks directly about certain things, but this does not get us very far; and indeed, unless more and more people can penetrate to the truth of the matter we shall never extricate ourselves from our present predicaments. Let us suppose that one of these great authorities says something along these lines: 'People are constantly talking about man having a body and a soul. This dualism of body and soul is fundamentally unsatisfactory. The only reason that we still speak about body and soul today is that we have to express ourselves through language, and we did not create our languages but inherited them from an earlier time when people were far more stupid than modern university professors. These stupid people still believed in the soul as distinct from the body. And when we speak about these matters today we have to make use of these words; we are the slaves of language and, through language, of the stupid people who were not blessed with clever professors like us.' And he continues: 'Thus we have to speak of body and soul, but there is no justification for doing so; for anyone speaking from a modern standpoint and without being misled by the views of former times may perhaps say: "Here I see a flower, and here I can see another human being. I can see the other person's form and complexion, just as I see the flower. Everything else I have to deduce for myself." But that is pure illusion. What I really receive when I experience a flower or a stone is a sense impression. The notion that something is living in the soul is a pure illusion. Nothing exists other than external relationships.'

You will be saying to yourselves that you cannot make head or tail of all this! Well, it is a good thing if you can make very little of it, for the whole argument is utter nonsense and the height of folly. And yet this crass stupidity is associated with all sorts of painstaking investigations undertaken in laboratories about the human brain, about all manner of clinical findings and so on. This means that the person concerned must be a fool. He is in a position to acquire good clinical results, because he has laboratories at his disposal; but what he says about it all is the purest folly. These fools are no rarity nowadays, and indeed they represent the norm. Of course, I do not make myself popular by saying such things. The lecture series which has been published in book form by the man in question—curiously, his name is Verworn,[10] though of course I must regard this as the chance legacy of physical circumstances—is entitled 'The Mechanism of Spiritual Life'. One might equally well write about the 'woodenness of iron' as about 'the mechanism of spiritual life'. Indeed, if our intellectual life is in its most enlightened representatives imbued with such 'acuity of thinking'—after all, Verworn describes what he sees, but he muddles everything with his own somewhat inane thoughts—we should not be surprised if those disciplines which do not have the fortune to have at least some bearing upon reality in the sense-perceptible world and lack a tangible, external content are completely unable to cope. Especially the political sciences, which lack the crutch of outward facts, would need to develop thoughts that are rooted in reality; but for the reasons that I have indicated in my previous lecture they are bereft of such thoughts. People have to have these things spelt out to them. I referred earlier on to a very capable person, the Swedish thinker Kjellén, who in many ways is quite outstanding. His book *The State as Organism* is of high quality; but towards the end he presents a remarkable idea which does not lead him anywhere but which no one else knows what to do with either. He quotes a certain Fustel de Coulanges,[11] who wrote *La cité antique*, and who points out in this book something which for him is quite remarkable, namely that if one studies pre-Christian political and social institutions one finds that virtually everything in the entire organization is based on ritual, on a social foundation of a spiritual nature. So, you see, people are forced to encounter certain facts; for I already told you in my previous lecture how the social order arose from the mysteries and really had a spiritual foundation. When people study these historical phenomena they encounter certain things; but they are unable to understand them and are at a loss to know how to relate to them. They can make nothing of what even history tells them when there is so little documentary evidence to rely on.

Still less are they able to make anything of the other idea that needs to be revived—an idea which we find in the mysteries and, as a miraculous echo of the mysteries, in Plato and which I referred to as a new path to Christ. If you read the works of Plato, you become aware of something quite remarkable. Plato places Socrates at the focal point of his dialogues, Socrates surrounded by his pupils; and what he wants to say is set within the framework of the conversation that he has with them. In his writings, Plato forms a connection with Socrates after his death. This is more than a mere literary device. It is, I would say, the continuation, the echo of what was practised in the mysteries, when the neophytes were guided towards communion with the dead, who continue to rule over the outer, sense-perceptible world from the world of the spirit. Plato develops his philosophy through his connection with the dead Socrates. This idea must be revived, it needs to become possible again; and I have already indicated how it can be done. We must find a way of reaching beyond a dry study of history, beyond the mere relating of outer events; we must be able to live with the dead and make it possible for the thoughts of the dead to arise once more within us. We must in this sense be able to take the idea of resurrection seriously. This is the path through which Christ reveals Himself in our inner soul experience, the path whereby He can demonstrate His true nature. But one aspect of this path is the development of what can be called the will in thinking. If you are only able to develop the kind of thoughts that you have when you perceive the sense-perceptible world, you will not engender thoughts that can truly relate to the dead. We need to acquire the capacity to derive thoughts directly from our own being. Our will must have the courage to unite with reality; and once it has become spiritualized in this way it will encounter spiritual beings, just as your hand encounters physical objects in the sense-perceptible world. And the first spiritual beings that we generally encounter are those dead people with whom we are in some way karmically connected. However, where these matters are concerned you should not be looking for the kind of guidance that can be written on a slip of paper and put in your waistcoat pocket. These things are not as simple as that. One encounters well-meaning people who ask: 'How can I distinguish between dream and reality?' One should not be aiming to apply a fixed rule to making this distinction in any particular case. One's whole soul should gradually become attuned to making a judgement in the individual case, just as in the sense-perceptible world one seeks to make a judgement about any specific instance. A dream may be very similar to having contact with reality, but one cannot in any particular instance state absolutely that this is how you distinguish between a mere dream and reality. It can even happen that what I am saying now is erroneous in certain specific cases, because other points of view need to be considered. The point is that one should always try to exercise a competence in making judgements about the spiritual world within the entirety of one's soul.

Let us take the very familiar case of someone who is dreaming or thinks he is dreaming; but people cannot so easily distinguish between dream and reality. Those who study dreams today think along the lines of people like Herr Verworn, who opts for an instructive experiment (and he gives the following experiment as an interesting example):[12] Someone is dreaming, and someone else goes up to the window with a pin and taps on the window pane. The sleeping person dreams, wakes up and says that he has heard rifle-fire. According to Verworn, the dream exaggerates everything. How can we explain this? We explain this, says Verworn, by acknowledging that in waking consciousness our brain is fully active. In dream consciousness the brain is in a diminished state of activity and only a peripheral consciousness is active; the cerebral cortex is not involved, and the brain's activity is at its least intense. This is why the dream is so bizarre; this is why the tapping of pins becomes rifle-fire, and why through the brain's activity the faint sounds of the pin are turned into a gun battle. Well, the members of the reading public are being innocently led up the garden path, because in one passage they are told that the dream exaggerates everything, and later on—not in the precise words that I have used—they are told that the brain is less active, which is why the dream appears bizarre; and by then the reader has already forgotten what was previously said. He therefore does not connect the two statements. His sole need is to believe that a person of authority who has been appointed by the state to know these things is saying this, and so he has to believe it. Now as you know, belief in authority is currently taboo. Someone who does not think in this way about the dream may say the following, which could well be the right approach. Let us suppose that you dream of a friend who has died. You dream, or believe you are dreaming, that you are sharing a situation with this friend—and then you wake up. Your first thought on waking is of course that he died long ago! But it did not occur to you in your dream that he was dead. Now you can find all sorts of clever explanations for the dream in Verworn's book. But if this is a dream, and the dream is not a recollection of everyday life, you will find it difficult to understand that the most prominent thought in your mind, namely the fact of your friend's death, plays no part in the dream when you have just been experiencing a situation which you know perfectly well you could not have been sharing with a living person. It would then be appropriate to say: I have now been experiencing something with X that I could not have experienced in life, something that I not only did not experience but, in terms of the relationship that I had with him, I could not have experienced, and yet I am now experiencing it. You may assume that the actual soul that has passed through the portal of death is behind this dream picture. It is, after all, clear enough that you are not sharing in his death experience. The soul has no reason to manifest itself to you as dead, since it lives on. If you take these two factors into consideration and perhaps connect them with something else, you will conclude that behind my image is concealed an actual meeting with the soul of this friend. And the reason why the thought of death does not occur to me is that I am not experiencing a recollection but the person who has died is drawing near to me. I am now experiencing something that is clothed in the form of a dream picture, but the situation that is portrayed could not have existed. Moreover, I do not think of death, because there is no reason for the thought of death to be evoked. You have every reason for saying that when you have a dream of this kind you are dwelling in a region where physical memory plays no part—and what I am saying now is extremely important; for it is a particular characteristic of our physical life that our physical memory remains intact. This kind of memory does not exist to the same extent or in a similar way in the world of the spirit which we enter; and we first have to develop the kind of memory which is necessary there. Physical memory is wedded to the physical body. Anyone who is familiar with this region knows that the physical memory does not extend there. It is not surprising that we are concerned not with a memory of the dead person but with a meeting with his living soul.

Those who are familiar with this say that what we call memory in physical life is something completely different in spiritual life. Anyone who has experienced Dante's great imagination of the *Divine Comedy* will, if he has some understanding of it, have no doubt that Dante had visions, that he was familiar with the spiritual world. Those who know the language of those people who were familiar with the spiritual world will find convincing proof in the introduction that Dante wrote for his *Commedia*. But Dante had knowledge of spiritual matters, he was no dilettante in the affairs of the spirit and was something of an expert in this field. He was someone who knew that ordinary memory does not extend to that sphere where we encounter the dead. Dante speaks much about the dead, and about how the dead live in the light of the spiritual world. You can find these beautiful words in his great poem about memory:

> O Light supreme, by mortal thought unscanned,
> Grant that Thy former aspect may return,
> Once more a little of Thyself relend.
> Make strong my tongue that in its words may burn
> One single spark of all Thy glory's light
> For future generations to discern.
> For if my memory but glimpse the sight
> Whereof these lines would now a little say,
> Men may the better estimate Thy might.[13]

Thus you can see that Dante knew that it is not possible to understand what could derive from spiritual realms with ordinary faculties of memory. Many people today ask why we should aspire to the spiritual world when we have quite enough to do here in the physical world; anyone with any competence will want to focus on coping with the problems of this world! Yes indeed, but are these people entitled to believe that those who were initiated into the mysteries in ancient times were any less prepared to do the physical world justice? After all, they knew that the spiritual world exerts an influence upon the physical world, and that one only creates confusion with these denials. Anyone who rejects the idea that those who have passed through the portal of death exert an influence upon this world is like a person who says that he doesn't believe it when he is told that a surface is hot and then burns himself on a hotplate. It is of course not so easy to demonstrate the harm that is caused if there is no awareness of the influence of the spiritual world upon the physical world and if people act on the basis that it is possible to ignore this influence. Our age is little inclined to build the bridge that must be built in order to reach that kingdom where the dead and the higher beings dwell. In many respects it even has a hatred, a really hateful attitude towards the spiritual world; and the spiritual scientist who seeks to approach these matters with honesty is obliged to draw attention to forces that are hostile to the development of anthroposophy. For there are profound reasons for this hostility, and they are the same reasons which underlie all the forces seeking to oppose the true progress of humanity in our time.[14]

NOTES

Sources of the Text and Previous Editions
Rudolf Steiner gave these lectures freely without notes (other than the quotations that they contain), and they were recorded in shorthand by Hedda Hummel and then printed in accordance with her shorthand report. For the second German edition of the whole of the present cycle of lectures (1982), the text was checked with the original shorthand report and, in the case of some of the lectures, compared with the shorthand notes of Johanna Arnold. The first edition dating from 1961 had been edited by Johann Waeger and Hella Wiesberger, and the present translation has been made from the 3rd edition of 1996, which—like the second edition—was edited by Hella Wiesberger and Ulla Trapp.

The first seven lectures were originally published in German in 1921 in Berlin under the title *Kosmische und menschliche Metamorphose* and in 1926 under a comparable title of *Cosmic and Human Metamorphoses* in English. Lecture 17 first appeared in Berlin in 1922, while lectures 8 to 15 were first published likewise in Berlin in 1931. A first English translation of lectures 8 to 15 was published in 1930 under the title *Building Stones for an Understanding of the Mystery of Golgotha*, and a new translation—including the two previously unpublished lectures—in 1972. The present translator wishes to acknowledge with gratitude the valuable work of both the German editors and the previous translators.

HUMAN LIFE IN A COSMIC CONTEXT

1. In his commentary to these meditative words in *Verses and Meditations* (RSP, 1961/1993)—his translation of which the present version should not be seen as a substitute but as enabling these words to be looked at in a fresh way—George Adams states that Rudolf Steiner indicated that the German word *Eure* (your/thy) refers in the first line to the human being(s) concerned and in the second line to their guardian spirits. This distinction has been drawn here through the respective use of 'your' and 'thy'.

Lecture 1

2. Rudolf Steiner had already spoken about it to the friends in Berlin in a lecture on 10 June 1915. See GA 157, *The Destinies of Individuals and Nations*.
3. Klara Motzkus (died 1916) had been a member of the German Theosophical Society in Berlin since 1895.
4. Sir Oliver Lodge (1857–1940), *Raymond, or Life and Death*, London 1916.
5. Frederic W.H. Myers (1843–1901), poet and essayist, spiritualist and friend of Sir Oliver Lodge; one of the founders of the Society for Psychical Research, London in 1882.

Lecture 2

1. *Theosophy. An Introduction to a Supersensible Knowledge of the World and the Destination of Man*, GA 9 (1904).

2. *Knowledge of the Higher Worlds. How is it Achieved?*, GA 10 (1904/5).

3. In this sentence up to this point, Rudolf Steiner is referring to attacks made by opponents on the grounds of his alleged Jewish descent.

Lecture 3

1. *Occult Science—An Outline*, GA 13 (1910).

2. Plutarch, *c.* AD 50–120, Greek writer. The quotation is missing in the shorthand report. Rudolf Steiner must have read the following passage: 'You are simply unaware that you are seeing daemons [creative geniuses]. This is how things stand. Every soul has a capacity for reason; there are none without some ability to think and reason. Nevertheless that part of it that enters into a connection with the bodily nature and its drives suffers a change and is transformed through joys and sorrows into an irrational force. Not everyone, however, relates to this in the same way; some become wholly immersed in the body and come completely to grief, torn by their passions; others are connected with this realm to some extent while also keeping the purest part of their being outside it, so that it hovers above it like a marker fastened to its upper end, touches the immersed human form only in the head region and keeps aloft that part of the soul which obeys and does not allow itself to be overwhelmed by passions and has thereby been preserved from complete immersion. What now stirs in the body in this submerged state one calls the soul; while that which eludes destruction most people call the reason, in the belief that it is living within them, as if the power of becoming that is visible in mirrors through reflection were contained in them, whereas those with the correct opinion call it—as something outside them—the daemon. In the stars that are apparently being extinguished ... you see the souls being immersed in the body; but when they as it were light up again and appear from out of the depths, shaking off the mist and darkness as obscuring grime, you see those who after death are floating upwards once again from their bodies; and those hovering in the heights are the daemons of the human beings of whom one says that they have the power of reason. Try to recognize the nature of the bond through which each person is connected with the soul.' From *Über Gott und Versehung, Dämonen und Weissagung* ('On Gods and Providence. Daemons and Prophecy'), the chapter entitled 'Regarding the Daemon of Socrates', section 22.

3. Theophrastus Bombastus Paracelsus von Hohenheim, 1493–1541.

4. This remarkable interpolation, which appears without obvious connection to the text on either side of it, played a crucial role in the founding of the Christian Community (the Movement for Religious Renewal founded by Friedrich Rittelmeyer with Rudolf Steiner's help in 1922). It is likely that Rittelmeyer and Emil Bock (another founding leader of the community) attended the lecture. When, four years later, a group of younger theology students met in order to discuss how best to ask Rudolf Steiner for his help in bringing about a renewal of Christian religious life, the distinction between

the respective tasks of the anthroposophical movement and religious activity that Steiner made in this lecture, which had only just been published, was a decisive help. On 22 May the students (Gottfried Husemann, Johannes Werner Klein, Ludwig Köhler and Gertrud Spörri) submitted a memorandum to Dr Steiner containing quotations from the cycle. His response was to offer the first course for theologians (June 1921), which was the first step leading to the foundation in September 1922. (The translator is indebted to the Revd Tom Ravetz, Lenker (Coordinator) of the Christian Community in Britain, for both this information and the above wording.)

5. See the chapter entitled 'The Soul in the Soul World after Death' in *Theosophy. An Introduction to a Supersensible Knowledge of the World and the Destination of Man*.

6. At this point there is a gap in the shorthand report. In an earlier English version the sentence is completed with the words 'away from the lower and lift it higher'. This makes perfectly good sense, even though the provenance of the added words remains a matter of conjecture.

7. Berlin, 17 February 1917 (GA 66). Available in English translation in Typescript Z 373, 'Destiny and the Human Soul'.

Lecture 4

1. The Kant-Laplace theory is a conception of the mechanistic origin of the world, named after Kant's *Allgemeine Naturgeschichte und Theorie des Himmels, oder Versuch von der Verfassung von dem Mechanischen Ursprunge des ganzen Weltgebäudes nach Newton'schen Grundsätzen* (General History and Theory of the Heavens, or an Attempt to Formulate a Mechanistic Origin of the Whole Fabric of the Universe in Accordance with Newtonian Principles), 1755, and Laplace's *Exposition du système du monde*, 1796.

2. Herman Grimm (1828 – 1901), Goethe-Vorlesungen, (Lectures on Goethe), vol.II, 23rd lecture, Berlin 1877.

3. See in this connection Rudolf Steiner's lectures of 10 September 1908 (GA 106), *Egyptian Myths and Mysteries*, and 21 December (GA 173), *The Karma of Untruthfulness*, vol. I (also included in *The Festivals and Their Meaning*).

4. Johann Valentin Andreae (1586–1654), *Die Chymische Hochzeit des Christian Rosenkreutz*. See also Rudolf Steiner's essay on the same theme in GA 35 (available in English translation under the title *The Chymical Wedding of Christian Rosenkreutz*).

5. Mechthild von Magdeburg, 1212–83. Compare Rudolf Steiner's lecture of 6 June 1912 in *Man in the Light of Occultism, Theosophy and Philosophy* (GA 137).

6. The lectures were given during the First World War (1914–18). On 22 January 1917 the American President, Woodrow Wilson, had given a speech by way of an answer to the Peace programme exchange of December 1916. In this speech the American principles of freedom, democracy and the self-determination of nations were proposed as principles for humanity as a whole.

7. August Wilhelm Hunzinger, Professor of Theology. The original title of the lectures referred to was *Hauptfragen der Lebensgestaltung*, Quelle Meyer Verlag, Leipzig 1916, no. 136 of a series entitled *Wissenschaft und Bildung* (Science and Culture).

8. See note 2 to this lecture.
9. In *Dichtung und Wahrheit* (Truth and Fiction), Book 11.
10. Immanuel Kant (1724–1804): *Kritik der reinen Vernunft* (Critique of Pure Reason), 1781. Foreword to the second edition, 'So I had to annul knowledge in order to arrive at faith...'
11. Johann Gottlieb Fichte (1762–1814), *Reden an die deutsche Nation* (Addresses to the German Nation), given in the winter of 1807/1808 in Berlin, Berlin 1808.

Lecture 5

1. See Plato, *Timaeus*.
2. The German word used here—*Bettschwere*—has the connotation in this context of drinking oneself into a state of being fit for nothing except going to bed: hence the association with sleep alluded to by Rudolf Steiner in the following sentence.
3. Rudolf Steiner characterizes the realm of which he is speaking here by the words *im Geistigen*.

Lecture 6

1. Compare the chapter entitled 'Die Vollendung der Uroffenbarung' in Otto Willmanns's book *Geschichte des Idealismus* (History of Idealism), vol. 2, Braunschweig 1894.
2. *The Portal of Initiation* (1910)—a Rosicrucian Mystery through Rudolf Steiner in *Four Mystery Plays* (1910–13), GA 14.
3. John 18:36.
4. 15 March 1917 (GA 66). Included in the new edition of *The Study of Man* (*The Foundations of Human Experience*) as an appendix.
5. Essay from the year 1907 originally published in *Lucifer-Gnosis* and included in GA 34. English translation available.

Lecture 7

1. Louis Claude de Saint-Martin (the 'unknown philosopher'), 1743–1803, *Des erreurs et de la vérité* (Of Errors and Truth, or a Retrospective Examination for Human Beings of the General Principle of all Knowledge), German edition Breslau 1782. See also *Beiträge zur Rudolf Steiner Gesamtausgabe*, vol. 32, Christmas 1970.
2. 'The book *Des erreurs et de la vérité* is a strange book, and scholars do not really know what to make of it, for it is not really understood; and one should of course understand what one purports to judge... I do not understand it properly either; but apart from the impression of superiority and reliability I also find in it a pure will, together with an unusual gentleness and dignity in its underlying convictions...'
3. 15 and 17 March 1917. See note 4 to lecture 6 (both lectures are available in this English volume).
4. 'First we find that the seed principle that is to serve the function of bodily reproduction is contained and developed in the lower abdomen. As one knows that the action of mercury is the foundation of all and every material form, it is

easy to see that the lower part of the body or the lower abdomen indeed represents an image of the action of the mercurial element. Secondly, the chest contains the heart or the fount of the blood, it is the principle of life or of the active element in the body. We also know that fire or sulphur is the principle of all growth and of all physical productivity; through it the relationship between the chest or the second stomach and the sulphur element is sufficiently clearly demonstrated.

'As for the third aspect or the head, it contains the source and the primitive or root-substance of the nerves, which in the bodies of animals are the organs of sensitivity; the property of salt to make everything sensitive is well known; it is also clear that their faculties are completely analogous, and that the head has an indisputable similarity to the third element or salt; and this harmonizes totally with what physiologists teach us about the position and the source of nervous fluid.' (Translated from the German edition, Stuttgart 1925.)

5. '...but in all this there is a mystery which, in my view, can never be buried deeply enough' (vol. I, p. 102).

6. Jean-Jacques Rousseau (1712–78), the political writings, especially his 'Discourse on the Origin of Inequality among Human Beings' and 'Social Contract'.

7. Lectures of 15, 17 and 22 March 1917. See note 3. The lecture of 22 March is not translated.

8. See further about this in *The Occult Movement in the Nineteenth Century and its Relation to Modern Culture*, GA 254.

9. Johann Albrecht Bengel (1687–1752), Swabian Protestant theologian. Accomplished significant work in the realm of researching and editing the Greek text of the New Testament. See also note 20.

10. Friedrich Christoph Oetinger (1702–82), Swabian Protestant theologian and theosophist, pupil of Bengel.

11. Christian Friedrich Daniel Schubart (1739–91), Swabian poet.

12. Philipp Matthäus Hahn (1739–90), Swabian theologian, mathematician, mechanician and astronomer.

13. Friedrich Christoph Steinhofer (1706–61), priest and writer.

14. Israel Hartmann (1725–1806), teacher at the orphanage in Ludwigsburg.

15. Johann Heinrich Jung (1740–1817), writer, optician and Professor of State Administration, known through his autobiography *Jung-Stillings Leben*.

16. Johann Jakob Moser (1701–85), Professor of Law in Tübingen, writer; wrote on juridical and theological subjects.

17. Carl August Auberlen (1824–64), Professor of Protestant Theology; wrote *Die Theosophie Friedrich Christoph Oetingers nach ihren Grundzügen*, Tübingen 1847.

18. Richard Rothe (1799–1867), Professor of Protestant Theology in Heidelberg. The quotations are from the preface to Auberlen's book referred to in note 17.

19. Leopold von Ranke (1795–1886), historian.

20. In his book *Erklärte Offenbarung Johannes* (The Book of Revelation Explained), Stuttgart 1740, Bengel calculated the time when the thousand-year captivity of the dragon (see Rev. ch. 20) will come to an end as being in the year 1836. Rudolf Steiner places the founding of Rome at the very beginning of the

fourth post-Atlantean age in 747 BC. 'That is the true date of the founding of Rome,' he says in the lecture given in Berlin on 30 July 1918 (GA 181), published in English translation in the *Golden Blade*, 2008.

21. See note 8.

22. Quotation from Goethe's *Faust*, part one, 'Night', 602. Translation by Philip Wayne, Penguin Classics, 1949.

23. See the lecture cycles on the Gospels:
    Menschheitsentwickelung und Christus-Erkenntnis, Kassel and Basel 1907 (GA 100)
    The Gospel of St John, Hamburg 1908 (GA 103)
    The Gospel of St John in Relation to the Three Other Gospels, especially to that of St Luke, Kassel 1909 (GA 112)
    The Gospel of St Luke, Basel 1909 (GA 114)
    Deeper Secrets of Human History in the Light of the Gospels, 1909 (GA 117)
    The Gospel of St Matthew, Bern 1910 (GA 123)
    The Gospel of St Mark, Basel 1912 (GA 139)

24. The actual phrase is: 'Die Leiblichkeit ist das Ende der Wege Gottes' ('The bodily nature is the end of the ways of God'). Although under 'body' in his *Biblisches Wörterbuch* (Biblical Dictionary) Oetinger writes, 'The bodily nature is the end of the works of God,' the sentence was quoted in the form as given above already in his lifetime. Cf. Rudolf Steiner's lecture of 14 December 1915 (GA 157), English translation included in *Forming of Destiny as Life after Death*.

25. *The Soul's Probation* (GA 14).

26. These are Saint-Martin's actual words: 'If one were wanting to resolve this difficulty, one would have to return to this natural human state; but then one would see that the physical form which an intelligent person regards as the most illogical part of his nature puts on for him the most humiliating spectacle imaginable; and that if he were to understand the principles of this form, he would be unable to look without blushing with shame, even though all parts of this body—in that each one of them has a different purpose and task—have not been fashioned to provoke the aforesaid reaction.'

27. Matthew 5:13.

28. See note 20.

BUILDING STONES FOR AN UNDERSTANDING OF THE MYSTERY OF GOLGOTHA

Lecture 8

1. Charles Januarius Acton (1803–47, Cardinal from 1842), uncle of the famous historian Lord John Acton (1834–1902). Rudolf Steiner's description would most likely have referred to the book *Die Memoiren Francesco Crispi's*, published in German in 1912. On pages 427–8 of this book in the last part of a letter from Cardinal G. von Hohenlohe to Pope Leo XIII delivered on 27 July 1889, we find these words: 'We cardinals have the strictest duty to tell the Pope this truth: the five million scudi that were deposited in the Castel Sant' Angelo were already lost at the time of Pius VI, but despite this every new cardinal vowed to look after these five million scudi that were no longer there. Cardinal

Acton alone finally in 1839 raised an objection to making this vow, and Pope
Gregory (XVI) could not but acknowledge his doubts as justified. Nevertheless, cardinals are still today required to make vows that cannot be sustained. This needs to be put right. I was obliged to say this to Your Holiness.'

2. Pope Pius VI (1775–99) had to pay out 36 million lire at the Peace of
Tolentino on 19 February 1797. See *Die Memoiren Francesco Crispi's*.

3. In this account—as with the description in the third lecture from the cycle on
the *Gospel of St Matthew* (GA 123)—Rudolf Steiner is drawing upon the study
by Chwolson, *Über die Frage, ob Jesus gelebt hat* ('Regarding the Question
whether Jesus ever lived'), Leipzig 1910. Daniel Chwolson (1820–1911), who
was an orientalist and a professor at St Petersburg, here expresses a view
contrary to that maintained by Arthur Drews and others in the *Berliner
Religionsgespräch* (1910), namely that Jesus never existed historically. See also
note 9 to lecture 9.

4. According to Chwolson there was an original version of St Matthew's Gospel
in Aramaic.

5. Talmud, Schabbat 116a/116b (see Daniel Chwolson, op. cit.).

6. See Daniel Chwolson, op. cit.

7. Saint-Martin's actual words, translated from the German edition published in
1925 in Stuttgart, are as follows: 'Man is older than any other being of nature;
he existed before the emergence of even the tiniest seeds, and yet nevertheless
he came into the world after them. But what raised him far above all these
beings is that they had to arise from a father and a mother, whereas man had
no mother. Their role was, moreover, to work in support of his role, which was
to engage in an endless struggle to bring disorder to an end and to lead
everything back to a unity; the role of these beings was to obey man. But
because the struggles that man had to deal with could be dangerous for him,
he was clothed with an impenetrable weapon whose function he could change
at will and from which he could make copies that were similar to and wholly
in conformity with the original.

'He was also armed with a lance, which was forged out of four metals that
were so well amalgamated that they can never be separated for as long as the
world endures. This lance had the distinctive quality of burning like fire;
moreover, it was so sharp that there was nothing that it could not penetrate,
and so active that it struck in two places at once. All these attributes were
combined with an infinite number of other endowments which man had
additionally received, making him truly strong and terrifying.

'The land where these human beings were to wage their battles was covered
with a wood formed of seven trees, each of which had 16 roots and 490
branches. Their fruits were constantly renewed and guaranteed the human
inhabitants the very best food, and the trees themselves served as a defensive
circle for them and made their posts inaccessible.

'Here in this charming landscape, the home of human bliss and the throne
of his glory, man would have been eternally happy and invincible; for he was
instructed to dwell in the centre of this place, and from there he could without
difficulty observe everything that happened around him, with the additional
advantage that he was able to perceive all the guile and all the assassination

attempts of his adversaries without ever being perceived by them; he maintained his natural ascendancy over everything else throughout the time that he guarded this post; he enjoyed a peace and a blessedness that would be beyond the comprehension of people today. But the moment that he left this post, he ceased to be master of it and another agent was sent to take his place. Man was then shamefully robbed of all his rights and cast down to the region of fathers and mothers where he has lived ever since, and has the sorrow and humiliation of being unrecognized and universally despised by all other beings of nature.

'It is impossible to conceive of a state sadder and more wretched than the unfortunate condition of man at the moment of his Fall; for he not only lost that terrible lance that nothing could withstand but the very armour with which he had been clad also forsook him, and it was for a time replaced by different armour which, because it was not impenetrable, was for him a source of constant danger.'

8. I Cor. 2:14–15; I Cor. 15:44–5; Thess. 5:23; Heb. 4:12.
9. See in this connection the three-volume work of the Catholic philosopher Otto Willmann—whom Rudolf Steiner greatly appreciated—entitled *Geschichte des Idealismus* (History of Idealism), first edition Braunschweig 1894. In section 54, 'Christian Idealism as the Fulfilment of the Idealism of Antiquity' (vol. II, p. 111), Willmann writes: 'The way that the Gnostics misappropriated the Pauline distinction between pneuma and psyche as elements in man's being, in that they represented the former as the expression of their own perfection while interpreting the latter as being associated with Christians who were ensnared in the laws of the Church, was instrumental in leading the Church explicitly to reject trichotomy.'
10. Wilhelm Wundt (1832–1920), philosopher and psychologist.
11. See note 1.
12. The addition 'filioque' (meaning 'and from the Son') to the creed of the Western or Roman Church means that the Holy Spirit proceeds from the Father *and* from the Son. This doctrine led to long debates within the Church and was a significant factor in the separation of the Eastern Church from Rome that took place in 1054. The Eastern Church, which called itself the 'Orthodox Church', acknowledges only the first seven Ecumenical Councils (until 787 AD) and has therefore never recognized the dogmas of the Eighth Council of 869 (see note 9).
13. Friedrich Engels, 1820–95.
14. Karl Marx, 1818–83.
15. 'I cannot say anything further about this subject without indiscretion; higher truths are not for all eyes' (op. cit., vol. 2, p. 64).

Lecture 9

1. See in this connection Rudolf Steiner's letter to Marie Steiner dated 14 March 1905 in Rudolf Steiner/Marie Steiner von Sivers, *Correspondence and Documents 1901–25* (GA 262).
2. Rudolf Eucken (1846–1924), Professor of Philosophy. Compare Rudolf Steiner, *The Riddles of Philosophy* (GA 18).

3. Aristotle (384–322 BC), 'Three Books concerning the Soul'.
4. Franz Brentano (1838–1917) wrote a book called *Die Psychologie des Aristoteles*, Mainz 1867. Compare Rudolf Steiner, *The Riddles of the Soul*, ch. 3: 'Franz Brentano. An Obituary' (GA 21). (This is omitted from *The Case for Anthroposophy*, RSP, 1970.) See also GA 213.
5. Eduard Zeller (1814–1908). Regarding the controversy between Brentano and Zeller see Brentano, 'Open Letter to Herr Professor Dr Eduard Zeller in connection with his Treatise about Aristotle's Doctrine of the Eternity of the Soul' (Leipzig 1883, Duncker and Humblot) and the same author's 'Aristotle's Doctrine of the Origin of the Human Spirit' (Leipzig 1911, Veit and Comp.).
6. Heraclitus of Ephesus (*c.* 535–475 BC), pre-Socratic philosopher. 'For the mysteries that are currently honoured amongst human beings are being celebrated in an unholy way', Fragment 14. See also Edmund Pfleiderer, *Die Philosophie des Heraklit von Ephesus im Lichte der Mysterienidee*, Berlin 1886.
7. AD 332–63, Roman Emperor 361–3.
8. This probably refers to a group of Protestant theologians active in Bremen at the beginning of the twentieth century (Albert Kalthoff, Friedrich Steudel, Friedrich Lipsius) who—like Arthur Drews (see the following note and note 11 to lecture 14)—disputed the historical existence of Jesus in their writings and lectures. Lectures and discussions on this theme were organized by the Bremen Protestant Society.
9. From 31 January until I February 1910 the German Marxist Association organized a religious conversation in Berlin where Protestant theologians had discussions with Arthur Drews (Professor of Philosophy) about his book *Die Christus-mythe* (The Myth of Christ). In this book Drews had tried to prove that a historical Jesus Christ had never existed. According to Drews the Gospels are not historical sources but biased ecclesiastical documents which clothed the ancient idea of a mythical pagan God-man in would-be historical form. He considered that the whole of Christianity was therefore based not on events whose truth could be demonstrated but on mythical ideas alone. The talks given at this event appeared in print under the title *Berliner Religionsgespräch—Hat Jesus gelebt?* (Berlin Conversation on Religion—Did Jesus Live?), Berlin 1910.
10. Firmicus Maternus, Latin author of the fourth century AD. *De errore profanarum religionum* (347 AD).
11. Rudolf Steiner here draws very freely on what Paul says, for what he actually wrote was the opposite (see I Cor. 3:18–19).
12. In his book *Des erreurs et de la vérité* (vol. 2, p. 57 in the German edition, Stuttgart 1925).
13. I Cor. 15:14, Jon Madsen's translation.
14. Luke, 23:34.
15. This is a reference to the Russian Revolution.

Lecture 10

1. Hermann Lotze (1817–81), *Grundzüge der Religionsphilosophie, Diktate aus den Vorlesungen*, 3rd edition 1894.

2. Matthew 21:21 (Jon Madsen's translation).
3. In the eighth lecture of the cycle on *The Gospel of St Luke* referring to Luke 8:40–4, Basel 1909 (GA 114).
4. See lecture 7 in this volume.
5. See his book *Welträtsel* (Riddles of the World), ch. 17, 'Wissenschaft und Christentum' (Science and Christianity).
6. Matthew 5:17–18.
7. The quotations from St Luke's Gospel are from chapter 4, verses 18, 23–7 and 28–9. The translation is by Jon Madsen.
8. Mark 1:34: '. . . and He did not allow the demons to speak, because they knew Him'. Mark 3:12: 'And He told them emphatically not to make Him known.' (Translation by Jon Madsen.)
9. Berlin, 22 March 1917 (GA 66).
10. Sir James Dewar (1842–1923), famous chemist, professor at the Royal Institution in London.
11. Previous editions state 'six thousand years'. The correction brings consistency to the meaning.
12. See Otto Willmann, *Geschichte des Idealismus*, vol. 2, p. 5: Tert. de praescr. hear. 36.
13. See Otto Willmann, op. cit., vol. 2, p. 5: Irenaeus adv. hear. III, 3,3.
14. *Des erreurs et de la vérité*, German edition Stuttgart 1925, vol. 2, p. 236.
15. This refers to those who were recording the lectures in shorthand.
16. See note 3 to lecture 9.
17. Ernst Haeckel, 1834–1919. *Die Welträtsel. Gemeinverständliche Studien über Monistische Philosophie*, ch. 13, 'Entwickelungsgeschichte der Welt' (Evolutionary History of the World).
18. Svante Arrhenius, 1859–1927, Swedish scientist. *Das Werden der Welten* (Worlds in the Becoming), Leipzig 1909.
19. Matthew 24:35; Mark 13:31; Luke 21:33.
20. I Corinthians 15:14.
21. See further in *From Jesus to Christ* (GA 131), lecture 7.

Lecture 11

1. See *Goethes Naturwissenschaftliche Schriften* (Goethe's Scientific Writings), vol. 1.
2. Aug. Joh. Georg Batsch (1761–1802), Professor of Natural History in Jena.
3. Franz Josef Schelver (1778–1832), Professor of Medicine in Jena and Heidelberg. Known for his books on botany.
4. Aug. Wilh. Ed. Theodor Henschel (1790–1856), Professor in Breslau, a specialist in botany, plant anatomy and physiology; pupil of Schelver.
5. Baubo tried to divert the sorrowing Demeter by cynical jests or obscene antics. Goethe applies the name elsewhere to an immodest merry-maker in the Roman Carnival, in *Faust*. She appears in the Walpurgis Night scene. (Reproduced from A.H. Parker's notes to the English edition of 1972.)
6. It would appear that this was not taken up again in greater detail.
7. Emil du Bois-Reymond (1818–1896). His Leipzig lecture 'Über die Grenzen des Naturerkennens' (Concerning the Limits of Knowledge), with its claim 'We shall never know—ignorabimus', was often mentioned by Rudolf Steiner.

8. See note 1.
9. Matthew 5:18.
10. The shorthand report does not contain any indications as to what is meant by this. Rudolf Steiner's observation could be understood as a general reference to Schelling's philosophy of nature, with which Hegel was known to be largely in agreement. The explicit statement that both philosophers said something of a similar nature might refer to the article 'Über das Verhältnis der Natur-philosophie zur Philosophie überhaupt' (Regarding the Relationship of the Philosophy of Nature to Philosophy in General), published in the journal *Kritisches Journal der Philosophie*, which Schelling and Hegel were co-editing around 1802, although the individual contributions were not identified with the names of the people who wrote them.

The phrase 'so much the worse for nature' has not hitherto been verified.
11. It has not been possible to identify who this was.
12. Luke 6:29–30; Matthew 5:39–42 and 7:12. Translations by Jon Madsen.

Lecture 12
1. In 'Raphael als Weltmacht' (Raphael as a World Power), *Fragmente*, second part, 1902.
2. Albrecht von Haller (1707–77), Swiss doctor, botanist and poet. 'Ins Innere der Natur...' forms part of the didactic poem *Die Falschheit der menschlichen Tugenden* (The Deceitfulness of Human Values), 1730.
3. Arthur Schopenhauer (1788–1860). 'The world is my idea' comes from *Die Welt als Wille und Vorstellung*. 'Without the eye there can be no colour, no light', or, more literally, '... that the colours with which ... objects appear to be clothed are only in the eye' is from Schopenhauer's introduction to his treatise *Über das Sehen und die Farben*.
4. See Rudolf Steiner, *Metamorphoses of the Soul/Transforming the Soul*, 7 lectures, Berlin 1909 and 1910 (GA 59), and *Aus dem mitteleuropäischen Geistesleben* (15 lectures, Berlin 1915 and 1916, GA 65).
5. This is a translation of the actual passage: 'The eye owes its existence to light. Out of indeterminate organs light has called forth an organ akin to itself, and so the eye is formed by the light for the light, so that the inner light may reach towards the outer light.' Goethe, *Entwurf einer Farbenlehre* (Outline of a Theory of Colour), 1810.
6. This quotation comes from A.W. Hunzinger, *Das Christentum im Weltanschauungskampf der Gegenwart*, Leipzig 1916, pp. 127–8.
7. See lecture 4 in the present volume.
8. GA 8 (1902).
9. The quotation from Plato comes from *Phaedo*.
10. GA 13 (1910).
11. 63 BC–AD 14. The title of Augustus was conferred on him in 27 BC.
12. Roman emperor, AD 37–41.
13. Roman emperor, AD 54–68.
14. Greek philosopher, 412–324 BC.
15. 1856–1939, the founder of psychoanalysis.
16. This quotation is from Maurice Barrès (1862–1923), and appears in an article

by André Germain entitled [in German] 'Abschied vom Führer der Jugend: Maurice Barrès' (Farewell from the Leader of Youth: Maurice Barrès) in *Internationale Rundschau*, year 1, vol. 3, 20 July 1915, Zurich.

Lecture 13

1. In this and the ensuing lectures Rudolf Steiner refers on several occasions to Ernst von Lasaulx, in particular to his article *Der Untergang des Hellenismus und die Einziehung seiner Tempelgüter durch die christlichen Kaiser* (The Decline of Hellenism and the Seizure of the Treasures of its Temples by the Christian Emperors). The page references in the following notes refer to the 1965 edition of this article.
2. See note 8 to lecture 10.
3. Roman emperor AD 14–37. See Lasaulx op. cit., p. 6.
4. Roman emperor AD 117–38. See Lasaulx op. cit., p. 12.
5. Lived *c.* 20 BC–AD 54. Greek philosopher of Jewish origin. The quotations have not been verified.
6. Emperor of the Eastern part of the Roman Empire, AD 313–25; Lasaulx op. cit., pp. 14–15.
7. Constantine (274–337), Roman Emperor, from AD 323 sole ruler. Under his rulership Christianity was in the year 313 elevated to being the official state religion.
8. See Lasaulx op. cit., pp. 14–15.
9. See Lasaulx op. cit., p. 14.
10. Roman emperor AD 222–35. See Lasaulx op. cit., p. 13.
11. Lived *c.* AD 182–253, Greek Church Father. See Lasaulx op. cit., p. 13.
12. Lived in the first century AD. Philosopher and magician. See Lasaulx op. cit., p. 13.
13. For example, in the lecture of 17 January 1915 in *Destinies of Individuals and of Nations*.
14. See Lasaulx op. cit., p. 30.

Lecture 14

1. See Lasaulx op. cit., p. 44.
2. ' "Contra solem ne loquaris" was not said by Pythagoras with regard to the visible Sun. It was the "Sun of Initiation" that was meant, in its triple form.' From H.P. Blavatsky, *The Secret Doctrine*, vol. 3.
3. AD 344–407, Church Father. 'The Occultists are quite ready to agree with St. Chrysostom, that the infidels—the *profane*, rather—being blinded "by sunlight, thus lose sight of the true Sun in the contemplation of the false one." ' From Blavatsky, *The Secret Doctrine*, vol. 3.
4. See Lasaulx op. cit., p. 44.
5. Compare *Spiritual-Scientific Explanations of Goethe's 'Faust'*, vol. 1, 'Faust, the Striving Human Being', lecture 2, GA 272. Rudolf Steiner gives a fuller description of Manichaeism in the lecture of 11 November 1904, *The Temple Legend* (GA 93).
6. Aurelius Augustinus, AD 354–430, Christian teacher. See also Rudolf Steiner, *Christianity as Mystical Fact and the Mysteries of Antiquity* (1902), GA 8.
7. Held in Berlin on 22 March 1917 (GA 66).

8. See lecture 10 in the present volume.
9. See lecture 4 in this volume.
10. This was entitled *Against the Galileans*.
11. Arthur Drews (1865–1935), Professor of Philosophy, advocated a monistic view of the world and rejected any belief in the hereafter. In his books (e.g. *Christusmythe*, 2 vols, 1909–1911) he denied the historical existence of Jesus and Peter. See also note 8 to lecture 9.
12. See note 23 to lecture 7.
13. Marcus Porcius Cato (234–194 BC), Roman statesman. 'They only chatter': in Ernst von Lasaulx's book *Die prophetische Kraft der menschlichen Seele in Dichtern und Denkern* this is quoted from Pliny.
14. Niccolò Machiavelli (1469–1527), statesman, historian and poet.
15. David Paul Drach (1791 Strasburg–1865 Rome), librarian and writer, studied in several Talmud schools, converted to Christianity in 1823. In 1827 he went to Rome, where on account of his great erudition he was nominated as the Librarian of Propaganda. Rudolf Steiner would be referring to his book *De l'harmonie entre l'église et de la synagogue ou perpétuité de la foi de la religion chrétienne*, 2 vols., Paris 1844.

Lecture 15

1. Clement of Alexandria (*c.* 160–*c.* 216), Origen (*c.* 182–253) and Tertullian (*c.* 160–222), Church Fathers.
2. Benedict of Nursia (*c.* 480–543) founded the original Benedictine monastery of Monte Cassino in 529.
3. 483–565, emperor of the Eastern Empire.
4. Wappler, *Geschichte der katholischen Kirche. Lehrbuch für Ober-Gymnasium und Ober-Realschulen* (History of the Catholic Church. Textbook for Sixth Form Students), third enlarged edition, Vienna 1875.
5. Church Father, lived in the second century AD.
6. Friedrich Hebbel (1813–63). What Hebbel wrote in his diary was this: 'After a transmigration of souls it is possible for Plato to be getting a hiding at school because—he cannot understand Plato.' (Diary no. 1335.)
7. Franz Brentano (1838–1917), an Austrian philosopher, published *Aristoteles und seine Weltanschauung* (Aristotle and his World-conception) in Leipzig in 1911.
8. *Concerning the Soul*, III, 5.
9. Dr Vincenz Knauer (1828–94), *Die Hauptprobleme der Philosophie in ihrer Entwickelung und teilweisen Lösung von Thales bis Robert Hamerling*, lectures given at Vienna University, Vienna and Leipzig, 1892, pp. 232 f.
10. See note 10 to lecture 4.
11. Brooks Adams (1848–1927), *The Law of Civilization and Decay*, 1895. Also wrote *The Dream and the Reality* (1917).

Lecture 16

1. Rudolf Kjellén (1864–1922), Swedish historian and statesman. *Der Staat als Lebensform*, Leipzig 1917.
2. Theophilus of Alexandria was bishop from 385 until AD 412.

3. See 'Untersberg-Sagen' in *Berechtesgadner Sagen*, Berechtesgaden 1911.
4. Friedrich Nietzsche (1844–1900). This quotation is the motto to *Die fröhliche Wissenschaft* (The Gay Science): 'Ich wohne in meinem eignen Haus,/Hab niemandem nie nichts nachgemacht,/Und—lachte noch jeden Meister aus,/ Der nicht sich selber ausgelacht.'
5. Hermann Bahr, 1863–1934. Quotation from 'Die Ideen von 1914' in *Schwarzgelb*, Berlin 1917, pages 167 and 164.
6. Max Scheler (1874–1928), philosopher. *Der Genius des Krieges and der deutsche Krieg*.
7. From the article entitled 'Max Scheler' in the journal *Hochland*, a monthly periodical for all areas of knowledge, literature and art, 14th year (April 1917–September 1917), vol. 7, April 1917.

Lecture 17
1. Otto Ludwig (1813–65), quotation from *Zum eignen Schaffen* in vol. 6 of his Collected Works.
2. Gustav Freytag (1816–95), quotation from the introduction to Otto Ludwig's Collected Works, Berlin (no date).
3. Compare *The Fall of the Spirits of Darkness*, 14 lectures, Dornach, 29 September until 28 October 1917 (GA 177).
4. Emanuel Swedenborg (1688–1772), Swedish scientist and theosophist.
5. Published in German under the title 'Der Verkehr zwischen Seele und Leib' in *Theologische Schriften*, Jena/Leipzig 1904.
6. René Descartes, 1596–1650.
7. Gottfried Wilhelm von Leibniz, 1646–1716.
8. Christian Freiherr von Wolff, 1679–1754.
9. Vincenz Knauer, quotation from *Die Hauptprobleme der Philosophie*, p. 202.
10. Max Verworn (1863–1921), physiologist and philosopher. Verworn's name very closely resembles the German word 'verworren', meaning 'confused' or 'muddled'—hence Rudolf Steiner's following comment.
11. Numa Denis Fustel de Coulanges (1830–89), French historian.
12. See *Mechanik des Geisteslebens*, the chapter entitled 'Schlaf und Traum', Leipzig 1910.
13. *The Divine Comedy*, Paradiso, Canto XXXIII, translation by Dorothy L. Sayers and Barbara Reynolds, Penguin Classics, 1962.
14. At the end of this lecture Rudolf Steiner spoke about an internal matter relating to the Society (the enmity of Max Seiling). Since the same observations were also made in other lectures and have, moreover, been published (e.g. GA 174b p. 199, GA 177, p. 54, German references), they will not be repeated here.

RUDOLF STEINER'S COLLECTED WORKS

The German Edition of Rudolf Steiner's Collected Works (the *Gesamtausgabe* [GA] published by Rudolf Steiner Verlag, Dornach, Switzerland) presently runs to 354 titles, organized either by type of work (written or spoken), chronology, audience (public or other), or subject (education, art, etc.). For ease of comparison, the Collected Works in English [CW] follows the German organization exactly. A complete listing of the CWs follows with literal translations of the German titles. Other than in the case of the books published in his lifetime, titles were rarely given by Rudolf Steiner himself, and were often provided by the editors of the German editions. The titles in English are not necessarily the same as the German; and, indeed, over the past seventy-five years have frequently been different, with the same book sometimes appearing under different titles.

For ease of identification and to avoid confusion, we suggest that readers looking for a title should do so by CW number. Because the work of creating the Collected Works of Rudolf Steiner is an ongoing process, with new titles being published every year, we have not indicated in this listing which books are presently available. To find out what titles in the Collected Works are currently in print, please check our website at www.rudolfsteinerpress.com (or www.steinerbooks.org for US readers).

Written Work

CW 1	Goethe: Natural-Scientific Writings, Introduction, with Footnotes and Explanations in the text by Rudolf Steiner
CW 2	Outlines of an Epistemology of the Goethean World View, with Special Consideration of Schiller
CW 3	Truth and Science
CW 4	The Philosophy of Freedom
CW 4a	Documents to 'The Philosophy of Freedom'
CW 5	Friedrich Nietzsche, A Fighter against His Time
CW 6	Goethe's Worldview
CW 6a	Now in CW 30
CW 7	Mysticism at the Dawn of Modern Spiritual Life and Its Relationship with Modern Worldviews
CW 8	Christianity as Mystical Fact and the Mysteries of Antiquity
CW 9	Theosophy: An Introduction into Supersensible World Knowledge and Human Purpose
CW 10	How Does One Attain Knowledge of Higher Worlds?
CW 11	From the Akasha-Chronicle

Public Lectures

CW 51	On Philosophy, History and Literature
CW 52	Spiritual Teachings Concerning the Soul and Observation of the World
CW 53	The Origin and Goal of the Human Being
CW 54	The Riddles of the World and Anthroposophy
CW 55	Knowledge of the Supersensible in Our Times and Its Meaning for Life Today
CW 56	Knowledge of the Soul and of the Spirit
CW 57	Where and How Does One Find the Spirit?
CW 58	The Metamorphoses of the Soul Life. Paths of Soul Experiences: Part One
CW 59	The Metamorphoses of the Soul Life. Paths of Soul Experiences: Part Two
CW 60	The Answers of Spiritual Science to the Biggest Questions of Existence
CW 61	Human History in the Light of Spiritual Research
CW 62	Results of Spiritual Research
CW 63	Spiritual Science as a Treasure for Life
CW 64	Out of Destiny-Burdened Times
CW 65	Out of Central European Spiritual Life
CW 66	Spirit and Matter, Life and Death
CW 67	The Eternal in the Human Soul. Immortality and Freedom
CW 68	Public lectures in various cities, 1906–1918
CW 69	Public lectures in various cities, 1906–1918
CW 70	Public lectures in various cities, 1906–1918
CW 71	Public lectures in various cities, 1906–1918
CW 72	Freedom—Immortality—Social Life
CW 73	The Supplementing of the Modern Sciences through Anthroposophy
CW 73a	Specialized Fields of Knowledge and Anthroposophy
CW 74	The Philosophy of Thomas Aquinas
CW 75	Public lectures in various cities, 1906–1918
CW 76	The Fructifying Effect of Anthroposophy on Specialized Fields
CW 77a	The Task of Anthroposophy in Relation to Science and Life: The Darmstadt College Course
CW 77b	Art and Anthroposophy. The Goetheanum-Impulse
CW 78	Anthroposophy, Its Roots of Knowledge and Fruits for Life
CW 79	The Reality of the Higher Worlds
CW 80	Public lectures in various cities, 1922
CW 81	Renewal-Impulses for Culture and Science—Berlin College Course
CW 82	So that the Human Being Can Become a Complete Human Being
CW 83	Western and Eastern World-Contrast. Paths to Understanding It through Anthroposophy
CW 84	What Did the Goetheanum Intend and What Should Anthroposophy Do?

Lectures to the Members of the Anthroposophical Society

SIGNIFICANT EVENTS IN THE LIFE OF
RUDOLF STEINER

1829:   June 23: birth of Johann Steiner (1829–1910)—Rudolf Steiner's father—in Geras, Lower Austria.

1834:   May 8: birth of Franciska Blie (1834–1918)—Rudolf Steiner's mother—in Horn, Lower Austria. 'My father and mother were both children of the glorious Lower Austrian forest district north of the Danube.'

1860:   May 16: marriage of Johann Steiner and Franciska Blie.

1861:   February 25: birth of *Rudolf Joseph Lorenz Steiner* in Kraljevec, Croatia, near the border with Hungary, where Johann Steiner works as a telegrapher for the South Austria Railroad. Rudolf Steiner is baptized two days later, February 27, the date usually given as his birthday.

1862:   Summer: the family moves to Mödling, Lower Austria.

1863:   The family moves to Pottschach, Lower Austria, near the Styrian border, where Johann Steiner becomes stationmaster. 'The view stretched to the mountains ... majestic peaks in the distance and the sweet charm of nature in the immediate surroundings.'

1864:   November 15: birth of Rudolf Steiner's sister, Leopoldine (d. November 1, 1927). She will become a seamstress and live with her parents for the rest of her life.

1866:   July 28: birth of Rudolf Steiner's deaf-mute brother, Gustav (d. May 1, 1941).

1867:   Rudolf Steiner enters the village school. Following a disagreement between his father and the schoolmaster, whose wife falsely accused the boy of causing a commotion, Rudolf Steiner is taken out of school and taught at home.

1868:   A critical experience. Unknown to the family, an aunt dies in a distant town. Sitting in the station waiting room, Rudolf Steiner sees her 'form,' which speaks to him, asking for help. 'Beginning with this experience, a new soul life began in the boy, one in which not only the outer trees and mountains spoke to him, but also the worlds that lay behind them. From this moment on, the boy began to live with the spirits of nature ...'

1869:   The family moves to the peaceful, rural village of Neudörfl, near Wiener-Neustadt in present-day Austria. Rudolf Steiner attends the village school. Because of the 'unorthodoxy' of his writing and spelling, he has to do 'extra lessons.'

1870:   Through a book lent to him by his tutor, he discovers geometry: 'To grasp something purely in the spirit brought me inner happiness. I know that I first learned happiness through geometry.' The same tutor allows him to draw, while other students still struggle with their reading and writing. 'An artistic element' thus enters his education.

1871: Though his parents are not religious, Rudolf Steiner becomes a 'church child,' a favourite of the priest, who was 'an exceptional character.' 'Up to the age of ten or eleven, among those I came to know, he was far and away the most significant.' Among other things, he introduces Steiner to Copernican, heliocentric cosmology. As an altar boy, Rudolf Steiner serves at Masses, funerals, and Corpus Christi processions. At year's end, after an incident in which he escapes a thrashing, his father forbids him to go to church.

1872: Rudolf Steiner transfers to grammar school in Wiener-Neustadt, a five-mile walk from home, which must be done in all weathers.

1873–75: Through his teachers and on his own, Rudolf Steiner has many wonderful experiences with science and mathematics. Outside school, he teaches himself analytic geometry, trigonometry, differential equations, and calculus.

1876: Rudolf Steiner begins tutoring other students. He learns bookbinding from his father. He also teaches himself stenography.

1877: Rudolf Steiner discovers Kant's *Critique of Pure Reason*, which he reads and rereads. He also discovers and reads von Rotteck's *World History*.

1878: He studies extensively in contemporary psychology and philosophy.

1879: Rudolf Steiner graduates from high school with honours. His father is transferred to Inzersdorf, near Vienna. He uses his first visit to Vienna 'to purchase a great number of philosophy books'—Kant, Fichte, Schelling, and Hegel, as well as numerous histories of philosophy. His aim: to find a path from the 'I' to nature.

October 1879–1883: Rudolf Steiner attends the Technical College in Vienna—to study mathematics, chemistry, physics, mineralogy, botany, zoology, biology, geology, and mechanics—with a scholarship. He also attends lectures in history and literature, while avidly reading philosophy on his own. His two favourite professors are Karl Julius Schröer (German language and literature) and Edmund Reitlinger (physics). He also audits lectures by Robert Zimmermann on aesthetics and Franz Brentano on philosophy. During this year he begins his friendship with Moritz Zitter (1861–1921), who will help support him financially when he is in Berlin.

1880: Rudolf Steiner attends lectures on Schiller and Goethe by Karl Julius Schröer, who becomes his mentor. Also 'through a remarkable combination of circumstances,' he meets Felix Koguzki, a 'herb gatherer' and healer, who could 'see deeply into the secrets of nature.' Rudolf Steiner will meet and study with this 'emissary of the Master' throughout his time in Vienna.

1881: January: '... I didn't sleep a wink. I was busy with philosophical problems until about 12:30 a.m. Then, finally, I threw myself down on my couch. All my striving during the previous year had been to research whether the following statement by Schelling was true or not: *Within everyone dwells a secret, marvelous capacity to draw back from the stream of time—out of the self clothed in all that comes to us from outside—into our innermost being and there, in the immutable form of the Eternal, to look into ourselves.* I believe, and I am still quite certain of it, that I discovered this capacity in myself; I had long had an inkling of it. Now the whole of idealist philosophy stood before me in modified form. What's a sleepless night compared to that!'

Rudolf Steiner begins communicating with leading thinkers of the day, who send him books in return, which he reads eagerly.

July: 'I am not one of those who dives into the day like an animal in human form. I pursue a quite specific goal, an idealistic aim—knowledge of the truth! This cannot be done offhandedly. It requires the greatest striving in the world, free of all egotism, and equally of all resignation.'

August: Steiner puts down on paper for the first time thoughts for a 'Philosophy of Freedom.' 'The striving for the absolute: this human yearning is freedom.' He also seeks to outline a 'peasant philosophy,' describing what the worldview of a 'peasant'—one who lives close to the earth and the old ways—really is.

1881–1882: Felix Koguzki, the herb gatherer, reveals himself to be the envoy of another, higher initiatory personality, who instructs Rudolf Steiner to penetrate Fichte's philosophy and to master modern scientific thinking as a preparation for right entry into the spirit. This 'Master' also teaches him the double (evolutionary and involutionary) nature of time.

1882:   Through the offices of Karl Julius Schröer, Rudolf Steiner is asked by Joseph Kürschner to edit Goethe's scientific works for the *Deutschen National-Literatur* edition. He writes 'A Possible Critique of Atomistic Concepts' and sends it to Friedrich Theodor Vischer.

1883:   Rudolf Steiner completes his college studies and begins work on the Goethe project.

1884:   First volume of Goethe's *Scientific Writings* (CW 1) appears (March). He lectures on Goethe and Lessing, and Goethe's approach to science. In July, he enters the household of Ladislaus and Pauline Specht as tutor to the four Specht boys. He will live there until 1890. At this time, he meets Josef Breuer (1842–1925), the co-author with Sigmund Freud of *Studies in Hysteria*, who is the Specht family doctor.

1885:   While continuing to edit Goethe's writings, Rudolf Steiner reads deeply in contemporary philosophy (Eduard von Hartmann, Johannes Volkelt, and Richard Wahle, among others).

1886:   May: Rudolf Steiner sends Kürschner the manuscript of *Outlines of Goethe's Theory of Knowledge* (CW 2), which appears in October, and which he sends out widely. He also meets the poet Marie Eugenie Delle Grazie and writes 'Nature and Our Ideals' for her. He attends her salon, where he meets many priests, theologians, and philosophers, who will become his friends. Meanwhile, the director of the Goethe Archive in Weimar requests his collaboration with the *Sophien* edition of Goethe's works, particularly the writings on colour.

1887:   At the beginning of the year, Rudolf Steiner is very sick. As the year progresses and his health improves, he becomes increasingly 'a man of letters,' lecturing, writing essays, and taking part in Austrian cultural life. In August–September, the second volume of Goethe's *Scientific Writings* appears.

1888: January–July: Rudolf Steiner assumes editorship of the 'German Weekly' (*Deutsche Wochenschrift*). He begins lecturing more intensively, giving, for example, a lecture titled 'Goethe as Father of a New Aesthetics.' He meets and becomes soul friends with Friedrich Eckstein (1861–1939), a vegetarian, philosopher of symbolism, alchemist, and musician, who will introduce him to various spiritual currents (including Theosophy) and with whom he will meditate and interpret esoteric and alchemical texts.

1889: Rudolf Steiner first reads Nietzsche (*Beyond Good and Evil*). He encounters Theosophy again and learns of Madame Blavatsky in the Theosophical circle around Marie Lang (1858–1934). Here he also meets well-known figures of Austrian life, as well as esoteric figures like the occultist Franz Hartmann and Karl Leinigen-Billigen (translator of C.G. Harrison's *The Transcendental Universe*). During this period, Steiner first reads A.P. Sinnett's *Esoteric Buddhism* and Mabel Collins's *Light on the Path*. He also begins travelling, visiting Budapest, Weimar, and Berlin (where he meets philosopher Eduard von Hartmann).

1890: Rudolf Steiner finishes volume 3 of Goethe's scientific writings. He begins his doctoral dissertation, which will become *Truth and Science* (CW 3). He also meets the poet and feminist Rosa Mayreder (1858–1938), with whom he can exchange his most intimate thoughts. In September, Rudolf Steiner moves to Weimar to work in the Goethe-Schiller Archive.

1891: Volume 3 of the Kürschner edition of Goethe appears. Meanwhile, Rudolf Steiner edits Goethe's studies in mineralogy and scientific writings for the *Sophien* edition. He meets Ludwig Laistner of the Cotta Publishing Company, who asks for a book on the basic question of metaphysics. From this will result, ultimately, *The Philosophy of Freedom* (CW 4), which will be published not by Cotta but by Emil Felber. In October, Rudolf Steiner takes the oral exam for a doctorate in philosophy, mathematics, and mechanics at Rostock University, receiving his doctorate on the twenty-sixth. In November, he gives his first lecture on Goethe's 'Fairy Tale' in Vienna.

1892: Rudolf Steiner continues work at the Goethe-Schiller Archive and on his *Philosophy of Freedom*. *Truth and Science*, his doctoral dissertation, is published. Steiner undertakes to write introductions to books on Schopenhauer and Jean Paul for Cotta. At year's end, he finds lodging with Anna Eunike, née Schulz (1853–1911), a widow with four daughters and a son. He also develops a friendship with Otto Erich Hartleben (1864–1905) with whom he shares literary interests.

1893: Rudolf Steiner begins his habit of producing many reviews and articles. In March, he gives a lecture titled 'Hypnotism, with Reference to Spiritism.' In September, volume 4 of the Kürschner edition is completed. In November, *The Philosophy of Freedom* appears. This year, too, he meets John Henry Mackay (1864–1933), the anarchist, and Max Stirner, a scholar and biographer.

1894: Rudolf Steiner meets Elisabeth Förster Nietzsche, the philosopher's sister, and begins to read Nietzsche in earnest, beginning with the as yet unpublished *Antichrist*. He also meets Ernst Haeckel (1834–1919). In the fall, he begins to write *Nietzsche, A Fighter against His Time* (CW 5).

1895:   May, *Nietzsche, A Fighter against His Time* appears.

1896:   January 22: Rudolf Steiner sees Friedrich Nietzsche for the first and only time. Moves between the Nietzsche and the Goethe-Schiller Archives, where he completes his work before year's end. He falls out with Elisabeth Förster Nietzsche, thus ending his association with the Nietzsche Archive.

1897:   Rudolf Steiner finishes the manuscript of *Goethe's Worldview* (CW 6). He moves to Berlin with Anna Eunike and begins editorship of the *Magazin für Literatur*. From now on, Steiner will write countless reviews, literary and philosophical articles, and so on. He begins lecturing at the 'Free Literary Society.' In September, he attends the Zionist Congress in Basel. He sides with Dreyfus in the Dreyfus affair.

1898:   Rudolf Steiner is very active as an editor in the political, artistic, and theatrical life of Berlin. He becomes friendly with John Henry Mackay and poet Ludwig Jacobowski (1868–1900). He joins Jacobowski's circle of writers, artists, and scientists—'The Coming Ones' (*Die Kommenden*)— and contributes lectures to the group until 1903. He also lectures at the 'League for College Pedagogy.' He writes an article for Goethe's sesquicentennial, 'Goethe's Secret Revelation,' on the 'Fairy Tale of the Green Snake and the Beautiful Lily.'

1898–99: 'This was a trying time for my soul as I looked at Christianity. . . . I was able to progress only by contemplating, by means of spiritual perception, the evolution of Christianity. . . . Conscious knowledge of real Christianity began to dawn in me around the turn of the century. This seed continued to develop. My soul trial occurred shortly before the beginning of the twentieth century. It was decisive for my soul's development that I stood spiritually before the Mystery of Golgotha in a deep and solemn celebration of knowledge.'

1899:   Rudolf Steiner begins teaching and giving lectures and lecture cycles at the Workers' College, founded by Wilhelm Liebknecht (1826–1900). He will continue to do so until 1904. Writes: *Literature and Spiritual Life in the Nineteenth Century; Individualism in Philosophy*; *Haeckel and His Opponents; Poetry in the Present;* and begins what will become (fifteen years later) *The Riddles of Philosophy* (CW 18). He also meets many artists and writers, including Käthe Kollwitz, Stefan Zweig, and Rainer Maria Rilke. On October 31, he marries Anna Eunike.

1900:   'I thought that the turn of the century must bring humanity a new light. It seemed to me that the separation of human thinking and willing from the spirit had peaked. A turn or reversal of direction in human evolution seemed to me a necessity.' Rudolf Steiner finishes *World and Life Views in the Nineteenth Century* (the second part of what will become *The Riddles of Philosophy*) and dedicates it to Ernst Haeckel. It is published in March. He continues lecturing at *Die Kommenden*, whose leadership he assumes after the death of Jacobowski. Also, he gives the Gutenberg Jubilee lecture before 7,000 typesetters and printers. In September, Rudolf Steiner is invited by Count and Countess Brockdorff to lecture in the Theosophical Library. His first lecture is on Nietzsche. His second lecture is titled 'Goethe's Secret Revelation.' October 6, he begins a lecture cycle on the mystics that will become *Mystics after Modernism* (CW 7). November-December: 'Marie von Sivers appears in the audience....' Also in November, Steiner gives his first lecture at the Giordano Bruno Bund (where he will continue to lecture until May, 1905). He speaks on Bruno and modern Rome, focusing on the importance of the philosophy of Thomas Aquinas as monism.

1901: In continual financial straits, Rudolf Steiner's early friends Moritz Zitter and Rosa Mayreder help support him. In October, he begins the lecture cycle *Christianity as Mystical Fact* (CW 8) at the Theosophical Library. In November, he gives his first 'Theosophical lecture' on Goethe's 'Fairy Tale' in Hamburg at the invitation of Wilhelm Hubbe-Schleiden. He also attends a gathering to celebrate the founding of the Theosophical Society at Count and Countess Brockdorff's. He gives a lecture cycle, 'From Buddha to Christ,' for the circle of the *Kommenden*. November 17, Marie von Sivers asks Rudolf Steiner if Theosophy needs a Western-Christian spiritual movement (to complement Theosophy's Eastern emphasis). 'The question was posed. Now, following spiritual laws, I could begin to give an answer....' In December, Rudolf Steiner writes his first article for a Theosophical publication. At year's end, the Brockdorffs and possibly Wilhelm Hubbe-Schleiden ask Rudolf Steiner to join the Theosophical Society and undertake the leadership of the German section. Rudolf Steiner agrees, on the condition that Marie von Sivers (then in Italy) work with him.

1902: Beginning in January, Rudolf Steiner attends the opening of the Workers' School in Spandau with Rosa Luxemburg (1870–1919). January 17, Rudolf Steiner joins the Theosophical Society. In April, he is asked to become general secretary of the German Section of the Theosophical Society, and works on preparations for its founding. In July, he visits London for a Theosophical congress. He meets Bertram Keightly, G.R.S. Mead, A.P. Sinnett, and Annie Besant, among others. In September, *Christianity as Mystical Fact* appears. In October, Rudolf Steiner gives his first public lecture on Theosophy ('Monism and Theosophy') to about three hundred people at the Giordano Bruno Bund. On October 19–21, the German Section of the Theosophical Society has its first meeting; Rudolf Steiner is the general secretary, and Annie Besant attends. Steiner lectures on practical karma studies. On October 23, Annie Besant inducts Rudolf Steiner into the Esoteric School of the Theosophical Society. On October 25, Steiner begins a weekly series of lectures: 'The Field of Theosophy.' During this year, Rudolf Steiner also first meets Ita Wegman (1876–1943), who will become his close collaborator in his final years.

1903: Rudolf Steiner holds about 300 lectures and seminars. In May, the first issue of the periodical *Luzifer* appears. In June, Rudolf Steiner visits

London for the first meeting of the Federation of the European Sections of the Theosophical Society, where he meets Colonel Olcott. He begins to write *Theosophy* (CW 9).

1904: Rudolf Steiner continues lecturing at the Workers' College and elsewhere (about 90 lectures), while lecturing intensively all over Germany among Theosophists (about 140 lectures). In February, he meets Carl Unger (1878–1929), who will become a member of the board of the Anthroposophical Society (1913). In March, he meets Michael Bauer (1871–1929), a Christian mystic, who will also be on the board. In May, *Theosophy* appears, with the dedication: 'To the spirit of Giordano Bruno.' Rudolf Steiner and Marie von Sivers visit London for meetings with Annie Besant. June: Rudolf Steiner and Marie von Sivers attend the meeting of the Federation of European Sections of the Theosophical Society in Amsterdam. In July, Steiner begins the articles in *Luzifer-Gnosis* that will become *How to Know Higher Worlds* (CW 10) and *Cosmic Memory* (CW 11). In September, Annie Besant visits Germany. In December, Steiner lectures on Freemasonry. He mentions the High Grade Masonry derived from John Yarker and represented by Theodore Reuss and Karl Kellner as a blank slate 'into which a good image could be placed.'

1905: This year, Steiner ends his non-Theosophical lecturing activity. Supported by Marie von Sivers, his Theosophical lecturing—both in public and in the Theosophical Society—increases significantly: 'The German Theosophical Movement is of exceptional importance.' Steiner recommends reading, among others, Fichte, Jacob Boehme, and Angelus Silesius. He begins to introduce Christian themes into Theosophy. He also begins to work with doctors (Felix Peipers and Ludwig Noll). In July, he is in London for the Federation of European Sections, where he attends a lecture by Annie Besant: 'I have seldom seen Mrs. Besant speak in so inward and heartfelt a manner....' 'Through Mrs. Besant I have found the way to H.P. Blavatsky.' September to October, he gives a course of thirty-one lectures for a small group of esoteric students. In October, the annual meeting of the German Section of the Theosophical Society, which still remains very small, takes place. Rudolf Steiner reports membership has risen from 121 to 377 members. In November, seeking to establish esoteric 'continuity,' Rudolf Steiner and Marie von Sivers participate in a 'Memphis-Misraim' Masonic ceremony. They pay forty-five marks for membership. 'Yesterday, you saw how little remains of former esoteric institutions.' 'We are dealing only with a "framework"... for the present, nothing lies behind it. The occult powers have completely withdrawn.'

1906: Expansion of Theosophical work. Rudolf Steiner gives about 245 lectures, only 44 of which take place in Berlin. Cycles are given in Paris, Leipzig, Stuttgart, and Munich. Esoteric work also intensifies. Rudolf Steiner begins writing *An Outline of Esoteric Science* (CW 13). In January, Rudolf Steiner receives permission (a patent) from the Great Orient of the Scottish A & A Thirty-Three Degree Rite of the Order of the Ancient

Freemasons of the Memphis-Misraim Rite to direct a chapter under the name 'Mystica Aeterna.' This will become the 'Cognitive-Ritual Section' (also called 'Misraim Service') of the Esoteric School. (See: *Freemasonry and Ritual Work: The Misraim Service*, CW 265). During this time, Steiner also meets Albert Schweitzer. In May, he is in Paris, where he visits Edouard Schuré. Many Russians attend his lectures (including Konstantin Balmont, Dimitri Mereszkovski, Zinaida Hippius, and Maximilian Woloshin). He attends the General Meeting of the European Federation of the Theosophical Society, at which Col. Olcott is present for the last time. He spends the year's end in Venice and Rome, where he writes and works on his translation of H.P. Blavatsky's *Key to Theosophy*.

1907: Further expansion of the German Theosophical Movement according to the Rosicrucian directive to 'introduce spirit into the world'—in education, in social questions, in art, and in science. In February, Col. Olcott dies in Adyar. Before he dies, Olcott indicates that 'the Masters' wish Annie Besant to succeed him: much politicking ensues. Rudolf Steiner supports Besant's candidacy. April-May: preparations for the Congress of the Federation of European Sections of the Theosophical Society—the great, watershed Whitsun 'Munich Congress,' attended by Annie Besant and others. Steiner decides to separate Eastern and Western (Christian-Rosicrucian) esoteric schools. He takes his esoteric school out of the Theosophical Society (Besant and Rudolf Steiner are 'in harmony' on this). Steiner makes his first lecture tours to Austria and Hungary. That summer, he is in Italy. In September, he visits Edouard Schuré, who will write the introduction to the French edition of *Christianity as Mystical Fact* in Barr, Alsace. Rudolf Steiner writes the autobiographical statement known as the 'Barr Document.' In *Luzifer-Gnosis*, 'The Education of the Child' appears.

1908: The movement grows (membership: 1,150). Lecturing expands. Steiner makes his first extended lecture tour to Holland and Scandinavia, as well as visits to Naples and Sicily. Themes: St. John's Gospel, the Apocalypse, Egypt, science, philosophy, and logic. *Luzifer-Gnosis* ceases publication. In Berlin, Marie von Sivers (with Johanna Mücke (1864–1949) forms the *Philosophisch-Theosophisch* (after 1915 *Philosophisch-Anthroposophisch*) *Verlag* to publish Steiner's work. Steiner gives lecture cycles titled *The Gospel of St. John* (CW 103) and *The Apocalypse* (104).

1909: *An Outline of Esoteric Science* appears. Lecturing and travel continues. Rudolf Steiner's spiritual research expands to include the polarity of Lucifer and Ahriman; the work of great individualities in history; the Maitreya Buddha and the Bodhisattvas; spiritual economy (CW 109); the work of the spiritual hierarchies in heaven and on earth (CW 110). He also deepens and intensifies his research into the Gospels, giving lectures on the Gospel of St. Luke (CW 114) with the first mention of two Jesus children. Meets and becomes friends with Christian Morgenstern (1871–1914). In April, he lays the foundation stone for the Malsch model—the building that will lead to the first Goetheanum. In May, the International Congress of the Federation of European Sections of the

Theosophical Society takes place in Budapest. Rudolf Steiner receives the Subba Row medal for *How to Know Higher Worlds*. During this time, Charles W. Leadbeater discovers Jiddu Krishnamurti (1895–1986) and proclaims him the future 'world teacher,' the bearer of the Maitreya Buddha and the 'reappearing Christ.' In October, Steiner delivers seminal lectures on 'anthroposophy,' which he will try, unsuccessfully, to rework over the next years into the unfinished work, *Anthroposophy (A Fragment)* (CW 45).

1910:   New themes: *The Reappearance of Christ in the Etheric* (CW 118); *The Fifth Gospel; The Mission of Folk Souls* (CW 121); *Occult History* (CW 126); the evolving development of etheric cognitive capacities. Rudolf Steiner continues his Gospel research with *The Gospel of St. Matthew* (CW 123). In January, his father dies. In April, he takes a month-long trip to Italy, including Rome, Monte Cassino, and Sicily. He also visits Scandinavia again. July–August, he writes the first mystery drama, *The Portal of Initiation* (CW 14). In November, he gives 'psychosophy' lectures. In December, he submits 'On the Psychological Foundations and Episte-mological Framework of Theosophy' to the International Philosophical Congress in Bologna.

1911:   The crisis in the Theosophical Society deepens. In January, 'The Order of the Rising Sun,' which will soon become 'The Order of the Star in the East,' is founded for the coming world teacher, Krishnamurti. At the same time, Marie von Sivers, Rudolf Steiner's co-worker, falls ill. Fewer lectures are given, but important new ground is broken. In Prague, in March, Steiner meets Franz Kafka (1883–1924) and Hugo Bergmann (1883-1975). In April, he delivers his paper to the Philosophical Con-gress. He writes the second mystery drama, *The Soul's Probation* (CW 14). Also, while Marie von Sivers is convalescing, Rudolf Steiner begins work on *Calendar 1912/1913*, which will contain the 'Calendar of the Soul' meditations. On March 19, Anna (Eunike) Steiner dies. In September, Rudolf Steiner visits Einsiedeln, birthplace of Paracelsus. In December, Friedrich Rittelmeyer, future founder of the Christian Community, meets Rudolf Steiner. The *Johannes-Bauverein*, the 'building committee,' which would lead to the first Goetheanum (first planned for Munich), is also founded, and a preliminary committee for the founding of an indepen-dent association is created that, in the following year, will become the Anthroposophical Society. Important lecture cycles include *Occult Phy-siology* (CW 128); *Wonders of the World* (CW 129); *From Jesus to Christ* (CW 131). Other themes: esoteric Christianity; Christian Rosenkreutz; the spiritual guidance of humanity; the sense world and the world of the spirit.

1912:   Despite the ongoing, now increasing crisis in the Theosophical Society, much is accomplished: *Calendar 1912/1913* is published; eurythmy is created; both the third mystery drama, *The Guardian of the Threshold* (CW 14) and *A Way of Self-Knowledge* (CW 16) are written. New (or renewed) themes included life between death and rebirth and karma and reincarnation. Other lecture cycles: *Spiritual Beings in the Heavenly Bodies and in the Kingdoms of Nature* (CW 136); *The Human Being in the Light of Occultism, Theosophy, and Philosophy* (CW 137); *The Gospel of St. Mark* (CW 139); and *The Bhagavad Gita and the Epistles of Paul* (CW 142). On May 8, Rudolf Steiner celebrates White Lotus Day, H.P. Blavatsky's death day, which he had faithfully observed for the past decade, for the last time. In August, Rudolf Steiner suggests the 'independent association' be called the 'Anthroposophical Society.' In September, the first eurythmy course takes place. In October, Rudolf Steiner declines recognition of a Theosophical Society lodge dedicated to the Star of the East and decides to expel all Theosophical Society members belonging to the order. Also, with Marie von Sivers, he first visits Dornach, near Basel, Switzerland, and they stand on the hill where the Goetheanum will be built. In November, a Theosophical Society lodge is opened by direct mandate from Adyar (Annie Besant). In December, a meeting of the German section occurs at which it is decided that belonging to the Order of the Star of the East is incompatible with membership in the Theosophical Society. December 28: informal founding of the Anthroposophical Society in Berlin.

1913:   Expulsion of the German section from the Theosophical Society. February 2–3: Foundation meeting of the Anthroposophical Society. Board members include: Marie von Sivers, Michael Bauer, and Carl Unger. September 20: Laying of the foundation stone for the *Johannes Bau* (Goetheanum) in Dornach. Building begins immediately. The third mystery drama, *The Soul's Awakening* (CW 14), is completed. Also: *The Threshold of the Spiritual World* (CW 147). Lecture cycles include: *The Bhagavad Gita and the Epistles of Paul* and *The Esoteric Meaning of the Bhagavad Gita* (CW 146), which the Russian philosopher Nikolai Berdyaev attends; *The Mysteries of the East and of Christianity* (CW 144); *The Effects of Esoteric Development* (CW 145); and *The Fifth Gospel* (CW 148). In May, Rudolf Steiner is in London and Paris, where anthroposophical work continues.

1914:   Building continues on the *Johannes Bau* (Goetheanum) in Dornach, with artists and co-workers from seventeen nations. The general assembly of the Anthroposophical Society takes place. In May, Rudolf Steiner visits Paris, as well as Chartres Cathedral. June 28: assassination in Sarajevo ('Now the catastrophe has happened!'). August 1: War is declared. Rudolf Steiner returns to Germany from Dornach—he will travel back and forth. He writes the last chapter of *The Riddles of Philosophy*. Lecture cycles include: *Human and Cosmic Thought* (CW 151); *Inner Being of Humanity between Death and a New Birth* (CW 153); *Occult Reading and Occult Hearing* (CW 156). December 24: marriage of Rudolf Steiner and Marie von Sivers.

1915:   Building continues. Life after death becomes a major theme, also art. Writes: *Thoughts during a Time of War* (CW 24). Lectures include: *The Secret of Death* (CW 159); *The Uniting of Humanity through the Christ Impulse* (CW 165).

1916:   Rudolf Steiner begins work with Edith Maryon (1872–1924) on the sculpture 'The Representative of Humanity' ('The Group'—Christ, Lucifer, and Ahriman). He also works with the alchemist Alexander von Bernus on the quarterly *Das Reich*. He writes *The Riddle of Humanity* (CW 20). Lectures include: *Necessity and Freedom in World History and Human Action* (CW 166); *Past and Present in the Human Spirit* (CW 167); *The Karma of Vocation* (CW 172); *The Karma of Untruthfulness* (CW 173).

1917: Russian Revolution. The U.S. enters the war. Building continues. Rudolf Steiner delineates the idea of the 'threefold nature of the human being' (in a public lecture March 15) and the 'threefold nature of the social organism' (hammered out in May–June with the help of Otto von Lerchenfeld and Ludwig Polzer-Hoditz in the form of two documents titled *Memoranda*, which were distributed in high places). August–September: Rudolf Steiner writes *The Riddles of the Soul* (CW 20). Also: commentary on 'The Chymical Wedding of Christian Rosenkreutz' for Alexander Bernus (*Das Reich*). Lectures include: *The Karma of Materialism* (CW 176); *The Spiritual Background of the Outer World: The Fall of the Spirits of Darkness* (CW 177).

1918: March 18: peace treaty of Brest-Litovsk—'Now everything will truly enter chaos! What is needed is cultural renewal.' June: Rudolf Steiner visits Karlstein (Grail) Castle outside Prague. Lecture cycle: *From Symptom to Reality in Modern History* (CW 185). In mid-November, Emil Molt, of the Waldorf-Astoria Cigarette Company, has the idea of founding a school for his workers' children.

1919: Focus on the threefold social organism: tireless travel, countless lectures, meetings, and publications. At the same time, a new public stage of Anthroposophy emerges as cultural renewal begins. The coming years will see initiatives in pedagogy, medicine, pharmacology, and agriculture. January 27: threefold meeting: ' We must first of all, with the money we have, found free schools that can bring people what they need.' February: first public eurythmy performance in Zurich. Also: 'Appeal to the German People' (CW 24), circulated March 6 as a newspaper insert. In April, *Towards Social Renewal* (CW 23) appears— 'perhaps the most widely read of all books on politics appearing since the war.' Rudolf Steiner is asked to undertake the 'direction and leadership' of the school founded by the Waldorf-Astoria Company. Rudolf Steiner begins to talk about the 'renewal' of education. May 30: a building is selected and purchased for the future Waldorf School. August–September, Rudolf Steiner gives a lecture course for Waldorf teachers, *The Foundations of Human Experience (Study of Man)* (CW 293). September 7: Opening of the first Waldorf School. December (into January): first science course, the *Light Course* (CW 320).

1920: The Waldorf School flourishes. New threefold initiatives. Founding of limited companies *Der Kommende Tag* and *Futurum A.G.* to infuse spiritual values into the economic realm. Rudolf Steiner also focuses on the sciences. Lectures: *Introducing Anthroposophical Medicine* (CW 312); *The Warmth Course* (CW 321); *The Boundaries of Natural Science* (CW 322); *The Redemption of Thinking* (CW 74). February: Johannes Werner

Klein—later a co-founder of the Christian Community—asks Rudolf Steiner about the possibility of a 'religious renewal,' a 'Johannine church.' In March, Rudolf Steiner gives the first course for doctors and medical students. In April, a divinity student asks Rudolf Steiner a second time about the possibility of religious renewal. September 27–October 16: anthroposophical 'university course.' December: lectures titled *The Search for the New Isis* (CW 202).

1921: Rudolf Steiner continues his intensive work on cultural renewal, including the uphill battle for the threefold social order. 'University' arts, scientific, theological, and medical courses include: *The Astronomy Course* (CW 323); *Observation, Mathematics, and Scientific Experiment* (CW 324); the *Second Medical Course* (CW 313); *Colour*. In June and September–October, Rudolf Steiner also gives the first two 'priests' courses' (CW 342 and 343). The 'youth movement' gains momentum. Magazines are founded: *Die Drei* (January), and—under the editorship of Albert Steffen (1884–1963)—the weekly, *Das Goetheanum* (August). In February–March, Rudolf Steiner takes his first trip outside Germany since the war (Holland). On April 7, Steiner receives a letter regarding 'religious renewal,' and May 22–23, he agrees to address the question in a practical way. In June, the Klinical-Therapeutic Institute opens in Arlesheim under the direction of Dr. Ita Wegman. In August, the Chemical-Pharmaceutical Laboratory opens in Arlesheim (Oskar Schmiedel and Ita Wegman are directors). The Clinical Therapeutic Institute is inaugurated in Stuttgart (Dr. Ludwig Noll is director); also the Research Laboratory in Dornach (Ehrenfried Pfeiffer and Günther Wachsmuth are directors). In November–December, Rudolf Steiner visits Norway.

1922: The first half of the year involves very active public lecturing (thousands attend); in the second half, Rudolf Steiner begins to withdraw and turn toward the Society—'The Society is asleep.' It is 'too weak' to do what is asked of it. The businesses—*Der Kommende Tag* and *Futurum A.G.*—fail. In January, with the help of an agent, Steiner undertakes a twelve-city German lecture tour, accompanied by eurythmy performances. In two weeks he speaks to more than 2,000 people. In April, he gives a 'university course' in The Hague. He also visits England. In June, he is in Vienna for the East–West Congress. In August–September, he is back in England for the Oxford Conference on Education. Returning to Dornach, he gives the lectures *Philosophy, Cosmology, and Religion* (CW 215), and gives the third priests' course (CW 344). On September 16, The Christian Community is founded. In October–November, Steiner is in Holland and England. He also speaks to the youth: *The Youth Course* (CW 217). In December, Steiner gives lectures titled *The Origins of Natural Science* (CW 326), and *Humanity and the World of Stars: The Spiritual Communion of Humanity* (CW 219). December 31: Fire at the Goetheanum, which is destroyed.

1923: Despite the fire, Rudolf Steiner continues his work unabated. A very hard year. Internal dispersion, dissension, and apathy abound. There is conflict—between old and new visions—within the Society. A wake-up call is needed, and Rudolf Steiner responds with renewed lecturing vitality. His focus: the spiritual context of human life; initiation science; the course of the year; and community building. As a foundation for an artistic school, he creates a series of pastel sketches. Lecture cycles: *The Anthroposophical Movement; Initiation Science* (CW 227) (in England at the Penmaenmawr Summer School); *The Four Seasons and the Archangels* (CW 229); *Harmony of the Creative Word* (CW 230); *The Supersensible Human* (CW 231), given in Holland for the founding of the Dutch society. On November 10, in response to the failed Hitler-Ludendorff putsch in Munich, Steiner closes his Berlin residence and moves the *Philosophisch-Anthroposophisch Verlag* (Press) to Dornach. On December 9, Steiner begins the serialization of his *Autobiography: The Course of My Life* (CW 28) in *Das Goetheanum*. It will continue to appear weekly, without a break, until his death. Late December–early January: Rudolf Steiner re-founds the Anthroposophical Society (about 12,000 members internationally) and takes over its leadership. The new board members are: Marie Steiner, Ita Wegman, Albert Steffen, Elisabeth Vreede, and Günther Wachsmuth. (See *The Christmas Meeting for the Founding of the General Anthroposophical Society*, CW 260). Accompanying lectures: *Mystery Knowledge and Mystery Centres* (CW 232); *World History in the Light of Anthroposophy* (CW 233). December 25: the Foundation Stone is laid (in the hearts of members) in the form of the 'Foundation Stone Meditation.'

1924:   January 1: having founded the Anthroposophical Society and taken over its leadership, Rudolf Steiner has the task of 'reforming' it. The process begins with a weekly newssheet ('What's Happening in the Anthroposophical Society') in which Rudolf Steiner's 'Letters to Members' and 'Anthroposophical Leading Thoughts' appear (CW 26). The next step is the creation of a new esoteric class, the 'first class' of the 'University of Spiritual Science' (which was to have been followed, had Rudolf Steiner lived longer, by two more advanced classes). Then comes a new language for Anthroposophy—practical, phenomenological, and direct; and Rudolf Steiner creates the model for the second Goetheanum. He begins the series of extensive 'karma' lectures (CW 235–40); and finally, responding to needs, he creates two new initiatives: biodynamic agriculture and curative education. After the middle of the year, rumours begin to circulate regarding Steiner's health. Lectures: January–February, *Anthroposophy* (CW 234); February: *Tone Eurythmy* (CW 278); June: *The Agriculture Course* (CW 327); June–July: *Speech Eurythmy* (CW 279); *Curative Education* (CW 317); August: (England, 'Second International Summer School'), *Initiation Consciousness: True and False Paths in Spiritual Investigation* (CW 243); September: *Pastoral Medicine* (CW 318). On September 26, for the first time, Rudolf Steiner cancels a lecture. On September 28, he gives his last lecture. On September 29, he withdraws to his studio in the carpenter's shop; now he is definitively ill. Cared for by Ita Wegman, he continues working, however, and writing the weekly installments of his *Autobiography* and *Letters to the Members/Leading Thoughts* (CW 26).

1925:   Rudolf Steiner, while continuing to work, continues to weaken. He finishes *Extending Practical Medicine* (CW 27) with Ita Wegman.
On March 30, around ten in the morning, Rudolf Steiner dies.

INDEX

368 * Building Stones for an Understanding...